R0061784070

03/2012

"I do not remember ever to have experienced a feeling of greater loneliness. It seemed as though we were deserted by all the world and rest of mankind."

— Confederate Major General Daniel Harvey Hill

UNHOLY

SABBATH

Brian M. Jordan

The Battle of South Mountain

in History and Memory

September 14, 1862

SB

Savas Beatie
New York and California

Cataloging-in-Publication Data is available from the Library of Congress.

ISBN-13: 978-1-611210-88-0

05 04 03 02 01   5 4 3 2 1
First edition, first printing

SB

Published by
Savas Beatie LLC
521 Fifth Avenue, Suite 1700
New York, NY 10175

Editorial Offices:

Savas Beatie LLC
P.O. Box 4527
El Dorado Hills, CA 95762
916-941-6896
sales@savasbeatie.com

Savas Beatie titles are available at special discounts for bulk purchases in the United States by corporations, institutions, and other organizations. For more details, please contact Special Sales, P.O. Box 4527, El Dorado Hills, CA 95762, or you may e-mail us at sales@savasbeatie.com, or visit our website at www.savasbeatie.com for additional information.

Printed in the United States of America

For my wife, Allison Elizabeth Jordan, with all of my love

and in loving memory of Richard Earl Klar (1932 – 2007).
How I wish we could share this, too.

An unposed photograph of Confederate troops from Robert E. Lee's Army of Northern Virginia marching through Frederick, Maryland, in September 1862. Like the photographer, the identity of the unit has not yet been determined. *Library of Congress*

Contents

Contents (continued)

Contents (continued)

Maps

Illustrations appear throughout the book
for the convenience of the reader

UNHOLY SABBATH

The Battle of

South Mountain

in

History and Memory,

September 14, 1862

BRIAN MATTHEW JORDAN

Introduction

The simple sound of the word "Antietam" yet sends an intuitive chill up the American spine. A dozen hours of combat in the cornfields, woods, and farm lanes near Sharpsburg, Maryland, one unassuming September day added some twenty-three thousand men to the Civil War's grisly register of killed, wounded, missing, or captured. Within a few days both George McClellan's Army of the Potomac and Robert E. Lee's Army of Northern Virginia had abandoned the battlefield, leaving behind a chilling panorama of death and destruction. Rows of stiffened, bullet-riddled and torn bodies outlined the Hagerstown Turnpike and littered the ground surrounding the simple sanctuary of the pacifist Dunkers, itself scathed by battle. For weeks vultures circled in merciless eddies in the sky above, charmed by Antietam's harvest of death.

In the battle's aftermath, celebrated photographer Alexander Gardner and his assistant, James Gibson, descended upon the war-torn landscape and captured in syrupy collodion these haunting images. Later that autumn, the photographers assembled these ghastly glimpses of war into a temporary exhibition entitled "The Dead of Antietam" on the second level of Mathew Brady's noted New York City photography studio and gallery. Then, as now, these images betrayed the incommunicability of war. As the *New York Times* noted on October 20, the exhibition brought home "the terrible reality and earnestness of war." Gallery-goers discovered that they had "a terrible fascination" with such scenes that made them "lo[a]th to leave" the haunting images behind.[1]

Historians, much like those New York spectators who wandered through the exhibit gallery, have been loath to leave behind the enormity of Antietam's carnage when penning the history of the Maryland Campaign of 1862. As Georgia veteran George D. Grattan recalled in an essay he published in the *Southern Historical Society Papers*, "the interest" in chronicling the campaign "centered upon the battle of Sharpsburg, which is generally conceded to have been the bloodiest and most stubbornly contested battle of the Civil War." The result of this focus, he concluded, "has served to almost obliterate the memory of the minor engagement at Boonsboro Gap, or South Mountain." John Watts de Peyster, a New York veteran and one of the nation's first military scientists, likewise recognized this lacunae in the historical narrative. When asked to contribute a selection on the Battle of Antietam for a series of essays chronicling the "decisive" battles of the Civil War, de Peyster argued that "it was impossible to treat of Antietam without devoting a large space to South Mountain or Boonsboro," for "whatever was won in the cornfields and woods of Antietam was decidedly initiated in the gaps of the South Mountain."[2]

Despite their sectional differences, veterans Grattan and de Peyster concluded there existed among the earliest chroniclers of the Civil War's military campaigns a propensity to assign significance to military events using the magnitude of slaughter as their only guide. In devising their "battles and leaders" view of the war, early historians infused the historical narrative with a sense of linear inevitability. These writers learned how to resolve the complicated consequences of war by subsuming them into a larger tale of the war's noble and millennial purpose. Dismissing the nagging incongruities and fierce contingencies of lived experience during wartime, these scholars effortlessly equated real significance with great slaughter. Even more recent students of the war, as historians Edward L. Ayers, Drew Gilpin Faust, and others point out, have followed in their footsteps. In an attempt to rationalize the war's catastrophic losses, these historians have "explained away" the

---

1   *New York Times*, 20 October 1862; William A. Frassanito, *Antietam: The Photographic Legacy of America's Bloodiest Day* (New York: Scribner's, 1978), 14-15.

2   George D. Grattan, "The Battle of Boonsboro Gap or South Mountain," in the *Southern Historical Society Papers*, 29 (Richmond, Virginia: Southern Historical Society, 1914): 31-44; John Watts de Peyster, "The Maryland Battles in September, 1862," *The Decisive Conflict of the Late Civil War, or Slaveholder's Rebellion*, no. 1 (New York: MacDonald & Co., Printers, 1867), 38-39.

staggering human and emotional costs of the conflict; their narrative histories valorize the mutual mettle of common soldiers and inform readers that the end of slavery and the future of freedom demanded such unprecedented sacrifices. They ameliorate, or at least sanitize, the tragedy of a battle by embracing reassuring explanations of what the harvest of death accomplished.[3]

When historians attend to the past not with hindsight but with the emotions of the historical participants, however, they usefully complicate foregone conclusions and restore unforeseen events to view. Moreover, by refusing to allow the size of an engagement to adjudicate its consequences, scholars can resist the temptation to underestimate the ability of small encounters to force large ripples in the stream of historical events. In this spirit, *Unholy Sabbath: The Battle of South Mountain in History and Memory, September 14, 1862* challenges traditional histories of the Maryland Campaign by restoring the combat on the slopes of South Mountain to the prominent place its veterans accorded it in their memories.

The Conventional Narrative

The conventional chronicle of the Maryland Campaign of 1862 begins with the Battle of Second Bull Run (Second Manassas), a decided tactical victory for Lee and his Army of Northern Virginia. Flushed with success in yet another military campaign in the Eastern Theater, Lee consulted with Confederate President Jefferson Davis and secured his approbation to make an offensive thrust north of the Potomac River aimed at the border state of Maryland. Traditional histories inform that this movement, undertaken with fewer than 40,000 men, personified Lee's alleged audacity in command.

Thereafter, according to the usual retelling of historians, Lee moved north to relieve war-torn Virginia for the upcoming harvest season. The Southern army commander gazed longingly at the defenses of Washington; hoped to shatter the morale of the federal army and northern civilians by bringing the war to their soil; and, by issuing a Proclamation to the People of Maryland, aspired to swell the ranks of his thinning command with pro-Confederate Marylanders ready to "throw off the oppression" of the Lincoln administration and its

---

3 See, for example, Edward L. Ayers, "Worrying About the Civil War," in *What Caused the Civil War? Reflections on the South and Southern History* (New York: W.W. Norton, 2005), 103-130, and Drew Gilpin Faust, "We Should Grow Too Fond of It: Why We Love the Civil War," *Civil War History*, 50, no. 4 (December 2004): 368-383.

unbridled abuses of civil liberties. Once in Maryland, Lee was pursued by the slothful George McClellan and his Army of the Potomac and decided to demonstrate his daring once more. In his Special Orders No. 191, Lee divided his army across a front thirty-five miles wide among the mountains of western Maryland. Recognizing the strategic and symbolic significance of the federal armory and arsenal at Harpers Ferry, Virginia, situated at the confluence of the Potomac and Shenandoah Rivers, Lee shuttled six of his nine divisions off to the federal garrison in an effort to bottle it up into a siege. The other divisions held Hagerstown, Maryland, and two passes of South Mountain, a spur of the Blue Ridge extending between Harpers Ferry and Frederick.

On September 13, the lethargic federal forces finally reached Frederick. Carelessness by a Confederate courier resulted in a stray copy of Special Orders No. 191 falling into the hands of the Union army. Despite possession of the enemy's strategic schematic, however, McClellan continued to move with his characteristic caution. He settled upon a plan to push through the South Mountain gaps and confront Lee's divided army, hoping to defeat its elements in detail. On Sunday, September 14, the right wing of the Union army, commanded by Major General Ambrose Burnside, assaulted Fox's and Turner's gaps on South Mountain. Six miles to the south, through the so-called "back door" to Harpers Ferry, Major General William Buel Franklin's Union Sixth Corps engaged the rebel forces at Crampton's Gap.

Tactically, the federal army defeated the Confederates defending the three South Mountain gaps in what amounted to prolonged and exceedingly heavy skirmishing. Strategically, however, the defenders won the day by keeping McClellan's army at bay for twenty-four precious hours. Delaying the blue coats on South Mountain sealed the fate of the Union garrison at Harpers Ferry, which the hapless Colonel Dixon Miles surrendered on Monday, September 15. Two days later, after both armies recuperated and reorganized, they met in the fields surrounding Sharpsburg for an inevitable showdown that ended in a bloody stalemate with some twenty-three thousand total casualties. Damaged by his heavy losses at Antietam, Lee reluctantly determined to end the campaign and to retire to Virginia. As a result, the federals billed the battle as a victory. This success delivered up the "moral courage" President Lincoln needed to issue a preliminary emancipation proclamation on September 22, 1862. The battle's spoils also convinced Great Britain and France to remain neutral, at least for the foreseeable future.

Ripe for Reassessment

Governed by this grand narrative, standard histories of the Maryland Campaign routinely consign South Mountain to a mere footnote in the enormous shadow of Antietam. In their popular histories of the campaign, historians James V. Murfin and Stephen W. Sears offer only brief chapters on the battle. Not until 1992, when John Michael Priest published *Before Antietam: The Battle for South Mountain*, did the engagement become the subject of a book-length study. Capitalizing on the success of his earlier and more popular volume on Antietam, Priest's 433-page prequel chronicled the opening days of the Maryland Campaign from an enlisted man's perspective. While uncovering a plethora of little-known human-interest stories relating to the battle, this focus limited the potential of Priest's monograph. Instead of situating the battle into a strategic context and considering the important consequences of the engagement, Priest instead offered—in rich though often confusing detail—a tactical overview of the battle illustrated with incomprehensible maps.[4]

In 1998 and again in 2004, historian Timothy J. Reese contributed to the historiography of the campaign with his thoughtful studies *Sealed with Their Lives: The Battle of Crampton's Gap* and *High Water Mark: The Maryland Campaign of 1862 in Strategic Perspective*. While Reese argued brilliantly for the strategic significance of the fight for the back door of Harpers Ferry, he too forcefully argued for an interpretive disconnection between the Crampton's Gap engagement and the battles for Fox's and Turner's gaps. As the following pages demonstrate, only by considering the histories of these geographically detached but strategically united engagements can one appreciate the significance of South Mountain to the fate of the Maryland Campaign.[5]

---

4 See John Michael Priest, *Before Antietam: The Battle for South Mountain* (Shippensburg, Pennsylvania: White Mane Publishing Co., Inc., 1992) and also D. Scott Hartwig's review of *Before Antietam*, in *Civil War History: A Journal of the Middle Period*, 40, no. 1 (March 1994): 84-86. My narrative is deeply indebted to and stands on the shoulders of Priest's pioneering work. Historian Ethan Rafuse has more recently contributed a guidebook to the Maryland Campaign which affords South Mountain considerable space. Finally, a few months before the publication of this book, historian John David Hoptak published his own treatment entitled *The Battle of South Mountain* (Charleston, South Carolina: The History Press, 2011). I did not have an opportunity to read John's work in time to utilize it for *Unholy Sabbath*.

5 Timothy J. Reese, *Sealed with Their Lives: The Battle for Crampton's Gap, September 14, 1862* (Baltimore: Butternut and Blue, 1998), and Timothy J. Reese, *High Water Mark: The 1862 Maryland Campaign in Strategic Perspective* (Baltimore: Butternut and Blue, 2004).

The narrative in *Unholy Sabbath* begins by considering the social, political, and military context of the campaign. Subsequent chapters attempt to revise the Maryland Campaign's contours by reconsidering Lee's motives in moving the war north. I conclude that Lee's true intention was not only to move his columns north of the Potomac River, but also to move them across the Mason-Dixon Line into Pennsylvania, where the mere presence of his army would be enough to enervate the wavering federal war effort. I analyze Lee's prim proclamations and his soaring rhetoric, suggesting that he intended with these documents to influence foreign observers on the threshold of diplomatic recognition of the Confederacy. Cognizant of the watchers overseas, and keenly aware of the upcoming federal elections that fall, Lee anticipated that one more "perfect" campaign would bring about a negotiated peace. Considering the physical state and sheer number of the invading forces, I conclude that Lee took a calculated risk by making such a foray above the Potomac. On the other hand, the Army of Northern Virginia's keen optimism after Second Manassas mediated some of these risks; thus, most importantly, as the campaign began, I argue that Lee and his army firmly maintained the initiative.

Lee assumed with justifiable logic that McClellan would once more move against his army in guarded fashion. However, in the five chapters treating the battle, I argue that McClellan, much to Lee's disbelief, overturned this judgment in an uncharacteristic display of confidence and cunning. Using a strategy of divide and defeat in detail, Burnside's wing of the Union army forced Fox's and Turner's gaps while William Franklin's Sixth Corps, while admittedly moving more lackadaisically, scored an easy victory at Crampton's Gap. On this unholy Sabbath, one of the first recorded incidents of hand-to-hand combat in the American Civil War occurred at Fox's Gap in fighting that involved two future presidents (one of whom, Rutherford B. Hayes, was seriously wounded), and on the slopes of Turner's Gap, the Iron Brigade earned its now immortal moniker.

As post-battle reports, diaries, and letters reveal, these clear-cut tactical victories transferred the energy and initiative to the Union army. "We yesterday gained a glorious and complete victory," McClellan wrote to his wife Ellen on September 15. "Every moment adds to its importance. . . . God has seldom given an army a greater victory than this."[6] Though buoyed by the welcome

---

6   George B. McClellan to Mary Ellen McClellan, Bolivar, Maryland, September 15, 1862, in Richard Wheeler, *Lee's Terrible Swift Sword* (New York: Harper Collins, 1992), 83.

news, the federal commander recognized what Lee also grasped: that the actions on South Mountain condemned the Confederate campaign to failure. As I point out, in stark contrast to his optimism at the outset of the invasion, Lee issued an unprecedented order for retreat on the evening of September 14. "The day has gone against us and this army will go by Sharpsburg and cross the [Potomac] river [into Virginia]," his assistant adjutant general wrote about eight o'clock.[7] Only the sanguine reports emanating from Thomas "Stonewall" Jackson a score of miles away at Harpers Ferry convinced Lee to rescind the order for retreat. Though Lee gathered his army at Sharpsburg, his design for Pennsylvania—like the initiative he once held so firmly—was forever lost. The rebel defeat at South Mountain exposed the gamble that Lee made with his anemic army, prevented him from sustaining operations north of the Potomac, and severed his path to Pennsylvania.

The final chapters round out the story of the battle. I consider the work of burying the dead and caring for the wounded, for these efforts began the process of remembering—or, conversely, forgetting—the fight. Finally, I draw some conclusions about the shifting historical reputation of the battle. Beginning with the instructive words of the participants themselves, I consider the battle's legacy and how it changed over time. Alongside the enduring allure of Antietam, several factors—including the triumph of the Lost Cause myth, widespread disdain for George McClellan, and the pitiable manner in which the battlefield was preserved—contributed to the process of excising the significance of the battle of South Mountain from modern memory.

*   *   *

Historian Isaac Heysinger remarked in 1912 that no military campaign of the Civil War was "so little understood" as the Maryland Campaign of 1862. Taking for "its central feature" the battle of Antietam, the story of the first rebel invasion of the North "bristle[d] from end to end, at every point, with questions which have never been answered."[8] *Unholy Sabbath* seeks to address a few of

---

7   Colonel R.H. Chilton to General Lafayette McLaws, Hagerstown, Maryland, September 14, 1862, in *The Wartime Papers of R..E. Lee*, Clifford Dowdey and Louis H. Manarin, eds. (New York: Bramhall House Publishers, 1961), 307-308, hereafter cited as *WPREL*.

8   Isaac Heysinger, "Introductory: Inaccuracy of All the Current Histories," in *Antietam and the Maryland and Virginia Campaigns of 1862* (1912), 19.

Heysinger's unanswered questions. More importantly, I hope it also raises new ones.

Acknowledgments

The length of these acknowledgments is a testament to the level of guidance, support, and assistance that is necessary in completing a book-length manuscript. Researching *Unholy Sabbath* would not have been possible without the helpful aid and assistance of the archives and libraries I scoured for material. At the Rutherford B. Hayes Presidential Center in Fremont, Ohio, perhaps the most scholar-friendly research library in the country, I spent many profitable hours rifling through the Civil War papers of Rutherford B. Hayes. The energetic curator of manuscripts, Nan J. Card, removed box after box of items from the stacks for me to search; Merv Hall pointed me to the diary of Lucy Elliot Keeler and helped track down the diary of E.W. Slocum.

At the Virginia Historical Society in Richmond, Greg Hansard and Janice Keesling were both helpful and courteous in retrieving items and making photocopies. I spent many afternoons writing and researching at The Kent State University Library in Kent, Ohio; the main branch of the Akron-Summit County, Ohio Public Library in Akron; the General Lucius V. Bierce Library at the University of Akron; and at the Musselman Library at Gettysburg College. Materials from the Ohio Historical Society in Columbus; the Western Reserve Historical Society in Cleveland; the U.S. Army War College Military History Institute in Carlisle, Pennsylvania; and the Library of Congress Manuscript Division were of great assistance.

My mother, Terri Jordan, served as an unofficial research assistant, struggling with microfilm readers and helping me scour contemporary newspapers. She perfectly transcribed accounts from the 18th Virginia Infantry and endured her fair share of my South Mountain obsession. My father, Ralph Jordan, frequently accompanied me on research trips: to Fremont and Columbus, Ohio; to South Mountain; and, on one memorable trip to the stacks of the Kent State University Library to pore through the *Confederate Veteran* and *Southern Historical Society Papers*. A tornado alarm sent us hurriedly down eight flights of stairs to the disaster shelter, each of us clutching a dozen volumes to be copied. For not complaining and for his copious and useful notes, he deserves much credit.

Christopher Labosky spent more than a few afternoons working on this project. He aided me in research, proofed footnotes, and edited an early draft of the manuscript. Along the way, I also received the unsolicited research aid of Brandon R. Roos, Ashley Towle, Bethany Canfield, and Allison Herrmann. So many other friends, too numerous to mention, have in the course of their own research, shared documents relating to South Mountain. For pointing me to these sources, I salute them.

I would be remiss to ignore four mentors. James W. Geary, Professor Emeritus of Library Science at Kent State University, and author of the definitive monograph on Civil War conscription in the North, has been a long-time friend and source of encouragement. My friend Michael J. Birkner, Professor of History at Gettysburg College, honed my research and writing skills in his rigorous methodology course. Gabor S. Boritt, Fluhrer Professor Emeritus Civil War Studies at Gettysburg College and the Director Emeritus of the Civil War Institute, has served as my teacher and my boss, but most importantly, a cherished friend. The same may be said of Allen C. Guelzo, the Henry R. Luce Professor of the Civil War Era at Gettysburg College and the dean of Lincoln scholars. Dr. Guelzo has taught me more about the nature and philosophy of history than perhaps anyone. My respect for him is beyond measure. I thank him as well for reading and commenting on an early draft of this manuscript, a curious but welcome role reversal for the two of us.

My friend from the Civil War Institute, Henry Ballone of Saddle Brook, New Jersey, spent a day on South Mountain with me shooting the beautiful photographs that illustrate the text. They appear here only after his painstaking editing and refinishing. I am also honored that the book is enhanced by the expert cartography provided by Civil War author and historian Bradley M. Gottfried.

Several individuals also deserve mention for their friendship, support, guidance, and scholarship through the years. Often, these people greeted me with, "How's the book coming?" They include, in no particular order, Judge Howard and Mary Ellen Whitehead; David, Susan, and Megan Herrmann; Dr. Matthew D. Norman; Catherine and Bill Bain; Cynthia and Bill Helfrich; Dr. Kerry Walters; Ashley Whitehead; Joseph Rizzo; Brandon Roos; Michael Catalano; Evan Rothera; Jackie Seymour; Marian Warner; Dr. Bill Jones; Antonio Marin-Rodriquez; Dr. Jack E. Ryan; Dr. Barbara Sommer; Mark Horner; Craig S. Bara; Beth Doney; Sue Langford; Kappy Sarver; Lisa Wilson; Kevin and Megan Bowman; Christopher Gwinn; Jay Hagerman; Derric Nolte; J. Gary Dillon; Tina M. Grim; Pamela J. Dalrymple; Diane Brennan; Susan Oyler; Carol Zeh; Bruce and Janet Caudill; William Adkins, Jr.; Vincent Batista; Charles E. Rush; Janie Holzer; Jessica Morrow; Jamie and Judy Raffensperger;

Lisa Kot; Mary Davis, and Erin Joyce; Iris Lukacevic, Olivia Vendetti, Sandra Peck-Beachell, and the remainder of the staff and regular customers of the Lincoln Diner in Gettysburg, where I worked many hours on this manuscript; Joseph, Judith, Thomas, and Betsey McCarthy; David Klar; Richard E. Klar, Jr., and Carol Klar; Nancy E. Klar, and Patricia J. Jordan.

Sean Joyce and the staff of the Bruegger's Bagels in the Amity section of New Haven refilled my coffee cup, brightened my day, and gave me a warm and welcoming place to finish this book.

Early on, Theodore P. Savas, managing director at Savas Beatie LLC, saw potential in this manuscript and personally worked patiently and diligently to improve it. I am also indebted to others at Savas Beatie who have worked hard on my behalf, including editor Rob Ayers, marketing director Sarah Keeney, and production manager Lee Meredith. I would also like to thank Ian Hughes for his excellent cover design. It is my pleasure to salute these talented individuals.

Finally, to my wife Allison. Her name on the dedication page grossly underestimates her tireless support and encouragement. She is not only the best thing that has ever happened to me, she is the reason this book became a reality.

Brian Matthew Jordan
New Haven, Connecticut
September 14, 2011

C hapter 1

"The divine will"

The War for the North, 1861-1862

F or Abraham Lincoln, Sunday, July 13, 1862, retrieved painful memories. Secretary of State William Henry Seward of New York and Secretary of the Navy Gideon Welles from Connecticut, the shrewdest and most politically savvy members of his cabinet, rode with him in the presidential carriage that morning. They were on their way to the expansive Oak Hill Cemetery overlooking the Rock Creek at Washington's edge, to offer condolences to Secretary of War Edwin McMasters Stanton, a veteran of the Buchanan administration and a conservative Ohio Democrat. The newly appointed Stanton was interring the remains of his infant son James, not all that far from where the president's eleven-year-old son Willie, who had succumbed to typhoid fever that February, was buried.[1]

During the carriage ride, Lincoln broached a discussion of an emancipation policy for the first time. The subject had burned inside him since his days in Illinois where, as a prairie attorney, he witnessed the specter of slavery hovering ominously over westward territorial expansion. For Lincoln, human bondage was a contagion that threatened to fracture history's most brilliant experiment in republican self-government. The institution threatened the country's moral and material growth and its place among the nations of the world.

---

1 Gideon Welles, *The Diary of Gideon Welles*, Howard K. Beale, ed. (New York: W.W. Norton and Company, 1960), 1:70-71.

For Lincoln, the self-educated lawyer who had risen through his own diligence and determination from the humility of a log cabin in the Kentucky backwoods to a place of esteem among the residents of Illinois' burgeoning capital city of Springfield, the notion of the American dream was real and transformative. The concept consumed Lincoln, and his political commitments expressed his devotion to progress. As a member of the Whig Party, he fastened himself firmly to the idea that internal infrastructure improvements within the rapidly expanding nation were incontrovertibly tied to the principles of self-advancement, an individual's attainment of property, and a legitimate opportunity for a "rise in life." If anything was antithetical to this formula, it was the Southern system of race-based slavery, "soiling the robes of republican liberty" and corrupting Jefferson's vision of a "more perfect union."[2]

Lincoln's secular faith in the American dream provided him with personal answers to the daunting questions of slavery. Shackling an entire race into suppression and subjugation deprived that entire race of the same "rise in life" that had propelled him to a "respectable" place in society. Lincoln did not consider slavery a mere "political" or "economic" issue, but a decidedly *moral* one. He would enlist his keen understanding of slavery's brutal contradiction to challenge his political foes and to expose their seemingly benign doctrines and compromises for what they were: temporary analgesics for the irksome paradox at the heart of freedom in America.

*   *   *

Although the slavery question had rocked Congress since James Monroe's presidency, when slaveholding Missouri threatened to overthrow the equilibrium of free and slave states, for Abraham Lincoln and the remainder of a deeply troubled country, 1854 proved a salient year in the progression of events. Senator Stephen Arnold Douglas, a Vermont-born Yankee turned Illinois Democrat, authored and pushed through Congress a piece of cunning legislation reopening the question of slavery in the territories both immediately and permanently. The Kansas-Nebraska Act carved two separate territories out

2   See also Gabor S. Boritt, *Lincoln and the Economics of the American Dream* (Memphis: Memphis State University Press, 1978; 2d edition, Chicago: University of Illinois Press, 1994); Daniel Walker Howe, *What Hath God Wrought: The Transformation of America, 1815-1848* (New York: Oxford University Press, 2008), and Eric Foner, *Free Soil, Free Labor, Free Men* (New York: Oxford University Press 1970).

'PRESIDENT LINCOLN AND HIS CABINET.

Abraham Lincoln and his cabinet: (left to right) Secretary of the Navy Gideon Welles, Secretary of the Treasury Salmon P. Chase, Postmaster General Montgomery Blair, Secretary of State William Seward, Secretary of the Interior Caleb Smith, Attorney General Edward Bates, and Secretary of War Edwin M. Stanton. *Library of Congress*

of the land originally acquired in the Louisiana Purchase of 1803. Despite the standing compromise that allowed Missouri to enter the Union without protracted conflict in 1820, providing for a line of demarcation to establish permanent bounds for the future admission of slave states, Douglas treated the precedent as moot. He opened up all of the western territories to the possibility of slavery under the auspices of "popular sovereignty." In other words, if local citizen majorities approved of human bondage, the territory in question would be admitted with slavery. Douglas provided the anti-slavery forces with a single uniting issue behind which to rally (and upon which they would eventually skewer themselves).

Lincoln immediately attacked the Douglas plan. On October 16, 1854, he delivered a speech at Peoria, Illinois, that helped other political rivals and allies identify him as a leading thinker and strong candidate for national office. Four years later Lincoln landed a position opposite Douglas on the stage at seven statewide debates in the race for an Illinois United States Senate seat. By challenging Douglas and exposing the flaws in his popular sovereignty ideology, Lincoln's ethical analysis became even clearer in these oratorical matches. Despite the moral underpinnings of Lincoln's stance on slavery, he also harbored what Doris Kearns Goodwin has called a consummate "political genius," which allowed him to assume a moderate public stance while allowing the logical flow of events and a providential view of history to sweep divine will into secular law.[3]

Because of that moderation, Lincoln could address the necessity of reassembling the Union first and at all costs, rather than encouraging a risky and dramatic ideological rift. Although this often discouraged the ardent northern evangelicals who yearned for these radical changes, like Oberlin College's Charles Grandison Finney, Lincoln remained unsure if emancipation was a necessary course of action—let alone one that would foster a rousing response from Northerners.[4] Like Finney, famous African-American intellectual, abolitionist, and newspaper editor Frederick Douglass became discouraged with Lincoln. Douglass, who as author David W. Blight argues consistently balanced his hopes and realities while keeping faith on the road to jubilee, invested his own "last best hope" in the Republican Party, clearly and presciently recognizing its anti-slavery tendencies.[5]

Yet, Lincoln's public image of apathy for the cause of emancipation and the administration's growing energy in support of the development of colonization—a scheme that would have deported blacks to Caribbean islands and encouraged the voluntary uprooting of free African-Americans—earnestly tested Douglass' hope. "Mr. Lincoln assumes the language and arguments of an itinerant Colonization lecturer showing all his inconsistencies, his pride of race and blood, his contempt for Negroes and his canting hypocrisy," Douglass vituperatively wrote in his newspaper.[6]

---

3 Doris Kearns Goodwin, *Team of Rivals: The Political Genius of Abraham Lincoln* (Simon & Schuster, 2005).

4 Allen Carl Guelzo, *The Crisis of the American Republic* (New York: St. Martins, 1995), 326.

5 David W. Blight, *Frederick Douglass' Civil War: Keeping Faith in Jubilee* (Baton Rouge: The Louisiana State University Press, 1989).

6 Frederick Douglass, "The President and His Speeches," in Philip S. Foner, ed., *The Life and Writings of Frederick Douglass*, (New York: International Publishers, 1952) 3:267-70.

With such scathing attacks beleaguering him—not only from those who supported the arrival of the war, like Douglass and Finney, but from a large population of democrats and war weary civilians in the North—Lincoln found himself "in the depths" of the crisis. Humiliating battlefield reverses, diplomatic blunders, and mounting casualties in the war's first sixteen months seemed to reconfirm the arguments offered by his opponents.

The first real exchange of blood on land came in June 1861 at Big Bethel, eight miles north of Fortress Monroe on the Virginia peninsula situated between the York and James rivers. While an embarrassing defeat, Big Bethel involved a relatively small number of troops. Infantry fighting began in earnest with the didactic battle at Manassas Junction in Virginia on Sunday, July 21, 1861. There, Brigadier General Irvin McDowell led federal troops donning a colorful menagerie of mismatched uniforms in a close-fought battle that turned against McDowell late in the day. The federal army fell back in a chaotic rout that handed the fields astride the muddy Bull Run to a victorious Confederate army led by Brigadier General Pierre Goustave Toutant Beauregard and 12,000 reinforcements brought to the field by rail under Brigadier General Joseph Eggleston Johnson. Nearly five hundred federals had been killed, a thousand wounded, and one thousand two hundred were missing and/or captured—a calamity of catastrophic scale. The hasty Northern demand for a manly prosecution of a romanticized war ceased. Innocence lifted into the air with the saltpeter at Manassas. In an ominous sign for those prone to see such things in random events, an ailing widow who lived on the hill most prominent in the battle, Judith Henry, was killed during the battle. She had been born in 1776.

In reality, the only positive effect of the Bull Run defeat for the federal army was what *did not* happen. Too nascent and disorganized itself, the Confederate army halted on the battlefield and passed up the opportunity to move against Washington. This allowed time for some much-needed administrative reorganization. Lincoln relieved McDowell of his command and in November cajoled Winfield Scott, a curmudgeonly relic of wars past and commander of all federal forces, into retirement. At the helm of both the Army of the Potomac, the North's principal army in the Eastern Theater, and of the entirety of the federal forces, Lincoln placed a thirty-five-year-old general with a reputation for lending organization to a body of men. He was also known for imbuing his forces with a formidable *espirit de corps*. His name was George Brinton McClellan.

The Philadelphia-born McClellan graduated second in the storied West Point Class of 1846. He earned two brevets during the Mexican War before

Major General George B. McClellan, commander of the Army of the Potomac.
Library of Congress

turning to the railroad industry, eventually serving as president of the Ohio & Mississippi Railroad on the eve of the war. Recognizing McClellan's apt administrative and organizational skills, when the Civil War broke out, Ohio Governor William Dennison tendered him an appointment as major general of the state's volunteers, an offer that propelled McClellan into the national spotlight. McClellan's forces earned several of the Northern war effort's early victories in the hills of western Virginia at Rich Mountain and Cheat Mountain that summer, checking Robert E. Lee and prompting the Confederate government to recall the Virginian—now disparagingly called "Granny"—back to Richmond. McClellan had earned the ardent respect and patronage of his men and, in addition to the success of his western Virginia campaign—a success that more rightfully belonged to his subordinate, William Starke Rosecrans—prompted Lincoln's offer to lead all federal armies.

Though McClellan's presence at the head of the army only portended greatness in the field, his devout adherence to the flawed tactical strategies of West Point's professor of military and civil engineering, Dennis Hart Mahan, plagued his command decisions. Unlike the Napoleonic approach to warfare, Mahan favored an army's assumption of a tenable defensive position that would in time provoke an enemy attack. Hence, Mahan's chief objective was not aggression, but resistance.[7] McClellan's adoption of the *Mahanite* tradition budded into a pattern of relentless caution, aided by what historian Joseph L. Harsh called the "heart of [his] policy"—waging war "within the limits of the Constitution," ensuring that nothing would hinder peace and reunion.[8] McClellan's practice of incessantly weighing risks tended to allow opportune moments to slip through his fingers, rendering the army, as Allen Guelzo has described it, a razor-sharp instrument dulled by unwarranted inaction. It was also an ailment exacerbated by McClellan's politics.

McClellan was a devout Democrat, and committed to a war of limited aggressiveness with a decided indifference to the ultimate fate of slavery. On May 26, 1861, he made this apparent with both a communiqué to the troops of the Department of the Ohio and a circular to the loyal men of western Virginia. "Your mission is to restore peace & confidence, to protect the majesty of the law . . . I place under the safeguard of your honor the persons & property of the Virginians," he instructed his men. "I know that you will respect their feelings & all their rights." Even more expressly, to the loyal slave-owners he gave the

---

7   See also Edward Hagerman, *The American Civil War and The Origins of Modern Warfare: Ideas, Organization, and Field Command* (Bloomington and Indianapolis: Indiana University Press, 1988), 4-12.

8   Joseph L. Harsh, "On the McClellan-Go-Round," *Civil War History: A Journal of the Middle Period* 19, no. 2 (June 1973): 117; George Brinton McClellan, *McClellan's Own Story. The War for the Union. The Soldiers Who Fought It, The Civilians Who Directed It, and His Relations to It and to Them,* William C. Prime, ed. (New York: 1887).

assurance that nothing would be done to disrupt their system of social control. "Not only will we abstain from all such interference but we will on the contrary with an iron hand, crush any attempt at insurrection on [the slaves'] part."[9]

At the same time, Lincoln clearly understood that public opinion would not permit him to interfere with slavery—at least not now. In the wake of the Bull Run fiasco that first summer of the war, Lincoln supported the joint resolution of Senators John J. Crittenden of Kentucky and Andrew Johnson of Tennessee that delineated the sole aim of the federal forces as the preservation of the Union, and not the liberation of the slave. Cognizant that slave-holding states Delaware, Kentucky, Maryland, and Missouri still remained in the Union, Lincoln knew that enlarging the war's limited boundaries could result in a simultaneous expansion of Confederate geography—a loss of these so-called "border states" of the Upper South. Kentucky seemed to be the most important of them all, situated along several key transportation and economic arteries. "I think to lose Kentucky is nearly the same as to lose the whole game," Lincoln wrote to his friend Orville Hickman Browning.[10] Thus, in order to maintain the declaration of neutrality offered by Governor Beriah Magoffin, he determined that the war could not become so ambitious so quickly. Ultimately, a keen sense of timing and a grasp of the topography of public opinion, buttressed by a faithful vision for moral progress, would lead Lincoln to resolve the war for Union with emancipation firmly in hand.

Another mortifying military debacle at Ball's Bluff on the Potomac River near Leesburg, Virginia, in October only contributed to Lincoln's troubles. The battle, which McClellan called "butchery," claimed the life of Colonel Edward D. Baker, a United States Senator from Oregon and one of Lincoln's close personal friends. A substantial percentage of the nearly one thousand casualties drowned in the Potomac River and during the subsequent days bobbed ashore in and near Washington, D.C. Most frustrating was the fact that no one assumed responsibility for the disaster. The crushing defeat was "entirely

---

9 McClellan to the Troops of the Department of the Ohio, May 26, 1861, and to The Union Men of Western Virginia, May 26, 1861, in *The Civil War Papers of George B. McClellan: Selected Correspondence, 1860-1865*, ed. Stephen W. Sears (New York: Ticknor & Fields, 1989), 25-26, hereafter cited as *McClellan Papers*.

10 Lincoln to Browning, September 22, 1861, in *Collected Works of Abraham Lincoln*, ed. Roy P. Basler (New Brunswick, New Jersey: Rutgers University Press, 1953) 4:532, hereafter cited *CWAL*.

unauthorized by me," McClellan wrote to his wife Ellen.[11] As a result, radical Republicans in Congress established a Joint Committee on the Conduct of the War that only presaged the political maneuvering and the ongoing, competitive struggle over the war's direction between the legislative and executive branches.

As if these problems were not onerous enough, Lincoln soon found himself engrossed in a precarious diplomatic situation. On November 7, Captain Charles Wilkes of the *U.S.S. San Jacinto* boarded the British mail steamer *Trent* off the coast of Cuba and captured James Mason and John Slidell, two Confederate envoys making their way across the Atlantic to meet with British officials. Although Wilkes released the *Trent*, Mason and Slidell were escorted to Fort Warren in Boston, where they faced imprisonment. Wilkes became something of a national hero for his action. "It was popular with the country, was considered right by the people, even if rash and irregular," wrote Secretary of the Navy Welles.[12] Congress even authorized a medal in honor of Wilkes' accomplishment. Nevertheless, the administration failed to foresee the precarious diplomatic confrontation sparked by the *Trent* affair.

When the first reports of the incident arrived in England on November 27, the citizenry erupted.[13] Already, much of the continent swarmed with secessionists and conservatives, many of whom excitedly anticipated a sweeping European intervention on behalf of the Confederacy that would at long last defeat the North's republicanism, egalitarianism, and radicalism—values they had long disdained.[14] Even substantial numbers within the abject laboring class in Europe found a rare moment of concurrence with the aristocrats on the issue of the war dividing the states. Starved of the Southern cotton needed to feed the textile mills, this already restless and unstable class now found themselves unemployed and destitute. As historians Lynn Case and Warren Spencer noted, "[t]he shot fired at Fort Sumter, like that

11 McClellan to Mary Ellen McClellan, October 25, 1862, in *McClellan Papers*. For more information on Ball's Bluff, see James Morgan, *"A Little Short of Boats:" The Civil War Battles of Ball's Bluff and Edward Ferry* (Savas Beatie, 2011).

12 Welles, diary, August 10, 1862, in Beale, ed., 1:73.

13 See also Jay Monaghan, *Diplomat in Carpet Slippers: Abraham Lincoln Deals with Foreign Affairs* (Indianapolis and New York: Bobbs Merrill, 1945), 173-193, and Howard Jones, *Blue and Gray Diplomacy: A History of Union and Confederate Foreign Relations* (Chapel Hill: University of North Carolina Press, 2010).

14 Lynn M. Case and Warren F. Spencer, *The United States and France: Civil War Diplomacy* (Philadelphia: University of Pennsylvania Press, 1970), 2.

at Concord, was heard around the world . . . its echoes reverberated in Europe down to the humble cottage."[15] Cognizant of the dangers of those reverberations, British Prime Minister Lord Henry Palmerston remained keenly aware of how closely the Confederacy's so-called struggle for the preservation of the status quo resembled European tensions.

As one Irish editorial wrote in support of the Northern war cause, "the present war has reduced England to a state of pauperism . . . we ask our countrymen in America to flock around the Stars and Stripes, with a generous alacrity. . . . for the preservation of the Union will be the salvation of Ireland." Proffering additional examples of the connectedness of American and European affairs, the editorial voiced:

> The breaking of the great Republic would be a fatal blow to the cause of freedom all over the world: it was a model of Democratic power and an instance of material progress which had no counterpart in any other country. It was a home for the oppressed of every land, who participated fully and freely in all its grand institutions. It was a rebuke and a terror to the despotic dynasties of the Old World. If ever a government was worth fighting for, it is that of the United States. . . . They are fighting not alone for America, but also for Ireland, for humanity, and universal freedom.[16]

Consequently, in recognition of the global implications of the conflict, Lord Palmerston issued a stern challenge to the Lincoln administration in the wake of the *Trent* affair. Not only did he demand the release of Mason and Slidell, but he also prepared some 7,000 British troops for deployment to Canada. Furthermore, British foreign minister Lord Lyons demanded an official apology from Secretary of State Seward, and likewise ordered the U.S. government to release Mason and Slidell. If the U.S. failed to comply, all diplomatic relations between the two nations would be effectively severed. The war that fractured the United States now imperiled the entire western hemisphere.

While the already immense contest between North and South threatened to evolve into a global conflict, the federal bureaucracy scrambled to adjust to the brisk and unpredictable pace of war. Although the infrastructural and economic

15 *Ibid.*

16 "A Friendly Voice from Ireland," originally published in the *Galway American*, reproduced in the *Dayton* [Ohio] *Daily Journal*, September 15, 1862.

conditions were considerably weaker below the Mason-Dixon Line, shortages, oversights, and costs still hindered the Northern war effort. Brigade after brigade of volunteer regiments added an even more complicating problem: the Union army was becoming a collection of raw recruits often led by partisan hacks lacking military acuity. Lincoln recognized these dilemmas, but his incisive political moderation, above all else, helped him avert an extended showdown with Britain that winter. With Seward in his prescribed role as diplomat-in-chief, Lincoln approved the release of Mason and Slidell, recognizing the inconsequential place of the two agents within the larger struggle. Although the president staved off an unwanted conflict, Britain and her neighbors could not yet be dismissed, as they still harbored the potential to determine the outcome of what was shaping up to be slaughter without end in sight. A broad spectrum of foreign observers continued to carefully document each advance and setback, each victory and defeat.

Despite propitious news from along the Atlantic coast, the North consistently lagged behind in the foreigners' tally of victories and advances against the Southern rebellion. With Winfield Scott finally in retirement and George McClellan now firmly in command, the "Young Napoleon" put forth his plan for peripheral attacks on the Confederacy in November 1861. He began with "combined operations"—joint navy and infantry expeditions up and down the Atlantic seaboard. Captain Samuel F. DuPont made short order of the South Carolina coast, capturing Port Royal Sound and Hilton Head Island. A Rhode Island soldier and inventor named Ambrose Everett Burnside did the corresponding work in North Carolina. Then, Quincy Adams Gilmore assailed and took Georgia's Fort Pulaski, a part of James Madison's original system of masonry coastal defenses, in April 1862.

To answer the supplications of eastern Tennessee loyalists Andrew Johnson and Horace Maynard, Don Carlos Buell and his 45,000 men in the Army of the Ohio followed orders to march through Kentucky and into Tennessee—first, to overthrow the secession government and then to buoy the burgeoning Union nucleus in the region as a precedent for other similarly loyal areas in the South. For himself and the Army of the Potomac in Virginia, McClellan proposed another combined operation. The federal navy would transport the infantry to Urbana, on the Rappahannock River, from which the foot soldiers would embark on a fifty-mile overland march to the Confederate capital at Richmond. Simultaneously, the Western Theater armies would thrust southward with the intention of uniting. "I will stake my life, my reputation on the result—more than that, I will stake upon it the success of our cause," McClellan boasted to Secretary of War Stanton on February 3, 1862.[17]

Beyond a gross overestimation of enemy strength around Manassas, incessant carping, and criticism of the administration, however, most of what McClellan offered was more braggadocio. He refused to move, fearing that he could not begin without the success of Buell, whose advance stood stymied in the backwoods of Kentucky. Meanwhile, Confederate troops on the Potomac River virtually blockaded the federal capital, and northerners summoned their largest Eastern Theater force to action. Exasperated with idle armies and a sharp-tongued general who harbored his own political ambitions, Lincoln issued a presidential directive ordering McClellan to commence a new campaign on George Washington's birthday, February 22, 1862. Lincoln would wait no longer.

On March 8, 1862, the president arranged a meeting with McClellan in the White House that finally precipitated action. Regrettably, even movement proved to be humiliating when McClellan advanced on the Confederate works outside of Manassas only to find them empty. Brigadier General Joseph Johnston's men had slipped out of their works and assumed a new line of defense along the Rappahannock River. With his so-called Urbana Plan now impossible to execute, McClellan adopted another combined strategy to approach Richmond from the opposite direction. In this new design, the navy would transport the roughly 100,000 men of the Army of the Potomac south of Richmond to the Virginia peninsula formed by the James and York rivers. Once the men landed at the tip at Fortress Monroe, they would creep up the peninsula to Richmond's "back door," and either capture it outright or lay siege to the symbolic heart of the Confederacy. Though Lincoln questioned the necessity of such an elaborate combined operation, he was relieved that the general proposed to do *something*. He authorized McClellan's plans, though the inclusion of an amendment that provided for the adequate defense of the District of Columbia signified Lincoln's reluctance to fully endorse them. McClellan offered Nathaniel Banks' Fifth Corps to operate as the capital guard. At last, the army was moving.

On March 17, the first components of McClellan's army embarked for Fortress Monroe. McClellan's plan to startle Richmond with the sudden arrival of the Army of the Potomac worked, though he allowed his trademark caution

---

17 McClellan to Stanton, February 3, 1862, in *McClellan Papers*, 167-71.

to render the surprise anti-climactic. At the outset, the federal forces confronted only a thin line of Confederate troops commanded by a West Point graduate with a penchant for acting named General John Bankhead Magruder. Outnumbered by the federals nearly four-to-one in the historic triangle bounded by Yorktown, Williamsburg, and Jamestown, Magruder employed his skills of dramatic improvisation once more. His grand theatrical production involved making his small force appear much larger than it was, and his Quaker guns seem as though they were powerful batteries of deadly artillery. His gambit worked and bought the Confederacy enough time to encircle reinforcements around Richmond. Instead of pushing his way through Magruder's troops and "on to Richmond," McClellan, slowly maneuvering up the Peninsula, condemned his troops to a pitched engagement for Yorktown, a sharp rearguard battle at Williamsburg, and, finally, a much larger defensive fight astride the Chickahominy River on May 31 and June 1, 1862, at Seven Pines (Fair Oaks). McClellan's adherence to Mahan's instructions had generated the most unwelcome outcome. Joseph Johnston, commander of the Confederate army in the botched large-scale offensive at Seven Pines, was severely wounded and required an extended leave of absence to recuperate. President Jefferson Davis turned to Robert Edward Lee and offered him command of the army on June 1. While altogether unexpected, it was a satisfying turn of events for the Confederacy.

The fourth child of the Revolutionary War hero "Light Horse Harry" Lee—the man who labeled his compatriot and confidant George Washington first in war, peace, and in the hearts of his countrymen—Robert was a prodigal son. Graduating second in his West Point class without a single demerit, he assumed a position on General Winfield Scott's staff during the Mexican War. Scott later wrote of Lee, "[He was] the best soldier I ever saw in the field."[18] When he returned to the states from Mexico a brevet colonel, Lee went on to serve as superintendent of West Point for three years. On the eve of the Civil War, the reserved Lee awaited the news of his beloved Virginia's fate from his stately mansion at Arlington, perched on the heights above the Potomac a short distance from the federal capital. When Virginia finally left the Union and joined the Confederacy, Lee also left the army. He declined President Lincoln's offer to command all federal troops and granted his services to the rebel army.

18 Winfield Scott, as quoted in Douglas Southall Freeman, *R. E. Lee*, 4 vols. (New York: Scribner's, 1934-1935), vol. 1., 294.

General Robert E. Lee, commander of the Army of Northern Virginia. *Library of Congress*

Now in command of what he named the Army of Northern Virginia, Lee decided on a bold offensive to turn McClellan's right flank and crush him. A week of rigorous battles followed near the Confederate capital during the waning days of June and on the first day of July. The Seven Days' Battles, with fights at places like Mechanicsburg, Chickahominy Bluff, Beaver Dam Creek, Savage's Station, White Oak Swamp, Glendale, and Malvern Hill, were the bloodiest to date in a war that was proving to be anything but predictable. The appalling casualties further awakened northern civilians to the unrelenting and costly nature of the conflict.[19] Despite inflicting substantial damage to the attacking Confederate army and tactically losing only the battle at Gaines' Mill, McClellan was, psychologically and strategically speaking, roundly defeated. With his right turned, McClellan ordered a retreat to the James River and the protection of the federal warships there. Convinced of the enemy's non-existent numerical superiority, he finally settled himself into a bivouac at Berkeley Plantation at Harrison's Landing.

As historian Brian K. Burton notes, this debacle (which followed the bloodbath at Shiloh in Tennessee that April) helped produce Democratic victories in the 1862 midterm elections, crushed Northern morale, bolstered the belief of the British and French that the North could not defeat the South militarily, and invigorated the same aristocrats and laborers to clamor more ardently for intervention. With casualty numbers swelling and their own interests interposed, intervention assumed a moral hue that placed both nations on intercession's threshold.[20]

Even worse, Lee had confirmed Lincoln's fears about the safety of Washington the month before the Seven Days' fighting when he convinced President Davis to release Major General Thomas J. Jackson and his 16,000 men to the Shenandoah Valley to make a threat against the federal capital. Lincoln hastily dispatched three separate federal forces, each commanded by generals of political pedigrees, into the Valley to contend with Jackson. Most importantly, Lincoln sent off the corps intended for the defense of the capital city, belonging to the former Speaker of the U.S. House of Representatives-turned-general Nathaniel Prentice Banks. Jackson's undertaking and Lincoln's response not only left the federal capital weakly defended, but prevented these forces from reinforcing McClellan just outside Richmond.

Along the macadamized Valley Turnpike, in a grueling campaign of surprise and audacious marching and maneuvers, Jackson became the stuff of legend against the 60,000 men of Banks, General James Shields, and General John Charles Frémont. A pair of impressive victories at the twin battles of

---

19 For the best treatment to date of the Seven Days campaign, see Brian K. Burton, *Extraordinary Circumstances: The Seven Days Battles* (Bloomington and Indianapolis: Indiana University Press, 2001).

20 *Ibid.*, 397

Cross Keys and Port Republic closed the campaign and caused the federal forces to withdraw. Jackson's foot cavalry betrayed their opponent's anemic battlefield leadership. Confederate morale bloated as the enemy grew more disillusioned.[21]

"We are in the depths now, permeated by disgust, saturated with gloomy thinking," New York lawyer and diarist George Templeton Strong observed in the weeks after the Seven Days.[22] For Lincoln, this observation consummately reflected the abominable atmosphere for the Northern war effort in the East during the summer of 1862. "There have been several occasions since those opening days of July that established so clearly the fact of General McClellan's failure to effect his purposes—when a well organized and vigorous effort of the enemy might have carried confusion and temporary panic into the National Army," Lincoln's secretary John Hay wrote pseudanonymously for the press on August 17.[23]

The war effort in the Western Theater was not as bleak. Commodore Andrew Hull Foote's flotilla captured the poorly designed Fort Henry on the Tennessee River in February. A short time later in conjunction with Foote's vessels, General Ulysses Simpson Grant's army achieved the stunning capture of Fort Donelson that included the unconditional surrender of the Confederate garrison.

During the first week of March, Major General Samuel Curtis defeated Confederate troops under Earl Van Dorn near the Elkhorn Tavern at the Battle of Pea Ridge in Arkansas. The victory essentially secured Union possession of Missouri for the next two years. Much farther to the west, at the end of March, the battle of Glorietta Pass shattered Southern Brigadier General Henry Hopkins Sibley's dream of achieving Confederate manifest destiny by seizing the federal foothold on the New Mexico Territory. Despite securing a tactical victory, the Confederates were compelled to retreat to Santa Fe—and eventually out of New Mexico.

---

21 On the 1862 Shenandoah Valley Campaign, see Peter Cozzens, *Shenandoah 1862* (Chapel Hill: University of North Carolina Press, 2008).

22 George Templeton Strong, diary entry, July 14, 1862, in *The Diary of George Templeton Strong*, eds. Allan Nevins and Milton Halsey Thomas (New York: The Macmillan Company, 1952).

23 John Hay, "Washington Correspondence, August 17, 1862," in *Lincoln's Journalist: John Hay's Anonymous Writings for the Press, 1860-1864*, ed. Michael Burlingame (Carbondale: Southern Illinois University Press, 1998), 291.

Days later along the Tennessee front on April 6, the war's bloodiest battle to date broke out at Shiloh Church near Pittsburg Landing. Grant's Union army was the victim of a massive surprise attack that first day and suffered appalling losses, but the fighting claimed the life of Confederate army commander General Albert Sidney Johnston, one of the South's most promising field commanders, and also decimated and disorganized the attacking Confederates. Instead of crumbling in defeat and retreating, Grant decided to make a resolute stance, welcomed the timely arrival of reinforcements, and went over to the attack, turning a pending federal disaster into a stunning Union victory. That same day, Union General John Pope took the fortified Confederate stronghold at Island Number 10 on the Mississippi River.

Promising news continued to trickle into Washington from the Western Theater. Admiral David Farragut landed a crushing blow by passing Forts Jackson and St. Philip on April 24, and the next day moving up river to capture the crucial city of New Orleans. Finally, General Beauregard (the former hero of Manassas) abandoned the all-important railroad junction at Corinth, Mississippi, that May. This was a welcome string of successes for anyone sympathetic to the northern war effort. Nevertheless, the press and European watchers were commenting almost exclusively on progress in the East, where the two capital cities dictated troop movements and battle lines and larger population centers panicked. Lincoln thought it extremely "unreasonable" that the series of successes along the Mississippi attracted little attention, yet a single reverse in the East could quickly become the epicenter of news over the wires. Despite this news, the Eastern Theater battlefield triumph Lincoln so desperately needed to instill confidence in the northern public remained elusive.[24]

For Lincoln, the emancipation policy he broached during that carriage ride to the cemetery seemed the only way to strike at the heart of the Confederacy and prevent the ship of the Union from capsizing. The horror of the Seven Days, which concluded the first dismal year of battlefield combat, awakened Lincoln to the earnestness of civil war and to the character of McClellan. Both awakenings seemed to demand a change in the war's direction. A conflict of this magnitude required the North to not only conquer the South militarily, but socially and politically as well.

24 Lincoln to Count Gasparin of France, August 4, 1862, in *CWAL*, 5:355-356.

Lincoln prodded General McClellan with exhasuting regularity to take the army on the offensive. "If, at any time, you feel able to take the offensive, you are not restrained from doing so," he wired his top general on the nation's birthday. Just three days before, he issued a call for three hundred thousand additional troops.[25]

Like Lincoln, the northern populace had also awakened. As the editors of a Massachusetts newspaper editorialized, "We suppose that all honest citizens are now convinced that the Union cannot be restored by the policy of conciliation and compromise." The editors recognized these policies had only resulted in "ruinous defeat" and demanded a new direction.[26]

Lincoln realized that in order to conquer the South, he would have to strike at its "cornerstone"—the institution of slavery. He recognized that Sunday afternoon that the nation "must free the slaves or be ourselves subdued," Gideon Welles recorded in his diary.[27] But he could not and would not move on an emancipation proclamation without the weight of northern public opinion behind him. And that, in turn, required a season of victory for the federal army in the Eastern Theater tantamount to the progress of arms in the West.

By the end of the summer, Lincoln was trying to reconcile this austere atmosphere. Withdrawing a scrap of paper, he composed the following meditation on the Divine Will:

> The will of God prevails. In great contests each party claims to act in accordance with the will of God. Both *may* be, and one *must* be wrong. God can not be *for*, and *against* the same thing at the same time. In the present civil war it is quite possible that God's purpose is something different from the purpose of either party—and yet the human instrumentalities, working just as they do, are of the best adaptation to effect His purpose. I am almost ready to say this is probably true—that God wills this contest, and wills that it shall not end yet. By his mere quiet power, on the minds of the now contestants, He could have either *saved* or *destroyed* the Union without a human contest. Yet the contest began. And having begun He could give the final victory to either side any day. Yet the contest proceeds.[28]

---

25 Abraham Lincoln to George Brinton McClellan, Washington, D.C., 4 July 1862, in *CWAL*, 5:296-297, 306.

26 Editorial, *Boston Evening Transcript*, 5 September 1862.

27 Welles, diary entry, 13 July 1862.

28 *CWAL*, 5:404-405.

For Lincoln, always the postmillennialist in practice, God had ordained this war. Yet His mere ordinance had not confirmed the superiority of one side or the other. The entire nation had sinned—the South in owning and trading human cargoes; the North in its blind complicity and relentless racism. That God had not predetermined one section's superiority was evident with a review of the Army of the Potomac's performance. There was more purging to do; more blood to be shed; more sins to repent. And just as this deadly and destructive war came, so it would proceed.

hapter 2

"Throwing off the oppression"

The War for the Confederacy, 1861-1862

Northerners faced considerable dilemmas, but Southern civilians in the nascent Confederacy confronted no less political strife and internal bickering—especially as the war came to demand greater physical and emotional sacrifices. To be sure, Southerners could point to a string of impressive military victories in the Eastern Theater, an achievement that eluded federal armies. And, unlike the Union, which had to defeat the enemy, conquer the South, and reconstruct the nation in order to celebrate victory, the Confederacy's route to independence required it to only fend off the invading armies. In other words, Southerners needed neither to conquer nor to defeat their opponent.

The loose alliance of rebel states had its fair share of predicaments, however. Confederate leaders needed to command the support of yeomen farmers, small planters, and poor whites—none of whom were certain of the immediate personal benefits of fighting a war to preserve the aristocratic institution of slavery. Southerners were also bound by their antebellum code of honor, which celebrated the moral authority of the community, the family, and public opinion. When the war came, rebel leaders found themselves in the awkward position of justifying the removal of fathers, sons, and brothers from their dutiful roles. The interests of the Southern patriarchal system and the demands of the military were at odds. Moreover, the Confederacy's political and military leaders realized far too late that sustaining and supplying field armies could never mesh easily with the overarching goals of a loosely constructed, decentralized government. Indeed, in order to succeed and earn its independence as a nation, the Confederacy would be forced to reestablish the same "oppressive" government its own collection of states had so defiantly left in 1860 and 1861.

For example, when the Conscription Act was signed into law on April 16, 1862, inaugurating the first military draft in American history, Georgia Governor Joseph E. Brown sharply denounced it as a violation of state sovereignty. Aggressive tax increases, levied to finance a war amidst skyrocketing inflation rates, only generated more internal censure. Both of these debates—along with the perfunctory performances of the Confederacy's Commissary General, Lucius B. Northrop, and his haphazard transportation and railroad division chiefs—provided for a legitimate questioning of its ability to generate nationalism, patriotism, and loyalty.[1]

Further criticism emanated from ordinary farmsteads and small plantations. Though endowed with a superior stock of able-bodied and able-minded volunteers and officers, the agricultural economy of the Southern states relied upon these same military-age men to perform labor, oversee slaves, and maintain plantations and farms of all sizes. When the war erupted and men left home, Southern women found themselves occupying a strange new world where everything seemed upside down. Forced by necessity to step outside of the domestic sphere, many Southern women rebelled and made their voices heard, condemning their new "nation" for betraying the time-honored promise of protection. The loyalty that generations of men pledged to the ladies of the South they now redirected to the Stars and Bars; this uncomfortable new arrangement demanded women to lay down their lives and antebellum gender roles on the "altar of sacrifice."[2] Vicious riots erupted in New Orleans, for example, where shouting, heckling, and spilled chamber pots led to Union

---

1   See also Drew Gilpin Faust, *The Creation of Confederate Nationalism: Ideology and Identity in the Civil War South* (Baton Rouge: Louisiana State University Press, 1988), passim chap. 1, "The Problem of Confederate Nationalism," 1-21; Anne Sarah Rubin, *A Shattered Nation* (Chapel Hill: The University of North Carolina Press, 2005); Paul D. Escott, *After Secession* (Baton Rouge: Louisiana State University Press, 1978).

2   See Faust, *Mothers of Invention: Women of The Slaveholding South in the American Civil War* (Chapel Hill: The University of North Carolina Press, 1996), Catherine Clinton and Nina Silber, eds., *Divided Houses: Gender and the Civil War* (New York and Oxford: Oxford University Press, 1992), and Drew Gilpin Faust, "Altars of Sacrifice: Confederate Women and the Narratives of War," in Clinton and Silber, eds., 171-199.

General Benjamin Franklin Butler's infamous General Orders Number 28, declaring the actions of these women to be on par with prostitution.

These rioting rebel women not only protested the absences of husbands, brothers, and fathers, but chronic shortages of food and sustenance. These shortages, exacerbated within the butternut ranks, led to hunger and frustration. Letters from home displayed desperation and often resulted in desertion— especially as Union armies captured more Southern land. Shortages also crept into the ledger books, with the Confederacy making appeals to European investors to underwrite bonds. Similar pleas were made for foreign agencies to run the federal naval blockade that was slowly squeezing life from the rebel nation.

That their letters and actions betrayed real rebel uncertainty was hardly surprising; forging a new nation was a monumental undertaking, and Southerners were bound to endure tremendous hardships. Creating the Confederacy was no trivial task. Secession was a gradual process, beginning with South Carolina's departure from the Union on December 20, 1860. Florida, Mississippi, Alabama, Georgia, and Louisiana absconded in January 1861, and Texas followed in February. In late April, Virginia, the most populous of all Southern states, a symbolic land rooted in history and tradition and home to much-needed natural resources and industries, seceded from the Union and fell into the hands of the newly formed government, which had claimed Montgomery, Alabama, as its capital nearly three months prior. The secession of Tennessee, Arkansas, and North Carolina completed the new confederation of states in May 1861. Secessionists accomplished this work— established a government, inaugurated former secretary of war and United States senator Jefferson Davis as president, endowed a new Constitution, and organized and armed an army and navy—all within the space of six months.

Both the destruction of the United States and the ideology upon which the new Confederacy was based received many welcome greetings in Europe. Not only did the shouts in defense of state sovereignty and slavery echo those of the aristocrats in Great Britain, but, as South Carolina Senator James Henry Hammond noted in a famous floor speech, cotton was "king."[3] The hawkish *Charleston* [South Carolina] *Mercury* proclaimed that the bankruptcy of every

---

3 James Henry Hammond's remarks are quoted in Frank L. Owsley, *King Cotton Diplomacy: Foreign Relations of the Confederate States of America*, revised by Harriet C. Owsley (Chicago: University of Chicago Press, 1959), 16.

Confederate President
Jefferson Davis

Library of Congress

textile mill in Great Britain and France would secure the most coveted of prizes: formal recognition as an independent nation-state.[4] Echoing the Southern senator, one merchant went to great lengths to assure noted English correspondent William Howard Russell that cotton would undoubtedly unlock British intervention. Russell recorded the exchange in his diary: "'Look out there,' he said, pointing to the wharf, on which were piled some cotton bales; 'there's the key that will open all our ports, and put us into John Bull's strong box, as well.'"[5]

Indeed, by the end of the summer of 1862, the lack of Southern cotton bales in England nearly scored the foreign intervention the Confederacy so deeply craved. Lord Palmerston wrote in a memo to Chancellor of the Exchequer William Gladstone, "It seems to [Foreign Secretary Lord John] Russell and me that the Time is fast approaching when some joint offer of Mediation by England, France, and Russia if She would be a Party to it, might be made with some Prospect of Success." Palmerston's pensive memo continued, describing the tribulations and hunger faced by unemployed Lancashire textile mill workers:

---

4   The *Charleston* [South Carolina] *Mercury* is quoted in Howard Jones, *Abraham Lincoln and a New Birth of Freedom: The Union and Slavery in the Diplomacy of the Civil War* (Lincoln: University of Nebraska Press, 1999), 8.

5   William Howard Russell, *My Diary North and South*, ed. Fletcher Pratt (New York, 1954), 69.

The populations of Lancashire have borne their sufferings with a fortitude and patience exceeding all example, and almost all belief. But if in any one of the great towns, resignation should, even for a single day, give place to excitement, and an outbreak should occur, our position in the face of America, and our influence for good might be seriously affected. . . . [6]

The recent machinations of Francis Napoleon III—who, with designs for empire in America deposed the Mexican government under Benito Juárez and installed as Mexico's new leader a French marionette—motivated Lord Palmerston to consider intervention. Napoleon III rightly theorized that permanent divisions between North and South would afford him an opportune moment to establish French colonies in North America. Thus Lord Palmerston, concerned for his nation's future both at home and abroad, and hoping to maintain some degree of influence over the continent where Britain had planted its thirteen colonies, recognized that he could not remain an impartial observer for long.[7]

While cautious, the prime minister—like his colleagues Russell and Gladstone—was decidedly in favor of recognizing Confederate independence. Perhaps nothing—not even a calming of internal political quarrels, a stilling of the restless Southern women, or an increase in military blows to the enemy— could have benefitted the Southern alliance more than this meaningful declaration of sentiments. Cognizant of the potential for unrest in Britain should she become entangled in the conflict, Palmerston assumed the language of moderation and caution—especially in his writings to Gladstone, the most visible of officials in his administration. Palmerston likewise knew that his endorsement of the Confederacy would ignite a firestorm amongst moral suasionist, New England abolitionists, who would undoubtedly affix labels of hypocrisy on the nation that had for several decades championed abolition.

The insincerity of Lord Palmerston's moderation emerged more clearly as the Confederacy continued to make exceptional progress on the battlefield.

---

6   Lord Palmerston to William Gladstone, 24 September 1862. In the Palmerston Papers, *Gladstone and Palmerston: Being the Correspondence of Lord Palmerston with Mr. Gladstone 1851-1865*, Philip Guedalla, ed. (London and Southampton: The Camelot Press Ltd., 1928), 232. Primary sources contained in this volume will hereafter be cited using the traditional method for written correspondence and *Palmerston Papers*.

7   See *ibid.*, 235, for a reference made by Palmerston on impartiality and Britain's North American interests.

After sending McClellan into a retreat down to Harrison's Landing along the James River following the Seven Days' Battles, the gray-clad soldiers readied for even greater victories, basking contentedly in the mounting evidence of desperation within the federal ranks.

The Lincoln administration effectively deposed McClellan by transferring large portions of his Army of the Potomac to the short-lived Army of Virginia led by Major General John Pope. The victor of Island No. 10 in the Western Theater also shared ancestors with George Washington and, for Lincoln at least, appeared to be something McClellan was not: a proven fighter. Freshly transferred east, Pope issued four general orders that debauched the Southern home front, held civilians to account for unconventional warfare, and demanded from them an oath of allegiance to the Union which, if not pledged, would result in the loss of their homes and possessions.[8]

Lincoln soon learned that Pope's braggadocio and acidic personality were as ineffective as his performance on the battlefield. On August 9, the Army of Virginia met Stonewall Jackson's men and tactical defeat at Cedar Mountain, Virginia.[9] "I hope your victory is but the precursor of others over our foe," Lee wrote Jackson.[10] Lee, who was seeking vengeance against the new federal commander and his callous orders, hoped that Cedar Mountain was only the beginning of a season of impressive battlefield victories. On August 20, Pope's men retreated across the Rappahannock River. In a broad strategic turning movement, Jackson's men marched more than fifty miles around Pope's right flank and met the enemy in a brief clash at Bristoe Station while the other wing of Lee's army, under Major General James Longstreet, moved to join Jackson. Two days of bloody fighting commenced on August 29 near the old Manassas battlefield where the men in blue and gray had first met in July 1861. The combat triggered especially vicious close-quarter fighting along an unfinished railroad cut near the hamlet of Groveton. The battle climaxed on Chinn Ridge, a short distance from the late Judith Henry's white clapboard home and the hill bearing her name. Longstreet's crushing counter attack broke Pope's army which, in a haunting reprise of the events of the previous year, retreated in

---

8 On John Pope's orders, see Mark Grimsley, *The Hard Hand of War: Union Military Policy Toward Southern Civilians, 1861-1865* (New York: Cambridge University Press, 1995), 85-95.

9 For the best treatment of the actions at Cedar Mountain, see Robert K. Krick, *Stonewall Jackson at Cedar Mountain* (Chapel Hill: The University of North Carolina Press, 1990).

10 Robert E. Lee to Thomas J. Jackson, August 12, 1862, in *WPREL*, 251.

confusion across the Bull Run to safety. There was "no denying," wrote civilian John Codman Ropes, "that we had lost prestige by the defeat of Manassas."[11]

"The army achieved today on the plains of Manassas a signal victory over combined forces of Generals McClellan and Pope," Lee telegraphed to President Davis. "We mourn the loss of our gallant dead, in every conflict[,] yet our gratitude to Almighty God for His mercies rises higher and higher each day, to Him and to the valour of our troops a nation's gratitude is due."[12] The Army of Northern Virginia stood at the pinnacle of its battlefield prowess. Confederate morale soared.

Across the Atlantic, meanwhile, Palmerston's government grew increasingly impatient on the question of recognition. On September 14, 1862 (the news of the upcoming Maryland invasion and battles north of the Potomac had not yet reached across the ocean), the prime minister sent the following note:

> My dear Russell,
>
> The detailed account given in the *Observer* to-day of the battles of August 29 and 30 between the Confederates and the Federals show that the latter got a very complete smashing; and it seems not altogether unlikely that still greater disasters await them, and that even Washington or Baltimore may fall into the hand of the Confederates. If this should happen, would it not be time for us to consider whether in such a State of things England and France might not address the contending parties and Recommend an arrangement upon the basis of separation? [13]

Russell seemed to concur. In the opening year of the war, the federal army had made "no progress in subduing the insurgent States," he replied three days later.[14] He recommended a cabinet meeting to settle on a course of action within the next two weeks. In a subsequent reply to this note, Palmerston was somewhat more candid about France's and Russia's place within the entire

---

11 John Codman Ropes, *The Army Under Pope* (New York: Charles Scribner's Sons, 1881), 144.

12 Robert E. Lee to Jefferson Davis, telegram, August 30, 1862, in *WPREL*, 268.

13 Lord Henry Palmerston to Lord John Russell, September 14, 1862. The Russell-Palmerston correspondence can be found in the appendices of James V. Murfin, *The Gleam of Bayonets: The Battle of Antietam and Robert E. Lee's Maryland Campaign September 1862* (Baton Rouge: Louisiana State University Press, 1965), 394-401.

14 Russell to Palmerston, September 17, 1862, in Murfin, *The Gleam of Bayonets*, 396.

scheme for intervention. After explaining that the courtesy should be paid to Russia by offering her a place within the mediation coalition, the prime minister concluded, "we should be better without her . . . she would be too favourable to the North; but on the other hand her participation in the offer might render the North the more willing to accept it."[15] Rendering foreign mediation palatable to Northerners had always been an important goal for Palmerston, for he knew that intervention of any kind would likely fracture the Union. As one widely circulated Northern editorial reflected, there is "no such thing as international sympathy." "Force is the only argument respected now a days. And if the nation fails in so glorious a cause as this, she will be held . . . and as a fit subject for the attacks of the rest of the world," the searing column concluded.[16]

Gladstone, for one, contentedly received news of the prime minister's position.[17] A few days later on October 7, the chancellor of the exchequer delivered a rousing speech at a political rally in Newcastle-on-Tyne, declaring: "Jefferson Davis and the other leaders of the South have made an army; they are making, it appears, a navy; and they have made what is more than either; *they have made a nation.*"[18]

*   *   *

Bolstered politically and spiritually, Jefferson Davis wasted little time capitalizing on Lee's stunning victory at Second Manassas. In a message to the Southern Congress, the Confederate president praised the general and his intrepid army. He also declared September 18 a National Day of Prayer and Thanksgiving. God, explained Davis, had once "again extended his shield over [the] patriotic Army."[19] Now, with full trust in Lee, Davis looked for the next

---

15 Palmerston to Russell, September 23, 1862, in Murfin, *The Gleam of Bayonets*, 399.

16 "The Opinion of Europe," editorial, September 24, 1862, *Canton Repository*, Canton, Ohio; Robert L. Reid, "William E. Gladstone's 'Insincere Neutrality' During the Civil War," *Civil War History: A Journal of the Middle Period* 15, no. 4 (December 1969).

17 Gladstone to Palmerston, September 25, 1862, *Palmerston Papers*, 233.

18 William E. Gladstone, speech, October 1862, emphasis added by this author; Robert L. Reid, ed., "William Gladstone's 'Insincere Neutrality' During the Civil War," 293.

19 Jefferson Davis, September 2, 1862, as quoted in Herman Hattaway and Richard E. Beringer, *Jefferson Davis, Confederate President* (Lawrence: The University Press of Kansas, 2002), 176.

campaign to use the psychological capital gained on Chinn Ridge. Ironically, like Lincoln (who was patiently awaiting the moment he could unveil his plan for emancipation), Jefferson Davis was looking forward to Lee's next major battlefield victory. Another significant federal defeat in the field, confirmed foreign leaders, would require "the iron" of intervention to be "struck while it is hot."[20]

*   *   *

Heavy rains escaped the clouds over Manassas Junction the night of August 30. The rainstorm slowed troop movements that evening and created a much-needed lull in the action for those Confederate troops who had committed to hard marching with Jackson's "Foot Cavalry" and had engaged in three battles in only one month. In a sweeping turning movement intended to flank and sever Pope's chaotic retreat, Confederate forces advanced to the Little River Turnpike the evening of August 31 and on the first day of September marched along that road to Fairfax Court House.[21] Another driving rain that evening saturated a pair of Confederate brigades as they advanced to ascertain the position of the retreating boys in blue near Ox Hill. The meeting commenced a heated skirmish that swelled to engage two Confederate divisions opposite two federal divisions.[22]

Thunder rolled and lighting crashed in sheets, adding color and syncopated rhythm to the pelting rain. General Isaac Ingalls Stevens, commanding a division in Major General Jesse Lee Reno's federal Ninth Corps, led an attack against the Confederate position that was initially successful and inflicted chaos in the ranks of one veteran Louisiana brigade holding down a portion of the line. In the middle of this attack, however, a bullet mortally wounded General Stevens and knocked him out of the saddle. The indiscriminate lead ball had claimed the life of both a soldier and a promising politician. President Franklin Pierce had appointed Stevens in the 1850s to head up the Pacific Railroad Survey, and the general went on to serve as the territorial governor of

---

20 Palmerston to Russell, September 23, 1862, in Murfin, *The Gleam of Bayonets*, 399.

21 General Robert E. Lee to [Adjutant and Inspector General] Samuel Cooper, official report of the Second Manassas Campaign, June 5, 1863, in *WPREL*, 275-285.

22 *Ibid.*

Washington and chairman of John Cabell Breckenridge's failed 1860 presidential campaign.[23]

Steven's death dealt a demoralizing blow to the Union troops. As historian David Welker notes, "the advancing [Union] line suddenly grew wild with fury and anger at their leader's death and they broke into a dead run for the Rebels in the woods."[24] Leading a division from General Heintzelman's Third Corps, Major General Phil Kearny sealed the breach in the federal command. The one-armed Kearny—his amputated right limb a souvenir of the fight for Mexico City—commanded the respect and loyalty of his men. According to early campaign historian Ropes, "In the field he was always ready, always skillful, always brave, always untiring, always hopeful, and always vigilant and alert."[25]

Darkness unfolded over the battlefield as Kearny galloped gallantly forward. Enraged and impatient in the heat of the battle, Kearny leapt into the middle of a cornfield near the Reid farmhouse. When he detected clattering and movement ahead of him, he called out to ascertain which federal regiment he had discovered. His uncertainty in the growing darkness and heavy rain turned to shock when the 49th Georgia of Colonel Edward L. Thomas' Brigade revealed itself from behind a hedgerow in front of him. The men recognized the rider as a federal officer and hurled nearly a dozen balls into the air, one of which struck Kearny's hip and flung him to the muddy Virginia soil.[26] "Of all who have fallen in this war[,] he is the only one for whom I have shed a tear," Michigan soldier Charles B. Hayden admitted. "I have to confess that in spite of pride the news quite unmanned me."[27]

With two general officers slain on the field, the darkness nearly complete, and the storm refusing to recede, the pitched conflict for the Little River

23 For a succinct sketch of Stevens' life and career, see Appendix 1 in Paul Taylor, *He Hath Loosed the Fateful Lightning: The Battle of Ox Hill (Chantilly) September 1, 1862* (Shippensburg: White Mane, 2003), 130-131.

24 David A. Welker, *Tempest at Ox Hill: The Battle of Chantilly* (Cambridge: Da Capo Press, 2002), 161.

25 Ropes, *The Army Under Pope*, 150.

26 "The Death of General Kearney," *Boston Evening Transcript*, Boston, Mass., September 5, 1862.

27 Charles B. Hayden, journal, in Stephen W. Sears, ed., *For Country, Cause, and Leader: The Civil War Journal of Charles B. Hayden* (New York: Ticknor & Fields, 1993), 282; see also Taylor, *Fateful Lightning*, 84-86.

Turnpike began to wane without a tactical victor garnering laurels. In a matter of two hours the Confederates lost nearly 500 men, while casualties on the federal side were slightly higher. "What a grand spectacle the Chantilly fight presented!" declared a Pennsylvania soldier. "A terrible rain storm with terrific thunder . . . this, combined with the booming of the cannon and rattle of musketry, made up a most indescribable scene, outrivaling pandemonium itself. It was a terrific, horrible, phantasmagoria."[28]

Strategically speaking, Pope's beaten army was on precarious ground, perilously close to the District of Columbia. By the next morning, according to Lee, "the enemy had conducted his retreat so rapidly that the attempt to intercept him was abandoned." Fearing a vigorous rebel pursuit, President Lincoln ordered clerks and employees of Washington's public buildings organized into companies and supplied with ammunition for the capital's defense. Lincoln's fear underscored his growing frustration. "The campaign of the army under Pope was ended," Ropes concluded.[29]

Pope's career leading the army in the East was also over. One he decided to depose Pope, the president turned to Ambrose Burnside, offering command of the largest Eastern Union army to the debonair Rhode Islander, who earlier in the war had secured the North Carolina coast for the federals. When Burnside refused (citing the immense pressure of "everything" resting on the military's performance on the battlefield), the president's secretary John Hay convinced Lincoln that he had only one resource upon which he could rely. Early on the morning of September 2, Halleck and Lincoln asked General George McClellan to assume command of the Washington defenses once again. The appointment to take the reins of the Army of the Potomac followed just three days later. McClellan conveyed the news to his wife Ellen in his usual vainglorious style: "Again I have been called upon to save the country." On September 7, Secretary of War Stanton issued General Orders No. 128, dismissing Pope and transferring him to head the Department of the Northwest, a largely inconsequential position that left him to subdue the vicious Sioux uprising in the Minnesota Territory.[30]

---

28 Pennsylvania soldier, as quoted in Taylor, *Fateful Lightning,* 70.

29 *WPREL,* 284. [Assistant Adjutant General] E.D. Townsend, 2 September 1862, Special Orders No. 218. Reproduced in *Messages and Papers of the Presidents,* James D. Richardson, comp. (New York: Bureau of National Literature, 1887), 5:332; Ropes, *The Army Under Pope,* 150.

30 George Brinton McClellan to Ellen McClellan, letter, 5 September 1862, *McClellan Papers.*

Many within the Lincoln administration harbored serious reservations about McClellan. The cabinet meeting on the afternoon Lincoln determined to reinstate the general became particularly heated, with Secretary of the Treasury Salmon Portland Chase and Secretary of War Stanton vigorously opposing the president's decision. These rivals distressed Lincoln with their fears of a "national calamity" and arguments that McClellan's return would only result in an encore of the disasters around Richmond.[31]

The administration may have harbored reservations about the bold decision, but the enlisted men did not. "From extreme sadness we passed in a twinkling to a delirium of delight," George Kimball of the 12th Massachusetts exclaimed when he learned of McClellan's return to command.[32] Affection for the reinstated commander was infectious and soon restored confidence to an overwhelmed and disorganized army. "McClellan took command of our forces at this critical juncture," confirmed an Ohio private. "Everything seemed to be restored to order, by his magic touch, on the instant. Confidence once more animated the breasts of our soldiers." He continued:

> Chaos and confusion in the ranks reduced to discipline and order, and in less than a week from the time he took command, McClellan had gathered around him one of the strongest, most splendid armies the world had ever seen, and taken the field against the enemy…the name that exercised the potent, all-powerful spell over the minds of the men composing our armies was McClellan's. Twas wonderful to see the implicit confidence, and devotion the men felt toward him. 'Give us McClellan and we're prepared to encounter the whole world.'[33]

Troops in Washington paraded past McClellan's residence on H Street to the rhythm of army bands, stirring paeans, and wild cheering. The Army of the Potomac "seemed to be itself again," Colonel Joseph J. Bartlett noted. Even the "despairing patriot officials of Washington seemed hopeful and buoyant once more," he continued, describing the cheers and waving handkerchiefs that

---

31 See also James M. McPherson, *Crossroads of Freedom: Antietam* (Oxford and New York: Oxford University Press, 2002), 86-87.

32 Kimball is quoted in John W. Schildt, *Roads to Antietam* (Hagerstown, Maryland: Antietam Publications, 1985), 7.

33 Letter dated September 19, 1862, Washington, D.C., printed in the *Summit County Beacon*, Akron, Ohio, September 25, 1862.

outlined the streets.[34] McClellan "had a personal touch," noted Jacob Dolson Cox, the Ohio general who would lead a IX Corps division in the upcoming campaign. "He went beyond the formal military salute, and gave his cap a little twirl, which with his bow and smile seemed to carry a little of personal good fellowship even to the humblest private soldier."[35]

Once more the men had hope, but the anticipation of a new campaign complicated their conflicted emotions. "There is every probability that the enemy, baffled in his intended capture of Washington, will cross the Potomac, and make a raid into Maryland or Pennsylvania," General-in-Chief Henry W. Halleck surmised on September 3. He ordered McClellan to ascertain the strength of the forces surrounding Washington and ready them for the impending defense of the capital.[36] That afternoon, the reinstated federal army commander ordered the Second, Ninth, and Twelfth corps to move north of the Potomac River.

*   *   *

Halleck's conclusion was indeed prescient. While the general-in-chief groomed his orders for McClellan, Robert E. Lee laid plans of his own. Sporting splints on both of his hands, Lee was forced to dictate his orders. On August 31, the general was standing in front of his horse when it became startled, causing Lee to trip over the reins and tumble to the ground. He suffered sprains in both hands, a broken bone in one, and excruciating pain that restricted his range of motion. The sight of Lee in dual splints fomented some excitement in the Northern press, which hastily circulated an account from a secessionist woman in Frederick, Maryland, who claimed that Lee had been wounded in battle.[37]

In his headquarters tent near Dranesville, Virginia, Lee began a thoughtful and contemplative correspondence with President Davis. "The present seems

---

34 Colonel Joseph J. Bartlett, letter, circa September 1862, *National Tribune*, December 19, 1862.

35 Jacob Dolson Cox, *Military Reminiscences of the Civil War* (New York: Charles Scribner's Sons, 1881), 1:243.

36 *The War of the Rebellion: The Official Records of the Union and Confederate Armies*, Series I, 19, 2:169, hereafter cited as *OR*. Unless otherwise noted, all references are to volume 19, "South Mountain and Antietam." The part numbers will be noted with each citation.

37 "General Lee Wounded," *Boston Daily Transcript*, 13 September 1862; also dispatched in the *Philadelphia Inquirer*, New York, and Baltimore papers, as well.

to be the most propitious time since the commencement of the war for the Confederate Army to enter Maryland," opined the general. "The two grand armies of the United States that have been operating in Virginia, though now united, are much weakened and demoralized. . . . If it is ever desired to give material aid to Maryland and afford her an opportunity of throwing off the oppression to which she is now subject, this would seem the most favorable."[38]

Since the outbreak of the rebellion, Maryland had straddled the sectional divide. Its counties were split between slave and free; those framing the District of Columbia and the Chesapeake Bay were ardently pro-Confederate. Despite caustic rhetoric from these secessionist strongholds, the state remained, albeit tepidly, in the Union. Like other slaveholding states whose stars continued to adorn the Union banner, Maryland repeatedly triggered heartburn for the Lincoln administration. Already it fielded several Confederate regiments, witnessed sharp anti-Union rioting when the 6th Massachusetts Volunteers attempted to pass through Baltimore, and felt the bitter dictates of wartime with Lincoln's suppression of the writ of *habeas corpus*.

Thus far, however, the one problem it had never seriously posed for Lincoln was the real threat of secession. "There was never a moment when Maryland's governor was willing that she should follow Virginia into secession," William Seabrook wrote when describing Maryland Governor Thomas Hicks. "When all other reasonable means . . . had been tried and failed, the governor was as decidedly in favor of prosecuting the war as was Lincoln himself."[39] Indeed, when a special session of the Maryland General Assembly was held on April 19, 1861, Hicks spoke of the essentiality of neutrality. "I honestly and most earnestly entertain the conviction that . . . the . . . safety of Maryland lies in preserving a neutral position between our brethren of the North and of the South," argued the governor. "I cannot counsel Maryland to take sides against the general government, until it shall commit outrages upon us which would justify us in resisting its authority."[40] The legislature took the governor's advice. "From the accounts of the Legislature, I don't think our

38 Lee to Davis, Dranesville, Virginia 3 September 1862, in *WPREL*, 292-293.

39 William L.W. Seabrook, *Maryland's Great Part in Saving the Union* (Westminster, Maryland: American Sentinel Company, 1913), 18-19; also quoted in Charles W. Mitchell, ed., *Maryland Voices of the Civil War* (Baltimore: Johns Hopkins University Press, 2007), 90-91.

40 Hicks, as quoted in the *Baltimore Sun*, April 29, 1861; also quoted in Mitchell, *Maryland Voices of the Civil War*, 86.

State will secede at least for the present," Baltimorean George Whitmarsh concluded in his diary. "The temporary vote yesterday was 13 for secession & 53 against."[41] Governor Hicks' successor concurred. In March 1862, Governor Augustus W. Bradford transmitted a series of state resolutions to President Lincoln that simultaneously denounced any attempt to meddle "with the domestic institutions of the States" and any thoughts of secession.[42] As one veteran remembered, any traces of secessionist rhetoric present in Maryland in April 1861

> had by [the summer of 1862] simmered down to a tepid sentimentalism which manifested itself in weak social snobbery, silly songs, intriguing, speculating, and blockade running . . . that living, practical faith which is willing to . . . take pay in Confederate promises, is totally lacking in Maryland. . . . In brief, except a few young Hotspurs attracted by the love of adventure, and a few cock-eyed politicians who have compromised themselves unwittingly, rebel Maryland seems to prefer the sideboard to the field, and from all accounts Lee will lose two by desertion where he gains one by recruiting.[43]

Lee clearly understood the slim chances of Maryland adopting an ordinance of secession, and he knew that few of its inhabitants could be cajoled into joining the rebellion. Still, the victorious Southern general refused to neglect the opportunity to carry the war north of the Potomac River. "Lee was a commander who habitually defied the odds," historian James M. McPherson noted succinctly.[44] As one veteran recalled of the Confederate army, "it must be their necessity, and not their hopes, which urges them to this desperate venture."[45]

Necessity played no small role in Lee's decision to move northward. "I am more fully persuaded of the benefits that will result from an expedition into

---

41 George Whitmarsh, diary entry, April 30, 1861, original in the Maryland Historical Society, Baltimore; also quoted in Mitchell, ed., *Maryland Voices of the Civil War*, 86-87.

42 Augustus W. Bradford to Abraham Lincoln, March 6, 1862; original in Executive Ledger Book, Maryland State Archives, quoted in Mitchell, ed., *Maryland Voices of the Civil War*, 4, 5-7.

43 "Personal Recollections of the War: Antietam," in *Harper's New Monthly Magazine*, 36 (February 1868): 276.

44 McPherson, *Crossroads of Freedom*, 88.

45 *Harper's New Monthly Magazine*, 36 (February 1868): 273.

Maryland," Lee wrote to Davis in his second communiqué.[46] Shifting the war onto Northern soil would proffer much needed relief to the war-torn Old Dominion, clearing the Shenandoah Valley of disruption during the fall harvest. Furthermore, a campaign into Maryland would offer Lee's poorly equipped army an assortment of war materiel, shoes, clothing, and well-fed animals to ride and pull wagons and artillery pieces, as well as a grand opportunity to collect additional supplies, subsistence, and possibly new recruits. In the 1860 census, Maryland's Washington and Frederick counties boasted 19,314 horses, 18,021 milking cows, 21,661 beef cattle, and 69,973 swine. These neighboring counties together produced nearly two million bushels of wheat and Indian corn. Indeed, these two counties outranked nearly every county in Virginia in terms of agricultural resources.[47] The allure of Maryland was enough to attenuate any lingering doubts about making the foray. "There is always hazard in military movements," Lee cautioned, "but we must decide between the positive loss of inactivity and the risk of action."[48]

Lee's haggard Army of Northern Virginia begged for fresh supplies. Many thousands of his men, like William W. Sherwood, who served in a Virginia infantry regiment, marched barefooted on blistered feet. "Our army is in a bad condition at present, the most of it is barefoot," George Washington Hall of the 14th Georgia observed. "I have no shoes nor clothes but what I have on my back."[49]

Some were hungry and toted empty canteens. Mary Bedinger Mitchell, a civilian in Shepherdstown, offered a poignant recollection:

> When I say that they were hungry, I convey no impression of the gaunt starvation that looked from their cavernous eyes. . . . I saw the troops march past us every summer for four years, and I know something of the appearance of a marching army, both Union

46 Lee to Davis, Leesburg, Virginia, 4 September 1862, in *WPREL*, 294.

47 For census figures and further data, see Joseph L. Harsh's indispensable reference volume, *Sounding the Shallows: A Confederate Companion for the Maryland Campaign of 1862* (Kent, Ohio: Kent State University Press, 2000), 148.

48 Lee to Davis, Leesburg, Virginia, 4 September 1862; Lee to Seddon, June 8, 1863, in *OR*, vol. 27, 3:868-869; Harsh, *Sounding the Shallows*, 132.

49 William W. Sherwood, diary, September 14, 1862, Virginia Historical Society, Richmond, Virginia; George Washington Hall, diary entry, September 11, 1862, in Miscellaneous Manuscripts Collection, Library of Congress, Manuscript Division, Washington, D.C.

and Southern. . . . Never were want and exhaustion more visibly put before my eyes, and that they could march or fight at all seemed incredible.[50]

Many in Lee's army had not changed clothes for weeks, and were infested with uninvited insects. In makeshift attempts to curb the infestation, many soldiers placed their garments in the bottom of shallow streams with rocks to hold them in place. This was a frequent ritual during the course of the Maryland Campaign of 1862. "Every evening in Maryland, when the army . . . bivouacked for the night, hundreds of the soldiers could be seen, sitting on the roads or fields, half denuded with their clothes in their laps busily cracking, between the two thumb-nails, these creeping nuisances," one Confederate soldier recounted.[51] The routine was suggestive of the hard life in camp and on the march, but it did not demoralize Hall. "When I wash my clothes I have to go naked till I wash and dry them or put them on wet, but I am in a just cause," he told his diary.[52] Of course, deficient of proper hygiene, the soldiers were frequently ill as well. "The whole country, from Warrenton to Leesburg, is filled with sick soldiers, abandoned on the wayside by the enemy," reported the 2nd New York Cavalry.[53]

Northern newspaper editors clearly and presciently recognized supplies and forage as the primary goals for Lee's incursion. "Our belief is that the rebel generals will essay to cross the river in hope of getting supplies and other assistance through a secession rising in Maryland, and thus be enabled to move on Baltimore rather than the federal metropolis, which they probably think too well fortified to be attacked," one editor explained.[54] Perhaps this stratagem was intended not only to "throw off the oppression" of eastern Maryland secessionists, but to throw off the oppression of his own depraved army, as well.

---

50 "The Battle of Sharpsburg," in *Southern Historical Society Papers*, 13 (Richmond, 1885): 512; Mary Bedinger Mitchell, as quoted in Robert K. Krick, "The Army of Northern Virginia in September 1862: Its Circumstances, Its Opportunities, and Why It Should Not Have Been at Sharpsburg," in Gary W. Gallagher, ed., *Antietam: Essays on the 1862 Maryland Campaign* (Kent, Ohio: Kent State University Press, 1989), 42-43.

51 "The Battle of Sharpsburg," 511.

52 Hall, diary entry, September 11, 1862.

53 *OR* 1:1092.

54 "Army Operations on Wednesday," *Boston Evening Transcript*, September 5, 1862.

By some strange fortune, the ragged condition of the rebel troops did not affect their combat performance. Even with only lukewarm assurance of replenished supplies and forage, Lee averred his confidence in the abilities of his troops. "How men famished and footsore could fight as they did was a question I asked myself over and over," C. E. Goldsborough marveled in the pages of a Union veterans' periodical.[55] By removing the largest of the rebel armies from the Confederacy and broaching conflict on enemy soil, Lee made a major investment using the triumphant record and soaring morale of his army as capital. And, if expended, Lee risked irreparable damage to his army's brilliant record and to the credibility that his men had so painstakingly garnered on battlefield after battlefield, convincing the world that they had made a nation. The Maryland expedition would transfer Lee from his customary and most comfortable interior lines and defensive fighting to unfamiliar roads and the offense. But he would not be idle. "[We must] endeavor to harass, if we cannot destroy them."[56] That harassment, according to Lee, had the potential to lead the armies into Pennsylvania, where they could set their eyes on the state capital at Harrisburg, or on the original national capital at Philadelphia.

By reaching into Pennsylvania, Lee hoped to affect the outcome of the 1862 midterm Congressional elections, confident that his campaign would expose the feckless federal prosecution of the war and Lincoln's inability to prevent the fighting from reaching and disrupting the lives of Northern civilians. This bold move could sweep enough conciliatory, anti-Lincoln Democrats into Congress to drastically inhibit Lincoln's ability to conduct the war. Already, "defeatism began to undermine Union morale and Democratic critics of the Lincoln administration stood to reap the harvest," historian Frank L. Klement wrote of the autumn of 1862. Now, according to Klement, with Kirby Smith's and Braxton Bragg's Southern armies also turning northward in the Western Theater, the situation beyond Virginia for the Union cause was "considerably worse" than the previous year. An economic recession in the upper Midwest and rampant racial prejudices seemed to afford a sound platform for the Democratic victories Lee aimed to bring about.[57]

55 C. E. Goldsborough, "Fighting Them Over," *National Tribune*, October 14, 1886.

56 Lee to Davis, Leesburg, Virginia, 4 September 1862, in *WPREL*, 294.

57 Frank L. Klement, *The Limits of Dissent: Clement L. Vallandigham and the Civil War* (Lexington: The University Press of Kentucky, 1970), 105-106.

*   *   *

If Lee had indeed selected a target for his incursion, then it was truly Pennsylvania, a fairly transparent conclusion that has since been obscured by more sensational claims that Lee intended to strike for the federal capital. "I had no intention of attacking him in his fortifications, and am not prepared to invest them," Lee wrote to Davis two days after Chantilly. "I considered it useless to attack the fortifications around Alexandria and Washington," he would confirm after the war. Confederate Chief of Ordnance Josiah Gorgas anticipated an advance into Pennsylvania. "Our army has crossed over into Maryland and is now I hope at Harrisburgh and on its way to Philadelphia," he confided to his diary.[58]

William Allan, who knew Lee and wrote one of the earliest histories of the campaign, summarized what the general had told him about the objectives of the campaign:

> As he was greatly outnumbered he must divide his adversaries; he must keep up, and increase if possible, their apprehensions for the safety of Washington. . . . while he drew the other part away and fought it *at a distance* from supports and strongholds. Large garrisons would be kept to secure the safety of Washington, Baltimore, and other important places, while public sentiment would demand that the remainder be promptly led against the invaders. Lee could then, probably, choose his battlefield and fight when and where he thought best.[59]

Dennis Tuttle of the 20th Indiana was similarly unfazed by Lee's designs and thought an invasion of Maryland improbable. "I should be surprised if they should make an attempt on Washington, or try to cross into Maryland," he wrote his wife on August 30. "Their situation is desperate."[60] John Hay, one of

---

58 The centrality of Pennsylvania to Lee's strategy will be explored in depth in a subsequent chapter; Lee to Davis, September 3, 1862, *OR*, 2:590; "Letter from General R. E. Lee," *Southern Historical Society Papers*, 7 (Richmond, 1879): 445; Josiah Gorgas, diary entry, September 14, 1862, in *The Journals of Josiah Gorgas 1857-1878*, ed. Sarah Woolfolk Wiggins (Tuscaloosa: University of Alabama Press, 1995), 52.

59 William Allan, "The Strategy of the Campaign of Sharpsburg or Antietam, September, 1862," in *Papers of the Military Historical Society of Massachusetts*, 3 (1888): 73-103. Emphasis in this passage added by author.

60 Dennis Tuttle to his wife, letter, August 30, 1862, in Dennis Tuttle Papers, Library of Congress, Manuscript Division, Washington, D.C.

Lincoln's personal secretaries, likewise had no anxieties over the matter. While Hay observed (under a pen name) that "Washington cannot be taken and the nation live," he also made observations about what he perceived to be the actual threat to the district. Even after Lee's army did cross the Potomac, Hay concluded that the capital would be free from harm. "I do not believe that Washington is to be taken. Trusting to that, I give myself no thought of this town, but look to . . . our army . . . . Our men are fresh, vigorous, healthy, well fed, well armed, perfectly equipped." He continued:

> Their rations are more than any man can eat, their marches have been short and easy, their clothing is comfortable, neat and soldierly. They are fighting in the best cause that ever blessed a banner . . . . They are opposed by a half-starved rabble, disorderly and miserable, perishing with disease and famine, gaunt, ragged and filthy, fired with whisky and fanatic hate, and led by perjured rebels and traitors. They subsist on what they can steal, and prepare in the intervals of their long and ruinous marches . . . the sharp stones are crimsoned with the blood of barefooted wretches, the moaning of disease and misery resound through the army . . .[61]

Though the road to Washington was, as Hay conceded, "open and unobstructed," it was threatened not by a serious force but a collection of ragged bandits more suited to harass than to beleaguer. By his own logic, the best Lee's army could do was "endeavor to harass."[62] Certainly, as Charles Marshall of Lee's personal staff had written, "General Lee's policy was not to capture any portion of Federal territory, but to protract the war by breaking up the enemy's campaigns. . . . At the same time he desired to increase the power of resistance of the South by keeping the enemy out of Confederate territory."[63]

Hay essentially suggested what one federal veteran posited after the war in the pages of *Harper's New Monthly*: the rebel incursion was one conceived of necessity. In spite of the condition of the enemy army, the presidential secretary subsequently lamented what he considered to be the "crowning shame and

---

61 John Hay, Washington correspondence, September 7, 1862, in *Lincoln's Journalist: John Hay's Anonymous Writings for the Press, 1860-1864*, ed. Michael Burlingame (Carbondale: Southern Illinois University Press, 1998), 306-307.

62 *Ibid.*, 305.

63 Charles Marshall, *An Aide-de-camp of Lee, Being the Papers of Colonel Charles Marshall, Sometimes Aide-de-camp, Military Secretary, and Assistant Adjutant General on the Staff of Robert E. Lee, 1862-1865*, Frederick Maurice, ed., (Boston: Little, Brown and Company, 1927), 145-146.

horror of the war": the defeats at Second Manassas and Chantilly.[64] With this commentary, Hay suggested that the federal army was sapped of both energy and morale. In this calculus, the Army of Northern Virginia scored victories simply because the boys in blue allowed the rebels to assert mastery over them.

And therein was the rub. Virtually nothing could approximate the ability of a battlefield victory to lift the self-esteem of the Army of the Potomac. Moreover, victory would not only emancipate the army, it would permit Lincoln to issue a document freeing the slaves. "Perhaps the time is coming when the President . . . will give the word long waited for, which will breathe the life that is needed, the fire that seems extinguished, in the breast of our men at arms," Hay wrote. In his next sentence, he clearly recognized the stakes. "If we are not gloriously victorious before the frosts of October redden the leaves, with their falling will fall our hopes and the hopes of liberty in the world."[65]

The ability of the Army of Northern Virginia to assert "mastery" over its opponents swelled appreciably the confidence of its commanders and fighting men. "[Lee] knew from events of the past that his army was equal to the service which he thought to call it, and ripe for the adventure," James Longstreet reflected. "We then possessed an army, which, if it had been kept together, the Federals would never dare attack," he recalled elsewhere. After the war, Lee told Edward Gordon that "he did not doubt . . . he could have crushed [the federal army]." Lee even allowed a morsel of hubris to stain his official report. "[The Army of Northern Virginia] was believed to be strong enough to detain the enemy upon the northern frontier until the approach of winter . . ."[66]

The physical condition of the Army of Northern Virginia at the end of the summer of 1862 offers the most convincing testimony of the heights to which Confederate rhetoric soared from the harsh realities of conditions on the ground. Now, necessity demanded a move for replenishment in the fertile valleys and plain fields of Maryland and Pennsylvania.

"Every where smiling fields of wheat, wide stretching acres of green corn with their yellow ears and crimson tassels met the eye; and on every hand were

---

64 Hay in *Lincoln's Journalist*, 307.

65 *Ibid*; see also Michael C. C. Adams, *Our Masters the Rebels: A Speculation on Union Military Failure in the East, 1861-1865* (Cambridge: Harvard University Press, 1978).

66 James Longstreet, *From Manassas to Appomattox: Memoirs of the Civil War in America* (Philadelphia: J. B. Lippincott Company, 1896), 200; Longstreet, as quoted in Harsh, *Sounding the Shallows*, 150; Lee, as quoted in *ibid*; OR 1:144.

the pasture lands teeming with clover, timothy, and broad waving blades of nourishing grass," Confederate soldier John Dooley recalled of Maryland's countryside. "Extensive orchards, the branches of whose trees swept the ground with their luscious burdens of pears, peaches, and apples, invited the stragglers who flocked in numbers from each brigade, as it marched by, to gather into their pickets and haversacks the refreshing fruit." These scenes stood in stark contrast to the "barren fields of Virginia." The Confederate army would at last have nourishment.[67]

On the wisdom of the incursion, Lee secured the sincere approbation of President Davis. Since the victory at First Manassas, Davis encouraged his generals to leave Confederate defensive strategy and its interior lines behind. In September 1862, he wrote that the Confederacy would be protected by "transferring the seat of war to that of [the] . . . enemy." Other politicians, including Secretary of State Robert Toombs, favored the commencement of an offensive campaign. The overwhelming Southern sentiments of aggression and the much-desired vision of horses watering on the Susquehanna metamorphosed Confederate military strategy.[68] Members of the Confederate Congress nearly unanimously supported a move across the Potomac into Maryland. Extending the campaign into Pennsylvania broached some debate, but thoughts of defeating the enemy army on its own soil were most alluring.[69]

Lee informed Davis that the army would begin fording the Potomac. Demonstrating once more his penchant for the offensive and his insistent hope for a battle of annihilation, Lee moved north. With another campaign exhibiting Southern aggressiveness, bold innovation, and superior strategy, Lee hoped that the watchers overseas would venture to "throw off the oppression," too.[70]

---

67 John Dooley, "South Mountain and Sharpsburg," in *John Dooley, Confederate Soldier: His War Journal*, ed. Joseph T. Durkin, S.J. (South Bend, Indiana: U. of Notre Dame Press, 1963), 31.

68 See Grady McWhiney, "'Who Whipped Whom?' Confederate Defeat Reexamined," *Civil War History: A Journal of the Middle Period* 11, no. 1 (March 1965): 17-18.

69 See *Richmond Dispatch*, September 13, 1862; Joseph L. Harsh, *Taken at the Flood*, 539n.5.

70 On Lee and the battle for annihilation, see Thomas L. Connelly and Archer Jones, *The Politics of Command, Factions and Ideas in Confederate Strategy* (Baton Rouge: Louisiana State University Press, 1973), 33; Lee to Davis, Leesburg, Virginia, September 5, 1862, in *WPREL*, 292-293.

C hapter 3

"Maryland, My Maryland"

Lee Invades the North

R umor and alarm, excitement and fear all competed in the pages of Northern newspapers the first week of September 1862. As journalists and editors drafted editorials, they carefully considered the confluence of military, political, and diplomatic affairs. Regular front-page columns updated readers not only as to the "excitement in Pennsylvania," the "position of the enemy," the "military matters of Washington," and the "strength of the enemy," but also informed them of European opinions and either opined or extolled the administration's conduct of the war. Lists of casualties in the most recent campaign, stretching from Cedar Mountain to Chantilly, consumed entire pages of the *New York Times*, presenting a deadly and earnest visualization of war's horrors.[1]

This season of heightened apprehension also renewed debates about the bounds, limits, and sacrifices of this terrible war. Some Republicans who expounded rather self-righteously about having furnished the "men and money" for the war realized their sacrifices had not been sufficient to thwart the invasion. Other Republicans explained away the perilous situation by attacking Democratic generals and commanders who led the principal armies and fought the major battles. For example, in a letter to Secretary of the Treasury Chase on

---

1 See *New York Times*, September 3, 1862.

September 14, Joseph Medill wrote, "The Union cause is in a dismal plight. . . . The President has allowed the Democratic party to shape the policy of the war and furnish the Generals to conduct it, while the Republicans have furnished the men and the money." Democrats retorted by defending their convictions about the appropriate limits of war in a republic. The conflict could not become too aggressive, too invasive, or too inhibitive of civil liberties and it certainly could not interfere with civilian 'property' rights, including human chattel.[2]

Some Republican newspaper editors instilled confidence into the hearts and minds of their readers by printing letters from Union troops ebullient at the prospect of turning rebel invaders from free soil. In an effort to maintain an optimistic outlook, other editors deliberately reduced the stakes. Noting the intense anxiety "everywhere," one feature held that "[a]lthough it will have a very marked effect upon the fortunes of the rebellion, it is not felt that an adverse result would be fatal to the Union cause." These optimists further defended their position by reminding readers of the gamble taken by the invaders. "[T]he defeat of the rebels . . . must be fatal. They have thrown upon Washington *the whole of their army*. . . . They will fight with desperation, undoubtedly, for they have everything staked upon the issue of the conflict. General Jackson is said to have made them a speech before going into action," the article continued, "in which he told them that their defeat would be the downfall of the Southern Confederacy, and that they must fight, therefore, as if they were fighting for life."[3]

But other editors, both Republican and Democrat, were more contemptuous and analytical. The September 5 edition of the *New York Times*, for example, explained that "there is a class of public men who think it highly unwise to admit that we have suffered any serious reverses." The column continued: "They have copious explanations of the apparent checks our forces have sustained, and abundant assurance that they are all to be redeemed in the immediate future. We regret that we cannot share their credulous confidence. Wherever we have met the Rebels . . . behind the earthworks . . . or in the open fields . . . they have beaten us."[4] The next day, in the same distrustful tone, the

---

2   Joseph Medill to Salmon P. Chase, letter, September 14, 1862, in *The Papers of Salmon P. Chase*, ed. John Niven (Kent, Ohio: Kent State University Press, 1996), 3:264-65.

3   "The Pending Battles," column, *New York Times*, September 2, 1862.

4   "Position of the Union Cause," editorial, *New York Times*, September 5, 1862.

Times commented on McClellan's restoration to full command. "Unless he wins victories, he is not the man for the place."[5]

While there existed no general agreement on what types of responses were more productive—patient optimism and hopeful anticipation or deep anxiety and genuine concern—this battle of words emphasized the significance that administration officials, editors, and their constituents consigned to the impending invasion. "The time has come therefore when the most herculean efforts must be put forth. . . . The enemy must be made to turn southward instead of northward," Secretary Chase wrote to George Denison in early September.[6]

Chase was not only speaking of affairs in the East. In the Western Theater, Confederate General Braxton Bragg and Major General Edmund Kirby Smith launched parallel invasions into Kentucky. Bragg's thrust, intended to offset the lonesome string of federal victories that had claimed a significant stretch of the Mississippi River, prompted a closer examination of the new Confederate strategy of northern incursions. Rebel "ferocity" was censured as barbarian and hopeless; it was as if the Confederates had "taken a leaf from the Aboriginals of our country" with its "terror striking" and "torments" the *New York Times* ranted.[7] The rebel tide was rising.

*   *   *

Despite all of this excitement and conflict, a relative and ironic calm hovered over the District of Columbia. Recent rumors about the intentions of the rebel forces were dismissed as "groundless."[8] As many had predicted, the Army of Northern Virginia splashed across the Potomac several scores of miles to the northeast at White's Ford, where the wide river was shallow and easily forded. More importantly, this crossing allowed the rebel army to protect its lines of communications and eschew the impregnable fortifications enclosing the federal capital. "It was decided to cross the Potomac east of the Blue Ridge,

5   *New York Times*, September 6, 1862.

6   Salmon P. Chase to George S. Denison, September 8, 1862, in *The Papers of Salmon P. Chase*, ed. John Niven, 3:262.

7   "A Barbarian Invasion of the North," *New York Times*, September 3, 1862; "Rebel Ferocity," September 4, 1862.

8   *New York Times*, September 4, 1862.

in order, by threatening Washington and Baltimore, to cause the enemy to withdraw from the south bank, where his presence endangered our communications," Lee reported.[9] Many Southerners were excited by the thought of turning to the offensive, penetrating north, and changing the war's course. "The winter of our discontent is turned to glorious summer," was how the *Richmond Examiner* characterized the move across the Potomac.[10]

The thought of an incursion into the North did not please all rebels. "I dont like the idea as I dont like to invade anybodys Country," Isaac Hirsh of the 30th Virginia scribbled in his diary.[11] Garland S. Ferguson, who penned the history of the 25th North Carolina, wrote, "When it was first made known to the men by General Lee's order that the army was to cross the Potomac there was a considerable murmur of disappointment in ranks." The men, Ferguson continued:

> said they had volunteered to resist invasion and not to invade, some did not believe it right to invade Northern territory, others thought that the same cause that brought the Southern army to the front would increase the Northern army, still others thought the war should be carried into the North; thus the men thought, talked and disagreed.[12]

Were these the thoughts of disgruntled Southerners, who considered the invasion to be yet another "breach" of the Confederacy's alleged commitment to limited authority, or was this merely the isolated grousing of a few tired war-torn soldiers? Whatever the reality, these murmuring soldiers likely remained uninformed of their commanders' strategic intentions for the campaign. Butternut-clad men engaged in wide conjecture as to why the war had carried them north. "Much speculation as to our destination," wrote Longstreet staff officer Osmun Latrobe.[13]

---

9   *OR* 1:145.

10   *Richmond Examiner*, Richmond, Virginia, September 5, 1862.

11   Isaac Hirsh, diary entry, September 5, 1862, as quoted in Harsh, *Sounding the Shallows*, 153.

12   Garland S. Ferguson, "Twenty-Fifth Infantry," in Walter Clark, ed., *Histories of the Several Regiments and Battalions from North Carolina in the Great War 1861-'65* (Goldsboro, North Carolina: Nash Brothers, 1901), 2:291-301. This passage has often been cited in the historiography of the Maryland Campaign, beginning with Douglas Southall Freeman.

13   Osmun Latrobe, diary entry, September 8, 1862, in Osmun Latrobe Papers, Virginia Historical Society, Richmond, Virginia.

Maj. Gen. James Longstreet

Library of Congress

———————————

*   *   *

The invading Army of Northern Virginia included some forty thousand men divided into two large wings of infantry. One wing was in the capable hands of Major General Thomas J. Jackson, with the other under Major General James Longstreet.[14] Conventional wisdom claims the command structure of the Army of Northern Virginia had been firmly established on the eve of the Maryland Campaign. Historian Joseph L. Harsh, however, offers a "less structured" view of the army. He reasonably suggests that the divisions of Daniel Harvey Hill, Richard Heron Anderson, Lafayette McLaws, and John Walker were not yet incorporated into the commands of either Longstreet or Jackson. For example,

---

14 Numbers are a precarious business in military history, but contemporary authors provide some clues that can encourage round estimates. William Allan estimated that Lee had 50,000 men on September 2; Walter H. Taylor estimated 35,255 Confederates present at the Battle of Sharpsburg on September 17, which would have placed the invasion force at just above 40,000; A. L. Long ventured there were no more than 45,000 men invading Maryland. Lee himself, wrote the following to President Davis: "Our ranks are very much diminished. I fear from a third to a half of the original numbers. . . ." If Lee is referring to his numbers after Second Manassas, generally accepted to be about 75,000 men, then Lee estimated his strength at the outset of the campaign to be somewhere between 37,500 and 50,000 men. See Allan, "Strategy of the Campaign of Sharpsburg or Antietam, September, 1862," in *Papers of the Military Historical Society of Massachusetts* 3 (1888): 75; Walter H. Taylor, *Four Years with General Lee*, ed. James I. Robertson, Jr. (Bloomington: Indiana University Press, 1962), 73; A. L. Long, *Memoirs of Robert E. Lee, His Military and Personal History* (Philadelphia: J. M. Stoddart & Co., 1886), 205; Lee to Davis, as quoted in Harsh, *Taken at the Flood*, 219-220. See also Harsh, *Sounding the Shallows*, 138-140.

during the Second Manassas Campaign, Richard H. Anderson's men operated as an infantry reserve command. Moreover, the remaining divisions denoted above were peeled out of Richmond to reinforce the Army of Northern Virginia between September 2 and September 5, when the army had already turned north.[15] Indeed, as artillerist Edward Porter Alexander wrote, "Confederate organization into corps was slowly developing." It was not until September 18, the day after the Battle of Antietam, that the Confederate Congress authorized the formal creation of "corps," into which it proposed placing a minimum of two divisions. Finally, this formal reorganization was not announced until November 6.[16]

The army's lack of a formal command organization was only one factor in its uneven profile. Another factor was the erosion of the officer corps, which had suffered considerable setbacks during the summer campaigning around Richmond. More than one-half of Jackson's fourteen brigades were led by colonels. One of Jackson's division commanders, Major General Ambrose Powell Hill, and one of Longstreet's, Brigadier General John Bell Hood, were under temporary arrest for bickering after Second Manassas. Losses in the lower echelons had been just as devastating. Thus, the army embarked upon a supreme test during a period of substantial transition and flux.[17]

If Lee could count on anything, it was the quality of his wing commanders. The right wing, led by forty-one-year-old James Longstreet, was composed initially of four divisions each containing three brigades. Further reorganization, however, merged Brigadier General James Lawson Kemper's Division into Brigadier General David Rumph Jones' Division.[18] Born in South Carolina, Longstreet graduated with the West Point Class of 1842. He proved himself capable of command, earning two brevets and receiving a wound during the Mexican War. Resigning his commission in June 1861, he first led a Confederate brigade at Blackburn's Ford and First Manassas. The next spring

---

15 *Ibid.*, 50-51.

16 E. Porter Alexander, *Military Memoirs of a Confederate: A Critical Narrative*, ed. T. Harry Williams (Bloomington: University of Indiana Press, 1962), 225; *OR* 2:618-619, 698-699; Harsh, *Sounding the Shallows*, 140-141; *Taken at the Flood: Robert E. Lee and Confederate Strategy in the Maryland Campaign of 1862* (Kent, Ohio: Kent State University Press, 1999).

17 On the Army of Northern Virginia in the Maryland Campaign, see Robert K. Krick, "The Army of Northern Virginia in September 1862," in Gallagher, ed., *Antietam: Essays on the 1862 Maryland Campaign*, 35-55.

18 Harsh, *Sounding the Shallows*, 53.

during the Peninsula Campaign Longstreet assumed division command, and by the end of the Seven Days' Battles effectively commanded half of the Army of Northern Virginia. In his role as a wing commander, Longstreet launched the timely counterattack against John Pope's Army of Virginia at Second Manassas, a humiliating hammerstroke that drove the Union off the field.

A tactically brilliant and courageous commander in whom Lee invested much confidence, Longstreet was "warm to brave the venture" north of the Potomac. With Lee still anxious as he pondered his food and resources, Longstreet shared his Mexican War experiences with the army commander. During that conflict, he explained, his division marched around the city of Monterey on two days' rations. "[I] said that it seemed to me that we could trust the fields of Maryland, laden with ripening corn and fruit, to do as much as those of Mexico," he reported.[19]

Longstreet's division commanders were likewise eager and proven. Due to the merger of his division with that of Kemper, General David Jones now led a large command of six brigades—the Georgians of Brigadier General Robert Augustus Toombs and Colonel George Thomas Anderson; the Georgians and South Carolinians of Brigadier General Thomas Fenwick Drayton; Kemper's and George Pickett's former brigade of Virginians; and the South Carolinians of Micah Jenkins' former brigade, now under the command of Colonel Joseph Walker. David Rumph Jones was born in Orangeburg District, South Carolina, on April 5, 1826, and a graduate of the famous West Point Class of 1846. Married to the niece of former President Zachary Taylor, the well-connected Jones served as chief of staff to Beauregard in Charleston Harbor. In that capacity, he had hauled down the federal flag flying over the bombarded Fort Sumter on April 12, 1861. Jones further burnished his name as a commanding officer in the army when he skillfully seized Thoroughfare Gap during the Second Manassas Campaign, an audacious move that allowed Longstreet to arrive with his divisions on the field in time to reinforce Stonewall Jackson's embattled command.[20]

Even more brave and reckless was Brigadier General John Bell Hood, who commanded a much smaller division composed of his former "Texas Brigade"

---

19 James Longstreet, *From Manassas to Appomattox: Memoirs of the Civil War in America* (Bloomington: Indiana University Press, 1960 ed.), 199; Harsh, *Sounding the Shallows*, 52-53.

20 Ezra J. Warner, *Generals in Gray: Lives of the Confederate Commanders* (Baton Rouge: Louisiana State University Press, 1959), 163-164.

Brig. Gen. John Bell Hood

National Archives

led by Colonel William Tatum Wofford, and Colonel Evander McIvor Law's Brigade. Graduating with the West Point Class of 1853, Hood earned a commission as a first lieutenant and served in California and Texas before the war erupted. He resigned his commission on April 17, 1861, and enlisted in the Confederate army as a cavalry captain. Within a matter of months he was promoted to colonel and took command of the 4th Texas Volunteer Infantry.

Hood earned his reputation as a fierce and feared commander on the Virginia peninsula where, at Gaines' Mill on June 27, he rallied his men and attacked, breaking through the Union lines above Boatswain Creek. His reward was the command of a division in Longstreet's Right Wing. Along with his aggressiveness as a fighter, however, came a petty streak. In the wake of Second Manassas, Hood engaged in a dispute with Brigadier General Nathan George Evans, his superior officer, about the disposition of captured wagons. The Texan was under arrest as his men turned their gaze northward into Maryland.[21]

Evans, known by his men as "Shanks," enjoyed an insatiable thirst for whiskey and shared Hood's stern and abrasive disposition. Born in Marion, South Carolina, on February 3, 1824, he graduated from West Point with the Class of 1848. After galloping across the frontier in the cavalry, Evans resigned

21 *Ibid.*, 142-143; see also Richard M. McMurry, *John Bell Hood and the War for Southern Independence* (Lincoln: University of Nebraska Press, 1992), and Brian Craig Miller, *John Bell Hood and the Fight for Civil War Memory* (Knoxville: University of Tennessee Press, 2010).

his commission and entered the Confederate service as a colonel. His brigade was holding the extreme Confederate left at First Manassas. After detecting McDowell's attempt to turn his flank, he shrewdly shifted his forces to meet and repulse the federal onslaught.

That October, Evans met the Union attack at Ball's Bluff, near Leesburg, Virginia, on the Potomac River. In recognition of this feat, which sent bloated bodies in blue coats down the river like flotsam, Evans received a brigadier general's commission. His brigade earned a reputation for proficiency in battle and was shuffled around to various armies. Nicknamed the "Tramp Brigade," Evans' command was dispatched south to assist in the coastal defenses around Charleston and met the enemy in the Battle of Secessionville, South Carolina, on June 16, 1862. It was sent back north again to join James Kemper's Division in time for Second Manassas. Evans retained an independent "divisional" command when Kemper's force was incorporated into Rumph Jones' Division. His command consisted of only his own brigade of South Carolinians.[22]

Lee's left wing was under the command of eccentric thirty-eight-year-old Major General Thomas J. "Stonewall" Jackson. The graduate of the West Point Class of 1846 displayed outstanding military talents in the Mexican War, during which he also first met Robert E. Lee. In 1851 he accepted a teaching position at the Virginia Military Institute in Lexington, Virginia, though he proved to be an uninspiring professor of artillery and natural philosophy and the butt of many jokes. Jackson resigned his commission in the U.S. Army and offered his services to the Confederacy. On the eve of the Maryland Campaign, he enjoyed the unyielding faith of Southerners across the Confederacy that heralded his postwar canonization as a saint of the Lost Cause.

In October 1861, Jackson was entrusted with command of the Valley District of the Department of Northern Virginia. In that role at the head of his own division and that of Richard S. Ewell, Jackson masterminded a campaign through the Shenandoah Valley of brilliant maneuvers, sharp deployments, hard marching, and stunning victories in May and June 1862, all of which earned him a hero's reputation. Shuffled east to fight for Richmond in what would be called the Seven Days' Battles, Jackson took temporary command of the divisions of Chase Whiting and D. H. Hill. Unlike the Jackson of the Valley,

---

22 Warner, *Generals in Gray*, 83-84; David S. and Jeanne T. Heidler, eds., *Encyclopedia of the American Civil War: A Political, Social, and Military History* (New York: W. W. Norton and Company, 2000), 662-663; Harsh, *Sounding the Shallows*, 59.

the Jackson of the Peninsula turned in an uncharacteristically lackluster performance usually attributed to sheer exhaustion. The former Jackson was on full display when Lee dispatched him to Gordonsville, where he would once again command the veterans of the Valley. A few weeks later, Major General Ambrose Powell Hill's "Light Division" was attached to his command, rounding out the three divisions he would lead into Maryland.[23]

Brigadier General John Robert Jones was given command of Jackson's former division of four brigades. One of the least known generals in the Confederate army, Jones was born in Harrisonburg, Virginia, in 1828. After attending the Virginia Military Institute, he taught in Virginia, Maryland, and Florida before mustering into the 33rd Virginia in June 1861. Jackson recommended him for promotion and Jones led a brigade during the Seven Days. A debilitating wound at Malvern Hill on July 1 kept Jones away from his command until September 6.

Much better known was Ambrose Powell (A. P.) Hill, the fiery leader of the "Light Division." The divisional *nom de plume* referred not to tactical or numerical weakness, but to Hill's ability to easily maneuver his six brigades. The well-structured division was a relatively recent formation (formed just before Seven Pines). Originally from Culpeper, Virginia, Hill graduated in the middle of his West Point Class of 1847. A career officer who fought in the Mexican and Seminole wars, he had something of a reputation for carousing. He eventually settled down with the sister of General John Hunt Morgan. Brave to a fault, Hill could be impulsive and reckless, and unafraid to move his division into a fight without adequate support. His bold assault from Mechanicsville toward Beaver Dam Creek opened the Seven Days fighting— but was a tactical disaster.

Richard Stoddart Ewell, on the other hand, was more cautious and calculating. Ewell led a division of Jackson's force until he lost a leg at Gainesville (Brawner Farm) during the opening salvo of Second Manassas. For the remainder of that battle and throughout the Maryland Campaign Ewell's division was led by Brigadier General Alexander Lawton, who was first and foremost a politician. Born in 1818 in South Carolina, Lawton practiced law in Savannah and served in both the Georgia State House of Representatives and Georgia State Senate. Upon the secession of his adopted state, Lawton became colonel of the 1st Georgia and aided in the seizure of Fort Pulaski. In April 1861, Lawton secured his Confederate commission and took charge of

---

23 Harsh, *Sounding the Shallows*, 59-60.

Georgia's coastal defenses. Leading the four veteran brigades of Ewell's Division would be his greatest test.[24]

As the Army of Northern Virginia commenced its invasion, perhaps its most conspicuous feature was not division into a pair of large infantry "wings" but the number of unattached and independently operating divisions. The smallest of these commands fell upon Brigadier General John George Walker, the son of Missouri's state treasurer. Brevetted for service in the Mexican War, he resigned his U.S. Army commission in July 1861 and entered Confederate service as a major of cavalry before promotion to division command. Walker led two brigades—his own under Colonel Vannoy Hartrog Manning of the 3rd Arkansas and the North Carolinians of Brigadier General Robert Ransom, Jr.[25]

Major General Richard Heron Anderson, a distinguished and determined fighter, headed a considerably larger division of six brigades. Anderson was born in Sumter County, South Carolina, on October 7, 1821, and graduated with the West Point Class of 1842. He earned a first lieutenant's brevet in the Mexican War and rose to the captaincy of the 2nd Dragoons upon his resignation from federal service the day before Lincoln's inauguration as president. Initially Anderson followed in the shadow of Pierre G. T. Beauregard, and so was present for the bombardment of Fort Sumter and the fighting at First Manassas. The next month, however, after a promotion to brigadier general, Anderson was dispatched to Pensacola, Florida, where he suffered a wound in the fighting on Santa Rosa Island. The following February Anderson was back in the Army of Northern Virginia. He delivered a sound performance on the peninsula and in the Seven Days, and followed it up with an impressive attack at Second Manassas.[26]

Richard Anderson's West Point classmate, Major General Lafayette McLaws, commanded four brigades in his own unattached division. Like Rumph Jones, McLaws was married to a niece of Zachary Taylor. Unlike many of his fellow division commanders, however, he left an undistinguished record in the Mexican War. After resigning from the army in March 1861, McLaws

---

24 Again, these biographical sketches have been informed by Jon Wakelyn, ed., *Biographical Dictionary of the Confederacy*, 228, 230, 278; Warner, *Generals in Gray*, 175-176; on John Robert Jones, see David S. and Jeanne T. Heidler, eds., *Encyclopedia of the American Civil War: A Political, Social, and Military History*, 1,090.

25 Harsh, *Sounding the Shallows*, 47-48.

26 Warner, *Generals in Gray*, 8-9.

assumed the colonelcy of the 10th Georgia Infantry. Still, McLaws rose quickly through the ranks and was promoted to brigadier general on September 25, 1861, and to major general on May 23, 1862, following his capable performance on the peninsula.[27]

Religious, insistent, and austere, division commander Daniel Harvey (D. H.) Hill boasted a record of competency and a long academic resume. His father, Solomon Hill, was a personal friend of South Carolina's ardent, fire-eating defender of states' rights, Senator John Caldwell Calhoun. Hailing from that state's York District, Hill graduated from West Point in 1842 and married a decade later. After fighting in the battles of Mexico's Contreras, Churubusco, and Chapultepec, he resigned his military commission to assume a position on the faculty at Washington College in Lexington, Virginia, where he taught mathematics. In 1854, he left Lexington for a position at North Carolina's Davidson College, where he remained for five years before assuming the superintendency of the North Carolina Military Institute in Charlotte.

A rabid secessionist who rejoiced as the Union dissolved, Hill cheerfully entered the Confederate service at the head of the 1st North Carolina Volunteers, leading his men in the first land engagement of the war at Big Bethel, Virginia. He fought as a major general under Joe Johnston at Yorktown, Seven Pines, and Williamsburg, but was perhaps best known for hammering out the details of a prisoner exchange cartel with Union Major General John A. Dix on July 22, 1862. In the Maryland Campaign, Harvey Hill's stable command contained the brigades of Brigadier Generals Robert Rodes, George Burgwyn Anderson, Samuel Garland, and Roswell Ripley, as well as the Georgia and Alabama brigade of Colonel Alfred Holt Colquitt.[28]

*   *   *

Jackson's wing was the first to ford the Potomac River early on the morning of September 4, 1862. "Our army was full of fight and confidence but in every other respect unfit for such a campaign as followed," Captain Samuel Buck of

---

27 *Ibid.*, 204; Jon L. Wakelyn, ed., *Biographical Dictionary of the Confederacy* (Westport, Connecticut: Greenwood Press, 1977), 300, 424, 238-239, 262, 75-76.

28 Warner, *Generals in Gray*, 136-137; Harsh, *Sounding the Shallows*, 74; see also Hal Bridges, *Lee's Maverick General: Daniel Harvey Hill* (New York: McGraw Hill, 1961; reprint, Lincoln: University of Nebraska Press, 1991); Cynthia B. Brown and Ellen Strong, biographical introduction to the Daniel Harvey Hill Papers, The College of William and Mary, Williamsburg, Virginia.

the 13th Virginia recalled. The Virginian went on to confirm their lack of sustenance when he wrote that a "small piece of bacon with a cup of coffee was a delicacy of which few could boast."[29]

As the men approached the Potomac River, they erupted into the dynamic strains of James Ryder Randall's secessionist favorite, "Maryland, My Maryland," delivered to the tune of "O Tannenbaum." Randall, a Maryland native, was living in Louisiana when he was inspired by the patriotic fervor sweeping the nation in the wake of the bombardment of Fort Sumter. One incident, in particular, moved him. Upon his native Maryland soil on April 19, 1861, blood was shed for the first time in the war when the 6th Massachusetts Volunteers marched through the streets of Baltimore for Washington, D.C. The fresh federal recruits stumbled innocently into a morass of incensed secessionists who proceeded to hurl stones and slurs. The conflict escalated, rounds were exchanged, and sixteen were left dead. Reading these details, the twenty-two-year-old secessionist poet composed nine stanzas, which began:

> The despot's heel is on thy shore
> Maryland!
> His torch is at thy temple door
> Maryland!

The Confederates ford the Potomac River. *Harper's Pictorial History of the Civil War*

29 Captain Samuel D. Buck, *With the Old Confeds, Actual Experiences of a Captain in the Line* (Baltimore: H.E. Houck and Co., 1925), 59.

Avenge the patriotic gore
That flecked the streets of Baltimore,
And be the battle-queen of yore,
Maryland, My Maryland![30]

Captain Buck remembered listening to the wading men signing the tune. "Every regiment [was] singing and as happy as if going to a ball," he recalled. Captain Henry L. P. King, of McLaws' staff, confided to his diary, "Finally General McLaws gave us the order—we are to cross White's Ford into Maryland in the morning at daylight. Hurrah! We go indeed at last to Maryland!"[31] Confederate cavalry chieftain James Ewell Brown (Jeb) Stuart's Chief of Staff, Major Heros Von Borcke, vividly recalled the scene of the gray-clad men consumed in song:

It was, indeed, a magnificent sight as the long column of many thousand horsemen stretched across this beautiful Potomac. The evening sun slanted upon its clear placid waters, and burnished them with gold, while arms of the soldiers, glittered and blazed in its radiance. There were few moments, perhaps, from the beginning to the close of the war, of excitement more intense, of exhilaration more delightful, than when we ascended the opposite bank to the familiar but now strangely thrilling music "Maryland, My Maryland."[32]

The strange thrill was supplemented with a general order from Lee announcing the progress of the Confederates in the Bluegrass State. "Soldiers, press onward!" Lee announced on September 6 after describing the August 30, 1862, victory scored by Kirby Smith at Richmond, Kentucky. "This great victory is simultaneous with your own at Manassas . . . let each man feel the responsibility now resting on him to pursue vigorously the success vouchsafed to us by Heaven." In the rebel capital, meanwhile, war clerk John B. Jones noted in his monumental diary that these concurrent victories were not accidental.

---

30 James Ryder Randall, "Maryland, My Maryland," 1861. All nine stanzas have been reproduced in John Cannan, *The Antietam Campaign: July-November, 1862* (New York: Wieser and Wieser, Inc., 1990), 71.

31 Captain Henry L. P. King, diary entry, 5 September 1862, as quoted in D. Scott Hartwig, "Robert E. Lee and the Maryland Campaign," in Gary W. Gallagher, ed., *Lee: The Soldier* (Lincoln: University of Nebraska Press, 1996), 331.

32 Major Heros Von Borcke, *Memoirs of the Confederate War for Independence* (New York, 1938), 1:185.

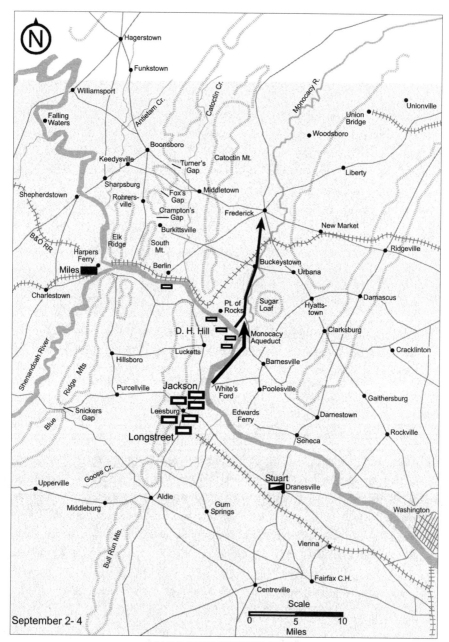

MAP 1. LEE MOVES NORTH

"This is not chance," he wrote. According to Jones, it was "God, to whom all the glory is due" who was responsible.[33] Here, then, was providence. "Great has the change been in our situation from the 26th of June to the present time," recorded George Washington Hall in his diary. "But the God on high give strength to our arms . . . our victorious army then proceeded to liberate Maryland, and they are now on its soil."[34]

For the first time, Lee connected Bragg's Kentucky invasion to his own army's actions, uniting the hopes of a desperate Confederacy. "Let the armies of the East and the West vie with each other in discipline, bravery, and activity, and our brethren of our sister States will soon be released from tyranny, and our independence be established upon a sure and abiding basis," he announced.[35] Though Lee was inhibited by what several historians have deemed a lack of knowledge of the war in the Western Theater, the commander who placed so much emphasis on his beloved Virginia clearly recognized the political parallels between his army and those under Bragg and Smith. As Thomas Connelly and Archer Jones aptly noted, President Davis' chief aim in the Kentucky gambit was to gain the Bluegrass State, justifying the movement with the mere prospect of its denizens "rising en masse" to join the Confederacy.[36]

The next day, Lee reported to Davis that all of his divisions had successfully crossed the Potomac. General Orders No. 102, issued in Leesburg on September 4, ordered commanders to reduce accouterments to necessities only and to select only the best animals for employment in the impending campaign. Stragglers and deserters, already a very real problem, would not be tolerated as they threatened to discredit Lee's "most important operations."[37] Furthermore, Brigadier General Lewis Addison Armistead was appointed provost marshal in an effort to impose at least some discipline and round up stragglers.

The president and Confederate legislature were just as confident of success as Lee. Jefferson Davis, accompanied by former Maryland Governor Enoch Lowe, traveled to Rapidan Station by rail on his way to Leesburg to conduct an

33 J. B. Jones, diary, September 10, 1862, in *A Rebel War Clerk's Diary*, Howard Swiggett, ed., (New York: Old Hickory Bookshop, 1935), 152.

34 George Washington Hall, diary entry, September 4, 1862, in Miscellaneous Manuscripts Collection, Library of Congress, Manuscript Division, Washington, D.C.

35 General Orders No. 103, September 6, 1862, OR 2:596.

36 Connelly and Jones, *The Politics of Command*, 38, 107.

37 General Orders No. 102, September 4, 1862, OR 2:592.

ostentatious interview with the army. "Congress has heard, with profound satisfaction, of the triumphant crossing of the Potomac by our victorious army," declared a House resolution, "and, assured of the wisdom of that military movement, could repose with entire confidence on the distinguished skill of the commanding general . . . to relieve oppressed Maryland, and to advance our standards into the territory of the enemy."[38]

As the butternut- and gray-clad men advanced into the fertile Maryland countryside and approached Frederick, panicked rumors swirled around Washington. At least one denizen was arrested for inducing panic.[39] Most of the excitement stemmed from a lack of knowledge about Lee's intentions in Maryland. "Great excitement has been caused in this city by the well authenticated report that the Confed. have crossed into Maryland in heavy force at Point of Rocks & Nolan's ford," wrote Baltimore resident Franklin Wilson. "It is uncertain what their intentions are, some believing that they intend to invade Pennsylvania, and let them feel the horrors of war; others that they will come to Baltimore."[40]

"Until the purposes of the Confs. develop themselves, & we see whether the fortune of war will make their occupation of Md. Permanent," Arthur Brown wrote his father the next day from the same city, "we are completely at sea in regard to the future. . . . Opinions differ as to whether they are bound for Penna or Washington, though present indications point to the former course."[41] Franklin Wilson recalled after the campaign that "Pennsylvania was thoroughly frightened . . . and volunteers met at Harrisburg & Chambersburg to repel the threatened invasion."[42] Many Unionists understandably feared vengeance and a war of retribution. The fetid and imposing column of rebels advancing along the Buckeystown Pike was itself enough to distress the

38 *Papers of Jefferson Davis*, ed. Lynda Lasswell Crist and Mary Seaton Dix (Baton Rouge: Louisiana State University Press, 1971-1995), 8:389n.1; "Proceedings of the First Confederate Congress," in *Southern Historical Society Papers*, 46 (1928): 106-125.

39 See Richard R. Duncan, "Marylanders and the Invasion of 1862," *Civil War History: A Journal of the Middle Period*, 11, no. 4 (December 1965), 370-383.

40 Franklin Wilson, September 7, 1862, Wilson Papers, Maryland Historical Society, as quoted in Mitchell, ed., *Maryland Voice of the Civil War*, 305-306.

41 Arthur Brown to George Brown, September 8, 1862, Brown Papers, Maryland Historical Society, as quoted in *Ibid.*, 308.

42 Franklin Wilson, September 22, 1862, Wilson Papers, Maryland Historical Society, as quoted in *Ibid.*, 318-319.

Marylanders. "Thousands of men, women[,] and children left during the night, many of them on foot[;] the roads to Pennsylvania and Baltimore [were] lined with fugitives," reported a journalist with the *New York Tribune*. "Many of the convalescents in the hospitals[,] dreading the horrors of a Richmond prison, started off and many of them were taken in by farmers along the roads."[43] Still others had their curiosity piqued by these Southern soldiers. "I was very much interested in seeing them," admitted Joshua Hering.[44]

*   *   *

The scruffy Southern soldiers continued along the Buckeystown Pike to the banks of the Monocacy River several miles south of the spires of Frederick. Along the way, near Adamstown, the hungry troops bivouacked and gorged themselves on ears of green corn and ripe fruit from the acres shaded by the Catoctin Mountains west of Frederick. As Longstreet's aide-de-camp G. Moxley Sorrel remembered, many of these green corn connoisseurs regretted their gluttony with the onset of diarrhea, which made an already difficult march even more challenging. "The cavalry and artillery were nearly all barefooted, while a portion of the infantry were in the same condition," one newspaper observed. "Some infantry had their feet tied up with rags or covered with raw hides, and others with dilapidated shoes, from which their toes were protruding."[45] No liberating force was this.

As the men approached the Monocacy, many removed their uniforms, bathing both themselves and their garb in the muddy waters just as they had done in the Potomac. The following day, September 6, with the "townspeople watching from the sidewalks," the rebels entered Frederick. It was about eleven o'clock.[46] Major Heros Von Borcke, a Prussian cavalryman serving in Lee's army, reflected on the rebels' entrance by noting the "tremendous state of excitement . . . flags and garlands of flowers . . . [and] singing and shouting in a

43 *New York Tribune*, September 9, 1862.

44 Joshua Hering, Hering Recollections, Hering Family Scrapbooks, Maryland Historical Society, as quoted in Mitchell, ed., *Maryland Voices of the Civil War*, 306-307.

45 *New York Times*, September 7-9, 1862, as quoted in Paul and Rita Gordon, *Never the Like Again: Frederick County, Maryland* (Frederick: n.p., 1995), 125.

46 Duncan, "Marylanders and the Invasion of 1862"; Anne Schaeffer, diary entry, September 6, 1862, as quoted in Mitchell, ed., *Maryland Voices of the Civil War*, 309-310.

paroxysm of joy and patriotic emotion" filling the air.[47] Lee's adjutant, Colonel Walter H. Taylor, was a bit more objective in his recording. "About here I think the population about equally divided in sentiment," he concluded. "I can judge only from what demonstrations I see."[48]

That same day, the purple-plumed and pompous Jeb Stuart, who commanded the three Confederate cavalry brigades under Brigadier Generals Wade Hampton, Fitzhugh Lee, and Colonel Thomas T. Munford, arrived in the sleepy crossroads village of Urbana about six miles southeast of the Monocacy. The brigades under Hampton and Lee trailed the rear of the army from Leesburg, making demonstrations along the way and crossing the Potomac on September 5. They reunited at Urbana with Munford's command, which on September 2 had misinterpreted an order and returned to the area of Chantilly, Virginia.[49]

*   *   *

The evening of September 6 found Jackson's foot soldiers bivouacked on the outskirts of Frederick. Longstreet's divisions arrived the next day.[50] Two of Jackson's divisions guarded the Baltimore and Ohio Railroad bridge spanning the Monocacy River, for the tracks continued along some forty miles to the federal capital. The rebels had already destroyed much of the track and had severed the telegraph lines outside of the city, though most of the railroad stock had been secured unscathed.[51]

While newspapers in the North tried to ascertain the positions of the invaders, printing and re-printing telegraph reports from Washington and Baltimore in front-page columns, Lee plotted the next strategic move on a new

---

47 Heros Von Borcke, as quoted in Cannan, *The Antietam Campaign*, 69.

48 Walter H. Taylor to Mary Lou Taylor, letter, September 7, 1862, Frederick, Maryland, in *Lee's Adjutant: The Wartime Letters of Colonel Walter Herron Taylor, 1862-1865*, R. Lockwood Tower, ed., (Columbia: University of South Carolina Press, 1995), 42-43.

49 *OR* 1:814-815.

50 *Ibid.*, 1:952-953; 1:839. Jones' Brigade, commanded by Bradley Tyler Johnson, did not bivouac with Jackson's troops on the outskirts of Frederick the evening of September 6 because Johnson, a native Marylander, had been appointed Provost Marshal and was responsible for overseeing the rebel occupation of the city.

51 *Boston Evening Transcript*, September 8, 1862.

chessboard of war. At his newly established headquarters near the Best Farm north of the Monocacy, Lee issued a proclamation to the people of Maryland. "It is right that you should know the purpose that brought the army under my command within the limits of your State, so far as that purpose concerns yourselves." He continued:

> The people of the Confederate States have long watched with the deepest sympathy the wrongs and outrages that have been inflicted upon the citizens of a commonwealth allied to the States of the South by the strongest social, political, and commercial ties.
>
> They have seen with profound indignation their sister State deprived of every right and reduced to the condition of a conquered province. Under the pretense of supporting the Constitution, but in violation of its most valuable provisions, your citizens have been arrested and imprisoned upon no charge and contrary to all forms of law. The faithful and manly protest against this outrage made by the venerable and illustrious Marylander, to whom in better days no citizen appeal for right in vain, was treated with scorn and contempt; the government of your chief city has been usurped by armed strangers; your legislature has been dissolved by the unlawful arrest of its members; freedom of the press and of speech has been suppressed; words have been declared offenses by an arbitrary decree of the Federal Executive, and citizens ordered to be tried by a military commission for what they may dare to speak. Believing that the people of Maryland possessed a spirit too lofty to submit to such a government, the people of the South have long wished to aid you in throwing off this foreign yoke, to enable you again to enjoy the inalienable rights of freemen, and restore independence and sovereignty to your State. In obedience to this wish, our army has come among you, and is prepared to assist you with the power of its arms in regaining the rights of which you have been despoiled.
>
> This, citizens of Maryland, is our mission, so far as you are concerned. No constrain upon your free will is intended; no intimidation will be allowed within the limits of this army, at least. Marylanders shall once more enjoy their ancient freedom of thought and speech. We know no enemies among you, and will protect all, of every opinion. It is for you to decide your destiny freely and without constraint. This army will respect your choice, whatever it may be; and while the Southern people will rejoice to welcome you to your natural position among them, they will only welcome you when you come of your own free will.[52]

---

52 Robert E. Lee, "Proclamation to the People of Maryland," September 8, 1862, OR 2:601-602.

Confederate Colonel Bradley Tyler Johnson, himself a native of Mayland, issued a similar pronouncement that same day in which he promised freedom to the people who had suffered "sixteen months of oppression more galling than the Austrian tyranny." Entreating his fellow Marylanders to remember the cells of Fort McHenry, and the dungeons of Fort Lafayette and of Fort Warren, Johnson's appeal, like Lee's proclamation, pulsed with anxious prudence and a sense of the war's heightening stakes. "Saw a proclamation from General Johnson calling on the Marylanders to flock to the Southern flag and help us to redeem their state from Northern oppression," William W. Sherwood of the 17th Virginia noted in his diary without further editorial comment on the matter. "We passed through Frederick City today," he continued. The Marylanders may not have been the only ones with shallow expectations of these posturing proclamations.[53]

Although Lee's mawkish, prim proclamation was addressed to the people of Maryland, it is altogether probable that President Davis intended it for an entirely different audience. In a communication written on September 7 and delivered several days after Lee's proclamation had already been issued, the president expounded on the tenets that he felt were important for Lee to reveal in the document. First, he urged Lee to clarify the war aims of the Confederate government, illuminating a war waged merely in self-defense. "It has no design of conquest, or any other purpose than to secure peace and the abandonment by the United States of their pretensions to govern a people who have never been their subjects." Second, Davis insisted that Lee explain the rebel attempt at peaceful negotiation with Washington. "This Government, at the very moment of its inauguration, sent commissioners to Washington to treat for a peaceful adjustment of all differences, but . . . these commissioners were not received, nor even allowed to communicate the object of their mission," Davis explained.[54]

The issue of a negotiated peace was obviously on the minds of both Davis and Lee, for on the same day Lee issued his proclamation, he penned a letter to the president discussing the propriety of such a proposal.[55] Furthermore, Lee included a description of an armistice in which the Southern states would

---

53 William W. Sherwood, diary entry, September 9, 1862, Virginia Historical Society, Richmond, Virginia.

54 Davis to Lee, September 7, 1862, in *OR* 2:598.

55 Lee to Davis, September 8, 1862, in *WPREL*, 301.

"pursue [their] own path[s] to happiness." According to Davis, Lee was to highlight that one way to achieve this bliss was through the invasion of Maryland, which would compel the Lincoln administration to "conclude a general peace." "Under these circumstances, we are driven to protect our own country by transferring the seat of war to that of an enemy, who pursues us with a relentless and, apparently, aimless hostility," he wrote. "The Confederate army, therefore, comes to occupy the territory of their enemies, and to make it the theater of hostilities." Finally, Davis recommended condemning the federal government for "subjugating a people over whom no right of dominion has ever been conferred, either by God or man."[56]

Lee seized the initiative and completed a proclamation which largely eschewed Davis' recommendations; Lee's document focused more specifically on the people of Maryland and was imbued with a military judgment which sought to calm, rather than to energize. The imagery of injustice, juxtaposed against rebel righteousness, only aimed to assuage fears of marauding invaders, offering little that could be construed as a recruitment device. There was to be "no constraint" upon free will, no intimidation in thought or word.

On September 13, Lee sent a note to the president. "You will perceive by the printed address to the people of Maryland which has been sent to you, that I have not gone contrary to the views expressed by you on the subject," he wrote. "Should there be anything in it to correct, please let me know."[57] Despite Lee's subtle efforts to convey the similarities between his finished product and Davis's desired document, he still failed to mask the stark differences between them. While Davis's stern language boasted a "transfer" of the "seat of war," Lee utilized neutral language intended simply to make a statement rather than attract attention. Had no disparity existed, the sentence imploring Davis to acknowledge the similarity would have been unnecessary, and any corrections rendered superfluous.

Unmistakably, Davis's instructions demonstrate that he intended the proclamation to be a sweeping statement about the revolutionary nature of the Confederacy, a conclusion substantiated by the important findings of historian Louis H. Manarin. Tucked away in the William B. Rodman Papers at the North Carolina State Archives in Raleigh, Manarin discovered a signed copy of Davis'

56 Davis to Lee, September 7, 1862, in *OR* 2: 598.

57 Lee to Davis, September 13, 1862, in *WPREL*, 306-307.

"proclamation" dated September 12, 1862. On the reverse side was written "The President to Gen'l R.E. Lee, instructing him to issue a proclamation to the people of _____ setting forth the motives and purposes of his presence among them at the head of an invading army." While the *Official Records* includes the same document (with the same blank to be filled) Manarin's version contained a single, hand-written word to fill the void: Pennsylvania.[58] Manarin's finding was unmistakable evidence of the true focus of the invasion, especially, as he points out, when coupled with the correspondence between Davis and Lee. On September 4, as the Confederates crossed the Potomac, Lee wrote to the president, "Should the results of the expedition justify it, I propose to enter Pennsylvania, unless you should deem it unadvisable on political or other grounds."[59]

While sending an army to subsist on Pennsylvania's abundant acres and potentially interrupt its influential infrastructure was a logical goal, any effort to garner political support for the Confederacy would be doomed to fail. Pennsylvania boasted the second largest population of any state in the Union, and recruited more volunteers to the federal cause than any other. With Andrew Gregg Curtin, a staunchly Republican advocate of the Lincoln administration, serving as governor, a proclamation attempting to entice the Keystone State into the Confederacy would have been an exercise in futility. Lee was certainly cognizant of that, as he made evident in his communication on September 4 proposing to enter Pennsylvania if politically practical; the question remains whether Davis, the astute former senator and secretary of war, shared Lee's awareness. But as the president's abstract proclamation read more like a piece of partisan literature, aimed squarely at exonerating the Confederacy of any blemish and defending its right to rank among the nations of the world, it is conceivable Davis clearly understood the invasion's political intentions.

Davis was virtually imploring Great Britain and France for mediation, which ultimately meant partisan intervention on the Confederacy's behalf. Acting in a manner akin to that employed by crafters of the "Lost Cause" mythology after Appomattox, the president refused to entertain slavery, the North's personal liberty laws, or *Herrenvolk* democracy as causes of the conflict, citing instead picayune legal disagreements and a fundamental Constitutional

---

58 Louis H. Manarin, "A Proclamation: 'To the People of _____'," *North Carolina Historical Review*, 41, no. 2 (April 1964): 246-251.

59 *OR* 2:592.

dispute as the genuine sources of strife. Ever aware of Great Britain's own history of emancipation, Davis manufactured an image intended not only to invite foreign sympathy, but preserve, protect, and defend his nation in the eyes of the rest of the world.

Markedly similar to the tenets proffered in Davis' proclamations are those put forth by Confederate agent James Mason to Great Britain's Earl Russell in the summer prior to the Maryland invasion. "The dissolution of the Union of the States of North America, by the withdrawal therefrom of certain of the Confederates, was not to be considered as a revolution in the ordinary acceptation of that term," Mason wrote on July 24. "This new Confederacy has now been in complete and successful operation as a Government for a period of nearly eighteen months; has proved itself capable of successful defense against every attempt to subdue or destroy it; and in a war conducted by its late confederates, on a scale to tax their utmost power, has presented everywhere a united people, determined at every cost to maintain the independence they had affirmed."[60] Mason exchanged another letter with Russell on August 1. "In a war such as that pending in America, where a party in possession of the Government is striving to subdue those who for reasons sufficient to themselves, have withdrawn from it, the contest will be carried on in the heat of blood and of popular excitement long after its object has become hopeless in the eyes of disinterested parties."[61]

Confederate Secretary of State Judah P. Benjamin used similar language. "In the code of modern international law, the nation which presents itself with an organized government and obedient people, with the institutions created by the free will of the citizens, and with numerous armies that crush all attempts of the most powerful foe to subjugate it, which is aiming at no conquest, seeking no advantages, and steadily bent on securing nothing but the inherent rights of self-government—such a nation may insist upon . . . its right of recognition," he wrote.[62] Just as Davis strove to convey in his proclamation, these Confederate diplomats offered a vision of a united government, defended by organized and

---

60 J. M. Mason to Earl Russell, Secretary of State for Foreign Affairs, July 24, 1862, in *The Messages and Papers of Jefferson Davis and the Confederacy, Including Diplomatic Correspondence 1861-1865*, ed. and comp. James D. Richardson (New York: Chelsea House-Robert Hector Publishers, 1966), 2:303-304.

61 Mason to Russell, August 1, 1862, in *ibid.*, 305-307.

62 Judah P. Benjamin to A. Dudley Mann, et al., August 14, 1862, in *ibid.*, 313-314.

obedient soldiers, who waged an increasingly unnecessary war of self-defense against an oppressive foe.

British papers lauded the efforts of both Davis and his soldiers. Commenting on an earlier piece penned by Davis, editors remarked that they "read with much pleasure the measured and statesmanlike language in which the Southern President pays a well earned tribute to the gallant and good conduct of his troops, deplores the desolating war, and expresses confidence of the final triumph of the desperate struggle against despotic usurpation." They were impressed by Davis and his "nation," for in "such a situation, they are able to speak and act with moderation and dignity. In the midst of reverses they can look forward with confidence to success."[63]

In his letter to Lee, Davis was looking for his general to replicate "moderation and dignity" with the subtle expression of confidence requisite to garner favorable opinion in London. By concealing this appeal in a proclamation addressed to Marylanders and Pennsylvanians—but made public nonetheless—he would eschew the inevitable charges of unpreparedness and desperation.

Perhaps Benjamin summarized the political and diplomatic stakes best. "Now, when appeal to the common sense of justice of the nations has failed to elicit any further response than a timid neutrality scarcely covering an evident dread of the power of our arrogant foe," he explained, "we prefer speaking in *other* tones and insisting that an admission into the family of nations is a right which we have conquered *by the sword.*" These *other* tones would soon be realized—through universal proclamations of independence, accompanied by an equally theatrical splash across the Potomac intended to conclude somewhere above the Mason-Dixon Line. Perhaps alluding to the upcoming invasion, Benjamin commented, "I have nothing of importance to add to my history of the events of the war," he began, "but I doubt not that long ere this dispatch can reach you you will have received news of other and important successes of our arms."[64]

Despite Davis' attempt to disguise his hopes for diplomacy, the Northern print media immediately recognized the proclamation as the covert petition the Confederate president had intended. One Ohio paper printed Lee's

63 Reprinted from the *London Times* in the *Capital City Fact*, September 17, 1862.

64 Judah P. Benjamin to A. Dudley Mann, et. al., August 14, 1862, in *Messages and Papers of the Confederacy*, ed. and comp. Richardson, 313-314.

proclamation in full with insightful editorial comment. Addressing it as "bombastic and hifalutin [*sic*]" the editor concluded it was "evidently intended more . . . for European ears than for those to whom it purports to have been addressed." The shrewd editor nonetheless surmised that it would have "just as much effect upon the one as upon the other."[65] Understandably, not all newspapers had immediate access to the entirety of Lee's proclamation. They made generalizations about it, merely reporting its friendly greetings to people of Maryland.[66]

*   *   *

Despite Lee's sincere effort to discourage pillaging and his intent that the army purchase its sorely needed clothes, shoes, and medical supplies in scrip, many shopkeepers in Frederick posted "SOLD OUT" signs in their windows to discourage the invaders. Frederick resident Anne Schaeffer recorded the scene of the Confederates moving into the city in her diary. "Soon the streets were swarming with ragged, filthy, worn out men. . . . Soon they were thronging the stores, offering their confederate notes, which not being regarded of much value in Maryland, about 4 P.M. most of the stores closed up."[67] Although some entrepreneurs willingly dealt with the rebels, most did not. According to historian Richard R. Duncan, "Coolness and indifference were far more pronounced than enthusiasm. Many Southern sympathizers, lacking confidence and assurance that Confederate forces could maintain control over the state, were cautious in their reception of Lee's army."[68]

Michael Shuler of the 33rd Virginia epitomized rebel optimism about the army's Maryland welcome in the pages of his diary on September 6th. "Citizens welcome us in Maryland. Many flocking in to join us . . . We are treated very kindly by the citizens. Strict orders in Regard to interrupting citizens." But another brief entry shed some light on a different, though related, issue: "Didn't get our Rations last night. . . . Soldiers [are] anxious to purchase at the stores in

65 "General Lee's Proclamation," *Summit County Beacon*, Akron, Ohio, September 25, 1862.

66 See, for example, the *Boston Evening Transcript*, September 10, 1862.

67 Schaeffer, diary entry, September 6, 1862, as quoted in Mitchell, ed., *Maryland Voices in the Civil War*, 309-310.

68 Duncan, "Marylanders and the Invasion of 1862."

town . . . not many open after Saturday."[69] In contrast to many of her neighbors, Schaeffer consistently noted the rebels' alleged admirable conduct and behavior. As trepidations grew, the citizens of Frederick wanted a return to normalcy, she recalled, but the Southerners were at least "polite strangers."[70]

Normalcy would seep back into Frederick on September 10 when Lee's men began to depart. "Their destination (*They* say) Pennsylvania," Schaeffer noted.[71] Most soldiers of course were unaware of where the next march would lead them. Maryland may have provided a limited amount of sustenance, but it had not proven a hospitable place to bivouac. It was not certain how much longer the rebel army would be able to remain in the state. Captain Samuel Buck explained away the rebels' mixed reception in Maryland as a symptom of a war-weariness among civilians. "War had become a reality, men were being killed by hundreds and thousands and the novelty had worn off," he admitted. "Had such an opportunity been presented the first year of the war we would have had the state of Maryland with us."[72]

*   *   *

On September 6, Jeb Stuart's cavalry corps reunited near Urbana, Maryland. There was, according to one of Stuart's biographers, "a holiday air about headquarters."[73] Indeed, when a local citizen delivered a dinner invitation to Stuart and his staff on the morning of September 7, the cavalry chieftain decided it was a prudent time for a respite from the constant campaigning that had consumed his troops and exhausted their mounts since the fording of the Potomac. Optimism about the impending campaign was not the only reason Stuart agreed to a night of celebration. In Urbana, the quixotic cavalryman had taken notice of an attractive New York gal named Anne Cockey, who was visiting her Maryland aunt and uncle who operated a small storefront situated on the town's main thoroughfare. Ever fond of merrymaking, Stuart's thoughts

---

69 Michael Shuler, diary entry, September 6, 1862, in Michael Shuler's Diary, Miscellaneous Manuscript Collection, Library of Congress, Manuscript Division, Washington, D.C.

70 Schaeffer, diary entry, September 9, 1862, in Mitchell, ed., 310.

71 Schaeffer, diary entry, September 10, 1862, in *ibid.*, 311.

72 Captain Samuel D. Buck, *With the Old Confeds*, 60.

73 Burke Davis, *J.E.B. Stuart: The Last Cavalier* (New York: Rinehart, 1957), 194.

Maj. Gen. Jeb Stuart

Antietam National Battlefield

turned toward the stately manor located just beyond the Cockey family store. "What a capital place for us to give a ball in honor of our arrival in Maryland!" he proclaimed.

And a capital place it surely was. Perched on a subtle grade and obscured from the Urbana Pike by a sprinkling of trees, the white clapboard mansion, known as Landon House, featured a two-story veranda that stretched the entire length of the grand structure. Originally constructed in 1754 outside of Fredericksburg, Virginia, where it was operated as a silk mill, the building was disassembled, transported north, and reconstructed piece by piece in Urbana in 1840. Now abandoned, Stuart commandeered its expansive rooms, printed invitations for the townspeople of Urbana, and entrusted Major Von Borcke with interior decorations, lighting, and the evening's dance card. The large halls astride the main entryway were cleaned, the walls were festooned with regimental flags and fresh roses, and the 18th Mississippi Infantry band of William Barksdale's Mississippi brigade set about to provide the musical accompaniment.[74]

Hours later, Urbana residents and Confederate cavalrymen, clad respectively in hoop skirts and frock coats, arrived for an evening of dancing and a surreal departure from the toils of the war. Von Borcke, serving as the master of ceremonies, and young Anne Cockey, the Queen, began the ball with a polka. For a few hours, cavalry sabers were stacked along with anguish and

74 *Ibid.*; "The Grand Ball at Urbana," in Cannan, *The Antietam Campaign*, p. 65.

fear. Before long, however, Stuart received word that the 1st New York Cavalry was exchanging rounds with the rebels near Hyattstown, news that summoned the troopers back into the saddle. After a brief engagement in which three Confederates were captured, the cavalrymen returned to Landon House along with the wounded. Though appalled at the sight of the bloodied butternuts, the ladies of the ball quickly attended to the injured.[75]

Despite the disruption, the evening of September 8 was a memorable one, although the modest engagement at Hyattstown foreshadowed the cavalry skirmishing that would continue the next day at Monocacy Church. A sharp skirmish emerged when two companies of the 8th Illinois Cavalry charged the 12th Virginia Cavalry. Nine confederates, several horses, and the colors of the 12th Virginia entered the list of casualties. That same day, up the road in Barnesville, the 8th Illinois joined several companies of the 3rd Indiana Cavalry and 4th Maine Artillery to meet the 9th Virginia in what proved to be a costly melee.[76] Samuel J. B. V. Gilpin of the 3rd Indiana Cavalry described the fight as a "brisk engagement," only to be followed the next day by more fighting "so violent."[77]

*   *   *

Historian James V. Murfin argues in his classic treatment of the Maryland campaign that Stuart's ball was "an affair that probably did more for Confederate public relations than Lee's eloquent proclamation."[78] Lee's document produced neither a meeting with the governor of Maryland nor did it foment any sizeable uprising of the disaffected. For the time being, however, Lee placed these disappointments aside. As the federal army at last began its pursuit, Lee shifted his sights toward striking "the telling and decisive blow of the war." He knew that if he was successful, it could very well alter the course of the conflict.[79] "We shall have to fight one more great battle to defeat that army

75 *Ibid.*

76 H. B. McClellan, 111; Priest, *Before Antietam*, 50-51; *OR* 2:218-219.

77 Samuel J.B.V. Gilpin, diary entries, September 8, 1862 and September 9, 1862, in E.N. Gilpin Papers, Library of Congress, Manuscript Division, Washington, D.C.

78 Murfin, *The Gleam of Bayonets*, 110.

79 *Richmond Daily Dispatch*, 9-13 September 1862.

now at & about Washington, & then the enemy will be completely prostrate at our feet," claimed munitions expert and Confederate chief of ordnance Josiah Gorgas. "God grant us this victory not for vengeance but for peace."[80]

---

80 Gorgas, diary entry, September 14, 1862, in Wiggins, ed., 52.

"Will send you trophies"

McClellan Pursues Lee's Army

W hen General Lee established his army headquarters in Frederick, Maryland, concern for the safety of Pennsylvania quickly replaced the spate of alarms about the fate of the nation's capital in the pages of Northern newspapers. The rebel general's motives became more transparent to anxious Northern civilians with each new wire report and editorial. On September 8, Lee, gesturing toward a local map, explained that the Pennsylvania state capital at Harrisburg was the principal objective of the army-size thrust north of the Potomac River. "After that I can turn my attention to Philadelphia, Baltimore, or Washington, as that may seem best for our interests," Lee declared. Even though the Southern army leader recognized that George McClellan was a cautious general and did not think he could be prepared for an offensive this early in September, Lee recognized that time was of the essence. Within three or four weeks, he hoped to be tenting his army on the banks of the Susquehanna.[1]

In Harrisburg, meanwhile, Pennsylvania's Governor Andrew Gregg Curtin faced the very real prospect of imminent plunder—or worse. A first-term Republican inaugurated on January 15, 1861, Curtin was deeply committed to the Union cause and throughout the war raised monies, visited hospitals, personally answered letters, and bickered with the War Department on behalf

---

1 *Battles and Leaders of the Civil War*, Robert Underwood Johnson and Clarence Buel, eds., 4 vols. (New York: Thomas Yoseloff, 1956), 2:605-606, hereafter cited as *B&L*.

Pennsylvania Governor
Andrew Gregg Curtin

Library of Congress

of his troops.[2] Though historian William Best Hesseltine once suggested the governor's inaugural address was "a triumph of oratory over consistency, and no one knew whether [he] was a radical or a conservative," no one could deny his fidelity to the cause.[3] With Lee's invaders just below his border, Curtin pledged that same devotion to the civilians of his Commonwealth.

With a tone of decided exigency, supplications from Harrisburg began streaming out of Pennsylvania and into the beleaguered War Department in Washington. "The people need something to restore confidence, in order to get them to step forward in support of the Government," urged one such dispatch fired east on the evening of September 8. The dispatch continued with a request that a brigade of troops be delivered to help safeguard Harrisburg.[4] The next dispatch left the Pennsylvania state capital a little more than an hour later with another request, this one an application for seven hundred carbines, slings, ammunition, and cavalry accouterments.[5] Still later, in a wire to Secretary Stanton, Governor Curtin, demanding an "explicit answer," explained that he

2 William B. Hesseltine, *Lincoln and the War Governors* (New York: Alfred A. Knopf, 1948), 344.

3 *Ibid.,* 122-123.

4 OR 2:214.

5 *Ibid.,* 2:215.

would "be ready to perform any duty that may be required of [him] in such an emergency."[6]

Perhaps most disconcerting for Curtin and those other anxious souls who surrounded the telegraph in Harrisburg, however, was Little Mac's noted indecisiveness. "My information about the enemy comes from unreliable sources, and it is vague and conflicting," McClellan wired to Curtin. Until now, the federal commander seemed content merely to rely upon rumor and preliminary probes of the enemy's position. Captain J. S. Ellen of the 23rd Ohio recalled that his regimental commander, Lieutenant Colonel Rutherford B. Hayes, told him that in responding to the emergency of the rebel invasion, "there were no orders, or directions from head quarters," and that "the army was floundering without a head."[7] While McClellan did not place much credence in the notion that Pennsylvania was the chief object of the rebel invasion, the agnostic commanding general nonetheless conceded to Governor Curtin this was merely guesswork on his part. "It would be well for you to push your investigations toward Frederick as far as possible," the governor importuned.[8]

Pressure on McClellan for reliable information mounted, and so too did fears for the safety of Pennsylvania. In the coming days, Lincoln and Halleck sent several dispatches to McClellan and spent anxious hours awaiting his replies. At the same time, a meeting of the Citizens' Bounty Fund Committee in Philadelphia, presided over by chairman Alexander Henry and vice-chairman Thomas Webster, adopted a preamble and two resolutions demanding aid in troops, arms, and material defense for the city, and called for a seasoned general to organize and discipline the militia in anticipation of a "sudden assault."[9] The mayor of Harrisburg likewise issued a proclamation, which forbade citizens from leaving town and threatened the arrests of those who refused to comply.[10]

Exacerbating these anxieties and the paucity of intelligence were several other factors, chief among them McClellan's caustic and predictable

---

6   *Ibid.*, 2:216.

7   Captain J. S. Ellen, unpublished typescript, "Battle of South Mountain," 2, Rutherford B. Hayes Papers, Hayes Presidential Center, Fremont, Ohio.

8   *Ibid.*; Murfin, *The Gleam of Bayonets*, 122.

9   OR 2:230-234.

10   "Affairs in Pennsylvania and Maryland," *Capital City Fact*, September 15, 1862.

personality. Thrust quickly back into command after the awkward and ultimately failed transfer of power to Major General John Pope, McClellan quickly began another round of grousing about the conduct of the war and his unpardonable treatment by the Lincoln administration. "You don't know what a task has been imposed on me!" he wrote his wife Mary Ellen. "I have been obliged to do the best I could with the broken and discouraged fragments of two armies defeated by no fault of mine."[11] The general's acidic comments about McDowell and Pope continued, only inflating his already bloated ego. "McDowell had to flee for his life . . . Pope had been foolish enough to try to throw the blame on the Army of the Potomac." The next day it was more of the same. "I hardly expect to equal the genius of Mr. Pope," McClellan wrote facetiously, "but hope to waste fewer lives and to accomplish something more than lame defeat."[12]

Some of McClellan's defensiveness emanated from the vocal Republicans in Congress and their newspaper organs who were actively plotting to destroy his reputation. On July 16, 1862, on the Senate floor and in the wake of the defeat that was the Seven Days' Battles, Michigan's Republican Senator Zachariah Chandler delivered an excoriation of McClellan's military performance and his idea of "strategy."[13] The speech was just one of many addresses, articles, and pamphlets devised by the radical wing of the Republican Party to discredit the Young Napoleon.[14] The amateur press, beholden to the romance of a quick and effortless military victory, refused to come to McClellan's aid. As one historian has noted, "war offered opportunity to the press but posed a problem . . . lacking expertise in observing war and lacking true professionalism, reporters hired for the purpose fell back on their store of

---

11 George McClellan to Mary Ellen McClellan, letter, September 8-9, 1862, *McClellan Papers*.

12 *Ibid.*, September 9, 1862.

13 See also Mark E. Neely, Jr., *The Union Divided, Party Conflict in the Civil War North* (Cambridge and London: Harvard University Press, 2002), 73-75.

14 One politico, Alexander Kelly McClure, describes these assaults in his classic *Abraham Lincoln and Men of War-Time* (Philadelphia: Times Publishing Co., 1892), 208. McClure also points out quite accurately McClellan's own wild fascination and belief that the Lincoln administration deliberately attempted to foil his military career. It should be at least considered, however, whether the end goals being pursued by McClellan and Lincoln were compatible. For a thoughtful analysis of McClellan and Civil War historiography, see Thomas J. Rowland, *George B. McClellan and Civil War History: In The Shadow of Grant and Sherman* (Kent: Kent State University Press, 1998).

general knowledge . . . when [they] left their accustomed realm of politics, they were literally at a loss for words."[15] By eagerly anticipating the achievement of a "sweeping and quick victory" in the Peninsula Campaign, the press (with its lofty unrealistic expectations) effectively condemned McClellan to failure.[16]

McClellan addressed yet another factor enervating the Northern military situation in a circular on September 9. Little Mac had done a remarkable job preparing the beaten army ringing Washington to fight again, but discipline was once again beginning to deteriorate within the ranks. McClellan commented on the alleged "frequent absence" of high-ranking officers from their commands while in camp and on the march. "The safety of the country depends upon what this army shall now achieve; it cannot be successful if its soldiers are one-half shirking to the rear, while the brunt of battle is borne by the other half, and its officers inattentive to observe and correct the grossest evils which are daily occurring under their eyes," he declared.[17] Hand-in-hand with this circular followed General Orders No. 55, which equated straggling with "cowardice, marauding, and theft." For many soldiers, such an affront to their manhood and sense of honor was as fearsome as death itself.[18]

Despite the federals' long litany of woes—reorganization issues, miscommunication with commanding officers, lackadaisical field commanders, straggling, the persistent demands hailing from Pennsylvania, and the seeming inability of the military or administration to allay those fears with their "vague and conflicting" reports of enemy operations—the commanding general, like the men of his army, remained generally optimistic. "I think we shall win for the men are now in good spirits—confident in their General & all united in sentiment," McClellan wrote to his wife on September 7. "You need not fear the result for I believe that God will give us the victory. . . . I hope with God's blessing, to justify the great confidence they now repose in me. A victory now," he concluded, "& we will soon be together."[19] New Jersey Colonel Robert

15 Neely, Jr., *The Union Divided*, 64, 69.

16 Eric T. Dean, Jr., "'We Live Under a Government of Men and Morning Newspapers': Image, Expectation, and the Peninsula Campaign of 1862," *The Virginia Magazine of History and Biography*, 103, no. 1 (January 1995): 5-28.

17 OR 2:225.

18 *Ibid.*, 226-227.

19 George McClellan to Mary Ellen McClellan, letter, September 7, 1862, and telegram, September 7, 1862, *McClellan Papers*.

McAllister concurred with his commanding officer. "I have no doubt but that Jackson will be defeated in his plans," he predicted. "McClellan has got hold of the army again and all will be right."[20] "The army is now better contented than it was," James Jenkins Gillette of the 71st New York Militia reported. "General McClellan their idol is restored to command. He is, in the opinion of all soldiers, the only honest and skillful leader we ever had. None other can replace him in the affection of the men."[21]

The Army of the Potomac was once again McClellan's army, and that news served to imbue the rank and file with at least a cautious optimism. Dennis Tuttle, who a few weeks before had reflected on the abject condition of the Army of Northern Virginia, anticipated a nearly effortless defeat of the gray-clad host. "It is my opinion the Rebel Army will be pretty much disposed of before they get away from before Washington. . . . It is success or ruin, now or never, with them, and they know it hence their bold and desperate moves. My hopes are quite sanguine that the Rebellion will be pretty much disposed of before Winter again sets in," Tuttle penned optimistically. "History is being made very rapidly and that too of most thrilling interest. God speed the right and all will be well."[22]

*   *   *

The "floundering army without a head" soon received its orders to break camp at Upton Hill near Washington and join in the general movement north by west. First, however, McClellan needed to unite the fragments of what remained, in effect, two armies. He divided his entire command into three wings, each of which tramped north out of the coiled defenses of Washington on parallel routes. Command of the left wing was conferred upon thirty-nine-year-old Major General William Buell Franklin, who led the VI Corps, augmented by the brigades of Brigadier Generals Charles Devens, Albion P. Howe, and John Cochran, from Darius Couch's division of the IV Corps.

20 Colonel Robert McAllister to Ellen McAllister, September 9, 1862, in *The Civil War Letters of General Robert McAllister*, James I. Robertson, Jr., ed. (New Brunswick, New Jersey: Rutgers University Press, 1965), 203-204.

21 James Jenkins Gillette to his mother, letter, September 8, 1862, in James Jenkins Gillette Papers, Library of Congress, Manuscript Division, Washington, D.C.

22 Dennis Tuttle to his wife, letter, September 3, 1862, Dennis Tuttle Papers.

Born on February 27, 1823, in York, Pennsylvania, Franklin secured an appointment to West Point, graduated as the valedictorian of the Class of 1843 and earned a commission in the prestigious Corps of Topographical Engineers. In this capacity he surveyed the Great Lakes and explored the South Pass of the Rocky Mountains. Franklin's adventures swept him off to war in Mexico and, attached to John Wool's column, he received a brevet for gallantry at Buena Vista. When the war ended Franklin returned to the nation's capital and served as the architectural engineer for the construction of the new dome over the United States Capitol Building. The Civil War broke out while he was overseeing the expansion of the old Treasury Department Building next to the Executive Mansion. Opportunity tapped Franklin once again when he was commissioned colonel of the 12th U.S. Infantry, a post he held for all of three short days. On May 17 he was promoted to brigadier general of volunteers. Nothing in Franklin's biography, however, suggested that he harbored any penchant for aggressiveness, and on the battlefield Franklin proved to be as indolent and slothful as his sponsor George McClellan.[23]

Franklin's VI Corps contained two divisions, each possessing three brigades. Major General Henry Warner Slocum led the first division. Descended from an Englishman who came to America in 1637, Slocum was born in the small Onondaga County village of Delphi Falls, New York, on September 24, 1827. At West Point Slocum roomed with Ohioan Philip Henry Sheridan and graduated with the Class of 1852. After seeing some action against Seminoles in Florida, Slocum determined he would rather practice law than lead troops in battle. He resigned his commission in 1856 and eventually used his Syracuse practice as a springboard into local politics. Slocum served his neighbors as county treasurer and a state legislator before mustering into the 27th New York Volunteers at Elmira on July 9, 1861. Slocum quickly earned the trust of Franklin, and when that general was offered command of the VI Corps, it was Slocum who assumed command of Franklin's former division.[24]

The trajectory of Major General William Farrar Smith's career mirrored that of Franklin. Affectionately known to his men as "Baldy," the commander

---

23 Ludwell H. Johnson, "William B. Franklin," in James W. Geary and John T. Hubbell, eds., *Biographical Dictionary of the Union: Northern Leaders of the Civil War* (Westport: Greenwood Press, 1995), 186-187; Ezra J. Warner, *Generals in Blue: Lives of the Union Commanders* (Baton Rouge: Louisiana State University Press, 1964), 159-160; Mark Snell, *From First to Last: The Life of Major General William B. Franklin* (New York: Fordham University Pres, 2002).

24 Warner, *Generals in Blue*, 451-452.

of the second division, born on February 17, 1824, in the tiny hamlet of St. Albans, Vermont, graduated with distinction from the West Point Class of 1845. Like Franklin, Smith's high showing secured him an assignment to the Corps of Topographical Engineers. Though not as widely traveled as Franklin—he slid into an instructorship at the Military Academy—Smith was a promising officer. He served on Major General Irvin McDowell's staff at First Manassas, and received his commission as brigadier general of volunteers after organizing the Vermont Brigade the following month. Breveted for gallantry at White Oak Swamp on the Virginia Peninsula, he assumed division command on July 4, 1862.[25]

McClellan assigned the center wing of his army to Major General Edwin Vose Sumner, a relic of the Black Hawk and Mexican Wars. At the age of sixty-five Sumner was the Civil War's oldest corps commander. A tenacious fighter who lacked the charisma needed to earn him a prominent place in the history books, "Bull" Sumner led the II Corps, with divisions under Major Generals Israel B. Richardson, John Sedgwick, and William French. McClellan coupled Sumner's II Corps with Major General Joseph K. Mansfield's XII Corps. Two able men, Brigadier Generals Alpheus "Starkey" Williams and George Sears Greene commanded Mansfield's divisions.

The right wing of the Army of the Potomac (the I Corps and IX Corps) Little Mac assigned to a debonair thirty-eight-year-old Rhode Islander named Major General Ambrose Everett Burnside. His politically connected father, a South Carolinian, owned slaves but freed them when he moved his family to Liberty, Indiana, a settlement in Union County. Burnside was born in the new family home on May 23, 1824. He may have remained there all of his life—he began an apprenticeship in a tailor's shop, which eventually led to a promising partnership—had his father's connections not secured him an appointment to West Point. He graduated with the Class of 1847 and made his way to garrison duty in Mexico City. After hostilities with Mexico ended Burnside was shifted west, and while patrolling the southwestern frontier was wounded in a skirmish with Apaches in 1849.

Growing weary of army life, Burnside resigned his commission four years later and migrated to Bristol, Rhode Island. There, he opened an arms manufactory and patented his concept for a breech-loading rifle. A few years later a hideous blaze consumed the factory along with his personal finances.

25 *Ibid.*, 462-463.

Major General Ambrose Everett Burnside. *Library of Congress*

This loss, coupled with a landslide defeat in his 1858 race for Congress as a Democrat, sent Burnside packing. He ventured west, met a railroad executive named George McClellan, and eventually became treasurer of the Illinois Central. War, however, once again interrupted Burnside's career. He assumed the rank of brigadier general in the Rhode Island Militia, raised a regiment, and quickly rose to brigade command in the Department of Northeast Virginia.

After an appearance at First Manassas, Burnside was promoted to brigadier general of volunteers in the new Army of the Potomac. In his role as commander of the Coast Division of that army, he scored some of the Union's lone victories in the East. His amphibious campaign along North Carolina's coast was inspiring and welcome news in early 1862. Work completed, his men transferred to the Virginia Theater, where they proudly filled the ranks of the IX Corps.[26]

McClellan expressed total confidence in his old friend. To better allow Burnside to concentrate on his duties as wing commander, McClellan transferred charge of the IX Corps to short and stocky Jesse Lee Reno, a Wheeling, Virginia (now West Virginia) native who graduated eighth in his West Point Class of 1846. Reno was assigned to the ordnance department and then shipped off to Mexico. He won brevets of first lieutenant and captain for his gallantry at Cerro Gordo and Chapultepec before returning to the academy as an instructor. Reno accompanied Albert Sidney Johnston on his expedition to the Utah Territory to confront the Mormons, and finally landed at Fort Leavenworth, Kansas, on the eve of the Civil War. In the fall of 1861, Reno received a commission to lead one of Burnside's brigades in the North Carolina campaigns.

Reno was curt, short-tempered, and aggressive. With no small dose of personal satisfaction, Rutherford B. Hayes, lieutenant colonel of the 23rd Ohio, vividly recollected one encounter with the general's unchecked temper. On the march from Washington, Eliakim Scammon's brigade of the Kanawha division, (which included Hayes' 23rd Ohio) bivouacked in a damp Maryland stubble field for the evening. After eying a stack of grain on a private parcel adjacent to the muddy field, the exhausted men reasoned that the owner of the grain must be loyal to the Union. Certainly he would have no objections to his hay being "carried by assault" and scattered on the ground to afford the boys in blue a more comfortable night of sleep. The men began spreading the haystack, only to have Reno gallop into the camp and inquire, "in no gentle voice, and in impermissible language," who was in command of such a lawless outfit. Hayes snapped to attention and responded that he was in charge of the regiment. The furious Reno insisted that private property must never be violated and dismissed out of hand Hayes' respectful rebuttal that the good health and

---

26 *Ibid.*, 57; on Burnside, see also William Marvel, *Burnside* (Chapel Hill: University of North Carolina Press, 1991).

comfort of men in the ranks necessitated their action. After a few hours Reno cooled down and issued a half-hearted apology. He even shook Hayes' hand and tried to explain his anger by noting that he was "held personally answerable to the general headquarters for the conduct and doings of his command."[27] It was this grit, historian William Marvel observed, that made Reno Burnside's "most experienced, capable, and dependable subordinate."[28]

Reno's IX Corps contained four divisions, each of which boasted two brigades. Brigadier General Orlando Bolivar Willcox, a Detroit-born graduate of West Point who received a commission in the 4th U.S. Artillery in 1847, commanded the First Division. Willcox served in the army during the tumultuous decade of the 1850s, chasing Indians on the frontiers in the Third Seminole War. After the conflict he resigned and returned to Michigan to practice law. When war broke out he was appointed to command the 1st Michigan Infantry and led a brigade at First Manassas, where he fell wounded before the rebels bagged him as their prisoner. For more than a year the

Confederates held Willcox as a hostage, seeking the release of rebel privateers the federals threatened to hang for piracy. When his release was secured more than a year later on August 19, 1862, Willcox was treated to a hero's welcome and parade, and commissioned as a brigadier general of volunteers.

Major General Jesse Lee Reno, beloved commander of the Army of the Potomac's IX Corps.

Library of Congress

27 This incident is recalled by Captain Ellen in his "South Mountain" unpublished typescript, Rutherford B. Hayes Papers; see also William F. McConnell, *Remember Reno: A Biography of Major General Jesse Lee Reno* (Mechanicsburg, Pennsylvania: White Mane, 1996).

28 William Marvel, "Jesse Lee Reno," in Geary and Hubbell, eds., *Biographical Dictionary of the Union: Northern Leaders of the Civil War* (Westport: Greenwood Press, 1995), 432; Warner, *Generals in Blue*, 394-395.

Willcox may have been canonized by rebel captivity, but Brigadier General Samuel Davis Sturgis from Shippensburg, Pennsylvania, was Reno's most trusted subordinate. In fact, the two were West Point roommates. Sturgis entered the 1st U.S. Dragoons after matriculating with the Class of 1846. After the Mexican War, he also fought Indians on the frontier until he landed command of Fort Smith, Arkansas. Despite the exodus of a number of his men to the Confederate ranks at the outbreak of the war, Sturgis refused to surrender the outpost. When federal commander Nathaniel Lyon became one of the first celebrated Union casualties at the nearby Battle of Wilson's Creek in Missouri on August 10, 1861, Sturgis succeeded him in command. The following March, Sturgis secured a promotion to brigadier general and headed east to the defenses of Washington. When Pope's Army of Virginia needed support at Manassas Junction in August, Sturgis' command was dispatched to the front. After he arrived on the battlefield and surveyed the army's bleak situation, he uttered a caustic assessment of its commander: "I don't care for John Pope one pinch of owl dung."[29]

Brigadier General Isaac Pearce Rodman, a devout Quaker from South Kingston, Rhode Island, who led Reno's third division, was much more restrained. Clinging to anti-slavery convictions and swept away by patriotic fervor, Rodman was a veteran of both chambers of the Rhode Island State Assembly. He set aside his pacifism and raised the 2nd Rhode Island Infantry when the war commenced. While serving under Burnside in North Carolina, seeing action at New Berne and Ft. Macon, he contracted typhoid fever and returned home to recuperate during the summer of 1862. He might have missed the Maryland Campaign entirely had Burnside not singled him out in a letter lamenting his lack of competent subordinates. A sickly Rodman returned just in time to command his troops in the imminent battles.[30]

Anti-slavery convictions also spurred Brigadier General Jacob Dolson Cox into the saddle. Born to American parents in Montreal on October 27, 1828, Cox matured in Ohio, where he attended the progressive Oberlin College in pursuit of the pulpit. While there, he marinated in both the radical abolitionism of the Western Reserve and the teachings of the revivalist Charles Grandison

---

29 Warner, *Generals in Blue*, 486-487; see also Robert Garth Scott, *Forgotten Valor: The Memoirs, Journals, and Civil War Letters of Orlando B. Willcox* (Kent, Ohio: Kent State University Press, 1999).

30 *Ibid.*, 409.

Brigadier General Jacob Dolson Cox, commander of the Kanawha Division.

Library of Congress

Finney. Ultimately, Cox decided to turn to the law, and after graduation began practicing in Warren, Ohio. In 1856, he served as a delegate to the organizing convention of the Ohio Republican Party. Four years later, while seated beside James A. Garfield in the State Senate in Columbus, Cox received command of a Union army recruiting camp outside of the capital city. Soon after, Cox was off to war in the hills of western Virginia, recently commissioned as a brigadier general. After a string of small victories in western Virginia, Cox's division— renamed for the Kanawha Valley where it had camped, marched, and fought— moved east on the eve of Second Manassas.[31]

McClellan's schematic attached the IX Corps to the I Corps, which was commanded by Major General Joseph Hooker. A grandson of a Revolutionary War captain, Hooker was born on November 13, 1814, in Hadley, Massachusetts. He graduated with a mediocre standing in his West Point Class of 1837 and as a staff officer under Generals P. F. Smith, Benjamin F. Butler, and Gideon J. Pillow, earned three brevets during the Mexican War. After the conflict Hooker vacated his post and moved to California to establish an agricultural and land speculation business. Instead of a professional reputation, he garnered infamy for gambling, liquoring, and revelry, wandering from town to town, in the words of one historian, as a hapless "beachcomber."

After the passage of nearly a decade, the drifter made his way east to receive command of Union troops. Hooker led a division in Samuel Heintzelman's

31 *Ibid.*, 97-98.

Third Corps as the Army of the Potomac crawled its way up the Virginia Peninsula in the spring of 1862. When, on May 5, 1862, his division received orders to move on Williamsburg, a dispatch from the front lines matter-of-factly reported, "Fighting—Joe Hooker." An error in transcription, however, omitted the dash and forever branded Hooker with his much-celebrated moniker. When the federal forces reorganized, "Fighting Joe" received command of the First Corps.[32]

Competent officers with experience commanding cavalry, artillery, and infantry led the three divisions in Hooker's I Corps, each of which contained three brigades. Brigadier General John Porter Hatch assumed command of the first division just hours before leading it into the Battle of South Mountain. Born in Oswego, New York, on January 9, 1822, Hatch graduated with the West Point Class of 1845. Twice breveted for gallantry in Mexico, the monotony of garrison duties in Oregon, Texas, and New Mexico marked Hatch's prewar years. The bombardment of Fort Sumter brought him east from the Department of New Mexico, where he had functioned as the chief commissary sergeant. Offered a commission as brigadier general of volunteers, he led Nathaniel Banks' cavalry as it galloped through the Shenandoah Valley in search of Stonewall Jackson during the spring of 1862.[33]

Tough-spirited Brigadier General James Brewerton Ricketts had the artillery experience. The New York City native born on June 21, 1817, commanded guns at Monterey and Buena Vista in Mexico. It was his battery at First Bull Run that defended Henry House Hill, only to be overrun in the rout of some of McDowell's infantry. In the melee that followed Ricketts, who held firm to his guns, received four wounds before being carted off to a rebel prison, where he remained until January 1862. A few months later he was promoted to brigadier general and assumed division command, leading troops at Cedar Mountain and, once again, into battle on the plains of Manassas.[34]

Brigadier General George Gordon Meade likewise distinguished himself in the first year of the war. Meade was born on December 31, 1815, in Cadiz, Spain, where his wealthy merchant father from Philadelphia was serving as a naval agent for the United States. Unfortunately, his father's allegiance to Spain

---

32 *Ibid.*, 233-235; see also John Bigelow, Jr., *The Campaign of Chancellorsville* (New Haven: Yale University Press, 1910).

33 *Ibid.*, 216-217.

34 *Ibid.*, 403-404.

in the Napoleonic Wars spelled financial ruin for the family. Overwhelmed and on the verge of bankruptcy, the elder Meade died unexpectedly in 1828, prompting the family's return to the United States. The young Meade prepared for West Point and secured a coveted appointment, graduating with the class of 1835. He resigned his commission to pursue a career in civil engineering, but when in 1842 his dreams floundered, Meade sought an appointment to the Corps of Topographical Engineers. He conducted coastal surveys and supervised lighthouse construction until the outbreak of the war with Mexico, where he fought at Palo Alto, Resaca de la Palma, and Monterey, earning a brevet to first lieutenant for his gallantry.

When President Lincoln called for volunteers to suppress the rebellion, Governor Andrew Curtin insisted on Meade's promotion to brigadier general of volunteers. Along with the commission, Meade received command of one of the three brigades of Pennsylvania Reserve Volunteers. Meade and the reserves threw up breastworks around Washington until they were pulled out to join McClellan's march up the Virginia Peninsula that spring. In the ensuing Seven Days' battles Meade's reputation blossomed—partly as a result of two wounds he suffered at Glendale on June 30. When the governor ordered John Reynolds, the commander of the division of Pennsylvania Reserves, home to oversee the defenses of the Commonwealth's capital city, George Gordon Meade received command of the entire division.[35]

*   *   *

McClellan's three wings quietly snaked their way northwest through Montgomery County toward Frederick, Franklin's left flank paralleling the Potomac River. Sumner's wing passed through Rockville and Gaithersburg, while Burnside's command assumed the most circuitous route due north of Washington through Leesboro and Brookeville before eventually bending westward to rendezvous with the other elements in Frederick. The momentum was unmistakable: McClellan was on the move.[36]

---

35 *Ibid.*, 315-31. For more on the lives of these commanding officers, see David J. and John H. Eicher, *Civil War High Commands* (Stanford: Stanford University Press, 2001); Heidler and Heidler, eds., *Encyclopedia of the American Civil War.*

36 Brian Holden Reid, *America's Civil War: The Operational Battlefield, 1861-1863* (Amherst, New York: Prometheus Books, 2008), 187-188.

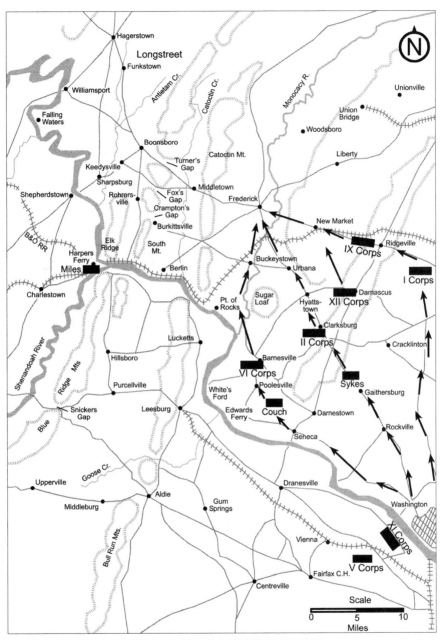

MAP 2. McCLELLAN MOVES NORTH

From his new headquarters near Rockville, "Little Mac" set about estimating the size of the invading Confederate army now operating less than forty miles from his own extended front. "The statements I get regarding the enemy's forces that have crossed to this side range from eighty to one hundred & fifty thousand," he wrote Lincoln. The next day, September 11, the estimate of enemy strength stabilized closer to the high end in a dispatch to General Halleck. "All the evidence . . . goes to prove most conclusively that almost the entire Rebel army in Virginia amounting to not less than 120,000 men is in the vicinity of Frederick City."[37]

Though McClellan invented self-defeating odds, he was keenly aware of the stakes of the impending campaign. "I believe this army fully appreciates the importance of a victory at this time, and will fight well," he scrawled. He closed the communiqué with the poignant observation: "if we defeat the army now arrayed before us, the rebellion is crushed; for I do not believe they can organize another army. But if we should be so unfortunate as to meet with defeat, our country is at their mercy."[38]

*   *   *

McClellan refused to recognize the extent to which Lee and his men were at *his* mercy. The Army of Northern Virginia fielded at most forty thousand men. Compared to the nearly ninety thousand men at the disposal of Army of the Potomac, Lee was heavily outnumbered. Moreover, the Confederate commander grossly underestimated the threat posed by the federal garrison at Harpers Ferry. Coupled with the cool reception his army received upon its arrival in Frederick, Lee felt compelled to write a letter on September 9 to President Davis, who toyed with the idea of journeying to Maryland to meet with his most successful general and army. Lee sternly cautioned against the journey, advising the Southern leader that the "difficulties and dangers" of the trip were far too great. Lee admitted the disparity between the romantic Confederate imagery of Maryland and the reality of sentiments on the ground, warning Davis that he would "not only encounter the hardships and fatigue of a

---

37 George B. McClellan to Abraham Lincoln, September 10, 1862, and McClellan to Halleck, September 11, 1862, *McClellan Papers*.

38 *Ibid.*

very disagreeable journey, but also run the risk of capture by the enemy."[39] The day before, Lee received a brief from Maryland Colonel Bradley Tyler Johnson about the political climate of west-central Maryland. "I impressed upon him emphatically the fact that a large portion of the people were ardent Unionists," Johnson later recalled. "They could not be expected to afford us material aid until we gave them assurance of an opportunity for relief, by an occupation promising at least some permanence."[40]

Despite these challenges, Lee devised one of his riskiest military strategems of the entire war. From his Frederick-based headquarters on September 9, he divided his forces for a specific strategic purpose and identified the various pieces of his soon-to-be-scattered army in Special Orders No. 191.[41] The loose nature of the Confederate command structure at the commencement of the Maryland Campaign allowed Lee to more easily divide and disperse his army in accordance with the new orders. Given his experiences dealing with McClellan, Lee anticipated a sluggish pursuit, and thus believed he had time to deal with the threat posed by Harpers Ferry and then slip into Pennsylvania unmolested.

Lee instructed Jackson and his command to advance through Frederick and Middletown, Maryland, assume the route toward Sharpsburg, cross the Potomac River, take possession of the Baltimore & Ohio Railroad, and strangle the federal arsenal and armory at Harpers Ferry, situated at the confluence of the Shenandoah and Potomac Rivers. The lower town of Harpers Ferry was nestled between three higher points—Maryland Heights to the northeast, Loudon Heights to the south, and Bolivar Heights to the west. Along School House Ridge, about one thousand yards behind Bolivar Heights, Jackson would situate the divisions of J. R. Jones, A. P. Hill, and Alexander Lawton. James Longstreet's command, meanwhile, was to advance as far as Boonsboro, where it would halt with the reserves and supply wagons.[42] Following Longstreet's main column as far as Middletown, McLaws and Anderson would march their divisions to Harpers Ferry and plant their commands on Maryland Heights.

---

39 OR 2:602-603.

40 Bradley Tyler Johnson, "Address on the First Maryland Campaign," in *Southern Historical Society Papers*, 12 (1882): 503-504.

41 Special Orders No. 191 became the focus for a book-length analysis of the military history of the Maryland Campaign: Donald R. Jermann, *Antietam: The Lost Order* (Gretna, Louisiana: Pelican Publishing Company, 2006).

42 James Longstreet was later ordered to continue directly to Hagerstown.

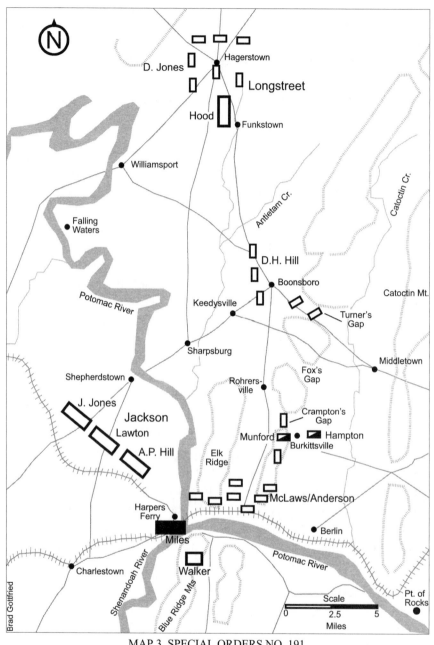

MAP 3. SPECIAL ORDERS NO. 191

Atop Loudon Heights, John Walker's small division would cooperate with McLaws and Jackson in the reduction of the key Union logistical post.

Daniel Harvey Hill's unattached division formed the army's rearguard and trailed behind Longstreet on the National Road. Jeb Stuart was ordered to detach troopers to accompany Longstreet, Jackson, and McLaws, but the main body of Southern cavalry would screen the National Road and gather up stragglers. Once Harpers Ferry was reduced, each infantry detachment would join the main body of the army at Boonsboro or Hagerstown, where the second phase of the invasion could be launched into Pennsylvania.[43]

Special Orders No. 191 committed six Confederate divisions to the reduction of Harpers Ferry. Such an investment was Lee's recognition that he could not hazard the solitary supply line connecting him to the Shenandoah Valley. If the campaign was to continue into Pennsylvania, the rebel columns could not advance with a threat posed to their rear by the sizeable federal Harpers Ferry garrison. Some fourteen thousand men under Colonel Dixon Miles guarded the arsenal and armory—the same place Lee "defended" in October 1859 following John Brown's failed raid. This federal garrison proved to be "a thorn in Lee's rear," a disconcerting distraction from the goals of the invasion.[44] The only way to continue the campaign he intended to push into Pennsylvania was to contend with the force that could potentially seal off the Shenandoah and invite a logistical disaster. And the best way to do that at this stage of the campaign, Lee reasoned, was to divide the disparate parts of his army.

Dividing the army and exposing its splinters across a front some twenty-five miles wide in the face of an advancing enemy did not sit well with General Longstreet, who could not overcome the nagging feeling that Lee was jeopardizing both the campaign and its initial objective. In a council with Jackson and Lee at Frederick, Longstreet made his case against the plan. "I thought it a venture not worth the game," Longstreet recalled. "As we were in the enemy's country and presence," he reasoned, "[the enemy] would be advised of any move that we made in a few hours after it was set on foot; that the Union army, though beaten, was not disorganized; that we knew a number

---

43 OR 2:603-604.

44 For quoted material, see Dennis E. Frye, "Drama between the Rivers: Harper's Ferry in the 1862 Maryland Campaign," in Gary W. Gallagher, ed., *Antietam: Essays on the 1862 Maryland Campaign*, 14-34; see also Reid, *America's Civil War: The Operational Battlefield*, 186-187.

of their officers who could put it in order and march against us, if they found us exposed, and make serious trouble before the capture could be accomplished; that our men were worn by very severe and protracted service, and in need of repose; that as long as we had them in hand we were masters of the situation, but dispersed into many fragments, our strength."[45] Lee would have none of it. "As their minds were settled firmly upon the enterprise, I offered no opposition further," Longstreet lamented.[46]

And so the Confederates marched out of their camps on September 10, with Jackson's command still in the lead. By all accounts it was a cheery day, and many of the high-spirited men in the ranks once again broke into song—this time "The Girl I Left Behind Me."[47]

The movement through Frederick in general, and Jackson's men in particular, inspired John Greenleaf Whittier's lyric and now legendary poem "Barbara Frietchie." The poem, which Whittier held was "no invention [of his]," having come from "completely reliable" sources, describes a "cool and clear September morn" when "up the street came a rebel tread, Stonewall Jackson riding ahead." From the attic window of her home, the ninety-six-year-old woman waved a Union banner at the "forty flags" with "silver stars" and "crimson bars," to demonstrate that her heart was loyal still. "'Shoot if you must, this old gray head,'" she allegedly snapped, "but spare your country's flag.'"[48]

*   *   *

With the advantage of a newly established signal station on Sugar Loaf Mountain, McClellan wired Halleck that the enemy had abandoned Frederick via the "Hagerstown & Harper's Ferry roads." Most importantly, though, his

---

45 James Longstreet, *From Manassas to Appomattox*, 201-205.

46 *Ibid.*

47 *Ibid.*, 205.

48 John Greenleaf Whittier, "Barbara Freitchie." Freitchie was born in Lancaster, Pennsylvania, on December 3, 1766. Her husband, John Casper Freitchie, whom she married on May 6, 1806, was a glove-maker in Frederick until his death on November 10, 1849. On Freitchie, see Conrad Reno, "General Jesse Lee Reno at Frederick: Barbara Fritchie and Her Flag," in *Civil War Papers Read Before the Commandery of the State of Massachusetts Military Order of the Loyal Legion of the United States* (Boston, 1900), 2:553-569.

own columns were "pushing on rapidly to Frederick."[49] The commanding general noted frequent stops were needed to "rest and rejuvenate" the army, which may have amounted to nothing more than lengthy loitering and gawking in "one of the most lovely regions" he had ever seen.[50] Letters from veterans of this march are almost comical in their reporting on the short cycles of marching and resting. These same men had just been reorganized after a stunning defeat from what had been two armies into three large wings, and were now pressing north and west in pursuit of a victorious invading enemy. Under the circumstances, McClellan was moving with remarkable and uncharacteristic speed. It was arguably his finest hour of the war.[51]

After days of panic and occupation, the sight of a federal army relieved the denizens of Frederick. "The people of Frederick turned out to welcome Burnside with the wildest enthusiasm," one newspaper wire story announced. They were especially excited to catch a glimpse of General McClellan the day after Burnside's arrival. "The people blocked up the streets so that it was difficult for him to reach his headquarters." After enduring the invasion of the rebels, these Marylanders were more than ready to demonstrate their loyalty to the Union. "When the Commander and Staff appeared the crowd became so demonstrative that we were forcibly brought to a halt," one soldier remembered. "The officers of the Staff received their due share of the floral honors, but the General and horse were absolutely covered with wreaths and bouquets; while old men, women, and children crowded around, anxious to touch his hand, or by some word or act to testify their enthusiasm for the leader of the National power."[52]

The *New York Times* reported that the lavish welcome afforded Generals McClellan and Burnside brought both men to tears, for it was "really the first loyal demonstration since the army entered Maryland." As a Baltimore paper put it, "The waving of flags and handkerchiefs was universal, and the women and children screamed words of welcome at the top of their voices." "[We] were welcomed with a spontaneous ovation that stirred every soul to its depths,"

---

49 McClellan to Halleck, September 12, 1862, *McClellan Papers*, 448.

50 McClellan offers this description in a letter to Mary Ellen McClellan, September 12, 1862, *McClellan Papers*.

51 Reid, *America's Civil War: The Operational Battlefield*, 188.

52 "Personal Recollections of the War—Antietam," in *Harper's New Monthly Magazine*, 36 (February 1868): 275.

Artist Edwin Forbes depicts General George B. McClellan's triumphant
arrival in Frederick, Maryland. *Library of Congress*

recalled a federal soldier. "The whole city was fluttering with national flags; while the streets through which we passed, from the sidewalks to the house-tops, shone with happy human faces. It seemed as if the whole population had turned out, wild with joy." The deeply felt joy was an unmasked expression of relief. "At some houses we noticed ladies attired in white dresses, wearing sashes of red, white, and blue," wrote a soldier whose name has been lost to history. "Some of them advanced to the streets and saluted our officers and men by waving flags . . . occasionally children, with miniature flags pinned to their dresses and flags in their hands came out into the road and tossed their flags to the tired and weary soldiers as they passed along," one letter observed. "One young lady in the intoxication of joy, jumped up and declared that she could kiss the whole army," remembered a veteran of the 12th Ohio Volunteer Infantry. Allegedly, an old sergeant overheard her claim and told her to begin with him, an offer that quickly stifled her enthusiasm.[53]

Many soldiers marveled at the sudden change in civilian sentiment. Only the week before, federal forces had passed through Poolesville and

---

53 *New York Times*, September 13, 1862; Baltimore wire report as reported in the *Boston Evening Transcript*, September 15, 1862; "Personal Recollections of the War—Antietam," 275; Unsigned letter, published in the *Capital City Fact*, September 16, 1862; J. E. D. Ward, *Twelfth Ohio Volunteer Infantry* (Ripley, Ohio: Published by Author, 1864), 57.

Darnestown, communities that now eagerly furnished supplies to the invading Confederate forces. Neither a "national flag" nor "a cheer" encountered the federals in that timorous region of "conditional unionism." Now, in Frederick, unionism was anything but tepid.[54]

"The Confederates have actually polluted this country and good old city with their detestable presence," James Jenkins Gillette wrote in a letter to his mother recalling a conversation he had with a Frederick civilian. He continued:

> The wretched half naked crowd that tainted the atmosphere with odors . . . They fairly stank so saturated with filth were they—these bunches of rags—these cough-racked, diseased and starved men. . . . I have no need to praise Confederate forbearance but the fact that we are confronted by an army perfectly under the control and discipline of tried officers is incontrovertible. . . . The charm is broken . . . The time of their stay was like a Sabbath on which no business is done and when people go about quiet and subdued. Not a welcome was given the soldiers who suspected an uprising. The rebels met icy coldness where they expected genial warmth and gratitude. Maryland is "all right" as I always said she was.[55]

The charm *was* broken. As Lieutenant Henry R. Brinkerhoff of the 30th Ohio Volunteers rhetorically asked a year later, "Can Frederick City ever forget this day? Can the old honest hero ever ask for a more heart-felt though boisterous reception? And can the regiment ask greater acclamations, at the hands of their countrymen, even at the deliverance of the Nation, than they received at Frederick City?"[56]

*   *   *

The 13th of September, a Saturday, was a seminal day in the Maryland Campaign and serves as a telling reminder of the power of contingency during any military operation. At dawn, federal cavalry commander Brigadier General Alfred Pleasonton rode out of Frederick in search of Lee's moving columns. A few hours later, along the Catoctin Mountains west of Frederick, the lances of

54 *New York Times*, September 13, 1862; *Boston Evening Transcript*, September 8, 1862.

55 James Jenkins Gillette to his mother, letter, September 13, 1862, James Jenkins Gillette Papers.

56 Henry R. Brinkerhoff, *Thirtieth Regiment Ohio Volunteer Infantry* (Columbus, Ohio: James W. Osgood, Printer, 1863), 41.

the 6th Pennsylvania Cavalry (Rush's Lancers) met up with Captain Roger P. Chew's horse artillery. A small engagement developed when the lancers received reinforcements in the form of Hawkins' Zouaves and six companies of the 103rd New York Infantry.[57]

Farther east, in the clover fields surrounding Frederick, the day began far less conspicuously. Near the banks of the Monocacy, the 27th Indiana, a XII Corps unit composed mostly of yeomen Hoosier farmers, bivouacked on ground recently vacated by the rebels. Ordered by their sergeant, John McKnight Bloss, to rest on what was uniformly described as a warm and beautiful day, Corporal Barton W. Mitchell, Private David B. Vance, and Private William H. Hostetter took advantage of the grassy shade and rested on the ground. After several minutes of conversation a bulky yellow envelope nestled in clover caught their attention. Inside it, the four men discovered three cigars and, more importantly, two folded sheets of parchment paper.[58]

As he skimmed through the document, Sergeant Bloss recognized the names of several rebel generals. The document appeared to be the marching orders of the Confederate army—one of nine copies of Special Orders No. 191. Recognizing the potential significance of his find, the sergeant carried the envelope to Captain Peter Kop, commander of Company F. After another reading by both Bloss and Kop, they forwarded the package to Colonel Silas Colgrove, the commander of the 27th Indiana. Brigadier General Nathan Kimball advised Colonel Colgrove to take the prize directly to General Williams, the commander of the XII Corps. In an almost impossible stroke of luck, Williams' assistant adjutant general, Captain Samuel E. Pittman, received Kimball and Colgrove and, as he recalled, "immediately identified the signature of Colonel R. H. Chilton, Lee's assistant adjutant general." Pittman worked

---

57 On the cavalry actions of September 13, see Timothy J. Reese, "The Cavalry Clash at Quebec Schoolhouse," *Blue and Gray Magazine* (February 1993), 24-30; "The Cavalry Fight at Boonsboro Graphically Described," *Richmond Dispatch*, July 16, 1897, and George Neese, *Three Years in the Confederate Horse Artillery* (New York: Neale Publishing Co., 1911).

58 The varied accounts of this incident are too numerous to mention and fall outside the purview of this study. Undertaking the historiography of the "lost order" incident is a considerable exercise, but one should begin with Wilbur Jones, *Giants in the Cornfield: The 27th Indiana Infantry* (Shippensburg: White Mane Publishing, Inc., 1997), 228-242. Jones also offers a helpful historiographical chronology in addition to his treatment of September 13, 1862. Jermann, *Antietam: The Lost Order*, 145-158, is somewhat less helpful, but offers a fine summary of events. For the Confederate perspective and how exactly the orders were "lost," see Harsh, *Sounding the Shallows*, 141-142, 159-162, 166-167, 170-175, 182. One should also consider J. Balsley, Co. H., 27th Indiana Volunteers, "Lee's Lost Order," *National Tribune*, March 26, 1908.

before the war as a teller at the bank in Detroit, Michigan, where Chilton, then the paymaster of the federal army, deposited countless checks endorsed with his signature. There was no doubt about it, confirmed Pittman. This was a genuine document.[59]

Williams' staffers took the order to Major General Randolph Marcy, McClellan's chief of staff, who slipped it into the hands of the Young Napoleon. Beaming with delight, McClellan declared that in misplacing the orders, the rebels had "made a gross error." "Here is a paper with which if I cannot whip 'Bobbie Lee' I will be willing to go home," he allegedly quipped to Brigadier General John Gibbon.[60] About noon, McClellan wired a confident message to Lincoln that demonstrated a newfound energy and zeal. "I have the whole Rebel force in front of me but am confident and no time shall be lost." He continued:

> I have a difficult task to perform but with God's blessing will accomplish it. I think Lee has made a gross mistake and that he will be severely punished for it. The Army is in motion as rapidly as possible. I hope for a great success if the plans of the Rebels remain unchanged. We have possession of Cotocktane [sic]. I have all the plans of the Rebels and will catch them in their own trap if my men are equal to the emergency. I now feel that I can count on them as of old. All forces of Pennsylvania should be placed to cooperate at Chambersburg. My respects to Mrs. Lincoln. Received most enthusiastically by the ladies [of Frederick]. Will send you trophies.
>
> All [is] well and with Gods Blessing [we] will accomplish it.
>
> Geo B. McClellan[61]

That Lincoln did not wire an immediate reply was no surprise. The president passed the day at his secluded cottage retreat on the expansive grounds of the Old Soldiers' Home on Washington's northern fringe. There, he composed a careful reply to a memorial in favor of national emancipation drafted by the Revs. William W. Patton and John Dempster of Chicago. On September 7, at an ecumenical meeting in Chicago, the reverends had adopted a

---

59 See Charles B. Dew, "How Samuel E. Pittman Validated Lee's 'Lost Orders' Prior to Antietam: A Historical Note," *Journal of Southern History*, 70, no. 4 (November 2004), 865-70.

60 Silas Colgrove, "The Finding of Lee's Lost Order," *B&L*, 2:603; John Gibbon, *Personal Recollections of the Civil War* (New York: G.P. Putnam's Sons, 1928), 73.

61 McClellan to Lincoln, telegraph, September 13, 1862, OR 2:281.

resolution in favor of abolition.[62] "It is my earnest desire to know the will of Providence in this matter. And if I can learn what it is I will do it!" Lincoln rejoined. "I have not decided against a proclamation of liberty to the slaves, but hold the matter under advisement. And I can assure you that the subject is on my mind, by day and night, more than any other. Whatever shall appear to be God's will I will do."[63]

Lincoln was certain God was not neutral between slavery and freedom. The thought of endangering the Union cause by issuing a war-changing proclamation devoid of material power, however, gave him pause. He weighed his options and resolved to let the document linger without further mention until Divine Will intervened. Until then, as in the response to Patton and Dempster, Lincoln resorted to tepidly sidestepping the issue. Knowing the topography of public opinion and how best to navigate it, Lincoln understood that he would have to wait to move on emancipation until his armies secured the military victory demanded by the Northern public. He could not act without some harbinger of ultimate success.[64] Now, McClellan was telling him that with God's will, that success would come. But would McClellan be equal to the task at hand? That was a question for which Lincoln did not have an answer.

*   *   *

"An order from General R. E. Lee, addressed to General D. H. Hill, which has accidentally come into my hands this evening—the authenticity of which is unquestionable—discloses some of the plans of the enemy, and shows most conclusively that the main rebel army is now before us," McClellan dispatched to Halleck that evening. "I expect a severe general engagement to-morrow."[65] About twenty minutes past six o'clock that evening, still gloating about his "full information" of the enemy's whereabouts, information that supposedly set the

---

62   *CWAL*, 5:419; on Lincoln and the Soldier's Home, see Matthew Pinsker, *Lincoln's Sanctuary* (New York: Oxford University Press, 2003).

63   *Ibid.*, 419-425.

64   The literature on Lincoln, emancipation, and black freedom is wide and varied, but one must begin with Allen C. Guelzo, *Lincoln's Emancipation Proclamation: The End of Slavery in America* (New York: Simon & Schuster, 2004); on the "limits of possible," see LaWanda F. Cox's important study, *Lincoln and Black Freedom: A Study in Presidential Leadership* (Columbia: University of South Carolina Press, 1981).

65   *OR* 2:281-282.

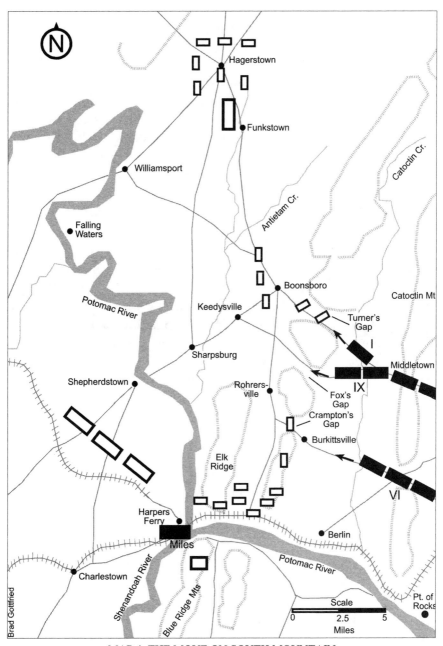

MAP 4. THE MOVE ON SOUTH MOUNTAIN

army in motion "as rapidly as possible," McClellan issued orders to Major General William Buel Franklin. "You will move at daybreak in the morning, by Jefferson and Burkittsville, upon the road to Rohrersville. If you find this pass [Crampton's Gap] held by the enemy in large force, make all your dispositions for the attack, and commence it," ordered McClellan. "Having gained the pass, your duty will be first to cut off, destroy, or capture McLaws' command and relieve Colonel Miles [at Harpers Ferry]. If you effect this, you will order him to join you at once with all of his disposable troops." And then McClellan gave Franklin free reign. "I believe I have sufficiently explained my intentions," he began. "I ask of you at this important moment all your intellect. . . . Knowing my views & intentions you are fully authorized to change any of the details of this order as circumstances may change, provided the purpose is carried out."[66]

By dusk on September 13, the core of McClellan's general strategy was complete. "My general idea is to cut the enemy in two and beat him in detail," he determined. Once more, the trust he had in his old friend Ambrose Burnside manifested itself when McClellan charged the Right Wing with the main assault. Little Mac's plan directed Burnside to mass the IX Corps and I Corps to the front and press on with a main assault toward Fox's and Turner's gaps in the South Mountain range. McClellan instructed the II Corps and XII Corps of the center wing, which still trailed behind, to join the rear of Burnside's vanguard. McClellan intended Burnside's attack to defeat D. H. Hill swiftly and carry the gaps, which would allow the insertion of four corps of the Union army on the far side of South Mountain. This, in turn, would prevent Hill's survivors and Longstreet's command from uniting with the divisions that were absent trying to reduce Harpers Ferry.

Franklin and the VI Corps fit into this scheme by offering a threat large enough to occupy the rebel divisions surrounding Harpers Ferry. If he was successful, Franklin's storming of Crampton's Gap would blockade the Confederate retreat route through Pleasant Valley, leaving the rebels no other option than to fight against tremendous odds or splash across the Potomac River in a hasty retreat. In other words, Franklin would defeat these commands in detail as Burnside supervised the hammering farther north. South Mountain was not merely the thoroughfare that led the armies into Pennsylvania; it was the spine of Union and Confederate grand strategy, and McClellan intended to snap it in half.

---

66 *Ibid.*, 1:45-46; McClellan to Franklin, September 13, 1862, *McClellan Papers.*

*   *   *

A dispatch arrived from Stuart during the early hours of September 14 informing Lee that a copy of the special orders had fallen into McClellan's hands.[67] Lee realized for the first time the absolute precariousness of his military situation. He had confidently believed for weeks that McClellan would continue to exercise his characteristic caution, just as he had during his lethargic move up the Virginia Peninsula that spring. "The hallucination that McClellan was not capable of serious work seemed to pervade our army," Longstreet remembered.[68] These preconceptions left the Army of Northern Virginia all the more unprepared to face the enemy, and all the more baffled when McClellan began to push forward toward South Mountain. Lee immediately summoned Longstreet to his headquarters tent, where the wing commander found Lee poring over maps of the mountain. The army leader preferred to make his stand at Turner's Gap, the northernmost of the three passes west of Frederick. Longstreet disagreed vehemently and boldly suggested abandoning the South Mountain range entirely. Although the heights offered the Confederates an enviable defensive position, he argued, it was much too late to march to Turner's Gap—let alone properly man the pass. "[I] expressed preference for concentrating D. H. Hill's and my own force behind the Antietam at Sharpsburg, where we could get together in season to make a strong defensive fight, and at the same time check McClellan's march towards Harpers Ferry," he recalled.[69]

Once more, Lee disagreed with his subordinate. Stung by his second rebuke in a single campaign, Longstreet retired to his headquarters tent to reflect upon affairs. "My mind was so disturbed that I could not rest," the general remembered. "As I studied, the perils seemed to grow, till at last I made a light and wrote to tell General Lee of my troubled thoughts, and appealed

---

67 Robert E. Lee to E. C. Gordon, February 15, 1868, as quoted in Harsh, *Sounding the Shallows*, 171.

68 Horace Greeley, "The American Conflict: Leading Incidents and Episodes of the War of the Rebellion," *National Tribune*, September 8, 1898; Longstreet, *From Manassas to Appomattox*, 220.

69 Longstreet, *From Manassas to Appomattox*, 219-220.

again for immediate concentration at Sharpsburg. To this no answer came, but it relieved my mind and gave me some rest."[70]

If indeed Longstreet rested that night, it would be a long while before he would be able to do so again.

---

70 *Ibid.*, 220.

hapter 5

"My God, be careful!"

The Morning Fight for Fox's Gap

Not till the lines seemed within a few yards of each other was the calm, radiant Sabbath morning broken by the crack of rifles. The battle was on.

— Adjutant V. E. Turner, 23rd North Carolina[1]

T he South Mountain range west of Frederick, Maryland, runs generally northeast to southwest and crests at an elevation of about 1,300 feet. Three gaps overlooked the spires of Frederick and the Catoctin Mountains farther east. The first, Turner's Gap near Boonsboro, was the northernmost of the trio. Fox's Gap was situated about one mile southwest of Turner's. The third and southernmost, Crampton's Gap, cut through the range opposite the small hamlet of Burkittsville.[2] Turner's Gap, named after Robert Turner, who had functioned as the overseer of roads in the Antietam Hundred as early as

---

1 V. E. Turner, "Twenty-Third Regiment," in Walter Clark, ed., *Histories of the Several Regiments and Battalions from North Carolina in the Great War, 1861-1865* (Goldsboro, North Carolina: Nash Bros. Printers, 1901), 2:220.

2 Ezra Carman, *The Maryland Campaign of September 1862*, ed. Joseph Pierro (New York: Routledge Press, 2008), 143. In this chapter, page references to the Carman manuscript refer to the Pierro edition, and not Carman's original pagination. The original manuscript is located in the Ezra Ayres Carman Papers, Manuscript Division, Library of Congress, Washington, D.C., Boxes 15-17. While the original manuscript of this seminal source for any student of the Maryland Campaign has also been microfilmed, Pierro's work is here cited because it will be the most accessible to future students of the campaign. After this manuscript was largely complete, Thomas Clemens, a student of Dr. Joseph Harsh, published a far superior edition of the Carman manuscript. The first of Clemens' two-volume edition, *The Maryland Campaign of 1862: Vol. 1: South Mountain*, was published in 2010 by Savas Beatie.

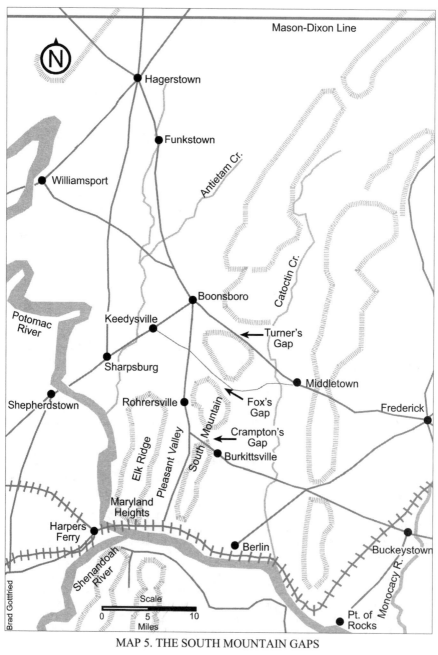

MAP 5. THE SOUTH MOUNTAIN GAPS

A modern view of the Mountain House, now the Old South Mountain Inn.

Henry F. Ballone

1748, was the most distinguished among the travelers and visitors to the area. On the summit was a stately tavern of corrugated gray stone known as the Old Mountain House. Nearby stood a hollow, barrel-shaped monument built of stone and mortar in 1827 as the nation's first commemoration of George Washington. The middle gap bore the name of an early deed holder, John Fox, who inhabited the mountain sometime before the 1760s. During the American Revolution, colonists funneled supplies from Berkeley and Frederick counties through Sharpsburg via this pass. Thomas Crampton arrived in Pleasant Valley before 1759 and constructed a wilderness road there, eventually lending his name to the third pass.[3]

A macadamized turnpike twenty-five feet wide spanned the length of the mountain. In November 1804, the Maryland General Assembly chartered the Baltimore and Fredericktown Turnpike Company to construct a proper road through Frederick and Middletown to Boonsboro. Work began and the company started taking subscriptions in 1805. In an effort to address the difficulties of overland travel from Maryland to the burgeoning settlements of the Ohio Valley, Congress in 1806 appropriated the funds to establish a road linking Cumberland, Maryland, to Wheeling, [West] Virginia. Eventually, Maryland banks financed a road connecting the state and federal highways, and by 1823 the path across the mountain became known as the National Road.[4]

The mountain was as picturesque as it was rough and wild. Sylvan patches and craggy rock formations obscured by untended groundcover punctuated open fields, partially wooded acres, and working farms. Several mountain roads

3   Curtis L. Older, *The Land Tracts of the Battlefield of South Mountain* (Westminster, Maryland: Willow Bend Books, 1999), 40-41, 45.

4   *Ibid.*, 51.

connecting these farms were so steep that just ascending them could be a dangerous undertaking. Stone walls, erected low to the ground, outlined many of the roads. "From Middletown the road runs in a westerly direction through a rather rough country, and strikes the abrupt rise of the mountain, at about three miles from the town," recalled veteran Thomas T. Ellis. "It here becomes very steep and stony; in some places the hill rises considerably above the road, on either side, forming a gulch rather than a road," he continued. "High and rough as the country is at this point, it is fenced, and near the summit of the mountain, at a point where the sides of the road are considerably higher than the road itself, a good stone wall runs around from the road to the right at right-angles, and crosses the field to the wood." A member of the famed Iron Brigade thought the land absolutely lovely. "There are few fairer landscapes in our country than this valley affords from its eastern range of hills," admitted Rufus R. Dawes of the 6th Wisconsin. Gilbert Frederick, who fought with a New York regiment, agreed with the Wisconsin officer. "[The landscape of South Mountain was] a picture of unrivaled beauty and grandeur. We have ascended mountains until lost in the clouds, followed forsaken paths and crossed rich green plains that resembled gardens decorated with flowers." The landscape we marched through "looked like a vale of Eden," gushed Gilbert Thompson of the U.S. Engineer Battalion.[5]

"The dreamy blue haze that covered, as with a gauzy veil, the mountain ranges; the deeper and brighter vapory covering that hung like a glory over the far-stretching valleys; the grass and the flowers, yet dripping and sparkling with nature's dewy baptism; the glad songs of the birds . . . all told of Sabbath—sweet, sacred Sabbath—the day of rest and peace!" William Lyle of the 11th Ohio waxed lyrically to his diary on September 14. "And we thought of home—Sabbaths, too, and the sanctuary of God, and the voice of prayer and the songs of praise." Indeed, being a lovely Sunday, some federals turned their thoughts to God during the march toward the enemy. "Many a prayer went up that morning from the embattled hosts of freedom for loved ones at home!," explained Lyle. Many soldiers "breathed the wish into God's own ear, that if no

5   Thomas T. Ellis, diary, September 1862, in *Leaves from the Diary of an Army Surgeon: or, Incidents of Field, Camp, and Hospital Life* (New York: John Bradburn, 1863), 312; Rufus R. Dawes, "Memoir of Rufus Dawes," in *Service with the Sixth Wisconsin Volunteers* (Marietta, Ohio: E.R. Alderman & Sons, 1890), 319; Gilbert Frederick, *The Story of a Regiment* (Chicago: C.H. Morgan Co., 1895), 83; Gilbert Thompson Papers, Manuscript Division, Library of Congress, Washington, D.C.

more earthly Sabbaths should see them and dear ones nestling once more at home, sweet home . . . where war's fierce tumults shall never be heard, and where the calm of an eternal Sabbath shall never be disturbed."[6]

*   *   *

"This morning the Sun rose bright and warm," one soldier recorded in his diary.[7] "It was a lovely morning. However much the passions of men might be raging," Lyle observed, "nature, at least, was calm, peaceful, and joyous."[8]

With daylight, which arrived eleven minutes before six, General Pleasonton and his federal cavalry division renewed efforts made the previous evening to reconnoiter the rolling, broken land before them. "Being soon satisfied that the enemy would defend his position at Turner's Gap with a large force, I sent back to General Burnside for some infantry," Pleasonton wrote in his official report.[9] Although Pleasonton suggested that he anticipated a general engagement that morning, the evidence suggests otherwise. "The notion that Pleasonton was authorized to put the infantry in position for an expected battle is wholly a mistake," cautioned General Jacob D. Cox of the IX Corps' Kanawha Division. "No battle was expected at Turner's Gap." Lieutenant Colonel Eugene Powell of the 66th Ohio agreed, recalling in 1895 that even the captured copy of Special Orders No. 191 suggested that a battle for the South Mountain passes would be unlikely. "That order revealed to McClellan the fact that the passes in the South Mountain beyond and through which he had to go would only be held by a rearguard, and that there Lee would not give battle."[10] Pleasonton, who only lightly reconnoitered in the direction of the passes on September 13, summoned the support of a "single brigade of infantry," which he assumed

6   William Lyle, *Lights and Shadows of Army Life* (Cincinnati: R.W. Carroll and Co., 1865), 124-125.

7   William W. Sherwood, diary entry, September 14, 1862, Virginia Historical Society, Richmond, Virginia.

8   William Lyle, *Lights and Shadows of Army Life*, 124.

9   *OR* 1:209.

10   Eugene Powell, "Recollections of Lee's First Invasion and the Battle of Antietam" (1895), handwritten manuscript in the Ezra A. Carman Papers, Box 17, folder no. 1, Manuscript Division, Library of Congress, Washington, D.C.

Alfred Waud's sketch of the Union army marching through Middletown, Maryland, on its way to the Battle of South Mountain, appeared in the October 25, 1862 edition of *Harper's Weekly*. *Library of Congress*

would be "enough to enable his cavalry to clear the way" of a Confederate "rear-guard" at Turner's Gap.

In response to Pleasonton's request, Cox detailed the 1,455 men of Colonel Eliakim P. Scammon's First Brigade. Scammon's command was composed of the 12th, 23rd, and 30th Ohio infantry regiments, two companies of West Virginia Cavalry (Gilmore's Company and Harrison's Company, commanded by Lieutenant James Abraham and Lieutenant Dennis Delaney, respectively), and a half-dozen 10-pound Parrotts of Captain James R. McMullin's First Ohio Light Artillery.[11] The men bivouacked in Middletown on the evening of September 13 and enjoyed breakfast the following morning on the banks of the lazy Catoctin Creek. Taking the lead from the dismounted cavalrymen, Scammon's brigade proceeded up the turnpike.[12] "As it had done from the time McClellan's army left Washington," Lieutenant Robert B. Wilson proudly

11 *OR* 1:209, 1:458-461; Hill, *B&L*, 2:563.

12 *Ibid*, 1:435, 458-459; Carman, *The Maryland Campaign*, 143; *B&L*, 2:585.

reported, "Scammon's Brigade with the 12th Ohio at the head of the column led the division."[13] The troops were "in the best of spirits and eager to meet the enemy and wipe out the Bull Run humiliation," admitted Sol Smith, also a veteran of Wilson's regiment.[14]

About 8:00 a.m., Pleasonton ordered Lieutenant Samuel N. Benjamin's Battery E of the Second U.S. Artillery, which was attached to the First Division of the IX Corps, to assume a position on a high knoll left of the turnpike. Benjamin wheeled his four 20-pound Parrotts into position near the crossroads village of Bolivar, about one-half mile in advance of the National Turnpike's intersection with the Old Sharpsburg Road.[15] Pleasonton also forwarded six 3-inch ordnance rifles of Batteries C and G belonging to Captain Horatio G. Gibson's Third U.S. Artillery to occupy this position. The federal guns began lobbing exploratory volleys north across the National Turnpike at Confederate artillery deployed there. Captain John Lane's Georgia battery returned the fire with two 20-pound Parrotts, three 10-pound Parrotts, and one British-made Whitworth rifle. The crest of the hill they occupied was several thousand yards north and east of the turnpike. Federal metal proved too much for Lanes' gunners, who were twice silenced by this long-range fire. Sol Smith, who watched the exchange of iron with his comrades, recalled how "The earth was shaken by the terrible thunder of artillery." In between exchanges, the Georgians took advantage of the lull to limber their pieces and move to a different position in an effort to avoid the deadly federal shells.[16]

It was only with this artillery support in place that Pleasonton felt comfortable enough to send troopers up the roads, followed by infantry, to more fully reconnoiter the mountain passes. General Cox moved forward with Scammon's brigade. Just after he splashed across Catoctin Creek, Cox noticed an officer alongside the National Turnpike. Upon closer inspection, the brigadier general recognized German-born Colonel Augustus Moor of the 28th Ohio, recently bagged as one of Wade Hampton's prisoners during a federal reconnaissance effort on September 12. Cox learned that Moor had walked to

13 Lieutenant R. B. Wilson to Ezra A. Carman, letter, July 11, 1899, in Ezra A. Carman Papers, Manuscript Division, Library of Congress, Washington, D.C.

14 Sol Smith, "South Mountain," *National Tribune*, January 17, 1895.

15 *OR* 1:209-210; 416-417; 435-436; Carman, *The Maryland Campaign*, 143.

16 *Ibid*.; *OR* 1:837; Smith, *National Tribune*, January 17, 1895.

Middletown that morning from the crest of South Mountain. The officer earned an honorable release under the parameters of the Dix-Hill Cartel.[17] "But where are you going?" Moor asked rather impatiently. When Cox replied that he was on a reconnaissance mission of South Mountain in support of Pleasonton's cavalry, Moor exclaimed, "My God, be careful!" He offered no further explanation of whatever dangers might have been lurking ahead in fear of violating his parole.[18]

Moor's caveat, however, was enough for Cox who, startled by the colonel's ominous admission, issued verbal warnings to each of his regimental commanders. "I went back along the column . . . warning them to be prepared for anything, big or little—it might be a skirmish, it might be a battle," he remembered.[19] Cox sought out Scammon and told him to follow the lead brigade with the regiments of Colonel George Crook's Second Brigade, which consisted of the 11th, 28th, and 36th Ohio Volunteer Infantry, Captain Frederick Schambeck's company of Chicago Dragoons, and the two 20-pound Parrotts and four, ten-pound Parrotts of Captain Seth J. Simmond's battery of Kentucky Light Artillery. "I suspected we should find the enemy in force on the mountain-top, and should go forward with both brigades instead of sending one," explained Cox. The division commander rushed back to camp and ordered his men to be ready to march at once. "We accordingly piled knapsacks and started on in pursuit," Lieutenant John Alexander Palmer of the 36th Ohio noted in his diary. Martin Sheets of the 11th Ohio also remembered leaving his knapsack behind and scurrying off toward the mountain top.[20]

Back in camp with the Kanawha Division, Cox fired a communiqué to his superior, IX Corps commander Jesse Reno, informing him of his latest orders.

---

17 On Moor's capture, see Ellison Capers, *South Carolina*, in *Confederate Military History* (Secaucus, New Jersey: Blue and Grey Press ed., 1993), 142-143; see also Cox, in *B&L*, 2:583-584; J. H. Horton and Solomon Teverbaugh, *A History of the Eleventh Regiment, Ohio Volunteer Infantry* (Dayton, Ohio: W.J. Shuey, 1866), 69-70; and Martin Sheets, diary entry, September 12, 1862, in Civil War Times Illustrated Collection, United States Army Military History Institute, Carlisle, Pennsylvania.

18 Cox, *B&L*, 2:585-586.

19 *Ibid.*

20 John Alexander Palmer, diary entry, September 14, 1862, transcribed in Lester L. Kempfer, *The Salem Light Guard: Company G, 36th Regiment Ohio Volunteer Infantry* (Chicago: Adams Press, 1973), 87; Sheets, diary entry, September 14, 1862, in Civil War Times Illustrated Collection, United States Army Military History Institute, Carlisle, Pennsylvania.

Reno pledged to bring up the balance of the corps to support Cox.[21] With his dispatch to Reno on its way Cox rode back up the National Turnpike to find Pleasonton, who now withdrew his previous assurances that Turner's Gap was occupied by only the enemy's rearguard. "I found that he was convinced that the enemy's position in the gap was too strong to be carried by a direct attack," Cox related. Pleasonton's reconnaissance also brought the local geography into sharper focus. The cavalryman was now aware of the Old Sharpsburg Road, which wound itself southwest around Fox's Gap. Additionally, Pleasonton noted the course of the road to Frosttown, on the opposite side of the main turnpike. These encircling road networks, he noted, "would assist us materially in turning the enemy's position."[22] Pleasonton decided to allow his cavalry to demonstrate on the main turnpike, supported by Benjamin's and Gibson's batteries, and ordered Scammon to ascend the mountain with his brigade up the Old Sharpsburg Road to the enemy's rear.

Cox convinced Pleasonton that deploying Crook's brigade during the approach was essential, and the Ohioans marched to support Scammon in his attempt to maneuver the federal column around the enemy, turn their right flank, and gain the mountain crest. Captain Simmond's two 20-pound Parrotts were too cumbersome to lug up the steep, weathered, and rock-littered mountain road being trudged by some of the infantry, so Cox positioned them in line with Benjamin and Gibson.[23]

The men marched slowly and rested several times during this portion of the advance, exhausted by the steep road grade and "the thick foliage of impenetrable woods." "Our progress was slow and rendered very difficult by reason of the dense growth of timber and underbrush," J. S. Ellen of the 23rd Ohio explained. "Up this slope, Colonel Hayes was dismounted, leading the way."[24]

*   *   *

21 Cox, B&L, 2:585-586.

22 OR 1:210.

23 Ibid., 1:458; Warren W. Hassler, Jr., "The Battle of South Mountain," Maryland Historical Magazine, 52 (March 1957): 53; Francis Winthrop Palfrey, The Antietam and Fredericksburg (New York, 1882), 33-34.

24 Ibid.; Smith, National Tribune, January 17, 1895; Ellen, typescript, Rutherford B. Hayes Papers, Hayes Presidential Center, Fremont, Ohio.

On the afternoon of September 13, Jeb Stuart's Confederate cavalrymen were tasked with observing, and if possible, slowing or repulsing any federal advance toward South Mountain. Although he "felt it important to check the enemy as much as possible in order to develop his force," D. H. Hill was sufficiently confident in the cavalry's ability to halt the enemy's attack. Hill was keenly aware of his own daunting task as the army's thinly dispersed rearguard. In obeying Lee's instructions in Special Orders No. 191, Hill preferred to keep his five infantry brigades neatly positioned in their camps west of Boonsboro. When the enemy began to appear in sizeable numbers before Stuart's troopers, Hill's decision to keep his men in place rekindled a long-standing feud between the cavalry chieftain and the infantry division commander. "The enemy soon appeared in force crossing the mountain, and a spirited engagement took place," Stuart wrote in his report of the actions on September 13. Overwhelmed by the oncoming federal infantry brigades, Stuart fired off a dispatch to Hill requesting a brigade of infantry to check the advance. Stuart's report offered a self-serving description of the "spirited" defense made by his unsupported horsemen that afternoon. "This was obviously no place for cavalry operations," fumed Stuart, "a single horseman passing from point to point on the mountain with difficulty."[25]

Not to be outdone, D. H. Hill dispatched not one but two brigades of infantry to Turner's Gap, the first under Colonel Alfred H. Colquitt (13th Alabama and 6th, 23rd, 27th, and 28th Georgia), and second under Brigadier General Samuel Garland Jr. (5th, 12th, 13th, 20th, and 23rd North Carolina). Hill also ordered Lane's and Captain J. W. Bondurant's artillery batteries to roll ahead and deploy in support of the infantry. Hill kept his remaining three brigades in the vicinity of Boonsboro, which anchored the mountain pass and concentrated the vanguard of available Confederate supplies. A short time later, one of those three brigades under Brigadier General Roswell S. Ripley received orders to occupy the Hamburg Pass Road, just three miles north of Turner's Gap.[26]

Colquitt fanned out his 1,400 men on either side of the turnpike, poised to aid Stuart in his reconnaissance operations. "I was ordered to move at once with my brigade," Colquitt reported. After proceeding along the National Pike about

---

25 *OR*, 1:816-817; Carman, *The Maryland Campaign*, 144-145.

26 *OR*, 1:1019; 1031.

two and one-half miles to a position about halfway down the slope, however, Colquitt discovered the Confederate cavalry falling back and Pleasonton's federal cavalry advancing against them. "The continued advance of the enemy rendered the execution of the order [to advance] impracticable," wrote the brigadier.[27]

When dusk fell on the 13th, Pleasonton pulled his blue-coated troopers back and decided to await dawn and the support of an infantry brigade. When it became apparent that the federals forming in the Middletown Valley below would not attack that evening, Stuart told Colquitt, whose brigade was positioned about halfway down the slope of the mountain, that he would "have no difficulty" holding the National Pike. An advance any farther would be unnecessarily risky. "The enemy's forces, he [Stuart] thought, consisted of cavalry and one or two brigades of infantry," Colquitt recalled. An indifferent Stuart galloped off toward Boonsboro. In his solitary display of concern for the defense of Turner's Gap, Stuart posted one section (two guns) of Captain John Pelham's Horse Artillery and Colonel Thomas Lafayette Rosser's 5th Virginia Cavalry from Brigadier General Fitzhugh Lee's Brigade near the turnpike, but neglected to inform Colquitt of their presence.[28]

General Lee did not share Stuart's perception that defending Turner's Gap would be a routine effort. Around midnight, Hill received a dispatch from the the army commander that indicated his growing unease with the situation on the National Pike and the overall strategic situation. "Learning that night that Harper's Ferry had not surrendered, and that the enemy was advancing more rapidly than convenient from Fredericktown," Lee later explained, "I determined to return with Longstreet's command to the Blue Ridge."[29] With the army so widely divided, holding the South Mountain passes was critical. Lee ordered Hill to report to the gap in person the next morning to assist Stuart in defending the passes. With Lee's orders in hand, Hill directed General Ripley,

---

27 Ibid., 1:1052; see also George D. Grattan, "The Battle of Boonsboro Gap, or South Mountain," Southern Historical Society Papers 39 (Richmond, 1914): 35-38.

28 Ibid., 1:1052; Colquitt to Hill, letter, July 4, 1885, as quoted in Hal Bridges, Lee's Maverick General: Daniel Harvey Hill (New York: McGraw Hill, 1961; reprint, Lincoln: University of Nebraska Press, 1991), 100-101.

29 Ibid.; OR 1:140-141; Lieutenant Colonel William Allan, "Strategy of the Campaign of Sharpsburg or Antietam," paper read December 10, 1888 before the Military Historical Society of Massachusetts, in Papers of the Military Historical Society of Massachusetts (originally published 1903; reprint, Wilmington, North Carolina: Broadfoot Publishing Co., Inc., 1989), 87-88.

who commanded a mixed brigade of Georgians and North Carolinians, to find Stuart. "I had not, up to this time, seen . . . Hill, but about midnight he sent General Ripley to me to get information concerning roads and gaps in a locality where General Hill had been lying for two days with his command," Stuart sarcastically observed. "All the information I had was cheerfully given."[30]

Hill reached the Old Mountain House at the summit of Turner's Gap between daylight and sunrise on the morning of September 14. Waiting for him there was a startling message from Stuart: "I repaired to Crampton's Gap, which I had reason to believe was as much threatened as any other." Not only had the horseman departed without warning for Crampton's Gap, six miles distant, but his decision left Turner's Gap without cavalry cover.[31]

The passage of time allowed Hill to absolve Stuart for this gross lapse in judgment. In a postwar piece for *Century* magazine, Hill explained that the cavalry chieftain was "too gallant a soldier to leave his post when a battle was imminent, and doubtless believed that there was but a small Federal force on the National Road." This was, of course, the precise assurance that Stuart had imparted to Colquitt the previous evening. Likewise, when Hill was preparing his article for *Century* magazine, the 5th Virginia' Colonel Rosser wrote him that Stuart assured Rosser that "he had been followed by only a small Federal force."[32]

Still, Colquitt's and Rosser's recollections and even the pardon of Harvey Hill does not exonerate Stuart for his actions on the evening of the 13th and morning of the 14th. It was Stuart who announced to General Lee that McClellan was in possession of Special Orders No. 191. The experienced cavalry leader certainly understood that a federal advance through the South Mountain passes was not only likely, but imminent. Indeed, his justification for moving to Crampton's Gap clarified that it "was as much threatened as any other" of the mountain passes. Stuart's report lends additional evidence to the suggestion that he fully anticipated the ensuing exigencies for the rebels on Fox's and Turner's gaps the next morning (September 14). "[Hill's] troops were duly notified of the advance of the enemy," he wrote. Inserting one final barb into Hill, the cavalryman noted that he "saw [Garland's and Colquitt's Brigades]

30 *OR* 1:816-817.

31 *Ibid.*; 1:1019-1020; *B&L*, 2:561-562.

32 *B&L*, 2:560-561.

in line of battle awaiting his approach, and . . . gave some general directions concerning the location of [Hill's] lines during the afternoon, *in his absence* [emphasis added]."[33] Only the gross underestimation of McClellan, as suggested by Longstreet, can explain Stuart's pronounced indifference with respect to the ensuing emergency Hill faced atop the lonely mountain.

Another explanation, even more condemnable, is that Stuart was still enraged by Hill's failure to support his reconnaissance efforts on Saturday afternoon. This personal frustration resulted not only in biting exchanges, but in a near-breakdown in communications. Except for Colonel Rosser's small regiment, Stuart deprived Hill of cavalry. Moreover, Stuart neglected to inform both Colquitt and Hill that Rosser's troopers were scouting the woods around Fox's Gap, a mile below Turner's Gap. "He, Rosser, was not directed to report to me, and I did not suspect his presence," Hill remembered.[34]

Significantly, General Lee not only assumed but *expected* Stuart to hold Turner's Gap (and by extension, the vital National Road) in force. According to Lieutenant Colonel William Allan, who served as a staff officer for the Southern army, Lee retained Hill's division with the "mass of his cavalry" to "watch the progress of McClellan" at least until the reduction of Harpers Ferry had been effected.[35] Lee himself offers the most significant evidence of his own assumptions and expectations. In an urgent message directing that the operations on Maryland Heights "be pushed on as rapidly as possible," Lee informed General McLaws that "General Stuart, with a portion of General D. H. Hill's forces, holds the gap between Boonsboro and Middletown."[36]

Colonel Cullen A. Battle of the 3rd Alabama succinctly summarized the Hill-Stuart controversy in his memoir. "The world had seen very few generals of cavalry superior to Jeb Stuart. Always alert, vigilant, sagacious and aggressive, his estimates of the strength of the enemy were usually wonderfully accurate; but, on this occasion, they were astoundingly inaccurate."[37]

---

33 *OR* 1:817.; *B&L*, 561-562.

34 *Ibid.*

35 Allan, "Strategy of the Campaign of Sharpsburg or Antietam," 81.

36 *OR* 2:608.

37 Cullen Andrews Battle, *Third Alabama! The Civil War Memoir of Brigadier General Cullen Andrews Battle*, CSA, Brandon H. Beck, ed. (Tuscaloosa: The University of Alabama Press, 2000), 52.

*   *   *

The morning sun of September 14 revealed an unpleasant reality for D. H. Hill that quickly morphed into stunned disbelief: Stuart had abandoned him. Hill's disbelief turned to dread when he took advantage of the vista afforded by the Old Mountain House and examined the terrain extending out below him. "An examination of the pass, very early on the morning of the 14th, satisfied me that it could only be held by a large force, and was wholly indefensible by a small one," he reported after the campaign.[38] The general was, just as Stuart had charged, largely ignorant of the geography and road networks. More than Garland's and Colquitt's small brigades were needed to properly defend

Facing pages illustration: Boonsboro, Maryland, and Turner's Gap from the west. *Harper's Pictorial History of the Civil War*

38 *OR*, 2:608, 1:1019.

Turner's Gap. Hill loathed the idea of extracting troops from the vicinity of Boonsboro—especially Ripley's Brigade at the Hamburg Pass Road— because they were defending the important roads leading to Hill's supply trains. Without support, however, Garland and Colquitt were doomed. Hill ordered up Brigadier General George Burgwyn Anderson's command (2nd, 4th, 14th, and 30th North Carolina), a modest-sized brigade totaling some 1,200 men.[39]

With at least some reinforcements on the way, Hill turned his attention back to the situation on the summit. He directed Colquitt to connect his brigade with Garland's line. Hill personally positioned Colquitt's 23rd and 28th Georgia regiments behind a stone wall on the north side of the turnpike, and across the road posted the remaining three regiments (6th Georgia, 27th Georgia, and 13th Alabama) in advance of the stone wall.[40]

39 OR 1:1019-1020.

40 Ibid., 1:1052-1053.

Hill maintained much later (erroneously) that he found Colquitt's men stationed at the foot of South Mountain, and that he recalled the brigade to its assumed position halfway up the slope. "I brought Colquitt's brigade back to a point near the summit," Hill wrote after the war. While Hill refused to condemn Stuart outright, his suggestions about Colquitt's initial position served much the same purpose. As historian Joseph Harsh has noted, the urgency with which Hill recounted the incident implied that he had detected and "corrected a significant error"—that Colquitt's men were insufficient to defend the mountain passes.[41]

Hill's postwar article emphasized Jeb Stuart's ineptness, not Alfred Colquitt's, as some have presumed. Noting the isolated nature of Colquitt's advanced position accentuated the degree of Stuart's error. According to Hill's narrative, Colquitt rather nobly assumed the absentee Stuart's reconnaissance role on the evening of the 13th and, in turn, Hill rescued his much-needed infantry to defend Turner's Gap. In a convincing account published after the war, George D. Grattan, Colquitt's adjutant, dismissed Hill's claim that he found the brigade at the foot of the mountain. Colquitt's report and Stuart's comments to him the evening of the 13th buttress Grattan's account. If scouting the enemy was made "impracticable" by "the enemy's cavalry advancing," the Confederate cavalry "gradually giving back," and, finally, the federals making "no further efforts to advance," settling in after dusk, Grattan wrote, "why, then, would Harvey Hill have discovered Colquitt's regiments at the base of South Mountain when he arrived on the morning of the fourteenth?"[42]

Hill intended to use Garland to defend Fox's Gap, but was still unsettled about exactly how to proceed without more information or cavalry support. Once Colquitt's men assumed their positions, Hill determined to do some reconnoitering of his own. "I went with Major Ratchford of my staff on a reconnaissance to our right," he wrote. Lieutenant James Wylie Ratchford, Hill's lieutenant aide-de-camp, donned a blue coat he had snatched from the Seven Pines battlefield that summer.[43] Riding down the slope of the

41 *B&L*, 2:561-562; see also Harsh, *Sounding the Shallows*, 177.

42 OR 1:1052.

43 *B&L*, 2:562; on Ratchford, see Robert E. L. Krick, *Staff Officers in Gray: A Biographical Register of the Staff Officers in the Army of Northern Virginia* (Chapel Hill: University of North Carolina Press, 2003), 250.

mountainside from the Old Mountain House, the two men encountered Tom Rosser's 5th Virginia Cavalry which, unbeknownst to Hill, Stuart had positioned to defend Fox's Gap one mile south of Turner's Gap. Hill and Ratchford also encountered two guns from Captain Pelham's horse artillery unlimbered along the Old Sharpsburg Road.[44]

His apprehension exacerbated by these discoveries, Hill terminated the reconnaissance and galloped back toward his headquarters at the Mountain House. On the way, the two officers encountered a civilian surrounded by his children in the yard of a small cabin. Still unsure of the road networks, Hill, aided in appearances by Ratchford's blue wardrobe, engaged the Unionist mountaineer in idle conversation. The man provided little information of use before a "shell came hurtling through the woods, and a little girl began crying." The child's screams moved Hill. "Having a little one at home of about the same age," he wrote, "I could not forbear stopping a moment to say a few soothing words to the frightened child, before hurrying off to the work of death."[45]

Back at the Mountain House, Hill explained the deteriorating situation to Samuel Garland, a thirty-one-year-old native of Lynchburg, Virginia. After being roughly handled at Gaines' Mill in late June, his entire veteran brigade now numbered just more than 1,000 survivors. Garland, the much admired grand-nephew of James Madison and a capable officer, had suffered tremendous losses of his own. His wife died in June 1861, and only three months later his infant son, Samuel Jr., also passed away. Many of his men worried about Garland's mental stability, concerned he may be careless with his own life on the battlefield.[46] The brigadier listened as Hill "explained the situation briefly to him." The division leader "directed him to sweep through the woods, reach the road, and hold it *at all hazards*, as the safety of Lee's large train depended upon its being held." Hill's language echoed that of the unsettled Lee on the eve of the Sabbath.[47] The rebels had no choice but to make a determined stand on the wooded and rocky slopes of South Mountain.

---

44 *Ibid.*; Carman, *The Maryland Campaign*, 145.

45 Daniel Harvey Hill, *Battles and Leaders of the Civil War*, 2:562.

46 Rev. Alexander D. Betts, *Experiences of a Confederate Chaplain, 1861-1864*, as quoted in Scott L. Mingus, Sr., *Human Interest Stories from Antietam* (Orrtanna, PA: Colecraft Industries, 2007), 26-27; Ezra Warner, *Generals in Gray* (Baton Rouge: Louisiana State University Press, 1959), 98-99.

47 Hill, *B&L*, 2:562.

Brigadier General Samuel Garland commanded a brigade of infantry in Daniel Harvey Hill's Division, Army of Northern Virginia. Garland was killed in action while leading his men. *Library of Congress*

Garland galloped off and led his North Carolinians to their positions atop Fox's Gap, which became the focal point of Hill's plan to defend both Turner's Gap and the supply wagons at Boonsboro. The brigade moved southward through the wooded hillside using an old mountain path called the "ridge road," which cut through the property of farmer Daniel Wise. The ridge road cut in a southerly direction before veering in a sharp angle to the west. West of the Old Sharpsburg Road and south of the ridge road, the stubble and corn fields attached to the Beachley properties provided a rare break from the dense woods and opened to a short plateau. The west edge of these fields was demarcated by another mountain path that originated farther to the south along the Old Sharpsburg Road.[48]

As Garland's Brigade filed into its initial lines, one of Pelham's Napoleon guns announced its position, and in doing so startled the North Carolinians. Just moments earlier Pelham announced to his gunners, "Men of the Horse Artillery, the safety of General Lee's wagon trains and the security of the whole army depend on our holding off the enemy until help can arrive. We must hold on at any cost. Now, to battery!"[49] Pelham and his artillerists enjoyed a grand view of the valley below and could see the approaching enemy infantry, but neither Pelham nor any of his gunners passed along the information to the assembling Confederate infantry.

Garland placed his largest regiment, the 5th North Carolina under Colonel Duncan K. McRae, at the intersection of the ridge road and the mountain path to the left of Pelham's two guns. McRae was now occupying the extreme right of the makeshift Confederate South Mountain line. Along the open ground, the 72 effectives of Captain Shugan Snow's 12th North Carolina supported McRae's left. Colonel Daniel H. Christie's 23rd North Carolina extended the line farther left behind an rambling stone wall outlining the ridge road. The crest of the ridge stood about fifty yards behind the wall.[50]

---

48 OR 1:1040, 1045; see also D. Scott Hartwig, "'My God! Be Careful!' Morning Fight at Fox's Gap, September 14, 1862," *Civil War Regiments: A Journal of the American Civil War*, Vol. 5, no. 3 (1996).

49 See William Woods Hassler, *Colonel John Pelham: Lee's Boy General* (Richmond: Garrett and Massie, Inc., 1960), 85; John Michael Priest, *Before Antietam: The Battle for South Mountain* (Shippensburg, Pennsylvania: White Mane Publishing Co., Inc., 1992), 134, 365n. 21.

50 *Ibid.*; Hill, *B&L*, 2:562; Carman, *The Maryland Campaign*, 146-147; R. B. Wilson to Ezra A. Carman, letter, July 22, 1889, in Ezra A. Carman Papers, Manuscript Division, Library of Congress, Washington, D.C; on the physical description of this portion of the battlefield, see

The nature of both the terrain and the emergency developing on the National Pike required Garland to disperse his already thin command across a hopelessly wide front. "From the nature of the ground and the duty to be performed, the regiments were not in contact with each other," Hill reported.[51] Garland's remaining pair of regiments, the 13th North Carolina under Lieutenant Colonel Thomas Ruffin Jr., and the 20th North Carolina under Colonel Alfred Iverson, took up a position on the northwest side of the Old Sharpsburg Road, well detached from the balance of the brigade. This alignment may have manifested itself psychologically, depriving soldiers of the battlefield phenomenon known as "the touch of the elbow." Individual soldiers "sustained one another's morale in a variety of ways," concludes one student of the Civil War's rank and file. For example, maintaining "tight tactical formations so that a man in the battle could get psychological comfort from the nearness of his comrades . . . the intimate bonds . . . the security of comradeship might have been the most pervasive and important support for battlefield morale."[52] Within a few hours these rebels would yearn for this security.

Garland's infantrymen were getting comfortable with their new positions when Captain J. W. Bondurant's Alabama battery rolled into the open field in front of the 23th North Carolina. Together with Garland's men, the battery reached the summit of Turner's Gap that morning from its camp west of Boonsboro. "[We] moved along a rough mountain road on the top of the mountain, passing a cabin," recalled gunner John Purifoy. "After passing the house, we reached a small clearing or field surrounded wholly or in part by a stone fence." Purifoy was describing the Beachley clearing adjacent to farmer Wise's south field. The artillerist cast a glance to his right down the Confederate line. "Immediately west of this clearing we found the infantry of Garland's brigade at rest, with arms stacked, in line, extending along the top of the depression in the mountain," Purifoy recalled.[53] Apparently the round fired by Pelham's Napoleon was not terribly instructive.

---

also John Purifoy to Carman, letter, July 21, 1900, in the Ezra A. Carman Papers, Manuscript Division, Library of Congress, Washington, D.C.

51 Hill, *B&L*, 2:563.

52 Earl J. Hess, *The Union Soldier in Battle: Enduring the Ordeal of Combat* (Lawrence: University Press of Kansas, 1997), 194.

53 *Ibid.* Purifoy to Carman, July 21, 1900; Hartwig, "'My God! Be Careful!'"

Concerned about the deployment of the brigade and with dense laurel obscuring the view of Middletown Valley, Bondurant wheeled his pieces to a point just east of where the ridge road began to abruptly turn away from the Old Sharpsburg Road. "My recollection is that this clearing was very limited in width as our right and left pieces were near the fence on each side," continued Purifoy. Bondurant's gunners aimed their pieces at the valley below. "We could be plainly seen from the valley, east of the mountain, and after, events satisfied me that we became an object of special interest."[54]

*   *   *

While Garland was shuttling his men into position, Scammon's and Crook's federal brigades continued their fitful climb up the Old Sharpsburg Road. Behind the leading 12th Ohio filed Hayes' 23rd Ohio, with Colonel Hugh Ewing's 30th Ohio bringing up the rear. The marching column approached the old Mentzer Saw Mill, "emerg[ing] from the wooded thicket into a clearing at the crest of the Mountain," when Bondurant's Jeff Davis artillery composed of two 3-inch ordnance rifles and one 12-pound Napoleon greeted them with a round of case shot.[55] "The Confederate battery at the crest of the mountain to the left opened fire . . . and the column immediately debouched to the left," remembered R. B. Wilson of the 12th Ohio. The unwelcome sound of the guns indicated that the Old Sharpsburg Road, the most direct route through Fox's Gap (and the one celebrated by Pleasonton) was held in force by the enemy. [56]

It was about 8:00 a.m. when some of Bondurant's Alabamians discerned skirmishers from Companies A and F of the 12th Ohio and the 30th Ohio farther left advancing before the Confederate center and left.[57] "We had not been in position long, say a half hour or hour at the most, before we discovered a few men slowly and stealthily approaching us near the north east corner of the

54 John Purifoy to Ezra A. Carman, letter, 15 July 1889, in Ezra A. Carman Papers, Manuscript Division, Library of Congress, Washington, D.C.

55 OR, 1:155, 809, 1024; Carman, The Maryland Campaign, 144; John Purifoy to Ezra A. Carman, letter, 7 August 1900, in Ezra A. Carman Papers, Manuscript Division, Library of Congress, Washington, D.C.; J.S. Ellen, typescript, "Battle of South Mountain," in Rutherford B. Hayes Papers, Hayes Presidential Center, Fremont, Ohio.

56 R. B. Wilson to Ezra A. Carman, letter, 11 July 1899, in Ezra A. Carman Papers, Manuscript Division, Library of Congress, Washington, D.C.

57 Ibid.

clearing," recalled Purifoy. "It did not take long to determine that they were not friends. This conclusion was formed, not from any hostile demonstration, but from their dress. They seemed to be satisfied at attracting and holding our attention." Bondurant dispatched a messenger to Garland with the news, but the rider returned a few minutes later unable to locate the general. Animated with the sense of urgency only imminent combat can generate, Bondurant attempted to find Garland himself. As Purifoy later recalled, however, the battery leader "failed to find anyone who felt authorized to take steps to relieve [the critical condition]."[58] The rough, foreign terrain made timely communication between the understrength and too widely dispersed Confederate units nearly impossible.

As it turned out, Bondurant could not find Garland because the brigadier was doing some reconnoitering of his own with the 5th North Carolina's Colonel McRae on the opposite end of the Confederate line. "General Garland and I had been but a few moments in the field when our attention was directed to persons moving at some distance upon [the mountain road at the base of the stubble field clearing]," reported the regimental commander. Because this road swept around the Confederate right flank, Garland feared the enemy was preparing to make a lodgment in that sector of the woods and turn his flank. He ordered McRae to advance fifty skirmishers from his 5th North Carolina into the underbrush. It was a blind venture, for neither Garland nor McRae had any idea of the strength or position of the federal infantry. Once he ordered the skirmishers forward, Garland galloped off to the left end of his line near the Wise cabin.[59]

McRae's skirmishers formed in the woods and faced by the rear rank. Several companies were out of place as they advanced down the hillside through the underbrush and over the rocky landscape.[60] They had barely advanced fifty steps when the clap of musketry rattled the air. Ahead of them were men from Company A from Hayes' 23rd Ohio. The tranquility of the Sabbath was broken. The battle for South Mountain was now truly underway.

---

58 John Purifoy to Ezra A. Carman, letters, July 15, 1899 and August 7, 1900, in Ezra A. Carman Papers, Manuscript Division, Library of Congress, Washington, D.C.

59 OR 1:1040; Carman, *The Maryland Campaign*, 146-147.

60 Rutherford B. Hayes, diary entry, September 14, 1862, in Charles Richard Williams, ed., *The Diary and Letters of Rutherford Birchard Hayes: Nineteenth President of the United States*, 5 vols. (Columbus: Ohio Archaeological and Historical Society, 1922-1926), 2:355.

Lieutenant Colonel
Rutherford B. Hayes of
the 23rd Ohio.

Rutherford B. Hayes
Presidential Center

*   *   *

After the initial artillery greeting, as the federal column shifted to the left and the 12th and 30th Ohio formed their lines of battle, Scammon ordered Hayes to turn the Confederate right and overrun the Southern artillery pieces. "I ordered the Twenty-third Regiment . . . to move through the woods on the right and rear of the right flank," was how Scammon would later report the move.[61] Before dispersing his troops, a worried Hayes inquired as to what he should do if he encountered "six guns and a strong support." "Take them anyhow!" the brigade commander replied.

Hayes deployed Company A in the front as his skirmishers while Companies I and F fanned out to the right and left, respectively, to draw up the skirmishers' flanks. Some of Lieutenant James Abraham's cavalrymen, led by Sergeant A. B. Farmer, screened the advance. "Deploying our cavalry as skirmishers at the base of the mountain we moved on and soon after commencing the ascent, encountered the rebel skirmishers in some fields," Abraham wrote. To the rear and left of the dismounted cavalrymen the Buckeyes of the 23rd Ohio prepared to advance. "Soon [we] saw from the opposite hill a strong force coming down towards us," Hayes wrote. A

61 *OR*, 1:461; Ward, *The Twelfth Ohio Volunteer Infantry*, 58.

An early lithographic depiction of the charge of the Kanawha Division at Fox's Gap on the morning of September 14, 1862. *Library of Congress*

"spattering fire" opened from a line of leveled Ohio muskets.[62] The proximity of the enemy surprised the North Carolinians. "The enemy's skirmishers had advanced almost to the very edge of the woods nearest us," Colonel McRae reported.[63]

The sudden collision and rough terrain threatened to disrupt both units. "I feared confusion; exhorted, swore, and threatened," wrote Hayes.[64] McRae recalled that he "found the growth very thick, so much so that it was impossible to advance in line of battle." Turning toward his men, Hayes shouted, "all right then, we'll take it!"[65] Hayes offered one more piece of encouragement to his fellow Ohioans: "Now, boys, remember you are the 23rd, and give them Hell. In these woods, the rebel's don't know but we are 10,000; and if we fight, and

---

62 Hayes, diary entry, September 14, 1862, in Williams, ed., 2:355; OR 1:1039-1043; James Abraham, *With the Army of West Virginia 1861-1864*, p. 17, copy of publication in United States Army Military History Institute, Carlisle, Pennsylvania. Priest, *Before Antietam*, 137.

63 *Ibid.*; OR 1:464-467; 1040.

64 Hayes, diary entry, September 14, 1862, in Williams, ed., 2:355.

65 OR 1:461; Hill, *B&L*, 2:586-587; T. Harry Williams, *Hayes of the Twenty-third: The Civil War Volunteer Officer* (New York: Alfred A. Knopf, 1965), 136-138.

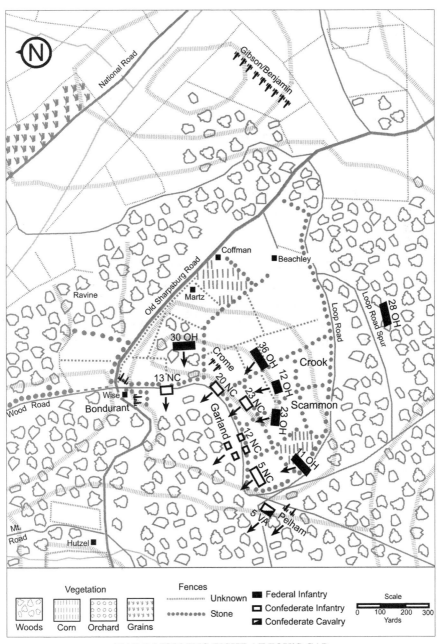

MAP 6. MORNING FIGHT AT FOX'S GAP

when we charge yell, we are as good as 10,000." He concluded emphatically, shouting "Give them Hell, boys, give them sons of bitches Hell!" Bayonets fixed and spirits afire, the attack stepped off.[66] Their position may have been vulnerable, but their spirit was invincible.

The fighting between the 5th North Carolina and 23rd Ohio's Company A became intense and desperate, exacerbated by the challenges posed by the daunting terrain. "The conformation of the ground was such that we could not use artillery only from the rear . . . the shells from which exploded over and among our own troops," Lieutenant Abraham recalled. "As our troops advanced the fighting grew desperate—the rebels giving ground foot by foot and clinging to every rock and tree with the most determined tenacity."[67] "The skirmishing at close quarters was very severe," observed Ezra Carman, the first historian of the campaign and a Union veteran.[68] "I sent 14 balls after them and if some of them didn't do execution it is not my fault," Robert B. Cornwall of Company A wrote. "Our company were deployed as skirmishers & killed 8 that I see before the Regt get up to us."[69]

Some of the men holding the right side of Garland's line of battle had never drilled let alone participated in combat, and began to break for the rear. "I immediately hastened back and rallied those retreating at our first position," McRae reported. He pulled back his men to re-form the line for another assault on the Ohioans.[70] As the North Carolinians regrouped, Hayes likewise halted. "I soon began to fear we could not stand it," he wrote.[71]

Remembering Scammon's instructions to turn the enemy right and capture the artillery, Hayes set about organizing another assault on the enemy line, only this time it would be a general advance made with the entire regiment. As he was doing so, the skirmishers of Company A drew the North Carolinians into the

---

66 Hayes, diary entry, September 14, 1862, in Williams, ed., 2:355; Hayes, diary entry, 8 December 1862, in Williams, ed., 2:373; Priest, *Before Antietam*, 137; T. Harry Williams, *Hayes of the Twenty-third*, 137.

67 James Abraham, *With the Army of West Virginia 1861-1864*, p. 17.

68 Carman, *The Maryland Campaign*, 146.

69 Robert B. Cornwall, letter, October 3, 1862, in Harrisburg Civil War Roundtable Collection, United States Army Military History Institute, Carlisle, Pennsylvania.

70 OR 1:1040.

71 Hayes, diary entry, September 14, 1862, in Williams, ed., 2:355-356.

open stubble fields near the summit.[72] "Our men halted at a fence near the edge of the woods and kept up a brisk fire upon the enemy, who were sheltering themselves behind stone walls and fences near the top of the hill," Hayes recalled.[73] "The assaulting line soon reached the fence on our right and a number of shots were fired at us at short range," one of Bondurant's gunners recalled.[74] A veteran of the 23rd Ohio did not remember the second charge fondly. "At this particular point was the 23rd's greatest loss," recalled J. S. Ellen. Company A's Robert Cornwall, who was so proud to have discharged fourteen rounds from his musket, was struck by an enemy round. "The ball went in on the inside of my leg and just touched the big artery. It was a very lucky shot for me," he reflected from a Washington, D.C. hospital several weeks later.[75]

With the right of his line under heavy pressure, Garland ordered the emaciated ranks of Colonel Shugan Snow's 12th North Carolina and Colonel Daniel Christie's 23rd North Carolina to support McRae. Minie balls whistled overhead, staggering the advances of both regiments and reducing them to closely concentrated columns—separated only by the stone-lined summit. "Slowly drawing nearer and nearer, came a dark-blue line," Adjutant V. E. Turner of the 23rd North Carolina recalled. Christie threw out a thin line of skirmishers to shield his advance, but they were thrown back under the weight and proximity of the Ohioans.[76]

Hayes was preparing to deliver a final blow and turn the enemy right when the dirty business of war overtook him. "Just as I gave the command to charge I felt a stunning blow and found a musket ball had struck my left arm just above the elbow," he noted in his diary. Hayes tumbled to the ground, unconscious for "a little while, a little delirious." He tried to stand, but was too lightheaded to

---

72 Rutherford Hayes, handwritten manuscript, "South Mountain," n.d., in Rutherford B. Hayes Papers, Hayes Presidential Center, Fremont, Ohio.

73 Hayes, diary entry, September 14, 1862, in Williams, ed., 2:355.

74 John Purifoy to Ezra A. Carman, letter, July 15, 1899, in Ezra A. Carman Papers, Manuscript Division, Library of Congress, Washington, D.C.

75 Ellen, typescript, Hayes Papers; see also OR 1:458-461; Robert Cornwall, letters, October 3, 1862 and October 9, 1862, in Harrisburg Civil War Roundtable Collection, United States Army Military History Institute, Carlisle, Pennsylvania.

76 V.E. Turner, "Twenty-Third Regiment," in Clark, ed., 2:220-221.

remain upright.[77] "Fearing that an artery might be cut, I asked a soldier near me to tie my handkerchief above the wound," he remembered. "I felt weak, faint, and sick at the stomach. I [lay] down and was pretty comfortable. . . . I was perhaps twenty feet behind the lines of my men, and could form a pretty accurate notion of the way the fighting was going. . . . I could see wounded men staggering or carried to the rear; but I felt sure our men were holding their own."[78]

As Hayes lay wounded, Colonel Rosser's dismounted 5th Virginia Cavalry added to the discomfiture of the advancing Ohioans by leveling a sharp fire into their left flank. With his 23rd Ohio facing fire from three directions, the wounded colonel attempted to stand once more to maneuver his embattled regiment to confront Rosser's fire. "I called out to Captain Drake, who was on the left, to let his company wheel backward so as to face the threatened attack," Hayes wrote. "His company fell back perhaps twenty yards, and the whole line gradually followed by example." Too weak to stand because of the loss of blood, Hayes fell back to the ground as Drake executed the maneuver. In doing so, however, he left the wounded colonel and future president of the United States between the opposing lines. Hayes remained there for the next twenty minutes, refusing to relinquish command of the regiment and belting out orders to Major James M. Comly as the fighting swelled.[79]

From his position between the lines, Hayes encountered a wounded North Carolinian. "We were right jolly and friendly," Hayes recalled. The exchange helped to ease the suffering and pain. Indeed, the soldier confided to Hayes that before the war, he had been a "Union man," but upon the secession of "his section," felt compelled to follow, obliged to the doctrine of "states' rights."[80] Hayes told the younger lad, "You came a good ways to fight us." The rebel inquired of Hayes' native state in response, and when he replied that he was from Ohio, the Southerner retorted, "well, you came a good ways to fight us!"[81]

---

77 Hayes, "South Mountain," Rutherford B. Hayes Papers, Hayes Presidential Center, Fremont, Ohio.

78 Hayes, diary entry, September 14, 1862, in Williams, ed., 2:355-356.

79 *Ibid.*

80 Hayes, "South Mountain," Rutherford B. Hayes Papers, Hayes Presidential Center, Fremont, Ohio.

81 *Ibid.*; Hayes, diary entry, September 14, 1862, in Williams, ed., 2:355-356.

From his prone position, Hayes did his best to discern how the fighting was going while balls passed near his face and pierced the coarse soil around him, animating flurries of dust, smoke, and dirt. After what must have seemed an interminable length of time, the sharp firing leveled off into a fitful lull. "After a few minutes' silence I began to doubt whether the enemy had disappeared or whether our men had gone farther back," he noted in his diary. "I called out, 'Hallo, Twenty-third men, are you going to leave your colonel here for the enemy?' In an instant, a half dozen or more men sprang forward to me saying, 'Oh, no, we will carry you wherever you want us to!'"

Lieutenant Benjamin W. Jackson of Company I finally appeared and removed his wounded superior from the range of gunfire, propped Hayes up against an old log, and offered him water from his canteen. The injured colonel was transported in an ambulance to the Widow Koogle farmstead on Lamb's Knoll, where doctors dressed his wound and he rested for several hours. Finally, he was transported, again by ambulance, the three and one-half miles to Middletown, where he was welcomed at the red-brick home of Jacob Rudy on West Main Street.[82]

Hayes had a telegraph message sent to his wife Lucy and to his beloved Uncle Sardis Birchard reporting his wounding at South Mountain. He begged for Lucy to journey to his bedside, though his telegraph merely announced that he was "here," rather than providing his exact location. Assuming that her husband was in one of the notorious general army hospitals dotting the District of Columbia, Lucy set off for the nation's capital and launched a grueling search for her wounded husband. Finally, after a federal worker traced the source of Hayes' telegraph to Middletown, Maryland, Lucy boarded a train to Frederick, the nearest depot. Once there, Lucy's brother Joseph, an army surgeon who had treated Hayes, took his sister on a disturbing carriage ride to the Rudy house past dead horses and the vestiges of the skirmishing that still lined the National Pike. Once she reached her wounded husband's bedside, Lucy teased Rutherford how she had always wanted to visit the nation's capital. Not long after the couple's joyful reunion, several Ohio surgeons visited with Hayes, who appeared to be in "the best of spirits." After the wounded colonel permitted the surgeon to examine his injured arm, Hayes reportedly sent them away with a patriotic proclamation, "tell Gov. [David] Tod that I'll be on hand again

---

82 *Ibid.* The red-brick home of Jacob Rudy still stands, unmarked, at 504 W. Main Street in Middletown.

The Jacob Rudy House in Middletown, Maryland, where Rutherford B. Hayes recovered from his wound. *Henry F. Ballone*

shortly."[83] In Jacob Rudy's upstairs bedroom, Hayes learned the details of the battle that had raged in his absence after his wounding during the morning's melee at Fox's Gap.

*   *   *

After the brief lull that allowed for Hayes to be removed from between the lines, skirmishers from Colonel Hugh Ewing's 30th Ohio on the right side of Scammon's brigade line poured "a storm of bullets" into Bondurant's battery, including one that wounded gunner John Purifoy. "I have a 'feeling' remembrance of that battle, having lost some blood there and barely escaping with my head whole," he later wrote.[84]

---

83 Russell Conwell, *Life and Public Services of Governor Rutherford B. Hayes* (Boston: B.B. Russell, 1876). This campaign biography, though any reader must navigate through the thickly-layered hyperbole, offers some useful material.

84 John Purifoy to Ezra A. Carman, letter, 15 July 1899, in Ezra A. Carman Papers, Manuscript Division, Library of Congress, Washington, D.C.

About this time, Colonel George Crook's Union brigade arrived in the rear of Scammon's troops. Through fields and an orchard the regiments formed up, "partly concealed by a strip of woods at the foot of the hill."[85] Lieutenant Colonel Augustus Coleman's 11th Ohio occupied the left of Crook's line, with Colonel Moor's former regiment, the 28th Ohio, behind the 12th Ohio. Lieutenant Colonel Melvin Clarke's 36th Ohio extended the brigade line near the left edge of the Old Sharpsburg Road.

By the time Samuel Garland reached Bondurant's position, the firing had again commenced hotly on the right. The brigadier passed along instructions to the gunners designed to both respond to the dilemma on the right and contend with the drama building before his left. "Garland from the direction we had come galloped up by us and gave the order to fire and retire from the right," Purifoy recalled. Each of the four guns was wheeled so that they would deliver enfilading rounds at a right oblique into the 12th and 23rd Ohio, attacking to their right front. This fire would likewise startle the skirmishers forming on the left. Finally, by withdrawing the guns, they would be sheltered from what seemed to be evidence of a federal attempt to wheel the left end of his line. One by one, Bondurant's guns roared their parting greetings. "The shots fired by the battery . . . did its work in aiding to check the assault," claimed Purifoy. While these methodically fired rounds may have momentarily checked Crook's already sluggish advance, Bondurant's ploy did not have the desired effect because by positioning the guns on a narrow axis, one behind the other, only one gun could fire at a time.[86]

While Bondurant delivered his rounds in his unusual tactical formation, an equally unusual event was transpiring downrange, where Quartermaster Sergeant Wilson of the 11th Ohio arrived on the field with regimental mail. With Lieutenant Colonel Coleman's permission, he distributed letters to anxious readers. "What hasty tearing open of envelopes!" recalled William Lyle. "What a fluttering of letters all along the line! Then what absorbed attention! Little did the writers of those 'love-notes' think, when writing them, that they would be opened and read amid the booming of artillery, and the explosions of shell that made the very earth tremble!" The explosions did not last long as the Southern gunners, heeding (though with much difficulty) Garland's orders,

---

85 William Lyle, *Lights and Shadows of Army Life* (Cincinnati: R.W. Carroll & Co., 1865), 126.

86 John Purifoy to Ezra A. Carman, July 15, 1899 and August 7, 1900, in Ezra A. Carman Papers, Manuscript Division, Library of Congress, Washington, D.C; *B&L*, 2:587.

assumed their new position on the higher ground to the north and west near Daniel Wise's cabin.[87]

Colonel Carr B. White's 12th Ohio deployed under fire in the center of the federal line to the right of Hayes' embattled 23rd Ohio regiment. "Under the withering effects of an awful musketry fire, a line was expeditiously formed," recalled the 12th Ohio's James E. D. Ward.[88] Hurrying back to his right, Garland ordered the 12th and 23rd North Carolina regiments to advance. Caught in a crossfire delivered by White's and Hayes's men, Colonel Shugan Snow's paltry 72 men managed but one volley before falling back into the woods. Impugned by one observer as "undisciplined gentlemen who thought themselves better than others," the North Carolinians fell back not only because of the enemy fire but from exhaustion, hunger, and thirst. As they turned to the rear, about one-half of the men ended up melting into the 13th

The Wise Farm atop Fox's Gap, scene of South Mountain's most grisly fighting. This view was taken from the Ridge Road looking south. The Wise cabin and surrounding stone wall are visible. *U.S. Army Military History Institute, Carlisle, PA.*

87 William Lyle, *Lights and Shadows of Army Life,* 126; John Purifoy to Ezra A. Carman, letters, July 15, 1899 and August 7, 1900, in Ezra A. Carman Papers, Manuscript Division, Library of Congress, Washington, D.C; *OR,* 1:1040-1041.

88 Carman, *The Maryland Campaign,* 146-147; Clark, *Histories of the Several Regiments and Battalions From North Carolina in the Great War 1861-1865,* 1:626-627; *OR* 1:464; Ward, *The Twelfth Ohio Volunteer Infantry,* 58.

North Carolina. Colonel Christie's regiments, meanwhile, prepared to advance and engage the 23rd Ohio. The North Carolinians moved up behind a stone wall and opened a brief but withering musketry fire on the Ohioans preparing to turn the rebel flank.[89]

After the defeat of the 12th North Carolina, and with the 23rd Ohio still pressing McRae's 5th North Carolina, Garland suggested that officer pull back his embattled regiment. McRae obeyed, as it was now clear to him that the 23rd Ohio, immediately in front before the stone wall, intended to flank the Confederate right. "I then stated to General Garland my belief that the enemy had massed a very large force in those woods, and were preparing to turn our right, and suggested that he might be dislodged," McRae reported. Unaware that Garland had ordered Bondurant's to redeploy his guns to the upper Wise fields, McRae proposed further pounding the woods on the right with artillery.[90]

His suggestion reminded Garland of his exposed and vulnerable left flank. Again attempting to contend with both dilemmas, Garland sent off for the 13th North Carolina and the 20th North Carolina, the two left-most regiments he had earlier positioned on the northwest side of the Old Sharpsburg Road some two hours before. The brigadier galloped back to the intersection of the ridge road and the Old Sharpsburg Road, halting in the south Wise fields on the extreme left of the brigade. With both flanks dangling in the air, Garland slid the 13th North Carolina, commanded by Lieutenant Colonel Thomas Ruffin Jr., to the right along the Ridge Road. Farther right, likely into the position previously held by Bondurant, Garland plugged in Colonel Alfred Iverson's 20th North Carolina. Iverson had orders to connect his right flank with the left side of Christie's 23rd North Carolina, but once more the difficult terrain and too few troops prevented Garland from cobbling together a cohesive line of battle.

The 20th North Carolina's tenuous situation was representative of the over-extension of Garland's brigade line. A gap of some 250 yards existed between the left flank of Iverson's 20th North Carolina and the right flank of Ruffin's 13th North Carolina. Iverson was unable to advance from his new position because it was directly in the line of enemy fire and without support on his flank, which would have been exposed had he advanced. As McRae later

---

89 *Ibid*; *OR*, 1:1040-1041; Hartwig, "'My God! Be Careful!'" 42.

90 *OR*, 1:1040.

noted in his report, the advanced position would have revealed this vulnerable "vacuum" to the advancing enemy skirmishers. Iverson fell in along the Ridge Road to the left of Christie's 23rd North Carolina. Even though Garland was generally familiar with his front and had rearranged his regiments accordingly, his line was still a haphazard affair with dangerous gaps and unanchored and weak flanks.[91]

Garland's federal counterparts, meanwhile, were also shifting regiments about to gain an offensive advantage. After having successfully thrown back the 12th North Carolina, the 12th Ohio advanced through the center against Colonel Iverson's newly arrived men. "We opened fire and then charged forward," Colonel White reported. The contest lasted about half an hour. "The enemy fled, leaving 15 to 20 dead and wounded, and we occupied the ground," the colonel continued.[92] Confusion reigned along the Confederate line. "It was a carnival of death; hell itself turned loose. . . . the Buckeyes carried everything before them, discomfiting and scattering their enemies," Sol Smith reflected.[93]

Awaiting orders for the general advance of Scammon's Brigade, White halted his Buckeyes and rested in the fields just beneath the summit.[94] They were obliged to remain still, for any noise or movement was detected by the clumped remnants of North Carolinians still just a handful of yards away. With their movement stalled, White needed fresh infantry or artillery support to help continue the advance. While the men were lying on the ground waiting for orders, a rattlesnake appeared and slowly slithered over some of the men, "getting inside their clothes, and performing in various other disagreeable ways, to their infinite horror and disgust," recalled one soldier, who went on to note that "the situation became every moment more terrible" when balanced between the unappetizing choice of being bitten by the snake or struck by

---

91 OR 1:1042, 1045; D. H. Hill, Jr., *North Carolina*, in *Confederate Military History* (Secaucus, New Jersey: Blue and Grey Press ed., 1993), 111; Carman, *The Maryland Campaign*, 147; Walter Clark, *Histories of the Several Regiments and Battalions From North Carolina in the Great War 1861-1865* (Goldsboro, North Carolina: Nash Bros. Printers, 1901), 1:219, 627; 2:115; on the over-extension of the brigade, see John Purifoy to Ezra Carman, letter, July 15, 1889, in the Ezra A. Carman Papers., Manuscript Division, Library of Congress, Washington, D.C. Hartwig, "'My God! Be Careful!'" 42-43.

92 OR 1:464; Sol Smith, "South Mountain," in *National Tribune*, January 17, 1895.

93 *Ibid.*

94 *Ibid.*; R. B. Wilson to Ezra A. Carman, letter, July 11, 1899, in the Ezra A. Carman Papers, Manuscript Division, Library of Congress, Washington, D.C.

enemy rounds. Unable to stand it any longer, one man jumped up and used the butt of his musket on the reptile, adding the rattlesnake to the list of casualties inflicted by the 12th Ohio. Somehow, the incident went undetected by the North Carolinians.[95]

As the 12th Ohio waited in the stubble, the firing continued on the flanks. "About ten o'clock, the tide rolled towards us," recalled Lieutenant Henry Brinkerhoff of Colonel Ewing's 30th Ohio on the far right side of the Union line. "For three hours after, our skirmishers kept up a brisk firing to our front, and in the meantime, heavy volleys could be heard on both flanks."[96] Ewing's Buckeyes no longer faced the threat of Bondurant's guns, but their advance precipitated showers of solid shot from Lane's relocated artillery on the ridge of Turner's Gap. The iron hail forced the regiment to fall back from an exposed rail fence to a position under cover. The infantry facing Ewing belonged to Colonel Ruffin's recently arrived 13th North Carolina. The Tar Heels could detect movement in the dense woods before them, but were incapable of distinguishing more precisely the dispositions or strength of the threatening federals.[97]

As the sputtering Union attack probed here and fell back there, Garland and his staff observed the action near the intersection of the mountain roads near the 13th North Carolina on the left side of the Confederate line.

Concerned about Garland's safety, Colonel Ruffin implored, "General, why do you stay here? You are in great danger!"

Garland replied simply, "I may as well be here as yourself."

Impatient and unsatisfied with his commander's response, Ruffin answered, "No, it is my duty to be here with my regiment, but you could better superintend your brigade from a safer position."

As if to confirm the hazards of the brigadier's position, a moment later a federal minié ball clipped the colonel's hip. Before he could alert Garland, another round struck the general, knocking the thirty-one-year-old to the ground with a mortal wound. He died on the field a short time later.[98] "I never

95 Ward, *The Twelfth Ohio Volunteer Infantry*, 59.

96 Henry Brinkerhoff, *History of the Thirtieth Ohio Volunteer Infantry* (Columbus, Ohio: J. W. Osgood, Printers, 1863), 42; OR 1:469; 1:1045-1046.

97 OR 1:461-462, 469, 1045-1046.

98 B&L, 2:563-564.

The site of Samuel Garland's mortal wounding.

Henry F. Ballone

knew a truer, better, braver man," Harvey Hill would eulogize. "Had he lived, his talents, pluck, energy, and purity of character must have put him in the front rank of his profession, whether in civil or military life."[99]

Garland's staff officers carried his corpse in a blanket to the Old Mountain House, where it became one of the first bodies to occupy the burgeoning field hospital. Almost immediately, rumors cropped up about his alleged obsession with death in the wake of his recent personal tragedies.[100]

After Garland's death, the 13th North Carolina was reeled up the hill about fifty yards until its left rested near Daniel Wise's cabin. Command of the brigade fell to Colonel McRae of the 23rd North Carolina, who "felt all the embarrassment which this situation was calculated to inspire."[101] McRae's words have the ring of truth in perhaps a way he did not intend. In the space of a few minutes he found himself in charge of a strung-out brigade with gaps in the line he surely did not fully comprehend, engaged in a confusing fight with a determined enemy several times larger, all of which was complicated by the loss

99 *Ibid.*, 2:562.

100 Byron L. Williams, *The Old South Mountain Inn* (Shippensburg, Pennsylvania: White Mane Publishers, Inc., 1990), 45.

101 OR 1:1039-1041; Carman, *The Maryland Campaign*, 147.

of a beloved commander. In the words of Harvey Hill, Garland's Brigade faced utter rout and dispersion."[102]

McRae promptly dispatched Garland's assistant adjutant general, Captain Don Peters Halsey, to request immediate reinforcements from D. H. Hill. "The force at my command was wholly inadequate to maintain the position," McRae later reported.[103] Fully understanding McRae's condition after the events of that morning, Hill turned to Brigadier General George Burgwyn Anderson's Brigade, which he ordered up from the west side of Boonsboro when making his initial deployment that morning. Hill divided Anderson's command. Leaving the 14th and 30th North Carolina just north of Turner's Gap, he instructed Colonel Charles C. Tew to detach and forward the 2nd and 4th North Carolina regiments to Duncan McRae along the Wood Road. "Filing some half mile to the right, we formed line of battle and moved in the direction of the firing," recalled a Tar Heel from the 4th regiment. As they approached the brow of the ridge, wounded men, as well as the makeshift stretcher bearing Garland's body made its way up the hillside toward the Old Mountain House, passed them by.[104]

By the time Colonel Tew's pair of regiments arrived on the far left of the Confederate line, a fretful McRae—already anxious to relinquish his responsibilities as the new head of Garland's Brigade—questioned Tew as to the date of his commission. Even though both were colonels Tew outranked McRae, although he was not about to make an issue of it on this day. Refusing to take command, Tew instead positioned his regiments as McRae directed, on the left side of Ruffin's vulnerable regiment. Once in place, Tew's pair of regiments (his own and the 4th North Carolina) opened fire on the 30th Ohio's skirmish line about 100 yards away. Because his own left was now largely exposed, Tew sent a request to General Anderson for reinforcements. The reply was as confusing today as it was then. As Tew later explained it, Anderson ordered his two regiments to move to the northwest, or "flank to the left." Tew passed on the order to McRae, who in turn sent Captain Charles Wood from

102 Hill, B&L, 2:567.

103 OR, 1:1041; see also Robert E.L. Krick, *Staff Officers in Gray: A Biographical Register of the Staff Officers in the Army of Northern Virginia* (Chapel Hill: The University of North Carolina Press, 2003), 146; Hartwig, "'My God! Be Careful!,'" 45.

104 Clark, ed., 1:244-245; OR, 1:1041, 1046.

Garland's staff to notify Hill of Anderson's inexplicable initiative and to request additional reinforcements.[105]

With Tew's regiments now maneuvering to the left, concern about the newly exposed 13th North Carolina rose once again. In a rather desperate effort to keep Ruffin's left attached to Anderson's reinforcements, McRae ordered Ruffin to shadow Tew's shifting regiments. This, in turn, opened a gap in the brigade line about 300 yards wide on Ruffin's right. McRae planned to seal the breach by recalling the 5th North Carolina on the right side of the line, now under the command of Captain Thomas M. Garrett. The decision was but a stopgap measure and risked the entire right flank should the 11th Ohio and 23rd Ohio decide to advance anew. When the firing once more swelled on the right, McRae realized "it was dangerous to withdraw it." Instead, the acting brigade commander decided to rely upon D. H. Hill to seal the openings in the brigade front before the "dark blue line" struck the porous line.[106]

The "dark blue line" was lying in the fields just below the crest awaiting artillery and Scammon's orders for a general advance. "It remained in this position for some time during which a gun from McMullin's battery was pulled up by hand through the lines of the 12th Ohio," R. B. Wilson remembered.[107] The unusual sight was the result of an unusual exchange. Hoping to finally break through the Confederate line about 11:00 a.m., Scammon called for a section of Captain James R. McMullin's 1st Ohio battery. Recognizing the assigned position as an "exceedingly dangerous one," McMullin demurred, "complaining that 'Old Granny' Scammon did not know what he was about." Once he was assured that the much-respected 12th Ohio would support the two 10-pounder Parrotts (McMullin allegedly once claimed that he would "trust his 'soul' in the keeping of that regiment"), the battery commander complied with Scammon's order and called up the pieces commanded by First Lieutenant George L. Crome.[108]

Somehow, Crome managed to deploy his guns as close as forty yards from the 20th North Carolina and then opened fire with canister. According to one

105 *Ibid.*; OR 1:1049; Clark, ed., 2:220-221; Krick, *Staff Officers in Gray*, 308; Hartwig, "'My God! Be Careful!,'" 47.

106 *OR* 1:1039-1041, 1042.

107 R. B. Wilson to Ezra A. Carman, letter, July 11, 1899, in Ezra A. Carman Papers, Manuscript Division, Library of Congress, Washington, D.C.

108 *Ibid.*; OR 1:463; Ward, *Twelfth Ohio Volunteer Infantry*, 58-59; Priest, *Before Antietam*, 153.

source, the artillery did "good service," and in many places stripped the trees of their leaves and sent branches tumbling to the ground. After discharging just four rounds, however, musketry from Captain James B. Atwell's company of the 20th North Carolina poured through the thick woods and silenced the guns. As it turned out, McMullin's first impression was right: this was no place for artillery. "It was, of necessity, advanced so near the enemy's lines," Scammon tried to explain in his report. Necessity or otherwise, according to Wilson, "The men about our gun were picked off rapidly, and their places were supplied from the ranks off the 12th." After five gunners had been shot down, Lieutenant Crome himself loaded one of the guns. He was turning to give the command to fire to a corporal from Company C of the 12th Ohio when a round aimed by an unnamed North Carolinian struck the lieutenant. "He fell dead behind his piece as the last shot was fired," Wilson remembered. "[I]t was a tragic scene that I shall never forget."[109]

By this time Cox was ready to order a general advance. With Crook's arrival, Cox had nearly 3,000 men on hand to drive uphill and capture the mountain. Major James M. Comly, now commanding the 23rd Ohio, was ordered to align his regiment on the left of the 12th Ohio to be in position to attack. Comly sent his men to ground and, "Concealed by the hill," they crawled forward to the left of their fellow Buckeyes. Still facing the threat of Tom Rosser's dismounted troopers on the rebel far right, Lieutenant Colonel Augustus Coleman's 11th Ohio, part of Crook's brigade, moved ahead to support the left flank of the 23rd Ohio. The 36th Ohio, also of Crook's command, was brought behind the 12th and 30th Ohio while Crook's remaining regiment, the 28th Ohio under Lieutenant Colonel Gottfried Becker, was positioned behind the main line and helped shore up the Union right flank.[110]

109 OR 1:458-459, 462, 463-464; James M. Comly, diary, September 14, 1862, in James M. Comly Papers, microfilm reel 1, Rutherford B. Hayes Presidential Center, Fremont, Ohio; R. B. Wilson to Ezra A. Carman, letters, July 11, 1899 and July 22, 1899, in Ezra A. Carman Papers, Manuscript Division, Library of Congress, Washington, D.C.; Ward, *Twelfth Ohio Volunteer Infantry*, 58-59; James Abraham, *With the Army of West Virginia, 1861-1864*, 17; Carman, *The Maryland Campaign*, 148; Priest, *Before Antietam*, 153.

110 OR 1:458-459; Cox, *B&L*, 586-588; John McNulty Clugston, diary entry, September 14, 1862, Rutherford B. Hayes Presidential Center, Fremont, Ohio; Hartwig, "'My God! Be Careful!,'" 46.

Up and down the federal line, crouched figures rose from the fields and trees, pulled their bayonets from their scabbards, and affixed them to the end of their rifled muskets with a sharp metallic clank. The anxious wait was over. "Immediately after this the orders to fix bayonets and then to charge were given," remembered Wilson. The line surged forward with a shout into the ranks of the North Carolinians. "As the line dashed over the short distance to the stone fence it received one murderous volley from the enemy, but before it had time to reload, our line was over the fence and among them with the bayonet."

Both sides "freely used" their bayonets. "This was the first authentic record of a hand-to-hand combat between Northern and Southern troops," the 23rd Ohio's Captain J. S. Ellen argued. Buckeye bayonets in Ellen's 23rd killed at least three Tar Heels in Colonel Christie's 23rd North Carolina. In return, the thrust of an opposing bayonet wielded by one of the Tar Heels brought down the 23rd Ohio's Sergeant Major Eugene L. Reynolds. "[O]f the many good men who fell that day in our command," eulogized Captain Ellen, "there was none more regretted than our brave, bright and youthful Sergeant Major Reynolds." His remains were found the following morning well in advance of any position held by his fellow troops.[111] Some members of the 23rd Ohio raised the stocks of their rifles over the stone wall as clubs, while others pulled their triggers at point-blank range, as if in a duel. The North Carolinians concurred. "The fight in front of the wall was of the stubbornest nature. Some of the Ohio men broke through a gap, and for a few seconds bayonets and clubbed muskets were brought into play."[112] According to one prominent authority, hand-to-hand combat was the "ultimate chaos of combat . . . so confusing, so threatening, and so unpredictable."[113] Whether this was the first hand-to-hand combat or not, the confusion usurped the sylvan innocence of Fox's Gap and provided the Civil War with a deadly precedent that, though rarely repeated, would come to represent the war's heated combat as portrayed in popular culture.

111 R. B. Wilson to Ezra A. Carman, July 22, 1899, in Ezra A. Carman Papers, Manuscript Division, Library of Congress, Washington, D.C.; James M. Comly, diary, September 1862, in James M. Comly Papers, microfilm reel 1, Rutherford B. Hayes Presidential Center, Fremont, Ohio; Carman, *The Maryland Campaign*, 148; J. S. Ellen, typescript, "South Mountain," in Rutherford B. Hayes Papers, Hayes Presidential Library, Fremont, Ohio.

112 Ellen, typescript, "South Mountain," in Rutherford B. Hayes Papers, Hayes Presidential Library, Fremont, Ohio; D. H. Hill, Jr., *North Carolina*, 112.

113 Hess, *The Union Soldier in Battle*, 51.

As the 23rd Ohio fought its way around and into the left ranks of Christie's 23rd North Carolina, Coleman's 11th Ohio pushed into the right side of Duncan McRae's 5th North Carolina. "From three sides came the leaden hail, rendering the position untenable," J. H. Horton and Solomon Teverbaugh, two veterans of the regiment, recalled. Once more, the terrain interrupted the flow of battle. "So dense was the laurel that the troops were obliged, in many places, to move in a single file, and our lines consequently became much broken." Coleman's men continued to move ahead on their own, many of them fighting alone or in small groups.[114] The pressure on the Southern line was mounting, and many in the ranks began to give way. "The enemy fled in confusion leaving their dead and wounded on the field," Martin Sheets would later note.[115]

On the right of the 11th Ohio, the Buckeyes of the 23rd Ohio did not face such a tangled maze of thick mountain laurel. The vicious exchange of volleys between the 23rd Ohio and Christie's 23rd North Carolina continued apace. When one of the zipping lead bullets struck Lieutenant Columbus C. Crouch of Christie's Company D, the disoriented officer exclaimed, "Boys, do tell me, ain't I killed! I know I'm <u>scared</u>, but ain't I killed?"[116] By this time, Christie's 23rd North Carolina was running dangerously low on ammunition and the regiment desperately needed reinforcements. Christie dispatched Adjutant V. E. Turner to find and relay the news to Colonel McRae, but there was no additional manpower available. The steady federal pressure had already splintered the regiment to Christie's right, where only remnants of the 5th North Carolina were still holding their ground.

Christie's men began to fall back. The gallant remnants of McRae's 5th regiment gave up the fight and fell back in confusion when the Ohioans' advance burst into their midst with "a long-extended yell." "Private Stevens, of Company K, alone, kill[ed] three men," one veteran of the 23rd Ohio boasted.[117] Endeavoring to rally the 5th North Carolina once more, Captain

---

114 J. H. Horton and Solomon Teverbaugh, *A History of the Eleventh Regiment, Ohio Volunteer Infantry* (Dayton, Ohio: W.J. Shuey, 1866), 71-72.

115 Martin Sheets, diary entry, September 14, 1862, in Civil War Times Illustrated Collection, United States Army Military History Institute, Carlisle, Pennsylvania.

116 Henry Clay Wall, *Historical Sketch of the Pee Dee Guards, Co. D, 23rd North Carolina* (Raleigh: Edwards, Broughton & Co., 1876), 42-43; OR 1:1042.

117 James M. Comly, diary, September 1862, in James M. Comly Papers, microfilm reel 1, Rutherford B. Hayes Presidential Center, Fremont, Ohio; Carman, *The Maryland Campaign*, 148;

Garrett placed his color bearer on the ridge road near the position the regiment had first held that morning. By this time, however, the onslaught was too great, the strength too overpowering. If there was any hope to hold, it ended when one of Buckeyes' rounds removed the color bearer from the field, leaving Garrett to explain he and his survivors were "compelled to fall back father down the hill." Rutherford Hayes' 23rd Ohio had finally smashed through the right side of Garland's weak and twisted line. Rosser's dismounted Virginia troopers, still dangling out on what had been the Confederate right flank, likewise fell back. "We completely routed the enemy," John McNulty Clugston of the 23rd Ohio told his diary. Still, the cost of their victory was considerable, with 32 men killed, 95 wounded, and three missing.[118]

The rout continued down the Confederate line as Scammon's and Crook's advancing regiments successively shattered the wavering North Carolinians. Together with the 36th Ohio, the 12th Ohio made one final charge into Colonel Iverson's 20th North Carolina. The Carolinians held for a short time, returning fire as best they could. Private Andrew Wykle, fighting with Company K of the 36th Ohio, ducked behind a rock as the "bullets flew thick and fast all around" him. Numbers told, however, and within minutes Iverson's troops were streaming rearward. "In this charge we drove the enemy in great confusion and inflicted serious loss upon him, killing several with the bayonet," Colonel White reported.[119]

This part of the fight for South Mountain along the center of the line proved just as intimate and deadly as it had been elsewhere. One of the 20th North Carolina's color bearers found himself surrounded by the Buckeyes and ordered to surrender. "Gentleman, I am a color sergeant and can not surrender," he declared. Thereafter, he produced a revolver and began firing. In short order a dozen balls pierced his body. "It was an instance of rash heroism which was admired by all who witnessed it," James E. D. Ward recalled. "Those who shot him did it with tears in their eyes."[120] Just ahead, Corporal Leonidas

---

Clark, ed., 2:220-221; J.S. Ellen, typescript, "South Mountain," in Rutherford B. Hayes Papers, Hayes Presidential Library, Fremont, Ohio.

118 OR 1:1,042, 466-467; John McNulty Clugston, diary entry, September 14, 1862, in collection of the Rutherford B. Hayes Presidential Center, Fremont, Ohio.

119 Andrew Wykle, "A Fighting Regiment: Four Years Service with the 36th Ohio," *National Tribune*, 9 January 1902.

120 OR 1:465; Ward, *Twelfth Ohio Volunteer Infantry*, 59.

H. Inscho, Company E, 12th Ohio, had just reached the stone wall at the crest when a musket ball struck his rifle stock and wounded his left hand. "A Confederate captain was on the other side and as he came near me, I caught him by the collar and told him to surrender," Inscho remembered. The captain refused, instead pointing his revolver at Inscho's head. "I caught it by the barrel and turned it up just as he fired," the corporal continued. "I clung to the revolver and disarmed him, and grabbing him by the shoulders began to pull him over the wall." The struggle continued for several minutes before Inscho finally knocked his opponent to the ground and induced his exhausted surrender. Having bagged his prisoner, the corporal stood up and turned to five Confederates taking refuge behind a clump of trees. "I pointed my revolver at them and demanded their surrender," he continued. Four of the North Carolinians dropped their weapons and ambled sullenly toward Inscho. The fifth man, however, raised his rifle and took aim at the revolver-wielding federal corporal as he dove for the cover of the stone wall. "He turned to run away and I at once rose from my position and emptied the contents of my revolver into him," Inscho proudly recounted. The Buckeye marched his five new prisoners off to Colonel White.[121] Elsewhere down the line, the Tar Heels were "closely pursued until both the pursued and the pursuers became scattered in the dense undergrowth." The 20th North Carolina was left in shambles, with seven dead, nine wounded, and 42 missing or captured.[122]

Garland's entire line had been reduced to just Colonel Ruffin's 13th North Carolina on the far left, which was still blazing away at Colonel Ewing's 30th Ohio. "And right there for about 45 minutes there was one of the most stubborn musketry duels that I witnessed during the war," recalled Joseph E. Walton, a private in Company I of the 30th Ohio.[123] One lieutenant in Walton's regiment was pierced by three balls, while another was mortally wounded after being struck twice. Both of the 30th's color bearers were shot dead as the

---

121 Leonidas H. Inscho, "Held on to the Rebel Captain," in W.F. Beyer and O.F. Keydel, eds., *Deeds of Valor* (Detroit: Perrin-Keydel Co., 1907), 1:71-72.

122 R. B. Wilson to Ezra A. Carman, letter, July 22, 1899, in Ezra A. Carman Papers, Manuscript Division, Library of Congress, Washington, D.C. On casualties, see D. Scott Hartwig, "'My God! Be Careful!' Morning Battle at Fox's Gap, September 14, 1862," *Civil War Regiments: A Journal of the American Civil War* 5, no. 3 (1996), 51.

123 Joseph E. Walton, "The 30th Ohio: Some Reminiscences of the Battle of Antietam," *National Tribune*, December 31, 1885.

national colors received sixteen bullet and buckshot holes and two fragments of grape shot hurled from Bondurant's guns in Wise's fields.[124]

Bondurant's position was about 600 yards to the front and right of the new ground won by Carr White's 12th Ohio. White received the order to charge the battery and end its molestation of the federal right. "I moved the regiment forward through a dense laurel under a heavy fire, and gained the rear of the battery," he reported.[125] The 12th Ohio's timing could not have been worse for Ruffin. Breaking under the pressure of the 30th Ohio, the commander of the 13th North Carolina sent an adjutant to the rear to chart an avenue for retreat. Within a few minutes his adjutant returned with a devastating litany of announcements: the rest of the brigade had collapsed, General Anderson had made off with the 2nd and 4th North Carolina regiments, and the federals were streaming into his rear. "The enemy in front was pressing us and I saw but one way out, and that was to charge those in my front, repel them, if possible, and then, before they could recover, make a dash at those in my rear and cut my way out," Ruffin planned.[126]

As the survivors of Ruffin's 13th North Carolina attempted to break away, a devastating new drama unfolded between them and the 12th Ohio near the Daniel Wise cabin. A small garden enclosed by low stone walls sat adjacent to the cabin. One of Ruffin's color bearers jumped on the garden's rear wall and, from that perch, furiously and defiantly waved his standard. After he refused numerous calls to surrender, including one from Lieutenant Colonel Coleman of the 11th Ohio, the flag bearer was summarily shot and fell inside the garden wall. Private Henry Hoagland of Company F, 12th Ohio, jumped over the garden wall and secured the flag. Coleman ordered Hoagland to deliver the flag to him, and afterward claimed the credit for its capture. "The little cabin and garden with its stone fence was the scene of the greatest and bloodiest conflict of the day," claimed R. B. Wilson. "The ground of the Garden was literally covered with the dead and wounded."[127]

---

124 OR 1:463; George H. Hildt, diary entry, September 22, 1862, in Hildt Papers, Ohio Historical Society, Columbus, Ohio.

125 OR 1:465; Carman, *The Maryland Campaign*, 149.

126 B&L 2:564.

127 R. B. Wilson to Ezra A. Carman, letter, July 22, 1899, in Ezra A. Carman Papers, Manuscript Division, Library of Congress, Washington, D.C.; Hartwig, "'My God! Be Careful!,'" 48. Priest, *Before Antietam*, 167.

Ruffin and his men were caught in the pincers of the 12th Ohio to their front and members of the 30th Ohio to their rear. In what must have been a final gasp of vigor and verve, Ruffin ordered his men to face north and charge across the Old Sharpsburg Road, where they hoped to reunite with Anderson's regiments. Somehow, the bold ploy worked. "He marched his regiment to the Old Sharpsburg Road and joined Anderson . . . taking position on Anderson's right and acting under his orders the rest of the day," wrote federal veteran and chronicler of the campaign Ezra Carman. "They retreated in confusion," Edward Schweitzer recorded. The cost to the 30th Ohio included 17 men killed and 60 men wounded. [128]

After the embattled North Carolinians cut their way out of Wise's fields, an exhausted Ruffin encountered D. H. Hill just north of the road. "I shall never forget the feelings of relief which I experienced when I first caught sight of you," he recalled. "You rode up to me, and, shaking my hand, said that you have given us up for lost and did not see how it was possible for us to have escaped." Not all of them were so lucky. Wilson of the 12th Ohio noted, "the slaughter was very great," and indeed it was. Of the 212 men who started the morning in the 13th North Carolina, 13 were killed, 19 were wounded, and 24 were captured.[129]

Ruffin's collapse left the Ohioans with a victory of heroic proportion. "The high knoll on the left was carried, the enemy's center was completely broken and driven down the mountain, while on the right our men pushed the routed Carolinians beyond the Sharpsburg road, through Wise's fields, and up the slope of the crest toward the Mountain House at Turner's Gap," Cox tersely summarized.[130] The three hours of fighting decimated Sam Garland's Confederate brigade, killing the general and 36 of his men and wounding 168 more. In addition, another 154 were captured or missing. The brigade lost nearly forty percent of its effective strength.[131] Hill's strategic defense of

---

128 *Ibid.*; OR 1:1046; *B&L* 2:564.

129 *B&L* 2:564.; Carman, *The Maryland Campaign*, 149; on casualties, see Hartwig, "'My God! Be Careful!' Morning Battle at Fox's Gap, September 14, 1862," *Civil War Regiments: A Journal of the American Civil War* 5, no. 3 (1996): 53; R. B. Wilson to Ezra A. Carman, letter, July 11, 1899, in Ezra A. Carman Papers, Manuscript Division, Library of Congress, Washington, D.C.

130 Cox, *B&L* 2:587.

131 These figures are those calculated by the first campaign historian, Ezra Carman. D. H. Hill's official report lists the official losses of Garland's Brigade at 46 killed, 210 wounded, and

Turner's Gap was in shambles and the road to the summit up that pass now stood wide open. Moreover, Jacob Cox's Kanawha Division had secured the strategic high ground. From these heights, the remainder of Hill's Southern division—and the reinforcements on the way to support him—would be most vulnerable to flanking maneuvers and subsequent efforts to gain the rear. Hill himself later described it "a serious repulse."[132]

Cox, too, had suffered considerable losses. "Our own losses had not been trifling," he admitted. Edwar Schweitzer reported 17 killed and 60 wounded in the 30th Ohio. Martin Sheets in the 11th Ohio calculated that seven men were killed in his regiment. All told, the Kanawha Division suffered 80 men killed, 265 wounded, and 11 missing or captured, comprising just more than ten percent of Cox's effective strength.[133]

*   *   *

A lull fell over the littered fields and roads of Fox's Gap. "We had several hundred prisoners in our hands, and learned from them that D. H. Hill's division, consisting of five brigades, was opposed to us," Cox wrote in a piece for the *Century* magazine. "Longstreet was said to be in near support . . . and it seemed wise to contract our lines a little, so that we might have some reserve and hold the crest we had won till the rest of the IX Corps should arrive." Cox determined to delay any new assault until the balance of the corps, which General Reno promised him earlier that morning, came to his aid.

Cox had no way of knowing that D. H. Hill's three supporting infantry brigades had not yet come up, and that a mere 1,200 exhausted and hungry Confederates stood between his victorious division and Turner's Gap. Lieutenant George Grattan, an aide to Colonel Alfred Colquitt, did not agree. "It is difficult to see why they did not follow [their assault] up by pushing their

---

187 missing (see *OR*, 1:1,026). Because Garland's Brigade was momentarily engaged three days later at the Battle of Antietam, Carman arrived at these figures by estimating that four-fifths of the "official" losses were incurred at South Mountain (see Carman, *The Maryland Campaign*, 449-450).

132 Hill, *B&L* 2:567.

133 Cox, *B&L* 2:587; *OR* 1:458-459, 471; Schweitzer, diary entry, September 14, 1862, in Civil War Times Illustrated Collection, United States Army Military History Institute, Carlisle, Pennsylvania; Martin Sheets, diary entry, September 14, 1862, in Civil War Times Illustrated Collection; *OR* 1:184-187; see also Carman, *The Maryland Campaign*, 447.

whole force down . . . to the Mountain House," he argued. "Fortunately for us, their evident timidity caused them to delay." On the ground, and after such a confusing and bloody fight, it would have been irresponsible for Cox to launch such a blind venture and risk losing what had been so arduously won that morning.[134]

General Scammon's after-action campaign report beamed with pride at all his men had accomplished. "In all this . . . there was no faltering," he boasted. "It was the thorough work of good soldiers."[135] "The conduct of both officers and men was everything that could be desired, and every one seemed stimulated by the determination not to be excelled in any soldierly quality," General Cox concluded of his brigades, Scammon's among them.[136] Northern newspapers quickly transmitted the stunning news of their mountain victory. "It appears that one of the North Carolina Brigades has been badly cut up by some Ohio Regiments," the wire report explained before going on to note that more than 200 prisoners had been captured. "A desperate fight took place . . . soon terminated in favor of the gallant Ohio regiments, the enemy scattering in great confusion."[137]

This excitement also buoyed the federal enlisted men. "The rebels had all the advantage of the ground but they still lost the most men," Schweitzer reflected. Not surprisingly, things looked different from the Confederate side of the hill. "Notwithstanding the disadvantage of position, the absence of artillery support, and the injurious effect produced by the death of its general, and the great superiority of the enemy's numbers," argued Colonel Duncan McRae, "this brigade maintained its ground for nearly three hours." McRae failed to mention several other plausible reasons that helped account for the untimely reverse, including but not limited to: the absence and perhaps negligence—deliberate or otherwise—of cavalry commander Jeb Stuart; lack of communication and coordination between officers and their staffs; poor deployment of regiments in thick laurel and woods without proper reconnaissance; the absence of "the touch of the elbow"; and, the naive notion

---

134 Cox, B&L 2:587; Judge George D. Grattan, "The Battle of Boonsboro Gap or South Mountain," in *Southern Historical Society Papers* 39 (Richmond, 1914): 39-40.

135 *OR* 1:461-462.

136 *Ibid.,* 1:460-461.

137 See, for example, *Summit County Beacon,* September 18, 1862.

that the federal army would continue to hesitate and falter before the gaps of South Mountain.[138]

The morning melee at Fox's Gap would be long remembered. "The fact that the 12th and 23rd Ohio were engaged with regiments with the same numbers has been a subject of comment from that day to this among the survivors," R. B. Wilson noted. One veteran of Bondurant's Confederate battery who moved to Texas after the war wrote to his old comrade John Purifoy, then the Examiner of Public Accounts for the State of Alabama. "I have thought and dreamed of the South Mountain fight for a day or two and can get no further than the first position after getting out of the scrape, where Garland was brought to us," he penned. "I can see him now with his buck gauntlets across his breast, after which memory fails to recount or to refer to anything that transpired until we awoke the next morning."[139]

But it was Harvey Hill's recollection that was perhaps the most significant—and certainly the most dramatic. "I do not remember ever to have experienced a feeling of greater loneliness. It seemed as though we were deserted by all the world and rest of mankind."[140]

---

138 Schweitzer, diary entry, September 14, 1862, in Civil War Times Illustrated Collection, United States Army Military History Institute, Carlisle, Pennsylvania; *OR* 1:1,041-1,043. Dennis E. Frye, one of the leading students of the Maryland Campaign of 1862, points out that the battle at South Mountain was the "first defensive fight," in *Antietam Revealed* (Collingswood, New Jersey: C. W. Historicals, 2004), 45.

139 R. B. Wilson to Ezra Carman, letter, July 22, 1899, in Ezra A. Carman Papers, Manuscript Division, Library of Congress, Washington, D.C.; John Purifoy to Carman, letter, August 7, 1900, in Carman Papers.

140 *B&L* 2:566.

C hapter 6

"Hallo, Sam, I am dead!"

The Afternoon Fight for Fox's Gap

A decided victory had been won over the veterans
of Lee's army; but we paid dearly for it.

— *Private Eugene Beauge, 45th Pennsylvania[1]*

It was now the noon hour, and a wave of utter helplessness swept over
Daniel Harvey Hill in his headquarters at the Old Mountain House. Indeed,
these morning hours had been the loneliest of his career. The heavily
outnumbered North Carolina brigade under Sam Garland had been routed
from Fox's Gap and its capable commander killed. The powerful enemy was
now just one mile below the thinly manned crest at Turner's Gap, and Hill knew
the federals could easily attack and secure the gap before reinforcements
arrived. The strategic situation was deteriorating by the hour. South Mountain
was slipping from the grasp of the Confederates, and its loss would jeopardize
not only the campaign into Maryland, but the existence of the widely dispersed
Army of Northern Virginia. And all of this was happening on Hill's watch.[2]

Still, Hill was nothing if not a determined fighter. He dispatched a message
to Gen. James Longstreet to send reinforcements as quickly as possible. In a
display that demonstrated the dire situation facing the Confederates, "a line of
dismounted staff-officers, couriers, teamsters, and cooks" is said to have

---

1 Eugene Beauge, "The Forty-Fifth at South Mountain," in *History of the Forty-Fifth Regiment Pennsylvania Veteran Volunteer Infantry*, Allen D. Albert, ed. (Williamsport, Pennsylvania: Grit Publishing Co., 1912), 54.

2 Hal Bridges, *Lee's Maverick General*, 110-111.

Major General Daniel Harvey Hill. *National Archives*

formed to offer the appearance of battery supports in front of his headquarters. As the minutes ticked past, and to Hill's great relief, it appeared as though Cox had suspended his advance until the arrival of his own reinforcements, which provided the Confederates with additional time to assemble a more credible defense.[3]

The lull in the infantry fighting, however, did not mean the fighting had stopped altogether. "About noon the combat was reduced to one of artillery," Cox explained. "The enemy's guns had so completely [showered] the range of the sloping fields behind us that their canister shot cut long furrows in the sod, with a noise like the cutting of a melon rind." Occupying a knoll north of the National Pike, Captain Lane's two 20-pound Parrotts and three 10-pound Parrotts greeted Cox's arriving reinforcements while Captain Thomas Carter's ten-pound Parrot, unlimbered at the Old Mountain House, shelled Seth Simmond's and Samuel Benjamin's guns down the turnpike. Bondurant's exhausted gunners were also active. After barely escaping from the desperate fighting near Daniel Wise's cabin, the battery assumed a third position and joined in the artillery duel Cox so vividly described.[4]

Private Frederick Pettit of the 100th Pennsylvania also remembered the noon-hour cannonading as he and his comrades approached South Mountain up the turnpike with Colonel Thomas Welsh's brigade of Brigadier General Orlando Willcox's IX Corps division. "We could see the batteries at work and hear the whizzing of the shells," wrote Pettit. "The enemy sent their shell among us thick and fast. They exploded above and all around us." The Pennsylvanians were ordered to halt and protect themselves under a bank along the side of the National Turnpike.[5]

In addition to slowing the enemy's advance up the mountain, the Confederate artillery allowed Hill to make adjustments to his lines. The first

3   *B&L*, 2:566-567; *OR* 1:1020; see also D. H. Hill, Jr., *North Carolina*, in *Confederate Military History*, 113. The supply vanguard was still west of Boonsboro, so it is unlikely that such services were at hand at the summit of South Mountain. This depiction of desperation, similar to the claim about recalling Alfred Colquitt's Brigade, may well be nothing more than another example of Lost Cause fiction.

4   *B&L* 2:587; John Purifoy to Ezra A. Carman, letter, July 15, 1899, in Ezra A. Carman Papers, Manuscript Division, Library of Congress, Washington, D.C.; Carman, *The Maryland Campaign*, 148-149.

5   Frederick Pettit, letter to "parents, brothers, and sisters," September 20, 1862, in Civil War Times Illustrated Collection, United States Army Military History Institute, Carlisle, Pennsylvania; Priest, *Before Antietam*, 175.

reinforcements that morning had arrived in the form of Brigadier General George B. Anderson's Brigade, followed by three regiments from Brigadier General Roswell Ripley's Brigade (Lieutenant Colonel Hamilton Brown's 1st North Carolina, Colonel William DeRosset's 3rd North Carolina, and Captain John Key's 44th Georgia). Ripley's last regiment, the 4th Georgia under Colonel George Doles, remained in the rear guarding the Hamburg Pass Road. About nine that morning, when the pressure was mounting against Fox's Gap, D. H. Hill—who was still loathe to strip away troops guarding his supply wagons— reluctantly ordered Ripley to forward his artillery to support the embattled Garland. Shortly thereafter, Hill directed Ripley "to move with the whole force to the main pass east of Boonsborough."[6]

When Ripley arrived at the Old Mountain House, Hill ordered him to form his infantry on G. B. Anderson's left. Anderson, who had arrived on the scene with two regiments only to shift them away from Garland's exposed left flank at a most inopportune time, was found on the Old Sharpsburg Road. "Upon coming up and communicating with that officer," reported Ripley, "it was arranged that he should extend along the Braddock Road [Old Sharpsburg Road] and make room for the troops of my command, and that an attack should be made upon the enemy."[7]

While these dispositions were underway, Hill arrived at the head of two brigades led by Colonel George "Tige" Anderson and Brigadier General Thomas Fenwick Drayton. "Tige" Anderson's Georgia command consisted of the 1st Georgia Regulars, and the 7th, 8th, 9th, and 11th Georgia regiments. Drayton's command added the 50th and 51st Georgia, 15th South Carolina, the Phillips Legion, and seven companies from the 3rd South Carolina Battalion. These 1,900 men from Brigadier General David R. Jones' Division of Longstreet's wing arrived at the Old Mountain House about 3:30 p.m.[8]

Once the enemy reorganized, Hill expected them to launch their main assault on the north side of the National Turnpike. Still, he remained unsettled about the presence of federal troops on his right after Garland's Brigade had been flanked and crushed. As a result, and needing room to accommodate the

---

6   OR 1:1031-1033; Carman, *The Maryland Campaign*, 150.

7   *Ibid.*

8   General G. Moxley Sorrel, *At the Right Hand of Longstreet: Recollections of a Confederate Staff Officer* (New York: Neal Publishing Company, 1905), 106; Carman, *The Maryland Campaign*, 150; OR 1:803-810, 1020-1021, 1032; B&L 2:569.

recent arrivals, Hill ordered G. B. Anderson and Ripley to move farther right until they reached Colonel Tom Rosser's original position in the woods (which had been on the far right beyond Garland's flank). Tige Anderson was ordered to follow them and form on Ripley's left, while Drayton's men would move behind Anderson and occupy the Confederate left. Before galloping back to his headquarters to await the arrival of Generals Robert E. Lee and James Longstreet, Hill notified Ripley that he, as the next senior officer, was now in command of the four brigades.

Ripley ordered the men to move by the right flank. In doing so, however, another gap opened in the Confederate line when Tige Anderson's men marched as ordered but Drayton did not follow him. As a result, and unbeknownst to Anderson, a yawning hole developed in the line as Anderson pulled away. "I had, by moving to the right under General Ripley's order, become separated at least 300 yards from General Drayton's right," Anderson explained.[9] The timing was unfortunate, for the federals were assembling farther down the slope and moving against Drayton, who had no choice but to deploy his brigade on the Confederate left around the Wise farm to repel any forthcoming attack.

* * *

The genesis of the attack against Drayton at Fox's Gap began earlier that morning when IX Corps commander General Jesse Reno assured Jacob Cox that the rest of the corps would advance to assist Cox's Kanawha Division in its fight for the gap. About eight that morning, the two brigades from Brigadier General Orlando Willcox's division were the first ordered up the turnpike from Middletown. They bivouacked about a mile and a half east of the village to enjoy a breakfast of roasted corn, crackers, and coffee. Colonel Benjamin Christ commanded the First Brigade, which included the 28th Massachusetts, 8th and 17th Michigan, 79th New York Highlanders, and 50th Pennsylvania. The Second Brigade under Colonel Thomas Welsh contained three regiments: the 46th New York and the 45th and 100th Pennsylvania.[10]

9 *Ibid.*; OR 1:908-909.

10 OR 1:177, 427-428, 459; Orlando Bolivar Willcox, "South Mountain and Antietam," in *Forgotten Valor: The Memoirs, Journals, and Letters of Orlando B. Willcox*, Robert Garth Scott, ed. (Kent, Ohio: Kent State University Press, 1999), 351-354; John Morton [Company F, 17th

As the men proceeded up the turnpike, they noticed the knapsacks of the Kanawha Division cast aside along the road.[11] "We were told that General Cox's 'Kanawha' division . . . was then engaged [with Garland], and that we were to follow in support," one veteran of the 79th New York Highlanders recalled.[12] Farther up the road, Willcox consulted with cavalry commander Alfred Pleasonton as to the intended disposition of his brigades. "The general indicated an attack along the slope of the mountain on the right of the main pike," Willcox recalled. With the 100th Pennsylvania thrown out as skirmishers, the brigades marched forward through the woods and up the slope to take position on the right side of the National Pike.[13]

About this time, Major General Ambrose Burnside, commanding the right wing of the Army of the Potomac, galloped up and ordered Willcox to withdraw his division, countermarch to the Old Sharpsburg Road, and assume a position there near Cox's resting brigades. After the war, Cox erroneously recalled that Willcox "would have been up considerably earlier but for a mistake in the delivery of a message," and that Willcox was recalled and given the correct direction by Reno. In any event, a considerable amount of time was lost countermarching Willcox's division. "We pushed steadily on and presently took a by-path that diverged to the left from the turnpike, and continued on over rough ground and wooded hill," Private Eugene Beauge of the 45th Pennsylvania remembered. According to Private William Todd of the 79th New York Highlanders, "shot and shell were dropping about us as we marched along the road." It was nearly 2:00 p.m. by the time Willcox halted his men under the eastern slope of the mountain and notified Jacob Cox of his arrival.[14]

Michigan Infantry], letter, September 24, 1862, in Civil War Miscellaneous Collection, United States Army Military History Institute, Carlisle, Pennsylvania; Beauge, "The Forty-Fifth At South Mountain," in *History of the Forty-Fifth Regiment Pennsylvania Veteran Volunteer Infantry,* 51.

11 Louis Crater, *History of the Fiftieth Regiment Pennsylvania Veteran Volunteers* (Reading: Coleman Printing House, 1884), 32.

12 William Todd, *The Seventy-Ninth Highlanders, New York Volunteers in the War of the Rebellion, 1861-1865* (Albany: Barton and Co., 1886), 230.

13 OR 1:427-428; see also Frederick Pettit, letter, September 20, 1862, in Civil War Times Illustrated Collection, United States Army Military History Institute, Carlisle, Pennsylvania.

14 Beauge, "The Forty-Fifth At South Mountain," 51; Crater, *History of the Fiftieth Regiment Pennsylvania Veteran Volunteers,* 32; Todd, *The Seventy-Ninth Highlanders,* 230; Ibid.; B&L 2:587-588. Unfortunately, General Pleasonton's report, in OR 1:208-209, sheds no further light on the sequence of events that led Willcox's division to countermarch back to the Old

As reinforcements from both sides were taking position for the next round of fighting, Captain Asa M. Cook's Eighth Battery of Massachusetts Light Artillery, which led Willcox's advance that morning, rolled forward one section of two 12-pound Napoleons into the fields just north (right) of the Old Sharpsburg Road to counter enemy artillery fire. Some men from the 79th New York, the lead regiment of Christ's brigade, helped the guns up the steep hillside until they found a suitable spot for them about 400 yards from the summit.

Willcox formed his line parallel to the Old Sharpsburg Road facing generally north to the National Turnpike. His left flank was behind Cox's right and refused enough so that the divisions did not connect. Upon request, Willcox peeled off the 8th Michigan and 50th Pennsylvania (which held the right of his line, along with the 28th Massachusetts) and sent them to bolster the left side of Cox's line, which at that time Cox believed was in danger of being turned. "Old soldiers only know how trying it is to be marched into a place which others have tried to hold," Adjutant Louis Crater later wrote. "The Fiftieth Regiment never refused to go where it was ordered . . . and though it seemed like marching into the very jaws of death, it took the position pointed out by General Willcox, and held it." Enfilading artillery fire welcomed the regiments. "It seemed as though the men were bound one to the other, arm to arm, and shoulder to shoulder," remembered Crater.[15]

Behind Captain Cook's pair of guns, Willcox's remaining infantry assumed secondary positions in support of the troops fighting farther up the slope. The 79th New York filed south and took up a position perpendicular to the Old Sharpsburg Road in the old Beachley farmyard. "We kept well under cover while the battery fired a few rounds," Todd noted as Cook's gunners unleashed their iron against Drayton's Georgians. The Massachusetts gunners only managed to fire four rounds before one of their Napoleons was disabled and forced to withdraw. Another gun was being pulled forward to replace it when enemy artillery fire commenced from another direction. This unexpected fire hailed from Bondurant's guns, which rained long-distance canister down upon the battery as a form of anti-personnel fire before switching to solid shot. "The enemy at once concentrated all his available artillery on Cook," Todd recalled.

Sharpsburg Road. Willcox's report has been accepted here as it is the most contemporaneous source.

15 Crater, *History of the Fiftieth Regiment Pennsylvania Veteran Volunteers*, 33; *B&L* 2:588; Carman, *The Maryland Campaign*, 150-151.

This fire, from about 600 yards away, also reached Cox's line. Private John Palmer, still occupying the approximate center of that line with the 36th Ohio, noted that "some half dozen men" from his regiment were "wounded very slightly with pieces of shell" that exploded over their heads. The enemy shelling also made work considerably more difficult for William Lyle and the surgeons of the 11th Ohio, who were busy consoling and treating the morning's wounded near the Coffman house along the Old Sharpsburg Road. The embattled crew began moving ambulance wagons to more secure locations.[16]

The Confederate artillery fire mortally wounded a pair of gunners, killed Private Frank A. Keene, and injured two more. One of Cook's horses drawing a limber wagon was also killed. Leaving two of his pieces behind, Captain Cook gave the order for his men to retire. The artillerists scrambled in a "temporary panic" for the shelter of the woods behind them. "The drivers with the limbers went wild to the rear," chronicled historian Ezra Carman.[17]

The sudden fire from Bondurant's guns opened just as Willcox's division was changing positions. Cox, the senior officer on the mountain, ordered Willcox to continue holding the Old Sharpsburg Road, but to also connect his left with Cox's right. "It looked for a few minutes as though a panic would ensue," admitted Private Beauge of the 45th Pennsylvania. "A number of cavalrymen and artillerists came rushing down upon us crying clear the road for the cannon we are beaten and just then the artillery came galloping down with the guns and caissons," Private Pettit remembered. Bondurant's gunners emptied their limber chests at the fleeing New Englanders while also lobbing shells and skipping solid shot down the hill and onto the Old Sharpsburg Road.[18] "And to make things worse the rebels were sending grape shot and shell amongst us in a perfect shower," Pettit continued. "The shells, which skimmed the crest and burst in the tree-tops at the lower side of the fields made a sound

16 John Palmer, diary entry, September 14, 1862, in Lester L. Kempfer, *The Salem Light Guard*, 87; William Lyle, *Lights and Shadows of Army Life*, 130-132; Priest, *Before Antietam*, 178, 178n.

17 Todd, *The Seventy-Ninth Highlanders*, 230-231; OR 1:433, 428-429, 437; see also *Massachusetts Soldiers, Sailors, and Marines in the Civil War*, 6 vols. (Norwood, Massachusetts: Norwood Press, 1933), 5:446-450; Carman, *The Maryland Campaign*, 151; Priest, *Before Antietam*, 178-179.

18 OR 1:428-429, 437; letter from John Purifoy to Ezra A. Carman, July 15, 1899, in Ezra A. Carman Papers, Manuscript Division, Library of Congress, Washington, D.C; Beauge, "The Forty-Fifth at South Mountain," 51-52; Frederick Pettit, letter, September 20, 1862, in Civil War Times Illustrated Collection, U.S. Army Military History Institute, Carlisle, Pennsylvania.

like the crashing and falling of some brittle substance, instead of the tough fiber of pine and oak," Cox remembered with poetic flair.[19]

With a section of Cook's guns at risk, Willcox ordered Lieutenant Colonel David Morrison's 79th New York and Colonel William H. Withington's 17th Michigan to change direction by the right flank, march at the double quick, and come to the defense of the unmanned artillery pieces. "This movement brought us in position behind a stone wall from which it would have been difficult for three times our number to have dislodged us," Todd wrote. The Highlanders' new position was to the left of both the road and Cook's abandoned guns. Enemy fire rattled over the tops of the stone walls, scattering individual rocks and sending them into the ranks of the regiment. Across the road, the 17th Michigan assumed a position to the right and rear of the Napoleons. According to Captain Gabriel Campbell of Company E, there was "a scramble up the sides of the ditch and out of range" as the regiment came to the defense of the guns. "We then lay still in a little patch of woods while the shot and shell poured down like rain bursting everywhere around us," recalled John Morton of Company F. Several horses tied to a rail fence behind the regiment were spooked by the blasts.[20]

These Michigan troops added a layer of naïveté, fear, and inexperience to the intensity of the moment. Their fresh blue kepis stood in stark contrast to the tattered uniforms of the veteran regiments, for these Wolverines had mustered into service just three weeks before at the Detroit Barracks. The regiment even fielded a full company composed entirely of students from the Ypsilanti Normal School. The Michiganders were under the command of Colonel William H. Withington who, like Willcox, had made an inmate's tour of Confederate prisons earlier in the war. Private David Lane of Company G described his regiment in the pages of his diary. "Dress coats buttoned to the chin; upon our heads a high-crowned hat with a feather stuck jauntily on one side. White gloves in our pockets; a wonder we did not put them on, so little know we of the etiquette of war," he scribbled. "Drill is the order of the day, as

19 Pettit, letter, September 20, 1862; Jacob Dolson Cox, *Military Reminiscences of the Civil War* (New York: Charles Scribner's Sons, 1900), 1:287.

20 OR 1:428, 437; Carman, *The Maryland Campaign*, 151; Todd, *The Seventy-Ninth Highlanders*, 231-232; Gabriel Campbell, letter, August 23, 1899, as quoted in Priest, *Before Antietam*, 179; original in the Ezra Carman Papers, Antietam National Battlefield, Sharpsburg, Maryland; John Morton, letter, September 24, 1862, in Civil War Miscellaneous Collection, United States Army Military History Institute, Carlisle, Pennsylvania.

it is the necessity of the hour." he continued when September dawned. "Officers and men have yet to learn the rudiments of military maneuvering. There is not a company officer who can put his men through company drill without making one, or more, ludicrous blunders."[21]

When the Sabbath dawned, the men of the fresh regiment were mystified by both the outline of South Mountain and the prospect that their baptism of fire might occur on a Sunday. "We had an inkling, how obtained I do not know; mental telepathy, perhaps, that occult, mysterious power that enables us to divine the most secret thoughts of men, that a mass meeting was to be held on that eminence to discuss the pros and cons of secession, and that we, the Seventeenth, had received a pressing invitation to be present," Lane told his diary.[22]

When they arrived on the field, Colonel Withington approached his old friend Willcox. "Glad to see you, Colonel. But what can you do?" asked the division commander.

"We can march by a flank and load and fire, General," the colonel responded.

In the immediacy of the moment, the reply was sufficient for Willcox. "All right, sir. You see that battery up in the gap?" he asked. "Now if you can steal up through the woods and pick off some of the cannoneers, that will help a good deal."

"All right," Withington answered.[23]

The Michiganders and the Highlanders from New York remained in place while the other units shifted into their proper positions. Colonel Thomas Welsh's brigade fell into line behind the New Yorkers to the left of the Old Sharpsburg Road. The men of the 45th Pennsylvania loosened their knapsacks and formed a line of battle near the Coffman's log house, the right of their line resting on the Old Sharpsburg Road. Private Beauge recalled a sight that must have given him pause: "surgeons with their knives, saws, probes and bandages had taken position close by." By lying down, Beauge and his comrades

---

21 Ypsilanti Normal School was a predecessor of modern-day Eastern Michigan University. David Lane, *A Soldier's Diary: The Story of A Volunteer, 1862-1865* (n.p., 1905), 8, 11; Orlando B. Willcox, "South Mountain and Antietam," in *Forgotten Valor: The Memoirs, Journals, and Letters of Orlando B. Willcox,* ed. Robert Garth Scott (Kent: Kent State University Press, 1999), 354.

22 *Ibid.* Lane, 11.

23 *Ibid.*

eschewed the "serious punishment" of the relentless Confederate batteries. Lieutenant Colonel Joseph Gerhardt's 46th New York guided his infantry into position behind the welcome cover of stone fencing on the left of the 45th Pennsylvania, extending the right side of Cox's division. The 100th Pennsylvania, which had been sent forward earlier as skirmishers, was held in reserve.[24]

After nearly three hours of fitful shelling the field fell silent yet again. It was about four o'clock. "Not a gun was heard," Beauge recalled. "The two giants were taking breath for the final tussle." Finally, the anticipated orders were heard. "Attention, battalion! Shoulder arms! Forward, guide center, march!" Companies A and K of the 45th Pennsylvania advanced as skirmishers. About twenty rods through the cornfields, "scattering shots were heard from the front and Minié balls began to zip through the air from that direction." The rounds came from Thomas Drayton's Confederates, who found themselves alone as Tige Anderson's Brigade marched away to the right.

Thomas Drayton's command—tired, confused, and hungry—occupied a meandering L-shaped front. The 50th and 51st Georgia and Phillips Legion held the brigade's left on the far side of the Old Sharpsburg Road facing east, where they availed themselves of the stone fences around the Daniel Wise property. To their right on the other side of the road rested the 3rd South Carolina Battalion and the 15th South Carolina closest to the Wise cabin, which extended the line to the right facing generally south. These men were positioned along a narrow wooded road leading to the Old Mountain House that intersected the Old Sharpsburg Road near the Wise Farm. Much of this front boasted low stone walls, meaning only gun barrels and heads were visible to the advancing federals. Both of Drayton's flanks, however, were "in the air," with 300 yards of empty hillside between his right flank and Tige Anderson's left flank.[25]

As the Pennsylvania skirmishers from the 45th regiment crested the hill, gunfire zipped through their ranks, courtesy of Captain Daniel B. Miller's Company F of the 3rd South Carolina Battalion. The under-strength Palmetto battalion had installed itself south of the Old Sharpsburg Road, forming an

24 OR 1:439-440, 441; Beauge, "The Forty-Fifth at South Mountain," 51-52; Carman, *The Maryland Campaign*, 151.

25 Carman, *The Maryland Campaign*, 151-152; D. Augustus Dickert, *History of Kershaw's Brigade* (Dayton, Ohio: Morningside Bookshop edition, 1976), 174.

unfastened arc around the eastern and southern perimeters of Wise's cleared field.[26]

As this skirmish fire heated up so did the artillery fire, so much so that Willcox was ordered to silence the Confederate batteries "at all hazards." Intending to storm the heights with the 79th New York, Willcox rode up to Lieutenant Colonel Morrison and conveyed the dispatch, which he told the regimental commander was direct from General McClellan. Morrison drew his sword. "Stand up and prepare to charge!" he commanded his troops. The regiment numbered barely 300 men. In addition to those killed and wounded during the war's opening contests, disease had further devastated its ranks. When the line of men slowly emerged from its recumbent position, Willcox queried, "Is this your regiment?"

Morrison shouted back, "Yes, General, but if you will give me more men we'll take that battery!"[27]

Willcox had no intention of pressing the enemy with such a thin line. "No, I'll send another regiment," he responded. "Yours is too small." He relieved the Highlanders from their advanced position with the larger 45th Pennsylvania, with the New Yorkers following in close support.[28]

The dispositions were quickly made, and the Wolverines of the 17th, now supported by Major John I. Curtin's 45th Pennsylvania on their left, leaped over the stone fences and pressed forward rapidly. Lieutenant Colonel Gerhardt's 46th New York, also of Welsh's brigade, advanced *en echelon* on the left of the Pennsylvanians, holding the left flank of the advancing line. Once again, their left approached the right side of Jacob Cox's line of battle, which was just in front of Drayton's infantry. "I ordered the regiment to assist our brothers in the fight, and with hurrah and double-quick they came to the relief of the Thirtieth Ohio," Gerhardt reported.[29]

Major Curtin intended to go into the fight on horseback. Frightened by the roaring combat ahead, his steed refused to mount the stone wall. The ranks pressed forward steadily, leaving their commander behind. A frustrated Curtin

---

26 *Ibid*; Byron L. Williams, *The Old South Mountain Inn*, 45; Beauge, "The Forty-Fifth at South Mountain," 53.

27 OR, 428-429; Todd, *The Seventy-Ninth Highlanders*, 226-227, 231-232; Carman, *The Maryland Campaign*, 151.

28 Todd, *The Seventh-Ninth Highlanders*, 232; Beauge, "The Forty-Fifth at South Mountain," 52.

29 *Ibid.*; Carman, *The Maryland Campaign*, 151-152; OR, 1:441-442.

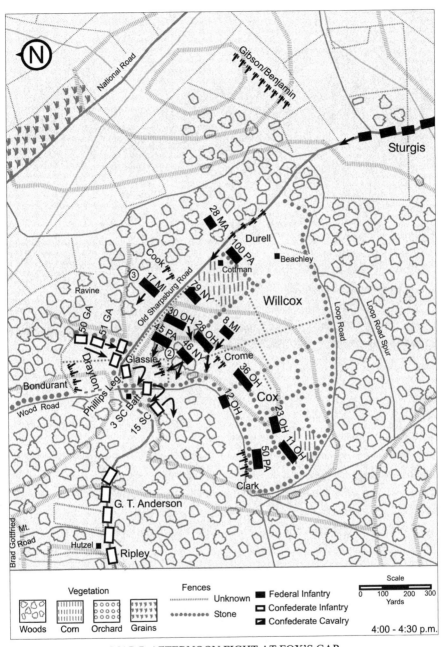

MAP 7. AFTERNOON FIGHT AT FOX'S GAP

dismounted and caught up with his regiment on foot as the riderless equine sought shelter in the woods.

"Steady, boys, keep cool!" shouted Curtin. Ahead, several of Drayton's men were spotted climbing over the fence outlining the crown of the hill and a spattering of musketry opened. In response, and without orders, the front ranks of the 45th Pennsylvania returned a volley. By doing so, they inadvertently instructed the Confederate gunners of the dimensions of their advance. Above the cracks and pops of the Harpers Ferry muskets, line officers pleaded with the men to cease firing. Private Andrew Bockus of Company G defiantly yelled back, "Don't care a damn! I saw a Johnny!"[30]

Shortly thereafter, Colonel Welsh gave the order to charge the rebel line. In gallant style and with shouts of enthusiasm erupting through the ranks, the men leapt forward. "The tangle of dense undergrowth in which they lay and through which they had to pass somewhat destroyed formation," historian Ezra Carman observed. "Notwithstanding the terrific fire from infantry and artillery . . . our troops continued to advance, utterly regardless of the slaughter in their ranks," Welsh reported. Branded with the peculiar ebullience conflict can produce, the

---

Above and facing page illustration: The ground across which the 17th Michigan made its memorable charge. *Henry F. Ballone*

30 *Ibid.*, 1:439-440; Beauge, "The Forty-Fifth at South Mountain," 52-53; Priest, *Before Antietam*, 195.

men "rushed down into the hollow, faced to the left, leaped over a stone fence," and came to the edge of the woods before Drayton's line, throwing his left flank into confusion.

"We rushed into them," recalled William Brearly of the 17th Michigan of Christ's brigade, "and all the time every man shouting as loud as he could—I got rather more excited than I wish to again." The fighting became desperate and determined. The Michiganders, according to Colonel Christ, "opened fire on the enemy with terrible effect, piling the road and field with his dead and wounded."[31]

Across the road on the Wolverines' left, Welsh's 45th Pennsylvania and 46th New York battled the 3rd South Carolina Battalion and perhaps part of the Phillips Legion at the tight distance of eighty yards. The two regiments rushed forward at an oblique to face the Confederates head on, with the Michiganders marching straight forward, parallel to the Old Sharpsburg Road. By doing do, the three-regiment attack formed a salient on the road. The line appeared to D. H. Hill as an inverted "V," reminding him of the formation of the 1st Mississippi Regiment at the Battle of Buena Vista during the Mexican War. "The V afforded a fine target from the pike, and I directed Captain Lane to open on it with his battery," Hill wrote.[32]

31 *Ibid.*; OR 1:428-429, 437-438; William Brearly, letter, September 26, 1862, as quoted in Bell Irvin Wiley, *The Life of Billy Yank* (Indianapolis: Bobbs Merrill, 1952), 84; Carman, *The Maryland Campaign*, 152; Willcox, "South Mountain and Antietam," in *Forgotten Valor*, 354-355.

32 Hill, *B&L* 2:571.

Lane's shells littered the ground in front of the 45th Pennsylvania, the fire increasing in frequency as the Confederates found the range and the regiment began taking casualties. "It was here that we sustained our heaviest loss," Beauge wrote. "Trees and fence rails were shivered to pieces by shells and grape and canister coming from the front or at right oblique. . . . Clouds of white-blue smoke hung over the field like a thick fog, and the air was stifling with the smell of gun-powder."[33]

The hellish combat had a deep impact on Beauge, for it was the regiment's "first pitched battle." Yet, for these men the charge of the nascent Michiganders advancing on their right was just as impressive. Isaac Steely, a veteran of Company C, wrote to Willcox nearly three decades after the South Mountain fight. "And by jabbers did you see the performance of the 17th Michigan on the right of the road," he asked. "I was of course somewhat occupied on our own side of the road. Yet I could not help keeping one eye on the Brave 17 Michigan. *God Bless Them,* I never saw the like; and not drilled troops either."[34]

Many of the inexperienced Wolverines stopped to fire from the relative defense of a natural hollow before climbing out to charge the wall as their supporting regiments pressed closer to the South Carolinians farther to the left. The bravery demonstrated by the 17th Michigan took its toll on the regiment as the battle line rolled forward toward Drayton's Georgians. Eli Sears, "the best, the most universally beloved" man of the 17th regiment, was one of those killed. According to a comrade, "a rifle ball, early in the engagement, struck him in the left breast and passed entirely through him." Sears could only speak in whispers by the time the comrade reached him. "He gave me his hand, with a pleasant smile, and told me he had but a few more hours to live . . . He died as heroes die . . ."[35]

*   *   *

As the musketry and artillery fighting for Fox's Gap continued, both sides brought up additional reinforcements to strengthen their lines. About 1:00

---

33 Beauge, "The Forty-Fifth at South Mountain," 53-54.

34 *Ibid.*; Isaac Steely to Orlando Bolivar Willcox, letter, July 13, 1891, in Robert Garth Scott, ed., *Forgotten Valor,* 355n.18.

35 Priest, *Before Antietam,* 193; David Lane, diary entry, October 9, 1862, in *A Soldier's Diary: The Story of a Volunteer, 1862-1865.*

p.m., Brigadier General Samuel D. Sturgis, commander of the Second Division of the IX Corps, was ordered to march from Middletown in the direction of Turner's Gap. Sturgis' division contained two brigades commanded by Brigadier Generals James Nagle and Edward Ferrero. Nagle's brigade included the 2nd Maryland, the 6th and 9th New Hampshire, and the 48th Pennsylvania. Ferrero's brigade was also composed of four regiments: the 21st and the 35th Massachusetts, the 51st New York, and the 51st Pennsylvania.[36]

"Fall in! Fall in!" The command echoed throughout the camp in the valley below the mountain. Captain Oliver Bosbyshell of the 48th Pennsylvania recalled the march through Middletown. "Quietly marching through the peaceful village of Middletown, thoughts of home were awakened in seeing the children going to Sabbath school, and their gathering seemed holy and happy, as viewed through the open door of the neat little church," wrote the captain. "How great the contrast—without and within—the troops marching to the field of mortal strife." The division made the march of five miles in two and a half hours, turning left off the National Turnpike about 3:30 p.m. to reach the field where the divisions of Orlando Willcox and Jacob Cox were engaged farther up the mountain with Thomas Drayton's Confederates. The 2nd Maryland and 6th New Hampshire continued up the turnpike toward Turner's Gap to reconnoiter. Meanwhile, the four 10-pound Parrotts of Captain Joseph C. Clark Jr.'s Battery E, 4th U.S. Artillery, were sent to support Cox's embattled right. The guns deployed facing northward in the direction of the National Turnpike.[37]

Ferrero's brigade led the division up the Old Sharpsburg Road. "Now, men, forward!" came the orders. "Right shoulder, shift! Quick time! Double quick!" Veterans from the 35th Massachusetts vividly recalled the experience. "We left the road, crossed the fields . . . and were soon close upon our batteries, which were fuming like furnaces, and sending shells into Turner's Pass on the right and up into the woods on the left." Halfway up the mountainside, the men met a wounded man carried on a stretcher and balanced on the shoulders of his comrades. One of his eyes had been shot out. "He shouted to us, as we

---

36 OR 1:178.

37 Oliver C. Bosbyshell, *The 48th in the War* (Philadelphia: Anvil Printing Co., 1895), 74. On the advance of the 48th Pennsylvania, see also Joseph Gould, *The Story of the Forty-Eighth* (Mt. Carmel, Pennsylvania: The 48th Pennsylvania Regimental Association, 1908), 77-78; Carman, *The Maryland Campaign*, 152; OR 1:443; Osborne, "Fourth Regiment," in Clark, ed., 1:245.

breathlessly hurried by: 'Forward, boys, forward! We're driving them! Don't let this scare you; give 'em hell! They can't stand cold steel!'" Just down the road, the stretcher made its way past the anxious men of the 21st Massachusetts. "The 17th is doing bully!" the wounded man shouted to the men of the approaching regiment.[38]

The Confederates also funneled additional men toward the escalating fight. When Drayton found himself on the receiving end of Willcox's onslaught, Colonel G. T. Anderson's Brigade was still following those of Roswell Ripley and George B. Anderson to the right. It was Ripley, it will be recalled, who ordered "Tige" Anderson to move by the right flank, which separated his (Anderson's) brigade from Drayton's right flank by at least 300 yards. When the first shots of the duel between Drayton and Willcox broke out, Ripley hastily ordered Anderson to reverse course and move by the left flank south of the Old Sharpsburg Road.[39]

Tige Anderson had already deployed the right wing of Colonel William J. Magill's 1st Georgia Regulars to the front as skirmishers. Unfortunately, no one thought to send an order recalling the Georgians or ordering them to change direction. The skirmish command, led by Captain Richard A. Wayne, continued moving to the front, where the captain and his men quickly became lost in the dense mountain laurels and rocky terrain. The balance of Anderson's command, meanwhile, thrashed its way back to close up with and support Drayton, but halted when Anderson recognized the danger facing Wayne's isolated skirmishers. A courier sent to find the skirmishers returned without success. Anderson continued on in accordance with his orders from Ripley.[40]

---

38 A Committee of the Regimental Association, *A History of the Thirty-fifth Regiment, Massachusetts Volunteers, 1862-1865* (Boston: Mills, Knight & Co., Printers, 1884), 26-27; James Pratt, Company H, 35th Massachusetts, letter, September 20, 1862, in James and Charlotte Pratt Collection, United States Army Military History Institute, Carlisle, Pennsylvania; Daniel Emerson Hurd, Company G, 9th New Hampshire Volunteers, "My Experiences in the Civil War," 19 August 1862 - 17 October 1863, typescript, in William Marvel Collection, United States Army Military History Institute, Carlisle, Pennsylvania; see also Edward O. Lord, ed., *History of the Ninth Regiment New Hampshire Volunteers* (Concord: Republican Press Association, 1895), 72, and William Marvel, *Race of the Soil: The Ninth New Hampshire Regiment in the Civil War* (Wilmington, North Carolina: Broadfoot Publishing, 1988), 39; Charles F. Walcott, *History of the 21st Massachusetts Volunteers in the War for the Preservation of the Union* (Boston: Houghton Mifflin, 1882), 189; Priest, *Before Antietam*, 197.

39 OR 1:908-909; Carman, *The Maryland Campaign*, 153.

40 *Ibid.*; Priest, *Before Antietam*, 196.

On the extreme Confederate right, meanwhile, George B. Anderson halted his brigade while Colonel Charles C. Tew advanced his own 2nd North Carolina and Captain Edwin A. Osborne's Company H of the 4th North Carolina to feel for the enemy. "Our progress was necessarily very slow, as the woods were very dense and the ground very rugged and mountainous," remembered Osborne. "We moved toward the south and swung around gradually toward the east, marching about three-fourths of a mile, when we discovered a heavy force of the enemy in a field on the crest of a ridge." Osborne informed General Anderson, who advanced his men toward the firing with caution, confidence, and care.[41]

The same assessment cannot be made of Roswell Ripley. The situation worsened considerably as Ripley pushed his brigade deeper into the woods and away from the escalating combat. Losing his connection with both George B. and George T. Anderson's brigades, Ripley embarked on a series of pharisaical marches and countermarches through the undergrowth. According to Colonel William L. DeRosset of the 3rd North Carolina, Ripley became so confused that at one point he advanced a "strong line" of skirmishers to his front, which allegedly detected the men of G. B. Anderson's Brigade instead of the enemy. Ripley only made matters worse when he sent a note to D. H. Hill indicating that he was "progressing finely." It was, of course, pure fiction, and Hill would never forget Ripley's inventive narrative. "Ripley did not draw trigger; why, I do not know," he documented in his report. After the war in his *Century* magazine piece, Hill issued the same abrupt indictment. "Before he returned the fighting was over, and his brigade did not fire a shot that day."[42]

In his own official report, Ripley attempted to pass the blame on to George B. Anderson for his own inept maneuvers. Ripley (who was in charge of all four brigades at that time), emphasized how far Anderson's command had extended to the right. "My own brigade had pressed up to within a short distance of the

---

41 *Ibid.*; Edwin A. Osborne, "Fourth Regiment," in Clark, ed., *Histories of the Several Regiments and Battalions from North Carolina in the Great War, 1861-1865*, 1:245-246.

42 *Ibid.*; OR 1:1020-1021; Hill, *B&L* 2:569; Colonel William L. DeRosset, 3rd North Carolina, "Ripley's Brigade at South Mountain," *Century Magazine* (December 1886): 308. The colonel's defense of Ripley's Brigade suggested that G. B. Anderson's Brigade was too far extended to the right, causing Ripley's Brigade to become easily lost. This feckless argument also suggests that not even the cautious and well-intentioned Anderson could navigate his way through the laurels of South Mountain; therefore, how could D. H. Hill expect Ripley to find the way? As noted in the main text, it was Ripley himself who first advanced this idea in his official report.

crest of the heights, and held its position under a noisy but comparatively harmless fire," he wrote. "But Anderson's Brigade having extended *far* to the right, it was for the time unsupported by any other troops." Perhaps Ripley failed to realize how this account of a "harmless fire" and Anderson's "unsupported" brigade only raised additional questions about his own decision-making that afternoon.[43]

Ripley's performance also impacted Tige Anderson. Having learned from Captain James G. Montgomery, his courier, that he was completely isolated and unsupported by Ripley's Brigade, and that Drayton's men were on the verge of collapse, Anderson re-crossed the road in an attempt to connect with Drayton's right flank. By then it was too late: heavy enemy columns were converging on the crest.[44]

*   *   *

The weight of the federal charge compressed its front lines in the fitful bloody journey up the slope of South Mountain. The Michiganders of the 17th moved to the left across the road and attached themselves to the right flank of the advancing 45th Pennsylvania, pressing the Pennsylvanians deeper into the woods. Lane's Battery ramped up its fire, snapping limbs and scattering leaves above the men while tearing others apart. As their limber chests grew lighter, their fire slackened. Almost as if permission had been granted to return, the 17th Michigan shifted right again to the east side of the road and continued slogging ahead.[45]

The arrival of the ten-pound Parrott rifles of Captain George W. Durell's Pennsylvania Light Artillery, attached to Sturgis' division, signaled the end of Lane's dominance over that part of the field. Durell's guns unlimbered on the right side of the road beyond Cook's pieces, which once more opened fire. "Durrell's Battery soon put a stop to this nonsense [of the Confederate artillery blasts]," Joseph Gould of the 48th Pennsylvania crowed. "The first shot it fired landed right over [one of the enemy guns], and a great scampering took place. Nothing could induce those fellows to return for their gun," he continued. D.

---

43 OR 1:1031-1032.

44 *Ibid.*, 1:909; Carman, *The Maryland Campaign*, 153.

45 *Ibid.*, 152; Priest, *Before Antietam*, 196.

H. Hill agreed. "The heavy batteries promptly replied, showing such excellent practice that Lane's guns were soon silenced."[46]

The Confederate artillery fire gradually fell away, but the infantry firing on both sides roared louder than ever. The federal lines were strengthened when Sturgis' division was finally called up to deploy for action. Colonel Ferrero's brigade would go into line on both sides of the Old Sharpsburg Road, encasing Durell's guns with supporting infantry. The 51st Pennsylvania aligned to its front, while the 51st New York went to ground behind the guns. "Our Regt lay in an open field near the edge of a wood into which the enemy had been driven, and had just got our position and laid down, when the enemy opened fire on us from the woods directly in front of us," George Washington Whitman of the 51st New York wrote home to his mother. "Our regt was ordered to lie close and not fire a shot untill the enemy advanced out of the woods and into the field where we lay."[47]

Also to the rear of Durell's guns but across the road, the 35th Massachusetts deployed its line of 800 effectives on the edge of a natural sunken road littered with dead and wounded Confederates. Farther to the rear, near the field hospital at the Coffman farm, the 21st Massachusetts rested its right flank on the western edge of the road. The 79th New York Highlanders had formed a parallel line ahead of them, pinching the Coffman farmhouse between their lines.[48] To support Ferrero, Brigadier General James Nagle sent in his remaining two regiments: the 900 men of the novice 9th New Hampshire and the anthracite coal miners of the veteran 48th Pennsylvania. These regiments filed off the Old Sharpsburg Road to the left. The Pennsylvanians lined up on the western boundary of the Martz farm, at that time parallel and ahead of the Highlanders. The Granite State men shifted into the Beachley clearing. The firing was hotter left of the road, so the men were ordered to load

46 Ibid.; Charles A. Cussel, Durell's Battery in the Civil War (Philadelphia: Craig, Finley, & Co., 1900), 73; Gould, The Story of the Forty-Eighth, 75; Hill, B&L 2:571; see also the Report of the Antietam Battlefield Memorial Commission of Pennsylvania and Ceremonies at the Dedication of the Monuments Erected by the Commonwealth of Pennsylvania (Harrisburg: State Printer, 1906), 216.

47 Ibid.; Priest, Before Antietam, 197-198; George Washington Whitman, letter to his mother, September 21, 1862, in Jerome M. Loving, ed., Civil War Letters of George Washington Whitman (Durham, North Carolina: Duke University Press, 1975), 66.

48 Ibid.; Committee of the Regimental Association, A History of the Thirty-fifth Regiment, Massachusetts Volunteers, 26-28; see also James Madison Stone, Company K, 21st Massachusetts, Personal Recollections of the Civil War (Boston: By the Author, 1918), 85.

their rifles. "Many of them had never been loaded and I presume we were clumsy at the job," Daniel Emerson Hurd of Company G admitted.[49]

It took Sturgis nearly an hour to deploy his division, which was still being positioned when the final division of the IX Corps arrived on the field. Brigadier General Isaac Rodman's two brigades left Frederick at 3:00 a.m. that morning and tramped into Middletown seven hours later. The men resumed their march at 2:00 p.m. and reached the pass in two or three hours. One member of the newly arriving troops belonged to Hawkins' Zouaves (9th New York) under Colonel Harrison S. Fairchild. He looked behind him and caught a glimpse of the advance, which he described as "a monstrous, crawling, blue-back snake, miles long, quilled with the silver slant of muskets at a 'shoulder,' its sluggish tail writhing slowly up over the distant eastern ridge, its bruised head weltering in the road and smoke upon the crest above."[50]

Colonel Fairchild commanded the division's first brigade, consisting of the 9th, 89th, and 103rd New York regiments, all of which were ordered to support Clark's guns on Cox's far left flank. Colonel Edward Harland led the second brigade of New Englanders consisting the 8th, 11th, and 16th Connecticut and the 4th Rhode Island. Harland's men were ordered to support Willcox's right, but they would not see much action.[51]

* * *

When the Michiganders re-acquired their position in the clearing north of the Old Sharpsburg Road, they did not remain in place for long. Using the terrain to maneuver with advantage, the right companies commenced a left wheel that their officers hoped would put them into a position to pour an enfilading musketry fire into the flank of Drayton's Georgia regiments, the left

---

49 OR 1:443, 445-446; Priest, *Before Antietam*, 198-199; Marvel, *Race of the Soil*, 37-42; Daniel Hurd, "My Experiences in the Civil War," William Marvel Collection, United States Army Military History Institute, Carlisle, Pennsylvania. The coal miners of the 48th Pennsylvania would earn a place in history July 30, 1864, when their colonel, a mining engineer named Henry Pleasants, devised an ingenious plan to burrow a narrow shaft leading underneath the Confederate lines at Petersburg, Virginia, more than 500 feet in length. The explosives planted below the Confederates detonated and formed a large depression. The federals rushed into the "horrid pit" and were slaughtered in what became known as the Battle of the Crater.

50 David L. Thompson, "Memoir of David L. Thompson," in *B&L* 2:558.

51 Carman, *The Maryland Campaign*, 153; OR 1:178, 449-450.

pair of which (the 50th and 51st) had turned to their right and taken up a position along the road to help repel the assault to the south. Even though this Southern fire was damaging, the Union fire and pressure was beginning to tell. "The Johnnies were ready to quit," Private Beauge of the 45th Pennsylvania observed as his regiment pressed along the Old Sharpsburg Road and closed with the enemy line. "Many of them were shot down while climbing the stone wall in their rear trying to get away."[52]

From their advanced position behind Wise's stone wall, Beauge's regiment put down a steady heavy fire that nearly expended its ammunition. The 100th Pennsylvania (also known as the "Round Heads") came up to relieve them on the firing line. One of the "Round Heads" was Private Pettit. The enemy, he explained, "were in a lane behind a stone fence and we were in the edge of a woods with a clear lot between us." The private recalled firing eleven rounds before the opponents to his front began streaming to the rear.[53]

Wounded Union men (and likely some that were not) were also pushing to the rear through the ranks of the 48th Pennsylvania. Sensing the nature of the fight ahead, the regiment shoved onward. "Forward, Forty-eighth!" the line officers bellowed. These Pennsylvanians wedged themselves into the line between the 100th Pennsylvania on their right, and Lieutenant Colonel Joseph Gerhardt's 46th New York on their left.[54]

Almost immediately after the Pennsylvanians advanced, a staff officer pulled in his mount before Colonel Enoch Q. Fellows of the 9th New Hampshire. Gerhardt's New Yorkers had also expended their ammunition and were beginning to retire. "Colonel! Hurry up those men. They're needed immediately," yelled the staff officer.[55] Fellows' New Englanders fixed bayonets, double-quicked through the cornfield to the front until they reached the stone wall near the crest, and assumed the position held by the 46th New York. "Bullets from the enemy were whistling just about our heads and were

---

52 Beauge, "The Forty-Fifth at South Mountain," 54.

53 *Ibid.*; Frederick Pettit, letter, September 20, 1862, in Civil War Times Illustrated Collection, United States Army Military History Institute, Carlisle, Pennsylvania.

54 Joseph Gould, *The Story of the Forty-Eighth*, 77-78; Oliver C. Bosbyshell, *The 48th in the War*, 75-76; see also John Michael Priest, ed., *Captain James Wren's Diary: From New Bern to Fredericksburg* (Shippensburg, Pennsylvania: White Mane Publishing Co., Inc., 1990), 65-66; Priest, *Before Antietam*, 203.

55 William Marvel, *Race of the Soil*, 39.

not particularly agreeable music," Daniel Hurd of Company G admitted. "A little way up in the cornfield we came to a large double stone wall, which we climbed as best we could, and soon reached a nearly level place of woody ground, and a Virginia rail fence, where we were ordered to fire."[56]

The early evening darkness of autumn was beginning to settle over the smoky wooded hillside, slowly obscuring the hotly contested combat. The men of the 17th Michigan, not as inexperienced as they had been a few hours earlier, completed their left wheel beyond Drayton's exposed left flank. The firing, coupled with the thousands of rounds pouring in from the front, unhinged the left side of Drayton's line. "Our boys sent them trembling helter skelter up the hill," John Morton noted in his diary. D. H. Hill echoed the federal private in his official report of the fighting along Drayton's front when he wrote, "His men were soon beaten and went streaming to the rear." Bondurant limbered his guns, ending his hours of effective harassment of the aggressive blue-clad enemy. The retreat spread through the Confederate ranks as hundreds of federals jumped the walls and fences to seize the high ground at Fox's Gap.

Other Confederate reinforcements were heading for the crest from the far side of the mountain, but they would not arrive in time to save Drayton's embattled position. Later, long after the fighting ended, artillerist John Purifoy penned a simple, chilling conclusion delivered ever so matter-of-factly: "The arrival of Longstreet and darkness saved us from annihilation."[57]

*   *   *

As Thomas Drayton's front crumbled and tumbled rearward, additional Confederate reinforcements were struggling their way to the crest. The two brigades belonged to Brigadier General John Bell Hood's veteran division. Their march up the mountainside "taxed to the utmost the energies of every man" remembered a member of the 4th Alabama. Hood's first brigade, the "Texas Brigade," was led by Colonel William T. Wofford and consisted of the

---

56 Daniel Emerson Hurd, "My Experiences in the Civil War," William Marvel Collection, United States Army Military History Institute, Carlisle, Pennsylvania; Carman, *The Maryland Campaign*, 154.

57 John Morton, letter, September 24, 1862, in Civil War Miscellaneous Collection, United States Army Military History Institute, Carlisle, Pennsylvania; OR 1:1021; John Purifoy to Ezra A. Carman, letters, July 21, 1900 and July 15, 1900, in Ezra Carman Papers, Manuscript Division, Library of Congress, Washington, D.C.

1st, 4th, and 5th Texas regiments, the 18th Georgia, and the South Carolina Hampton Legion. Colonel Evander M. Law led Hood's other brigade, which included the 4th Alabama, 2nd and 11th Mississippi, and the 6th North Carolina.[58]

Although he was with his division as it marched along the narrow winding roads, Hood rode in the rear under arrest. He was detained on August 30 on the march from the Second Manassas battlefield after an argument with Brigadier General Nathan G. "Shanks" Evans about the ownership of captured federal ambulance wagons. Simply put, Shanks (who ranked Hood via the date of his commission) demanded Hood turn the wagons over to him. Providing them to the army was one thing, but Hood believed giving them to another brigadier who had no right to them was something else altogether. The fiery Texas brigadier refused the demand and Evans placed him under arrest. General Lee allowed Hood to remain with his men, but not in command of them. "The ambulances I had captured were destined to cause me somewhat of annoyance, which I had nowise anticipated at the time I assigned them to my troops for the use of their sick and wounded," Hood recalled in his memoir.[59]

"I could hear the men, as they filed up the ascent, cry out along the line, and 'Give us Hood!'" the Texas general recollected. As his men drew near the base of the mountain, Hood was approached by Colonel Robert H. Chilton, Lee's assistant adjutant general. Chilton slipped the brigadier a note informing him that General Lee wished to speak with him. Hood dismounted and walked to meet with Lee, who had ridden to the base of South Mountain with James Longstreet.

"General," Lee began, "I am just upon the eve of entering into battle, and with one of my best officers under arrest. If you will merely say that you regret this occurrence, I will release you and restore you to the command of your division." It was a generous offer, and one that underscored just how much Lee wanted Hood back at the head of his veteran troops.

58 R. T. Coles, *From Huntsville to Appomattox*, ed. Jeffrey D. Stocker (Knoxville: The University of Tennessee Press, 1996), 62-63; OR 1:805.

59 John Bell Hood, *Advance and Retreat: Personal Experiences in the United States and Confederate States Armies* (New Orleans: For the Hood Orphan Memorial Fund by G. T. Beauregard, 1880; reprint, Lincoln: The University of Nebraska Press, 1996), 38-39; Donald E. Everett, ed., *Chaplain Davis and Hood's Brigade* (San Antonio: Principia Press of Trinity University, 1962), 124-125. See also Richard M. McMurry, *John Bell Hood and the War for Southern Independence* (Lincoln: University of Nebraska Press, 1982), 56-59.

Hood refused. "I am unable to do so, since I cannot admit or see the justness of General Evans's demand for the ambulances my men have captured," the stubborn brigadier responded, who went on to argue in his own defense.

The frustrated army commander finally outmaneuvered his subordinate by concluding, "Well, I will suspend your arrest till the impending battle is decided."

With a kind welcome from his troops, an elated Hood remounted and galloped to the front of his column. Longstreet, who by now had reached the summit of South Mountain, ordered Hood's men to oblique to the right and fall into line in an effort to support Drayton. But it was too late.[60] "We met Drayton's brigade falling back in confusion, stating that they had been flanked," Adjutant Robert T. Coles of the 4th Alabama recalled. When he learned of Drayton's fate, Hood ordered Wofford and Law to move their brigades to the left and fix bayonets. "We marched on through the wood as rapidly as the obstacles in our passage would admit," Hood wrote. "Each step forward brought nearer and nearer to us the heavy Federal lines, as they advanced, cheering over their success and the possession of our dead and wounded."[61]

When the federals appeared to be about seventy-five yards in advance of his division, Hood ordered his infantry to charge. They swept through the woods with a hearty rebel yell, pushing back the federals and regaining some of the lost ground. "Several attempts were made to charge our lines," Chaplain Davis of Hood's command recalled, "but they were only able to utter a few huzzas and move up but a few paces." The gloomy dusk was making it more difficult to not only identify who was who, but to wage effective combat. Another lull engulfed the gap. For better protection and some rest, many of Hood's men slipped into a shallow sunken road. Among the few early casualties was Lieutenant Colonel Owen K. McLemore of the 4th Alabama, shot through the shoulder.[62]

*   *   *

60 *Ibid.*

61 Coles, *From Huntsville to Appomattox*, 63; Hood, *Advance and Retreat*, 59-60; Everett, ed., *Chaplain Davis and Hood's Texas Brigade*, 123; OR 1:922; Priest, *Before Antietam*, 187-188.

62 Coles, *From Huntsville to Appomattox*, 63-64; Hood, *Advance and Retreat*, 40-41; Everett, ed., *Chaplain Davis and Hood's Texas Brigade*, 123-124; Carman, *The Maryland Campaign*, 154.

By this time G. B. Anderson's Brigade had finally maneuvered its way back (left) to the top of the mountain in search of an enemy to strike or a Confederate line to support. Because of the trees, rocks, laurel, and growing darkness, however, no one could see anything down the hillside. Anderson ordered a skirmish line to slip slope to ascertain the location of the enemy. An aide returned a short time later to explain the brigade was on the enemy's left flank and that a quick strike could overrun an enemy battery (Clark's) and maybe roll up the federal flank.

What G. B. Anderson did not know was that the enemy was there in strength, and Colonel Fairchild's brigade line was waiting for them. "The brigade was formed like the letter L," noted Matthew J. Graham, the historian of the 9th New York (Hawkins' Zouaves). The long leg of the "L" was shaped by the Zouaves (9th New York) supporting Clark's battery, their line running generally east to west. Bending back perpendicular was the shorter stem held by the 89th and 103rd New York regiments. They had orders to hold fire until commanded to do otherwise. "This was being done and I was wondering that still no enemy was visible," Charles F. Johnson of Company I of the 9th New York recalled, "when a long rattling volley of musketry burst upon us."[63]

At nearly the same moment, a skirmish line from the 4th North Carolina under Captain Edwin A. Osborne fumbled through the dense undergrowth and ensuing darkness on the left of G.B. Anderson's line. Discovered by the men of Lieutenant Colonel Joshua Sigfried's 48th Pennsylvania amidst the tangled mountain laurel, "they opened upon [us] a heavy fire," recalled Osborne. "Our men received them firmly, returning their fire with spirit."[64]

Gunfire erupted at both ends of G. B. Anderson's line, and he ordered an aggressive push forward. His right two regiments, the 2nd and 13th North Carolina, fired a ragged round toward Clark's gunners during their approach. The shadows were growing so long that the neighboring men of the 9th New Hampshire could not easily discern the scattered enemy from Sigfried's own troops. "[They imagined] that the battle had opened & the whole regiment opened fire & fired direct into my line of skirmishers in the frunt," Company

63 Matthew J. Graham, *History of the Ninth New York Volunteers (Hawkins' Zouaves): Being a History of the Regiment and Veteran Association from 1860 to 1900* (New York: E.P. Coby & Co., 1900), 271-272; Carman, *The Maryland Campaign*, 154; OR, 1:449-450; Charles F. Johnson, *The Long Roll* (East Aurora, New York: The Roycrofters, 1911), 184-186.

64 Priest, ed. *From New Bern to Fredericksburg*, 65-66; Osborne, "Fourth Regiment," in Clark, ed., 1:245-246.

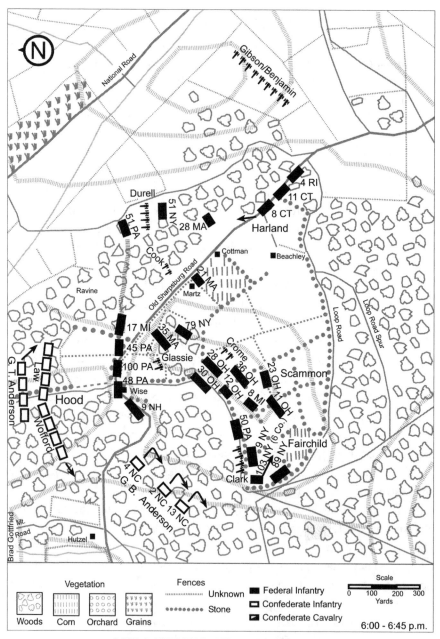

MAP 8. EVENING FIGHT AT FOX'S GAP

B's Captain James Wren of the 48th Pennsylvania recalled. Not all the Granite State volunteers fired into the friendly ranks. "Part of our regiment saw someone to fire at, no doubt, but I didn't," Daniel Hurd admitted. "You must remember that 900 men strung out in double file would reach some distance and while the firing from the enemy left no doubt they were not far away, they were not in sight of where our part of the regiment [was] at that moment."[65]

The "long rattling volley" was the result of an aggressive push by Anderson, who had deployed his men in line and shoved them forward. The 4th North Carolina, which formed Anderson's left, may have veered to the left and struck the left flank of the 9th New Hampshire of James Nagle's brigade, which fell back before collecting itself and exchanging fire with the Tar Heels of the 4th until darkness ended the fighting.

Anderson's right two regiments, the 2nd and 13th North Carlina, fired a ragged round toward Clark's gunners during their approach. The sudden shock of the enemy's irregular firing sent tremors throughout the battery and the ranks of Fairchild's just-arrived brigade. Many in the 103rd New York, holding the center of the line, bolted for the rear while most of Fairchild's other men, including those in the 89th New York, dropped flat on their faces as the first volley passed uncomfortably close above them. "They were coming at us like a pack of Blood-Hounds," Sgt. George Magusta Englis of Company K explained. Major Edward Jardine, their commander, stood and roared, "Eighty-ninth New York, what in hell are you about?" Despite the orders to hold fire until a command to do so had been issued, the 89th's Corporal Charles Curie of Company C, who was acting as the left-general guide, cocked his musket and prepared to fire. Jardine heard Curie's lock click as it snapped back. "Put down that hammer!" bellowed the officer. "You know what the orders are. We want to meet the charge with the bayonet."[66]

When the immediate shock of the enemy fire subsided, Jardine issued the command for which Curie and so many others had been waiting: "[open] a steady, well-directed fire." According to Sergeant Englis, the volley that followed sent the rebels "howling in every direction." Another wrote home, "after they fired the first round we rose up and let it into them . . . and they skedaddled." Some in the 103rd New York joined their comrades and began

---

65 *Ibid.*; Daniel Emerson Hurd, "My Experiences in the Civil War," in William Marvel Collection, United States Army Military History Institute, Carlisle, Pennsylvania.

66 *Ibid.*

"firing volley after volley" into the North Carolinians. "For a moment bullets seemed to fill the air and matters assumed a serious aspect," Graham wrote from the post of the 9th New York. At one point, Johnson remembered a "shower" of bullets rushing "madly" over his head. Clark's men joined in with double-canister rounds, as did the 50th Pennsylvania aligned to the right of the embattled battery. Within a handful of minutes the sharp fighting ended almost as quickly as it began. Johnson of the 9th New York recalled the rebel recoil with clever, if dry, wit. "I could hardly help laughing at the precipitant retreat of the supernumeraries down the hill," he wrote. A North Carolinian noted simply, "Night drew on and put a stop to the engagement. We then returned to the road from whence we had started early in the afternoon." The 89th New York collected 150 stands of arms and thirty prisoners at a cost of just two killed and eighteen wounded.[67]

Likewise, the push of Confederates across the Wise property against the 48th Pennsylvania and 9th New Hampshire ended just as "suddenly and unexpectedly" with the obscurity of night. In the 9th New Hampshire, Daniel Hurd reported 26 men wounded or missing. For Captain James Wren in the 48th Pennsylvania, the large pile of enemy knapsacks approximated the value of the 89th New York's newly acquired armory. "In this Battle I Captured a large pile of knapsacks belonging to the enemy," he gloated. Ironically, in sifting through the heap of possessions, he uncovered a number of his own regiment's knapsacks that had been captured at Second Manassas just two weeks earlier. "Now we are even with the Johnnys in capturing of Knapsacks," he concluded with smug satisfaction.[68]

Beaming with the same pride, the Zouaves of the 9th New York congratulated their equally happy comrades in the 89th New York, both part of Fairchild's command. As far as they were concerned, the enemy had been pushed off the mountain and the battle won. Moments later, however, the fitful silence was again broken on the federal right. "We were engaged in applauding

67 *Ibid.*; George Magusta Englis, letter, September 20, 1862, in Eileen Mae Knapp Patch, ed., *This From George: The Civil War Letters of Sergeant George Magusta English, Company K, 89th New York Regiment of Volunteer Infantry* (Binghamton, New York: Broome County Historical Society, 2001), 39; Graham, *Ninth New York Volunteers*, 272-273; Osborne, "Fourth Regiment," in Clark, ed., 1:245-246.

68 Daniel Emerson Hurd, "My Experiences in the Civil War," in William Marvel Collection, United States Army Military History Institute, Carlisle, Pennsylvania; Priest, ed., *From New Bern to Fredericksburg*, 66.

the gallant Eighty-ninth for its noble conduct," recalled one of the Zouaves, "when again the sound of musketry rattled harshly, but more distantly, upon our ears."[69]

*   *   *

The sun was setting and the federals were firmly in possession of the terrain previously held by the Confederates. Like their comrades in Fairchild's brigade on the federal left, Captain Gabriel Campbell and a squad of men from the 17th Michigan near the intersection of the ridge road and the Old Sharpsburg Road likewise concluded the enemy was in retreat and the battle won. They began scouring the woods for their wounded comrades. Many in Ferrero's brigade— which was again drawn up in a column of lines with the 51st New York and 51st Pennsylvania strung out in front and the 21st Massachusetts to the rear—also supposed the enemy had disappeared and the fighting was at an end. Colonel John F. Hartranft ordered his 51st Pennsylvania to cross to the opposite side of the Old Sharpsburg Road, stack arms, and make coffee for the evening. As they moved to do so, his men took note of the grisly evidence of the afternoon's battle that surrounded them including a "heap of rebel bodies"—forty-seven in a space of thirty by ten feet. Another pile contained ninety-seven stiffening corpses piled up across one another.[70]

General Reno rode up behind the brigade, escorted by his medical doctor Calvin Cutter, and Martin Ficken and Alexander H. Wood, two orderlies from Company L of the 6th New York Cavalry. Reno had spent the morning and afternoon with Generals McClellan, Burnside, and Pleasonton at army headquarters in the valley. With the situation seemingly under control on this end of the battlefield, Reno's purposes in now appearing on the mountaintop were twofold. First, he arrived to congratulate the victorious brigades of his corps for having pushed back the rebels. Second, and perhaps most important, he wanted to survey the ground for himself because he did not fully understand why his men were unable to press farther up the mountain to the summit of

69 Johnson, *The Long Roll*, 186.

70 Priest, *Before Antietam*, 212-213; *History of the 35th Regiment Massachusetts Volunteers*, 29-30; Thomas H. Parker, *History of the 51st Regiment of Pennsylvania Volunteers and Veteran Volunteers* (Philadelphia: King and Baird Printers, 1869), 225; see also *Report of the Antietam Battlefield Memorial Commission of Pennsylvania*, 100-102.

Turner's Gap. After a brief consultation with Jacob Cox, Reno set out to uncover—and potentially to help unravel—whatever obstacle remained before his victorious forces. "I met General Reno and two orderlies riding up the road," recalled a private in the 30th Ohio of Scammon's brigade. "He stopped and asked me what troops were in front." The IX Corps commander had motioned toward the woods where Hood's lines were concealed before riding on without comment.[71]

As Campbell and his comrades of the 17th Michigan continued searching for bodies, a contingent of unarmed Confederates appeared in the woods at the corner of Wise's field. Upon closer inspection, Campbell noticed they were looting bodies. A few of the rifles the rebs discovered broke the stillness. Campbell yelled at them to cease firing; Southern curses replaced flying minie balls. Nearby and unsettled by the demonstration, General Willcox ordered Ferrero to scout Wise's woods. The brigade commander called forward Colonel Edward A. Wild's 35th Massachusetts, a decision that upset Captain Charles F. Walcott of the 21st Massachusetts. "Just as sun set, the 35th Massachusetts were ordered to feel the woods in front, while the three old regiments of the brigade were formed in the cleared space," explained Walcott. "General Ferrero had no right to assign a new regiment to this duty," he continued, citing their want of drill and "utter fighting inexperience."[72]

Following orders, the Bay Staters barreled into the woods. "Here was a scene of unavoidable confusion," admitted the regiment's historian. "Such a shouting of company letters, 'Company A!' 'Company B!' 'Company C!' etc., was never heard before nor since." The heavy undergrowth dissolved the already tenuous cohesion between these companies of untried soldiers. After plunging some distance into the woods in the thickening darkness and not stumbling into any enemy, the men turned back; the left companies began massing to the rear of Walcott's 21st Massachusetts, extending their lines farther right. Their noisy foray, however, had awakened the recoiled troops of "Tige" Anderson, who moved up on Hood's left with a certain renewed vigor. The 35th Massachusetts was filtering back to Ferrero's column when General

---

71 Carman, *The Maryland Campaign*, 154; *National Tribune*, August 23, 1883; A. H. Wood, "How Reno Fell," *National Tribune*, July 6, 1883.

72 *Ibid.*; Priest, *Before Antietam*, 212-213; Charles Walcott, *History of the 21st Massachusetts Volunteers in the War for the Preservation of the Union, 1861-1865* (Boston: Houghton Mifflin, 1882), 189, 189n2.

Reno completed his gallop to the front line, ready to establish outposts for the night. The 51st New York left or below the Old Sharpsburg Road was ordered to lie close together and not fire a shot. Company H of the 51st Pennsylvania was leading the regiment across the Old Sharpsburg Road. "Right face, forward, march!" a line officer shouted. "File right!" Companies A, F, D, and I made it across the road with a portion of the color company (Company C) when a tight hail of musketry fire cut through the gloomy darkness from a distance of about thirty yards.[73]

"The surprise was complete," recalled a veteran of the 35th Massachusetts. "The darkening forest was lined with flashes of the hostile guns, and their bullets cut the earth about our feet." "There was a sudden fusillade—five or six shots in about a couple of seconds," recalled Captain Gabriel Campbell. "There was at once commotion among the Reno horsemen, a dismounting and a catching of someone." Campbell continued:

> Evidently the rebels had begun to form behind the stone fence. Quickly an orderly [came] back leading several horses. To my inquiry, 'what happened,' he answered, 'Reno is shot!' Immediately men bearing the General on a blanket follow[ed]. They pause[d] as they [met] me, and [were] glad of a little assistance in carrying the middle of the blanket . . . [74]

A fatal bullet had passed through Reno's chest while another round entered his thigh and groin. As he tumbled to the ground, the wounded general noticed Brigadier General Samuel Davis Sturgis, his West Point classmate and personal friend. "Is it anything serious, Jesse?" the division commander called out.

"Hallo, Sam, I am dead!" Reno replied, gasping for breath. Sturgis refused to accept Reno's dismal assessment and replied, "Oh, no, General, not so bad as that, I hope!"

"Sam, it's all up with me," the fatally struck general continued. "Yes, yes, I'm dead—good-bye!" The makeshift stretcher bearers placed the fallen officer under a tree at the foot of a hill. "Boys, I can be with you no longer in body, but I

---

73 *Ibid*; Walcott, *History of the 21st Massachusetts Volunteer Infantry*, 190; *History of the 35th Regiment Massachusetts Volunteers*, 29; James Pratt, diary entry, September 20, 1862, in James and Charlotte Pratt Collection, United States Military History Institute, Carlisle, Pennsylvania; see also Robert West, "Reno's Death," *National Tribune*, August 9, 1883; OR 1:909.

74 Gabriel Campbell, letter to Ezra Carman, August 23, 1899, Carman Papers, Antietam National Battlefield Site, Sharpsburg, Maryland, as quoted in Priest, *Before Antietam*, 216-218.

am with you in spirit," Reno uttered. "He fell, and from that moment seemed to have a knowledge that he could not survive," recorded surgeon Thomas Ellis. "He was at once carried to the rear and attended by his surgeon, Dr. Cutter."

It was just after 7:00 p.m. when Jesse Lee Reno died. His body was taken to Baltimore, where it was embalmed before making the journey back to Boston, where his newly widowed Mary awaited her husband's final arrival with their two sons.[75]

The suddenness of the musketry attack that claimed Reno's life threw the Bay Staters into a deeper confusion. "Fire! Fire!" some of the line officers shouted. More calmly and to no avail, others ordered the same men to cease firing. The result was a confused, indiscriminate pattering of small arms fire in several directions wherever any enlisted man believed he witnessed enemy movement.[76]

The situation was exacerbated when a ball shattered Colonel Wild's left arm. "When word spread that Colonel Wild was hit, there was some hesitation as to who should succeed him, the lieutenant-colonel not being found at first," recalled the 35th's regimental historian. Captain Stephen Andrews, commanding Company A, finally took charge of the floundering men. The reaction of the Massachusetts men to the wounding of their colonel was an increase in the intensity of their fire. Unfortunately, much of it was into the ranks of the four companies of the 51st Pennsylvania that had made it across the Old Sharpsburg Road. When the New Yorkers of the 51st heard the firing, they "sprang to their feet," wrote Private George Washington Whitman to his mother, who added that he could "hear the bullets whiz all around." The New Yorkers interposed themselves between the two regiments and threatened to

75 Parker, *History of the 51st Regiment of Pennsylvania Volunteers and Veteran Volunteers*, 227; see also Todd, *The Seventy-Ninth Highlanders*, 234-235; Gould, *The Story of the Forty-Eighth*, 78-79; OR 1:418; Thomas T. Ellis, *Leaves from the Diary of an Army Surgeon, or Incidents of Field, Camp, and Hospital Life* (New York: John Bradburn, 1863), 257; for the heretofore best treatment of the life of Major General Jesse Lee Reno, see William F. McConnell, *Remember Reno: A Biography of Major General Jesse Lee Reno* (Shippensburg: White Mane Publishing Co., Inc., 1996), 80-87; *Norwalk* (Ohio) *Weekly Register*, 30 September 1862.

76 Walcott, *History of the 21st Massachusetts Volunteer Infantry*, 190; *History of the 35th Regiment Massachusetts Volunteers*, 29; James Pratt, diary entry, September 20, 1862, in James and Charlotte Pratt Collection, United States Military History Institute, Carlisle, Pennsylvania; see also Robert West, "Reno's Death," *National Tribune*, August 9, 1883; OR 1:909; George Washington Whitman, letter to his mother, September 21, 1862, in Jerome M. Loving, ed., *Civil War Letters of George Washington Whitman*, 66.

fire upon the 35th Massachusetts if its members did not cease firing. Only then did the New Englanders cease pulling triggers.[77]

It took about fifteen minutes for the enemy fire to slacken and then fall off altogether. The field was quiet once again. "While the enemy's musketry was dying away, we lay with bayonets fixed, peering into the darkness over the stone wall . . . awaiting the flank attack which did not come," recorded the history of the 35th Massachusetts. The fighting was finally over. "We knew [the enemy] had [fallen] back out of range so we ceased firing and lay down again until daylight when we found there was no enemy in sight," a Pennsylvania private wrote home.[78] "The rebels were again obliged to fall back, leaving their wounded, and some prisoners, in our hands," confirmed Surgeon Thomas Ellis.[79] The debris of war littered the ground and told its own story, concluded federal   Thomas Livermore. "A lot of gray clothes, old knapsacks, and equipments thrown down by the road showed us how precipitate had been the retreat of the rebels."[80]

*   *   *

The unfortunate friendly fire episode launched by the inexperienced men of the 35th Massachusetts has been misappropriated to suggest that General Reno was not shot by Hood's men, but was instead felled by his own. Figuring most prominently into this meme was Charles F. Walcott, a captain in the 21st Massachusetts and the outfit's regimental historian. Walcott's work claimed that Reno was shot by his fellow New Englanders. The captain harbored an acerbic disdain for the 35th Massachusetts. For example, his lengthy criticism of

---

77 *Ibid.*; Carman, *The Maryland Campaign*, 155; Parker, *History of the 51st Regiment of Pennsylvania Volunteers*, 225-226. Wild's arm was amputated at the shoulder. He later won fame as the general in command of "Wild's African Brigade" and for a period was placed in command of the contraband camp on Roanoke Island, North Carolina, described as an early "rehearsal for Reconstruction." See also Richard Alden Huebner, ed., *Meserve Civil War Record* (Oak Park, Michigan: RAH Publications, 1987), 13-16; Priest, *Before Antietam*, 219.

78 *History of the 35th Regiment Massachusetts Volunteers*, 30-31; George Washington Whitman, letter to his mother, 21 September 1862, in Jerome M. Loving, ed., *Civil War Letters of George Washington Whitman*, 67; see also Walcott, *History of the 21st Massachusetts*, 190.

79 Ellis, *Leaves from the Diary of an Army Surgeon*, 257.

80 Thomas Leonard Livermore, "Memoir of Thomas Leonard Livermore," in *Days and Events*, 1860-1866 (Boston: Houghton, Mifflin & Co., 1920), 121.

that regiment's assignment by Ferrero to reconnoiter the woods was jaundiced by a streak of jealousy. The 21st Massachusetts' position in the rear forced the men to "hug the ground" and thus prevented them from engaging the enemy. Decades later, Walcott infused his prose with a longing to have participated more actively in the battle. At the very least he allowed the substantiation of one unfortunate encounter to stand as evidence of an even more fatal occurrence.

Walcott was not the only participant to claim that Reno fell victim to friendly fire. Another account, first published in the *Boston Journal*, suggested that an enlisted man from the 23rd Ohio killed Reno to prevent a court-martial of Rutherford Hayes over the stubble-field incident. This motive, however, was dismissed outright by Colonel Scammon in an 1888 address delivered at a regimental reunion.[81] An enlisted man from the 6th New Hampshire perpetuated the allegation. Although his regiment had been detached from its division and the action surrounding Reno's death, Private Albert A. Batchelder wrote to his father, "General Reno was killed by a Massachusetts Regiment by mistake he was in front of the lines."[82] A *National Tribune* article published by a pair of Reno's orderlies on July 6, 1883, also recalled the early evening episode. According to Sergeant Alexander H. Wood and Private Martin Ficken, an enlisted man in the 35th Massachusetts screamed "Rebel Cavalry!" Before anyone could command the regiment to hold its fire, six rifle shots rang out in rapid succession. One of the bullets, claimed the orderlies, bounced off Reno's scabbard and lodged in his chest.[83] Even Orlando B. Willcox claimed as much, recalling in his memoirs that during his final moments Reno wheezed out, "Willcox, I am killed. Shot by our own men."[84]

Not everyone agreed with this tenuous claim. "[Reno] had gone to the skirmish line to examine the situation there," Kanawha division commander Jacob Cox penned in the *Century* magazine, "and had been shot down by the enemy posted among the rocks and trees." Ezra Carman, the campaign's first

81 See Walcott, *History of the Twenty-First Regiment Massachusetts Volunteers*, 185; E.P. Scammon, "Address," August 22, 1888, Rutherford B. Hayes Presidential Center, Fremont, Ohio.

82 Batchelder as quoted in John Michael Priest, "The Death of Jesse Reno," *Civil War* (May-June 1992), 44.

83 "How Reno Fell," *National Tribune*, July 6, 1883.

84 Orlando B. Willcox, "South Mountain and Antietam," 355; see also Gabriel Campbell's letter to Ezra Carman, August 23, 1899, which provides additional evidence supporting Willcox's recollection.

The Jesse Reno Monument, dedicated in 1889, was the first memorial erected to commemorate the Maryland Campaign of 1862. *Henry F. Ballone*

historian, specifically cited the "sudden rain of bullets" from the woods where "Hood's men opened fire," resulting in the mortal wounding of Jesse Reno.[85] The widespread reports of Reno's death by friendly fire shed more light on the existence of the ever-present gossip mill than on the event itself. The simple fact

85 *B&L* 2:589; Carman, *The Maryland Campaign,* 155.

is that the rampant confusion generated by the sudden fusillade of bullets fired in a gloomy shadow-laden dusk after a hard-fought combat when everyone was on edge makes it impossible to say with any degree of certainty *who* was responsible for Reno's untimely demise.

For the men themselves, the most immediate result was the loss of their beloved corps commander. They wept, vowed to avenge his death, and exhibited genuine grief. "His loss will be deplored by all who knew him," General Burnside wrote in his effusive official announcement of Reno's death. After explaining that the country had lost "one of its most devoted patriots," Burnside paid tribute to Reno's "high character and the kindly qualities of his heart in private life," which along with "personal daring" had "marked him as a soldier." General McClellan agreed: "In General Reno the nation lost one of its best general officers. He was a skillful soldier, a brave and honest man."[86] Cavalry commander Alfred Pleasonton eulogized that the fallen leader "was eminently successful in driving the enemy until he fell at the moment he was gallantly leading his command to a crowning victory. At his loss a master mind had passed away."[87] "General Reno, I hear, is killed; another of our best men gone," one federal soldier confided to his diary. "Some are so uncharitable as to accuse General McClellan of willfully and unnecessarily ordering him to a position from which escape from death was almost impossible. I will not believe it."[88] Surgeon Thomas Ellis assumed a broader pragmatic view of the macabre work that September when he concluded, "The country can ill afford to lose such men as Kearney, Stevens, and Reno."[89]

---

86 Edward O. Lord, ed., *History of the Ninth Regiment New Hampshire Volunteers in the War of the Rebellion* (Concord: Republican Press Association, 1895), 76; McClellan as quoted in Hassler, Jr., 57; Ellis, 257-258.

87 Pleasonton's report was quoted by Orlando B. Willcox, "South Mountain and Antietam," 356.

88 Alfred Lewis Castleman, *The Army of the Potomac, Behind the Scenes: A Diary of Unwritten History from the Organization of the Army to the Close of the Campaign in Virginia, About the First Day of January, 1863* (Milwaukee, Wisconsin: Strickland & Co., 1863), 223-224.

89 Ellis, *Leaves from the Diary of an Army Surgeon*, 257-258. Three days later while preparing to cross Antietam Creek at the Rohrbach Bridge (forever after referred to as Burnside's Bridge), the men of the IX Corps shouted a tribute to their former commander: "Remember Reno! Remember Reno!" After an entire morning of costly failed attempts to cross the shallow creek on that narrow choke point, it was the 51st New York and the 51st Pennsylvania that led the way over the stone bridge. McConnell, *Remember Reno*, p. x.

Wise's Field and a large oak tree near the site of Reno's death came to symbolize the calamitous cost of the fight at South Mountain. These locations were more permanently memorialized when a handsome monument was dedicated at the site on September 14, 1889—the first monument erected in commemoration of the Maryland Campaign. Although the weather was cold and rainy, nearly 1,000 people attended to hear the chief orator for the solemn occasion, Major General Orlando Bolivar Willcox: "Be this his epitaph: A skillful soldier, a brave and honest man."[90]

Commemoration of the fallen hero spread well beyond the bloody fields of South Mountain. In Wyoming, the first fort on the Bozeman Trail was named Fort Reno in 1865. It would burn three years later. On February 26, 1867, the Kansas state legislature named a county near Wichita in Reno's honor. At the behest of Irvin McDowell, Charles Crocker, the superintendent of railroad construction for the Central Pacific Railroad named the dusty Nevada crossroads on the Truckee River for the fallen general, and a town in northern Pennsylvania and a fort and city in Oklahoma would also bear his name.[91]

*   *   *

The grisly evidence of the costly day at Fox's Gap littered the ground of a federal victory that was both impressive and decisive. All told, the IX Corps, with its nearly 13,500 men, lost 889 (157 killed, 691 wounded, and 41 missing/captured). The Confederates, with about 7,000 effectives, suffered nearly 900 losses from all causes (96 killed, 406 wounded, and 370 missing/captured).[92]

A general examination of some of the respective losses is instructive. The fighting at Fox's Gap devastated Thomas Drayton's Confederate brigade. Of

90 See C. H. Barney, ed., *The Reno Memorial, South Mountain, Maryland, Unveiled September 14, 1889: Its Inception, Erection and Dedication* (Portland, Maine: Society of the Burnside Expedition and the Ninth Army Corps, 1891), 12.

91 For years, largely due to the 1913 history of the state of Nevada written by Samuel Davis, many have erroneously assumed that the Nevada town was named for Marcus Reno. See Darwin L. Flaherty, "The Naming of Reno, Nevada: A Century Old Mystery," Nevada Historical Society Quarterly 27, no. 3 (1984): 154-181, and Nevada State Archivist Guy Rocha, "Wanted: The Real Reno," *Sierra Sage* (September 2007), 23.

92 Casualty figures have been culled from Carman, *The Maryland Campaign*, 155, official records, and John Michael Priest, *Before Antietam*, 325-326.

the nearly 650 men Drayton marched into battle that afternoon, 49 were killed, 164 were wounded, and another 176 either captured or missing, for losses approaching sixty percent.[93] Holding the gap was nearly impossible, but turning the Confederate flank was also a costly venture. The 45th Pennsylvania lost 136 officers and men (21 killed and 115 wounded), and many of those unfortunate wounded later died. According to the 45th Pennsylvania's Captain William Chase and Lieutenant Thomas Davies, the bloody tally at Fox' Gap extracted the highest number of casualties the regiment would suffer during any single engagement for the remainder of the war. The next morning, in a little trench just above a log cabin where the ranks first formed, the Pennsylvania corpses were wrapped in blankets and laid to rest in South Mountain's rocky soil. The 17th Michigan suffered nearly as heavily, adding 17 killed and more than 100 wounded to the casualty rolls.[94]

Many were eager to attach effusive praise to the Wolverine regiment. For example, General Orlando Willcox wrote in his official report that "the Seventeenth Michigan, Colonel Withington, performed a feat that may vie with any recorded in the annals of war, and set an example to the oldest of troops."[95] Youth and combat innocence didn't stop the 17th from mounting and maintaining a charge, and eventually driving back veteran South Carolinians and Georgians. "I will only add that the Forty-fifth Pennsylvania of my brigade and the Seventeenth Michigan of the first brigade sustained the brunt of the battle with a bravery and constancy seldom equaled in modern warfare," was the encomium Colonel Welsh delivered in concluding his report. Even General McClellan weighed in, remembering the Michiganders favorably in his memoirs.[96]

---

93 These numbers for Drayton's Brigade are from Ezra Carman in his appendix, "Confederate Losses at Turner's Gap and Fox's Gap," in *The Maryland Campaign*, 449. Longstreet's official report of the Maryland Campaign of 1862 presents an aggregate loss for Drayton of 541 (82 killed, 280 wounded, and 179 missing or captured; see OR 1:843). Carman's extensive correspondence with survivors of this brigade revealed that the losses on September 17 were 33 killed, 106 wounded, and three missing. Deducting these figures from Longstreet's aggregate allows one to arrive at the casualty rate presented herein. See also Priest, *Before Antietam*, 325.

94 Todd, *The Seventy-Ninth Highlanders*, 233; see also OR 1:186.

95 *OR*, 1:428-429.

96 *Ibid.*, 1:440; George B. McClellan, *McClellan's Own Story: The War for the Union, the Soldiers Who Fought It, the Civilians Who Directed It, and His Relations to It and Them* (New York: Charles Webster and Company, 1886), 578.

The soldiers recognized their transformation almost immediately, baptized as it was in the blood of their comrades. The tale of their charge at South Mountain circulated in Northern newspapers, offering civilians a glimpse of the virtues and values embodied on the fields of war. "Of our exploits on South Mountain I will not write," Private David Lane of the 17th Wisconsin's Company G scribbled into his diary. "They will be woven into history and will be within the reach of all."[97]

In 1903, at the apogee of the so-called "strenuous manhood" period epitomized by President Theodore Roosevelt, Captain Gabriel Campbell published a narrative poem in *Dartmouth Magazine* celebrating the charge of what became known as the "Stonewall Regiment."[98] "A sultry, dull, September, Sabbath morn woke us unrested, much inclined to scorn," began former Captain Campbell. His poetry continued, following quick rations and sprung rammers, buckled waist-belts and slung knapsacks, and the command given to advance. The sights of South Mountain, he waxed on, "aspire[d] to heaven," as "traitor shells" unleashed their deafening sound. With enlarged hearts, the men rallied for the charge. "On sweeps the line of Union men, with bristling bayonet all. Three volleys and a charge! Great God!" Campbell wrote. Neither "rebel steel, nor walls of stone" could check the Michiganders "loyal flood." They had, he concluded, "struck one blow for God and Liberty."[99]

*   *   *

As dramatic and prolonged as it was, the bloody fight for Fox's Gap was but one element of the momentous struggle to seize the mountain's trio of passes and tear asunder General Lee's Army of Northern Virginia in an effort to thwart its invasion north of the Potomac River. Just a short distance to the north, both sides fought for control of Turner's Gap. Farther south, more fighting was about to erupt at Crampton's Gap.

---

97 Lane, *A Soldier's Diary: The Story of A Volunteer, 1862-1865*, p. 12.

98 On "strenuous manhood," see E. Anthony Rotundo, *American Manhood* (New York: Basic Books, 1993), passim; see also Nina Silber, *The Romance of Reunion: Northerners and the South, 1865-1900* (Chapel Hill: University of North Carolina Press, 1993), passim.

99 Gabriel Campbell, "The Charge at South Mountain by the Stonewall Regiment: A Poem by the Captain of a Company of Students, Seventeenth Michigan Infantry," imprint from *Dartmouth Magazine* (1903), Western Reserve Historical Society, Cleveland, Ohio.

C hapter 7

"The worst looking place to take"

The Fight for Turner's Gap:
Meade Assaults Rodes and Evans

"The place where the reserve fought at South Mountain was the worst looking place
to take ever I seen. . . . They met us at the top of the hill and they held [their]
ground for a while but they had to give way and we had to follow them
down the side of the pass over rocks and stone fences . . ."

— *John McQuaide, 8th Pennsylvania Reserves*[1]

A t dawn on September 14, Major General Joseph Hooker started the ten
thousand federals comprising his First Corps from their encampment
on the banks of the Monocacy River. "Marched at 6 a.m.," Lieutenant Martin
Swarthout of Company H, 20th New York, recorded in his diary. "A little after
daybreak this morning an orderly came to my tent to announce that we were to
march at once; but, while tents were packing, we had plenty of time for
breakfast," was how Captain George Freeman Noyes of the 76th New York
remembered the start of what would be one of the army's memorable days.

The soldiers spotted the spires of Frederick as they approached, and soon
passed through the city on a morning that had dawned clear and warm. "The
bells of the city of Frederick were all ringing. It was a rejoicing at the advent of
the host for her deliverance, the Army of the Potomac," believed Major Rufus
R. Dawes of the 6th Wisconsin. "From right to left along the valley below us,

1 John McQuaide, letter to Thomas McQuaide, September 22, 1862, in Civil War Times
Illustrated Collection, United States Army Military History Institute, Carlisle, Pennsylvania.

were stretched the swarming camps of the blue coats." Noyes noted that it was a good day for marching. "Every one was in good spirits," he commented.[2]

Dawes described the procession through Frederick as triumphal. "The stars and stripes floated from every building and hung from every window. The joyful people thronged the streets to greet and cheer the veterans of the Army of the Potomac," he wrote. "Little children stood at nearly every door, freely offering cool water, cakes, pies and dainties. The jibes and insults of the women of Virginia, to which our men had become accustomed, had here a striking contrast in a generous and enthusiastic welcome by the ladies of Frederick City." Sergeant Major E. M. Woodward of the 2nd Pennsylvania Reserves likewise recalled the colorful and patriotic array of flags and multitudes gathered in doorways. "Patriotism, with these good people was no abstract theory, but a living fact," recalled Franklin B. Hough, the historian of Duryee's brigade. "It was the Sabbath day, and like good Christians they had closed all places of business; yet notices of 'Sold out,' 'Closed up,' . . . gave reasons to suspect, that piety was not altogether the motive which led to this strict observance of Sunday."[3]

The tossing of bouquets and the waving of handkerchiefs—"a perfect ovation" of "wild enthusiasm"—buoyed the spirits of the enlisted men. Along with many others, Colonel William F. Rogers of the 21st New York noted the "marked contrast" in this march through Maryland with those made in Virginia. "I calculate that the net value to us in the South Mountain battle of this new inspiration which came upon us from the eyes and fingers of our fair friends in Frederick was equal to about one thousand fresh men," Captain Noyes concluded. "One can scarcely estimate the value of such a reception, upon the

2   OR 1:213-214; Carman, *The Maryland Campaign*, 155; Martin Swarthout, diary entry, September 14, 1862, in Northwest Corner Civil War Roundtable Collection, United States Army Military History Institute, Carlisle, Pennsylvania; John Harrison Mills, *Chronicles of the Twenty-first Regiment, New York State Volunteers* (Buffalo: 21st Regiment Veteran Association, 1887), 279; George Freeman Noyes, *The Bivouac and the Battlefield; Or, Campaign Sketches in Virginia and Maryland* (New York: Harper & Brothers, Publishers, 1863), 165; Rufus R. Dawes, *Service with the Sixth Wisconsin Volunteers* (originally published 1890; reprint, Dayton, Ohio: Morningside Bookshop, 1996), 79.

3   Dawes, *Service with the Sixth Wisconsin Volunteers*, 79; E. Morrison Woodward, *Our Campaigns: The Second Regiment Pennsylvania Reserve Volunteers, 1861-1864* (Philadelphia: J.E. Porter, 1865), 195; Franklin B. Hough, *History of Duryee's Brigade* (Albany, New York: J. Munsell, 1864), 110-111; on the march through Frederick, see also Theodore B. Gates, *The Ulster Guard* (New York: Benjamin H. Tyrrel, 1879), 294-295; Isaac Hall, *History of the Ninety-Seventh Regiment, New York Volunteers* (Utica: L.C. Childs & Son, 1870), 86-87.

very eve of the terrible battle of South Mountain," the 76th New York's Abram Smith echoed. "The men not only had friends at home to protect with their lives; but a new inspiration urged them forward, as they thought of these loyal daughters of a State around which the monster of secession had attempted to wind his deadly coil."[4]

By eleven o'clock that morning, most of the men reached the village of Middletown, striding along to the distant cadences of exploding artillery. "We could see arising the smoke of battle," Dawes recalled. "We hurried along down the road toward the scene of action, every gun of which we could see and hear." According to Franklin Hough, "every few seconds, a puff of light blue smoke, a little white cloud" suddenly appeared in the sky. Clusters of soldiers halted at the spectacle. Abram Smith wrote that though the men were "steady and determined," there were some "who gazed upon the curling wreaths of smoke, as they arose from the mountainside before them . . . and thought of the dear ones in their distant homes." The sight of so many of the men, women, and children of Middletown gathering with no little anxiety along the road side only encouraged these yearnings for far off loved ones. "The people were more excited as the cannon boomed loud and near," soldier Isaac Hall wrote. The "evidences of conflict" also presented themselves more visibly in the village. Already, the townspeople opened their houses, churches, and the music academy as makeshift hospitals to care for the wounded. "Pillows and bedding, the best their dwellings afforded, were freely brought and offered, for the wounded and dying, and their last moments were soothed with comforting words and delicate attentions."[5]

Hooker's three divisions halted at 1:00 p.m. about one mile west of Middletown along the banks of Catoctin Creek. Brigadier General John P. Hatch's First Division included the brigades of Colonel Walter Phelps, Jr., and Brigadier Generals Abner Doubleday, Marsena R. Patrick, and John Gibbon. Brigadier General James B. Ricketts commanded Hooker's Second Division. These men, from New York, Massachusetts, and Pennsylvania, were divided

---

4 Noyes, *The Bivouac and the Battlefield*, 165-166; William P. Maxson, *Camp Fires of the Twenty-third* (New York: Davies & Kent, 1863), 98; William F. Rogers as quoted in John Harrison Mills, *Chronicles of the Twenty-first Regiment, New York State Volunteers*, 278; Abram P. Smith, *History of the Seventy-Sixth Regiment New York Volunteers* (Cortland, New York: Truain, Smith, and Miles Printers,1876), 140-150.

5 Dawes, *Service with the Sixth Wisconsin Volunteers*, 79; Franklin Hough, *History of Duryee's Brigade*, 111; Isaac Hall, *History of the Ninety-Seventh Regiment*, 86.

into the brigades of Colonel William A. Christian and Brigadier Generals Abram Duryee and George L. Hartsuff. Massed into the brigades of Brigadier General Truman Seymour and Colonels Albert L. Magilton and Thomas F. Gallagher, the Pennsylvania Reserve regiments constituted the Third Division under Brigadier General George Gordon Meade. The Pennsylvania Reserves were the product of an acute political rivalry in the Keystone State. When Pennsylvania surpassed its quota of federal volunteers in April 1861, Secretary of War Simon Cameron, an arch enemy of Republican Governor Andrew Gregg Curtin, refused to accept the additional regiments from his native commonwealth. Cameron insisted that the War Department could not afford to outfit the excess troops. In response (and ready to best Cameron), the governor called for thirteen regiments to be organized by the state and mustered into federal service. Cameron grudgingly accepted the troops into active service as part of the V Corps.[6]

Ricketts' division remained long enough to be reviewed by General George McClellan. "It was the first time that the commander had been seen by [Duryee's] Brigade, and he was welcomed by enthusiastic cheers," historian Hough wrote. The army commander, who was escorted by Captain Daniel P. Mann's Independent Company of the Oneida Cavalry, as well as Companies A and E of the 4th United States Cavalry, "at once created a favorable impression" with his "earnest, active appearance, youthful look and eagle eye" gazing to the north and west—toward the rocky slopes of South Mountain.[7]

*   *   *

"In front of us was South Mountain," General Hooker reported. "Its slopes are precipitous, rugged, and wooded, and difficult of ascent to an infantry force, even in the absence of a foe in front." The National Turnpike—the route from Middletown to the summit—cut across the mountain "through a gentle depression," passing at nearly right angles through Turner's Gap. "On the north side of the road, the mountain is divided longitudinally into two crests

6   OR 1:170-172; Samuel P. Bates, *History of the Pennsylvania Volunteers* (Harrisburg: B. Singerly, State Printer, 1869; reprint, Wilmington, North Carolina: Broadfoot Publishing, Inc., 1993), 1:539-544.

7   Hough, *History of Duryee's Brigade*, 112; Hall, *History of the Ninety-Seventh Regiment*, 86; see also Priest, *Before Antietam*, 225.

Turner's Gap, looking southeast from the Mountain House. *Battles and Leaders of the Civil War*

---

by a narrow valley," explained Lieutenant Colonel Theodore B. Gates of the 20th New York State Militia. The undulating ground beneath these commanding crests formed deep ravines and high ledges. As cavalry commander Alfred Pleasonton discovered much earlier that morning, two country roads diverged from the National Pike on their way to the respective gaps: the Old Sharpsburg Road to the left wound its way to Fox's Gap, and to the right, the Old Hagerstown Road ran to Turner's Gap and the two crests described by Gates.[8]

Soldiers encountered plenty of evidence along the National Turnpike suggestive of the eventful morning. "Some barns filled with grain along the route had been destroyed by fire, and the bridge over Catoctin Creek had been burned," one veteran recalled. Ahead and to the left, the sights and smells of

---

8   OR 1:214-215, 266-267; Gates, *The Ulster Guard*, 294-295; Hooker, as quoted in Carman, *The Maryland Campaign*, 155-156.

battle still lingered from Scammon's and Crook's morning melee with Garland's North Carolinians.[9]

As described earlier, the morning's engagement created serious problems for Confederate Major General D. H. Hill. In desperation, he ordered up George Burgwyn Anderson's Brigade, stationed at that time near Boonsboro, to support Samuel Garland's and Alfred Colquitt's men positioned near the summit of Turner's Gap in close proximity to General Hill's Old Mountain House headquarters. Hill was initially reluctant to summon the additional brigades under Roswell Ripley and Robert Rodes from their important roles guarding the division's supply arteries, but when Jacob Cox began rolling up Garland's outnumbered Tarheels, Hill had no other viable alternative other than to reinforce the gap accordingly. After first calling forward Ripley's artillery, during which the fighting increased and claimed the life of the capable Garland, Hill relented and ordered up Ripley's infantry. These regiments followed G. B. Anderson, and were in turn reinforced by the two advance brigades of Longstreet's command.

One-half mile west of Boonsboro, Robert Emmett Rodes' Brigade of Alabamians overtook and held the vital position vacated by G. B. Anderson's men. But the 1,200 troops of the 3rd, 5th, 6th, 12th, and 26th Alabama regiments would not remain there very long. In the ultimate expression of his feeling of "loneliness," Hill changed his mind and directed his last brigade to move up and assume a position to the left of Colquitt to better secure the high ground north of the National Turnpike and the Dahlgren Road. "With characteristic promptness, Gen Rhodes . . . ordered us into line, and had the brigade moving at the double quick for the scene of action," S. Q. Hale of the 6th Alabama recalled. "After looking over the field of battle, I was ordered by Major General Hill to take position on the ridge immediately to the left of the gap through which the main road runs," reported Rodes. "There was a solitary peak on the left," Colonel Cullen Andrews Battle of the 3rd Alabama remembered, "which, if gained by the enemy, would given them control of the ridge commanding the pike." Rodes anchored his right flank, held by Colonel Briston B. Gayle's 12th Alabama, near the National Turnpike. To its left, Colonel Edward A. O'Neal's 26th Alabama extended the line northward. Down the line, Major E. L. Hobson's 5th Alabama, Colonel Battle's 5th

9   Hall, *History of the Ninety-Seventh Regiment*, 86.

Brigadier General Robert E. Rodes. *National Archives*

Alabama, and Colonel John Brown Gordon's 6th Alabama rounded out the extended line of battle.[10]

Rodes had just thrown out his sharpshooters as skirmishers to the left and to the front when artillery in Lieutenant Samuel Benjamin's, Captain Horatio Gibson's, and Captain James McMullin's batteries to the southeast opened a cannonade that kept the Middletown Valley flushed with action. "Affairs were now very serious on our left," D. H. Hill remembered. Spying the federal columns filing down the National Turnpike *en masse*, the Southern general knew how difficult it would be to hold his positions if the federals made a serious attempt to dislodge him. The battle was well underway that morning farther south at Fox's Gap, and now Hooker was moving in strength to attack the Confederate left at Turner's Gap. To Hill's dismay, it became readily apparent that the enemy would extend well beyond the left of Rodes' rather isolated brigade. Hill also learned after another survey of the terrain north of the National Turnpike that he had failed to fully appreciate South Mountain's complex topography. While the high ground straddling the old road was important, the second crest, about three-quarters of a mile farther north, was just as vital. If the federals seized it, they would not only command the gorge between the crests, but would be in fine position to deliver the enfilading fire necessary to roll up Rodes' exposed line and open the National Turnpike for thousands of waiting enemy infantry.[11]

About forty-five minutes into the cannonade, which Hill assumed presaged a federal advance, Rodes shifted his Alabamians to the northern crest. The movement was peppered by federal shot and shell. Colonel Gordon's men scrambled up the slopes of the undefended high ground as the remainder of Rodes' line redeployed, still in the same order, to the south and west through the "deep gorge" of Frosttown.[12]

Neither Hill nor Rodes seem to have fully understood the obvious consequence of this relocation. The move opened a substantial breach in the line between Colquitt's left flank and Rodes' right, leaving the high ground

---

10 OR 1:1019-1020, 1033-1034; S. Q. Hale, as quoted in Darrell L. Collins, *Major General Robert E. Rodes of the Army of Northern Virginia: A Biography* (New York and California: Savas Beatie, 2008), 157; Beck, ed., *Third Alabama! The Civil War Memoir of Brigadier General Cullen Andrews Battles*, CSA, 52-56.

11 *Ibid.*; Carman, *The Maryland Campaign*, 155-157.

12 *Ibid.*

astride the National Turnpike virtually defenseless. Additionally, Captain John Lane's Georgia Battery, whose guns had unlimbered on the hill first occupied by Rodes not far from the Mountain House, was now unsupported. As Hooker's men continued forming and the enemy artillery fire persisted, an alarmed Hill identified the error and ordered Rodes to send some infantry support back to seal the breach.

Like his commander, Rodes was also anxious about his new position. "By this time the enemy's line of battle was pretty well developed and in full view," the brigadier recalled. "It became evident that he intended to attack with a line covering both ridges and the gorge." Rodes asked Hill to place artillery supports on the second crest, a plea answered with a single gun from Lane's Battery. Unsatisfied, Rodes peeled off the 12th Alabama to support the balance of Lane's gunners on the first eminence and determined that the only way to prevent the enemy from rolling up his line was to extend it farther left (south), a move that effectively gambled everything on the northern hill and the gorge below. There were simply too few men to man the length of line that required defending.

The only consolation for the defending Confederates was the rugged terrain, which in many respects favored their efforts to defend the important mountain pass. The federal attackers would have to keep their formations intact while mounting a steep series of rough ridges interrupted by boulders, underbrush, and trees. Josiah Sypher, who authored the first full history of the Pennsylvania Reserve Corps, described the challenging landscape before General Meade's infantrymen as "a succession of parallel ridges, alternated with deep irregular valleys and broken ravines. The hills increased in height, and their eastern slopes became more abrupt and rugged, as they neared the mountain crest."[13]

Hooker, of course, did not know the strength of the enemy waiting for him with any certainty. He did, however, appreciate the difficult topography, which explains much of the corps leader's caution as he prepared his men to assault the high ground north of the National Turnpike. A year after the battle, in the wake of the fiasco at Fredericksburg in late 1862, General Burnside—who was then in command of the Army of the Potomac—sought to distract his critics by challenging the performance of his subordinates in recent engagements.

---

13 OR 1:1019-1020, 1033-1034; Josiah Sypher, *History of the Pennsylvania Reserve Corps* (Lancaster, Pennsylvania: Elias Barr & Co., 1865), 367-368.

Brigadier General George Gordon Meade. *Library of Congress*

Burnside alleged that Hooker unnecessarily delayed his attack at Turner's Gap, and responded tartly when Hooker submitted his official report of the battle. "It partakes of something worse than untruthfulness," he determined. "General Hooker should remember that I had to order him four separate times to move his command into action, and that I had to myself order his leading division to start before he would go."

Burnside's own record, of course, gave him little authority to condemn alleged caution on the part of others. Although Hooker's report included several significant errors—Jacob Cox had not yet been in command of a corps, and had not yet fallen back—these discrepancies should not raise suspicion about his caution that afternoon. The orders Hooker received from McClellan instructed him to hold his corps "in readiness." Likewise, Hooker was aware that his movements were intended to create "a diversion in favor of Reno," who was fighting farther south at Fox's Gap. Moreover, when Hooker threw out the 1st Massachusetts Cavalry into a cornfield north of the National Turnpike, the troopers suffered under the fire of Lane's Georgia guns. "Here we sat on our horses for two hours," complained Adjutant Charles Francis Adams, Jr. His regiment was "unpleasantly exposed with the shells hurtling over us like mad, and now and then falling around us."[14]

Indeed, it was "in readiness" that Meade's division of Pennsylvania Reserves led the corps on this Sabbath, having left camp along the Monocacy with the sunrise and halted in Middletown by one that afternoon. "About 3 O'clock we were moved some distance to the gap through which the turnpike passed," wrote Lieutenant Colonel Adonriam Judson Warner, commanding the 10th Reserves. Ahead, Sturgis' division of Jesse Reno's IX Corps was marching up the National Turnpike to reinforce the left side of Orlando Willcox's line of battle moving against Fox's Gap. Sturgis' troops diverted left off the main road, allowing Meade's infantry to continue tramping westward toward Mount Tabor Church.[15]

At the stone sanctuary he claimed as a headquarters, Hooker awaited Meade's arrival. Truman Seymour's brigade led Meade's division along the Old Hagerstown Road. Seymour ordered Colonel Hugh W. McNeil's 13th Pennsylvania Reserves, complete with buck tails affixed to their kepis, forward as skirmishers. They advanced across a broad front with their left running along

---

14 OR 1:214-215, 422-423; Benjamin W. Crowinshield, *A History of the First Regiment of Massachusetts Cavalry Volunteers* (Boston: Houghton, Mifflin and Co., 1891), 74-75; Charles Francis Adams Jr. to his mother, letter, 25 September 1862, in Worthington Chauncey Ford, ed., *A Cycle of Adams Letters*, vol. 1 (Boston: Houghton, Mifflin and Co., 1920), 188-189; Priest, *Before Antietam*, 227.

15 OR 1:266-267; John W. Urban, *My Experiences Mid Shot and Shell and in Rebel Den* (Lancaster, Pennsylvania: n.p., 1882), 204; Warner, as quoted in James B. Casey, ed., "The Ordeal of Adoniram Judson Warner: His Minutes of South Mountain and Antietam," *Civil War History*, 28, no. 3 (September 1982), 217.

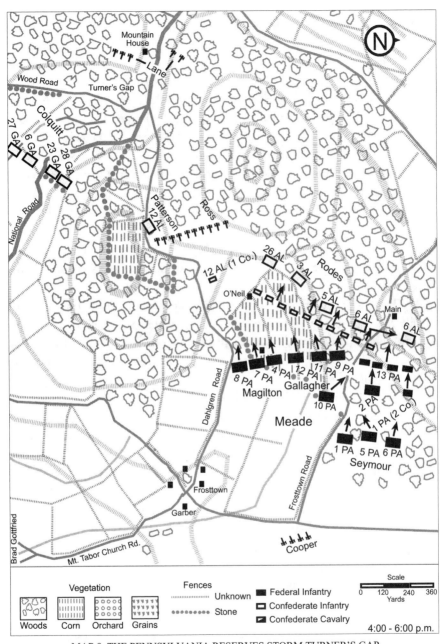

Scale

0   120   240   360
Yards

4:00 - 6:00 p.m.

MAP 9. THE PENNSYLVANIA RESERVES STORM TURNER'S GAP

the Frosttown Road. The 13th was supported fifty yards to the rear by Captain James N. Byrnes' 2nd Pennsylvania Reserves and two companies of Colonel Richard B. Roberts' 1st Pennsylvania Reserves. Along the road beyond the intersection with the Zittlestown Road, which cut toward the crest, Colonel William Sinclair's 6th Pennsylvania Reserves held the right flank. Colonel Joseph W. Fisher, commanding the 5th Reserves, held the center of Seymour's line, with the remaining companies of Roberts' regiment to the left.[16]

Colonel Thomas F. Gallagher organized his regiments on Seymour's left on the far side of the Frosttown Road at the foot of the valley. Lieutenant Colonel Robert Anderson's 9th Pennsylvania Reserves held the brigade right near the roadbed. Lieutenant Colonel Samuel M. Jackson's 11th Pennsylvania Reserves and Captain Richard Gustin's 12th Pennsylvania Reserves held the center and the left, respectively. The 10th Pennsylvania Reserves under Lieutenant Colonel Adoniram Judson Warner was held in reserve about 100 yards behind the right-center of the line along the Old Hagerstown Road.

Colonel Albert L. Magilton, who assumed command of the brigade when Meade was promoted to lead the division, aligned his men behind Gallagher's left with his regiments running through the scattered buildings of Frosttown, where the various major roads intersected. Major John Nyce led Magilton's former regiment, the 4th Pennsylvania Reserves, which formed along the Old Hagerstown Road left of and behind Gallagher's line. Colonel Henry C. Bolinger's 7th Pennsylvania Reserves and Major Silas M. Bailey's 8th Pennsylvania Reserves extended the line to the left. Meade ordered the 3rd Pennsylvania Reserves under Lieutenant Colonel John Clark to advance about three-quarters of a mile north of Magilton's brigade to guard the right side of the entire division.[17]

As Bailey's 8th Pennsylvania Reserves deployed on the far left side of Magilton's line, Lieutenant William M. Carter of Company B turned to Company D's Captain Cyrus Conner and exclaimed, "Captain, I think there will be a fight!"

"No doubt there will be," he replied.

---

16 *Ibid.*; OR 1:214-215, 272; Samuel P. Bates, *History of Pennsylvania Volunteers*, 1:584, 2:918; Priest, *Before Antietam*, 231; see also D. Scott Hartwig, "'It Looked Like a Task To Storm': The Pennsylvania Reserves Assault South Mountain," *North & South* 5, no. 7 (October 2002), 36-49.

17 *Ibid*; OR 1:273; Carman, *The Maryland Campaign*, 155-157; Bates, *History of Pennsylvania Volunteers*, 1:614.

Carter's face was ashen. "Captain," he repeated, earnestly, "I know I shall be shot." Though Conner attempted to calm his fellow officer, Carter only grew more insistent. "But I will," he insisted. "I am an unlucky mortal. I was shot while on the Peninsula almost the first chance I got—I was only wounded there; today, I will be killed. I know it."

Unsettled by the lieutenant's eerie premonition, Conner attempted yet again to interject a ray of optimism. "Come now, lieutenant," he started. "It's only a foolish notion that has got into your head. Get rid of it, cheer up. You will come out all right."

"I wish I could think so," Carter responded. "I will fall doing my duty, captain," he said as he turned away, melted into the battle line, and prepared to storm the mountain.[18]

*   *   *

"He was always in deadly earnest, and he eschewed all trifling," D. H. Hill once wrote of division commander George Gordon Meade, an officer Hill described as "one of our most dreaded foes." The Confederates were about to witness Hill's fears firsthand.

Captain James H. Cooper's Company B of the 1st Pennsylvania Artillery unlimbered its four 3-inch ordnance rifles on a hill near the base of the mountain below the intersection of the Frosttown and Old Hagerstown roads about 3:30 p.m. His responsibility was to support George Meade's powerful 4,000-man, three-brigade front. Immediately after deploying into battery, the gunners unleashed thirty rounds of case shot up the slope toward the enemy defenders.[19]

Farther south, division leaders John Porter Hatch and James Brewerton Ricketts digested orders to follow Meade's division up the slopes with their own commands. Additional orders from the adjutant general's office in Washington transferring command of the First Division of Hooker's I Corps to Hatch had also just arrived. (Its former commander, Rufus King, had suffered an epileptic seizure during the Second Manassas Campaign, and was not fit for further field

---

18 Archibald F. Hill, *Our Boys* (Philadelphia: John E. Potter, 1864), 395; Priest, *Before Antietam*, 232.

19 *Ibid.*; OR 1: 271, 274-275; Bates, *History of Pennsylvania Volunteers*, 1:639; 2:726, 760-761, 790, 850, 884.

duty.) The slope these divisions were preparing to scale were foreboding indeed. "Before us the mountain rose somewhat abruptly, so much so as to render the ascent on horseback very difficult, and to require the aid of shrubs, saplings, and stumps to assist in climbing," Edward Barnes of the 95th New York remembered.[20]

*   *   *

The noisy and very visible assembly of Meade's three brigades confirmed for Robert Rodes that he was in for the fight of his life. It is difficult to overemphasize the enormity of his task at South Mountain. By this time Rodes was well aware that federal attacks that morning farther south at Fox's Gap had either punched through or rolled up the defending Confederates. Now, outnumbered nearly four to one, his own men had to defend a lengthy gap-filled line and prevent history from repeating itself. "In view of the great force approaching to attack him his fight seemed almost hopeless," Longstreet reflected in his memoir. For Hill, the sight of the federal onslaught was both majestic and terrifying. "The sight was grand and sublime, but the elements of the pretty and the picturesque did not enter into it," recalled Hill. "Doubtless the Hebrew poet whose idea of the awe-inspiring is expressed by the phrase, 'terrible as an army with banners,' had his view of the enemy from the top of a mountain."[21]

Rodes ordered Colonel Briston B. Gayle to select skirmishers from the ranks of the 12th Alabama to spread out well in front of the brigade. Gayle called forward Lieutenant Robert E. Park of Company F, who selected forty men—four from each company—to scout the ground below the line of battle. "I hastily deployed the men, and we moved down the mountain side," recalled Park. "On our way we could see the enemy in the valley below advancing, preceded by their dense line of skirmishers." The Alabama colonel concealed the skirmishers behind trees, rocks, and bushes as they slipped down the mountain and through the gorge to the north and the east. "We awaited with

---

20 *OR*, 1:221, 241; Mills, *Chronicles of the Twenty-first Regiment*, 279; Edward L. Barnes, "The 95th New York at South Mountain," *National Tribune*, January 7, 1886; *OR* Atlas, Plate 27, Map 3; Sypher, *History of the Pennsylvania Reserve Corps*, 368; *B&L*, 2:574; Joseph Gibbs, *Three Years in the 'Bloody Eleventh': The Campaigns of a Pennsylvania Reserves Regiment* (University Park: The Pennsylvania State University Press, 2002), 173-174.

21 *B&L*, 2:573-574; *OR* 1:1034-1036; Longstreet, *From Manassas to Appomattox*, 224.

bated breath and beating hearts, the sure and steady approach," remembered Park.[22]

As Rodes' skirmishers fanned out, the single field piece Lane rushed to the second eminence lobbed a shell into the ranks of the oncoming Pennsylvanians. Private Bates Alexander of Company C, 7th Pennsylvania Reserves, watched as the shell hurtled over the Gaber Farm, situated at the intersection of the Frosttown and Old Hagerstown roads. The Gabers were not the only civilians whose lives had been interrupted and endangered by this meeting of the armies. That morning, scores of men and women who lived on the mountain moved along with the Reserves in their column of regiments. Now, with the fighting heating up, their collective excitement and anticipation metamorphosed into something approaching terror. "While moving to this position, the enemy opened upon us . . . throwing their shell in close proximity, which caused great consternation among the citizens, who accompanied us to see the fun," sarcastically observed Sergeant Major E. Morrison Woodward of the 2nd Pennsylvania Reserves. "The children lay down upon the ground, the women shrieked, and the men displayed wondrous agility in leaping the fences."[23]

Excitement also rippled through the blue line of skirmishers, especially along Seymour's front. "Pour your fire upon those rocks!" Colonel Hugh McNeil shouted at his Bucktails. When his men hesitated, the colonel screamed "Fire!" Many men in the 2nd Pennsylvania Reserves fifty yards to the rear heard the command advanced to carry out the order and melted into the lines of the Bucktails.[24]

On the opposing skirmish line, Lieutenant Park issued the much-anticipated order: "Fire!" Southern rifled-muskets cracked out a hard greeting to the approaching Pennsylvanians. Some of the bullets found their mark and men began to go down. "Nearly every bullet did fatal work," exaggerated Park.

---

22 Robert E. Park, "Anniversary of the Battle of Boonsboro, Maryland," in *Southern Historical Society Papers*, 33:278-279; Carman, *The Maryland Campaign*, 157.

23 Bates Alexander, "One of Our Constituents: What a Pennsylvania Man Thinks of Our Paper," *National Tribune*, December 12, 1889; Priest, *Before Antietam*, 229; E. Morrison Woodward, *Our Campaigns: The Second Regiment Pennsylvania Reserve Volunteers, 1861-1864*, ed. Stanley W. Zamonski (Philadelphia: J.E. Porter, 1865; reprint, Shippensburg: Burd Street Press, 1995), 152.

24 OR 1:272; "An Incident of Battle, Colonel McNeil at South Mountain," *Wellsboro Agitator*, 10 December 1862; Sypher, *History of the Pennsylvania Reserve Corps*, 372; Bates, *History of Pennsylvania Volunteers*, 1:584.

Though the Reserves were "checked for some minutes," they reordered themselves and advanced anew. Colonel McNeil was exhorting his men to continue forward when Park ordered his men to conduct a slow withdrawal. Four of his Alabamians received wounds—and six more frightened skirmishers fled to the rear.[25]

When Truman Seymour discovered the enemy skirmishers falling back, he pointed to that part of the hill where Rodes had formed his left flank and shouted to Colonel Roberts, commander of the 1st Pennsylvania Reserves, "Can't your regiment take that height?" The colonel gave the command for his men to move forward and the regiment "rushed on with a yell" into the woods ahead. Although their exposure was considerable, admitted Private Otis Smith of the 6th Alabama, their fire "was terrific." The Alabamian recalled how "the pat, pat of the bullets against the rocks sounded like hail."[26]

Seymour, meanwhile, reported to Meade that his brigade could easily take the northern crest, deliver enfilading volleys from behind part of the enemy line, advance through the Frosttown gorge, and secure the second ridge. It was now about 4:00 p.m. With Hooker committed to the assault, Meade ordered Seymour to go ahead and do so. The division commander also ordered Colonels Thomas Gallagher and Albert Magilton to advance against the enemy on Seymour's left in a coordinated assault across the entire divisional front. The terrain interrupted unit cohesion, however, and the main assault gradually devolved into three staggered thrusts, each brigade slowly forcing its way up the slopes on its own hook. "All order and regularity of the lines were soon destroyed," one of the first historians of the Pennsylvania Reserves noted.[27]

Many of the Alabamians also realized their own line was anything but solid and ready to repulse a determined attack. The mountainous landscape punctured their regimental cohesion. Rodes instructed his men to hold their fire until the enemy approached within 100 yards of their line.[28] The woods filled with clouds of suffocating powder smoke as Seymour's men advanced farther to the right and reached an open cornfield "full of rebels." Believing this to be a

---

25 *B&L* 2:572-573.

26 Otis Smith as quoted in Hartwig, "It Looked Like a Task to Storm," 44; OR 1:272; Bates, *History of Pennsylvania Volunteers*, 1:549.

27 OR 1:266-267, 272, 273, 274; Bates, *History of Pennsylvania Volunteers*, 1:584.

28 OR 1:1034-1035; Darrell Collins, *Major General Robert E. Rodes of the Army of Northern Virginia*, 60.

critical moment in the fighting, Seymour turned to Colonel Joseph Fisher, whose men of the 5th Pennsylvania Reserves were filing into the field as if on dress parade, and shouted, "Colonel, put your regiment into that cornfield and hurt somebody!"

"I will, General, and I'll catch one alive for you," came the colonel's cool reply.

Cheering, Fisher's 357 men leaped over the stone wall with the men of the 2nd and 6th Pennsylvania Reserves. The colonel quickly made good on his promise when his regiment bagged and sent back to Seymour eleven prisoners.[29]

By this time the firing was heavy and general across Seymour's front. Colonel William Sinclair rushed out on the right flank with his 6th Pennsylvania Reserves in an attempt to turn the rebel line. The movement was detected by Colonel Gordon's 6th Alabama, which shuttled farther north to hold the threatened ground with a tenacious determination. Severed from the left flank of the 5th Alabama by several hundred yards, Gordon's men delivered a steady but heavy fire into the Pennsylvanians. The volume and location of the defensive fire convinced Meade that Rodes was extending his lines north in an effort to turn the federal right, rather than to defend his own exposed left flank. Meade sent a courier to Hooker seeking reinforcements, and the commanding general responded by forwarding Duryee's brigade from Ricketts' division. These three New York regiments, along with one regiment from Pennsylvania, were halted along the National Turnpike, and several hours would elapse before they arrived.[30]

The Reserves, meanwhile, kept up a persistent and determined advance in an effort to turn Rodes' right. Captains William Ent and Charles Roush, commanding Companies A and B, respectively, of the 6th Pennsylvania Reserves, were ordered to sweep into the woods ahead and turn the enemy flank. Forming to their left, Companies C, D, and E moved to support them.[31]

*   *   *

29 Bates, *History of Pennsylvania Volunteers*, 2:669.

30 *Ibid.*; OR 1:215, 266-267; Hough, *History of Duryee's Brigade*, 113-114; H. W. Burlingame, letter, February 8, 1904, in S. Roger Keeler, *Crossroads of War: Washington County, Maryland in the Civil War* (Shippensburg, Pennsylvania: Burd Street Press, 1997), 105-107.

31 *Ibid.*; Bates, *History of Pennsylvania Volunteers*, 2:669; Priest, *Before Antietam*, 234.

As Seymour was moving on the right to flank Rodes' Alabama brigade, Gallagher and Magilton continued their advance farther south on Seymour's left. Gallagher's brigade, with its commander riding along the front of his line to direct his troops, moved obliquely to the right in an attempt to close a gap that had developed and thus reconnect with Seymour's regiments. The 9th Pennsylvania Reserves holding Gallagher's right found shelter from Rodes' deadly musketry under the cover of a low stone wall. For about twenty minutes, these Pennsylvanians slugged it out with their counterparts of the 5th Alabama until their ammunition was nearly expended. During this fighting, a musket ball shattered Gallagher's arm and forced him from the field. As he passed to the rear, he transferred command of his brigade to the 9th's Lieutenant Colonel Robert Anderson; Captain Samuel B. Dick of Company F assumed command of the 9th regiment.[32]

Meade's worry that his own right flank was being turned once again concerned him. "A report came that the rebels were flanking us on the right," explained Lieutenant Colonel Warner of the 10th Pennsylvania Reserves in his "minutes" of the battle. "[Meade] directed me to move out in that direction which I did on double quick." Warner rallied his regiment and expected to reinforce a faltering and endangered front line of battle. Instead of finding retreating chaos, however, he discovered that "The 1st Brigade was making their way up the mountain." Warner halted his men and reported his findings to General Meade. "Go in and help our men in there!" he snapped back, motioning toward the emerging gap between Seymour's left and Gallagher's right.

The 10th Pennsylvania Reserves moved forward into what was described as "a shower of bullets" from across the ravine. "We opened fire, part of the men moving rapidly up under cover and firing evenly on the rebels as they showed themselves among the rocks," Warner recollected after the war. The men in blue entered the ravine, but "unsurely faltered" in places where they were exposed to a sharp enemy fire. "This was the effect of the defeat at Bull Run," concluded Warner. "I did all in my power to push them rapidly forward and soon nearly all were in the ravine and beyond it and the rebels were running." About halfway up the slope, a rebel ball killed Warner's horse. The physically and mentally exhausted men hesitated once again, but additional

---

32 *Ibid.*; Bates, *History of Pennsylvania Volunteers*, 2:790, 850; OR 1:268, 274-275.

urging from Warner and their line officers got them going again toward the ridge.[33]

Farther left, Colonel Samuel Jackson rallied his 11th Pennsylvania Reserves. In the midst of their rocky ascent, Sergeant William D. Kuhns of Company B, "like a cock uttering the note of triumph," crowed loudly above the roar of the musketry. The sergeant from rural Indiana County, known for his powers of impersonation, had a wild effect on his men. His swaggering sounds punctuated the random pauses in the battle, so inspiring the men that they "went forward with renewed zeal to assured victory," wrote one eyewitness. In the words of enlisted man James H. McIlwain, it was "a hard fight."[34]

Gallagher's heavy and unrelenting pressure was beginning to tell on the loosely arranged lines of the 3rd and 5th Alabama regiments. The left of the 3rd Alabama (led by its appropriately named Colonel Cullen Andrews Battle) covered the bottom of the Frosttown gorge, where Colonel Battle deployed Captain R. M. Sands' Company K (the Mobile Rifles) as skirmishers. "[T]here were a number of houses [at the bottom of the gorge] . . . that must be held at all hazards," Battle reported, so he dispatched the 50 men of Company I (Wetumpka Guards) under Captain Edward S. Ready to secure the structures. The decisive nature of the federal attack struck quickly and hard. "In the first attack of the enemy up the bottom of the gorge," Rodes reported, "they pushed on so vigorously as to catch Captain Ready and a portion of his party of skirmishers."

Colonel Battle observed the storm from the perch of a high rock. Just minutes into the fight, the surviving members of the Wetumpka Guards fell back. With Ready a prisoner, command devolved upon Lieutenant J. J. Lake. When the lieutenant returned with his skirmishers, Battle left his observation post to say, "Lieutenant, when a man does his duty as you have today, he ought to at least know that he has the approbation of his commander." Just as Lake lifted his cap to recognize the compliment, a ball struck him. "He fell dead at my

33 Adoniram Judson Warner, as quoted in James B. Casey, ed., "The Ordeal of Adoniram Judson Warner: His Minutes of South Mountain and Antietam," *Civil War History*, 28, no. 3 (September 1982), 217-218; Bates, *History of Pennsylvania Volunteers*, 2:819; OR 1:266-267, 274-275.

34 *Ibid.*; Priest, *Before Antietam*, 233; Carman, *The Maryland Campaign*, 157; Bates, *History of Pennsylvania Volunteers*, 2:850, 858; James H. McIlwain, letter, September 16, 1862, United States Army Military History Institute Collection, Carlisle, Pennsylvania.

feet," the colonel wrote. "He was a splendid young man; as good as he was brave."

Thrusting their way up the mountains, the Reserves penetrated the Confederate line, separating Major Hobson's 5th Alabama from Battle's 3rd regiment. "From behind every rock, tree, and log, they forced the enemy with ball and bayonet," wrote Pennsylvania Reserve Corps historian Josiah Sypher.[35] "The firing now became general," Battle wrote. "In and around the houses, the struggle was terrific. The gorge had become another Thermopylae," he waxed poetically, "and Ready was its Leonidas." According to John S. Tucker of the 5th Alabama, the Alabamians were "cut all to pieces" and many of the men were taken prisoners. "Never saw so many straggling in all my life," he noted.[36]

General Rodes observed the unfolding debacle while peering through gaps in the rocks from behind the 12th Alabama. He was conversing behind the lines with Colonel Bristor B. Gayle and Lieutenant Colonel Samuel B. Pickens when the line began cracking apart. "What troops are those?" Rodes inquired when he caught a glimpse of the federal onslaught.

"I don't know, sir, I'll see," replied Colonel Gayle, who hoisted himself onto a rocky ledge in an effort to steal a better view. A moment later he exclaimed loudly, "My God, it's the Pennsylvania Reserves!" Pickens jumped up to take a look for himself. As he did so, Gayle shouted once more, "We are flanked, boys, but let us die in our tracks!" The fighting drew closer, and within minutes musket balls pierced both officers. Gayle was killed; Pickens was carried from the field mortally wounded.[37]

As the men of the 3rd and 5th Alabama regiments began falling back, Rodes attempted to rally the demoralized forces while also seeking help from D. H. Hill. "I renewed again, and yet again, my application for re-enforcements," he later complained, "but none came." Accompanied by Colonel Battle, Rodes guided his horse across the gorge while beseeching his

---

35 *Ibid.*; Sypher, *History of the Pennsylvania Reserve Corps*, 369; OR 1:267-268, 272.

36 *Ibid.*; OR 1:1035; Cullen Andrews Battle, "Boonsborough and Sharpsburg," in Brandon H. Beck, ed., *Third Alabama! The Civil War Memoir of Brigadier General Cullen Andrews Battle, CSA*, 55; John S. Tucker, diary entry, September 14, 1862, in G. Ward Hubbs, ed., *Voices from Company D: Diaries by the Greensboro Guards, Fifth Alabama Infantry Regiment, Army of Northern Virginia* (Athens: University of Georgia Press, 2003), 109.

37 Robert E. Park, "Anniversary of the Battle of Boonsboro, Maryland," in *Southern Historical Society Papers* 33:279; see also Priest, *Before Antietam*, 244; Collins, *Major General Robert E. Rodes of the Army of Northern Virginia*, 160, 432n23.

fleeing Alabamians—like those observed by John S. Tucker—to halt, organize, and make another stand. Together, he and Battle directed the "straggling" soldiers to pay attention to the crumbling left, where Seymour's Pennsylvanians were hammering away. Seymour's Reserve troops "dashed like steel," their rousing cheers heard rolling down the mountainside, were swinging around to the Confederate rear to make their way toward the head of the gorge. The only regiment poised to throw back the heavy attack was Colonel John Gordon's 6th Alabama, which leveled its muskets and opened fire.

The sight of Gordon's "last stand" was enough to encourage many of the stragglers to coalesce around the Rodes and Battle, who somehow managed to organize one final line of defense. When Rodes reached Gordon, he instructed him to move his regiment to the right and rear, while filling in the gaps with those who had returned to the ranks to form what he later described as "an embryonic line." Once in place, the veterans opened fire on the approaching federals. The sun was now setting, and it was so gloomy the men found it difficult to see much beyond musket range.[38]

Rodes' desperate situation was about to get worse. The reinforcements Meade had requested three hours earlier—Duryee's brigade from Ricketts' division—were arriving on the field. Up came the 97th New York, commanded by Major Charles Northrup; the 104th and 105th New York regiments, commanded by Major Lewis C. Skinner and Lieutenant Colonel Howard Carroll, respectively; and Captain James MacThomson's 107th Pennsylvania. The brigade ascended the mountain with bayonets fixed, bagging pockets of prisoners hiding behind rocks and trees along the way. The 97th New York alone reported capturing "about sixty of the enemy" during its ascent to the front line. It was, as brigade historian Franklin Hough observed, "a critical moment, and Duryee's brigade was just in time to strike a decisive blow."[39]

And the blow was delivered almost without firing a shot. Meade formed Duryee's regiments into a line of battle and advanced them behind the left-center of his divisional line. They were moving in when the embattled Alabamians reached the end of their defensive endurance. Beneath the full cover of darkness, Rodes and Battle decided to fall back and establish another

---

38 OR 1:1035-1036; B&L, 2:574; Bates, *History of Pennsylvania Volunteers*, 1:584, 2:698; Carman, *The Maryland Campaign*, 158; Collins, *Major General Robert E. Rodes*, 160-161.

39 OR 1;1036; Hall, *History of the Ninety-Seventh Regiment*, 87; Hough, *History of Duryee's Brigade*, 113-114.

line. Despite Gordon's stout defense and the impressive last minute rally on the far left, Seymour's federals finally turned their flank and gained control of the northern crest. An "immense number" of Confederates fell into the welcoming hands of Duryee's brigade farther left. Clothing, weapons, and knapsacks littered the roads, woods, and fields.[40]

Throughout this phase of the fighting, the firing along Gallagher's front (on Seymour's immediate left) was "incessant on both sides," and the federals there met with similar success. Because of the confusing and heavy terrain, opposing soldiers sometimes found themselves face-to-face, which resulted in hand-to-hand fighting. Colonel Edward A. O'Neal's 26th Alabama was fighting between the 3rd and 12th Alabama. A politician-turned-soldier, O'Neal had been severely injured by a shell fragment at Seven Pines on May 31, and as he was directing his men on the mountainside on this day, one of the federal bullets struck him in the thigh. Like most of the others, his survivors soon also streamed for the rear, their morale disintegrating along with every formation in the brigade. Even Rodes admitted that by this point, his troops were "completely demoralized" and mingling in "utter confusion." Wounded Lieutenant Troup K. Randle of Company D, 3rd Alabama, who supposedly "only 'cussed' by way of emphasis," as Colonel Battle remembered, "cussed old General Hill out of his boots." The soldiers who had dislodged them had little left inside to continue after them. "My men, like myself, were almost ready to sink down from complete exhaustion," recalled the 10th Pennsylvania Reserves' Lieutenant Colonel Adoniram Warner.[41]

*   *   *

Lieutenant Randle was not the only Confederate who wanted to cuss D. H. Hill "out of his boots" that day. Rodes spent much of the afternoon reporting his impossible position to Hill while pleading for reinforcements. Despite even the most adroit deployment of his regiments, Rodes was a good enough soldier to know his brigade could only buy some time. After Rodes' men were fighting

---

40 *Ibid.*; OR 1:267-268, 272.

41 OR 1:274, 1035; Gibbs, *Three Years with the Bloody Eleventh*, 174-176; Cullen Battle, "Boonsborough and Sharpsburg," in Beck, ed., *Third Alabama!*, 56; Adoniram Judson Warner, as quoted in James B. Casey, ed., "The Ordeal of Adoniram Judson Warner: His Minutes of South Mountain and Antietam," *Civil War History*, 28, no. 3 (September 1982): 217-218.

for their lives, reinforcements in the form of Brigadier General Thomas Drayton's and Brigadier General George "Tige" Anderson's brigades, from Longstreet's command, arrived on the field. Two additional brigades under Brigadier General John Bell Hood and the independent command of Brigadier General Nathan G. Evans also approached the crest of South Mountain. Drayton, Anderson, and Hood's men scurried south to shore up the crumbled defenses of Fox's Gap. Only the South Carolinians received orders to lend a hand to Rodes.

Rodes later reported that he had no assistance, although he did mention that he "heard that some Confederate troops had joined my right very nearly." The "confederate troops" to whom Rodes referred belonged to Nathan Evans' brigade of South Carolinians. General Hill, probably still seething from the perfunctory performance turned in by Jeb Stuart, nearly echoed Rodes in his postwar piece for *Century* magazine. In his article, Hill observed that Evans' men "got on the ground too late to effect anything else" besides saving Rodes from "being entirely surrounded." While both statements are true as far as written, both also diminish the effort these men made and the difficult position into which they were thrust.[42]

The 550 men of Evans' independent "tramp" brigade—the 17th South Carolina, commanded by Colonel F. W. McMaster; the 18th South Carolina, commanded by Colonel W. H. Wallace; Lieutenant Colonel T. C. Watkins' 22nd South Carolina; Captain S. A. Durham's 23rd South Carolina; and Colonel Peter F. Stevens' Holcombe Legion—were under Stevens' command on September 14. Longstreet ordered the brigade to report to D. H. Hill at the Old Mountain House. Stevens arrived at Turner's Gap at the head of his brigade between 4:00 and 4:30 p.m. and was conducted to Hill by Major John W. Fairfax, a member of Longstreet's staff.

Almost certainly as a result of Rodes' repeated requests, D. H. Hill directed Stevens to support the embattled Alabama brigade. According to the Palmetto brigade commander, his men had "accomplished about half the distance" when he received an order from Evans to halt. As the minutes ticked past and with the battle raging at full fury, the colonel grew anxious and sent a dispatch to Rodes explaining why he had stopped. He also sent a courier dashing back to Evans demanding instructions. At the same time, a rider from Rodes' staff galloped up to Stevens and urged him to move his men forward. The enemy was pressing

---

42 OR 1:1035-1036; *B&L*, 2:574.

the Alabamians from the valley below, his men were beginning to fall back, and there was no time to spare. Without waiting for Evans to reply, Stevens took it upon himself to throw out his own Holcombe Legion to the right as skirmishers, advanced the balance of the small brigade, and prepared for contact with the advancing enemy. The South Carolinians went in on Rodes' right facing east across the Frosttown gorge against Colonel Magilton's Pennsylvania troops. The 23rd South Carolina, on the left of the brigade front, "very nearly" met Rodes' right under the 12th Alabama. The 22nd, 18th, and 17th South Carolina regiments moved into place to extend the line to the right. Within minutes the federals shoved back the Holcombe Legion skirmishers.[43]

Stevens ordered a general movement into the gorge. Magilton's men poured a heavy fire into the Confederates, who, according to one federal, held their ground with "remarkable obstinacy." The small arms fire was delivered within fifty yards—and sometimes closer. Colonel Bolinger of the 7th Pennsylvania Reserves was urging his men forward when one of the rebel balls tore the flesh off the right arm and passed through his right breast. Command of the regiment fell to Major Chauncey A. Lyman.

Immediately to the left of the 7th, members of Major Silas M. Bailey's 8th Pennsylvania Reserves selected specific South Carolinians to shoot down. "I remember taking deliberate aim at a tall South Carolinian, who was standing with his side to me loading his gun," Sergeant Alonzo Hill wrote. "I fired, and he fell into a crevice between two rocks." The sergeant made his way toward his victim. "On my arrival thither, he arose to a sitting posture, and I was convinced he was not dead yet." A pool of blood collected on the rock ledge to his side, gushing from a wound in his neck. His arm was fixed, still extended vertically from having sent his ramrod home. "He arose to his feet, and I was pleased to find him able to walk," Hill continued. He sent the Confederate to the rear—his name recorded in the "captured" column instead of being added to the growing list of the "killed." Little by little the South Carolinians fell back or tumbled to the earth. "Poor fellows!" Sergeant Hill wrote. "I almost pitied them, to see them sink down by the dozens at every discharge!"[44]

Fighting with Sergeant Hill's 8th Pennsylvania, Lieutenant William M. Carter of Company B and Company D's Captain Cyrus Conner sprang over a

---

43 OR 1: 839, 885-886, 894-895, 899-900, 939, 941, 945; Carman, *The Maryland Campaign*, 159.

44 Carman, *The Maryland Campaign*, 159-160; Bates, *History of Pennsylvania Volunteers*, 2:726, 761; Archibald F. Hill, *Our Boys*, 395-397; Priest, *Before Antietam*, 244.

stone wall within a few feet of each other—close enough, at least, for Conner to see his comrade's prophesy come true: an enemy ball struck Carter in the head, killing him instantly.[45]

A few paces from Carter's body Conner discovered a wounded Confederate major with an injury to his thigh resting on the ground. "You are wounded, are you not?" inquired the federal captain.

"Yes, in the thigh—and badly," came the rebel's reply.

"What's your name?" asked Conner.

"I am Major Means of the Seventeenth South Carolina. May I ask you the same question?" When Conner replied with his name and regiment, the Southern major replied, "Well, captain, your men fight like devils; they are driving our men right up this steep mountain; I never could have believed it!"

"Ah, major," consoled Conner, "there is blood in Pennsylvania as well as in South Carolina."[46]

Rodes' men were falling back along with the South Carolinians as darkness engulfed the mountainside. Colonel McMaster ordered the 17th South Carolina to continue firing during their withdrawal. The other regiments were already breaking hastily for the rear, in some cases reduced to mere handfuls of men. The sounds of retreat resoundingly confirmed for the Pennsylvania Reserves what they already instinctively knew: they had won the tactical battle for control of the crests north of the National Turnpike.

As Captain Conner confessed to the wounded Major Means, the Pennsylvanians had indeed been bloodied that afternoon. The effort to drive away the Alabamians and South Carolinians and capture the craggy wooded heights cost Meade a reported loss of 392 men from all causes. The losses were essentially evenly distributed between the three brigades, although Seymour's command sustained the heaviest losses with 38 killed and 133 wounded. Gallagher's regiments suffered losses of 32 killed and 100 wounded, and Magilton reported 25 killed, 63 wounded, and one captured. Magilton's losses clearly demonstrate that Evans' South Carolinians put up quite a fight given their untimely arrival and impossible task. The 8th Pennsylvania Reserves took the brunt of the assault when the South Carolinians poured into the gorge against the extreme left of Magilton's line, counting 17 killed and 37 wounded

---

45 *Ibid.*; Priest, *Before Antietam*, 249-250.

46 Hill, *Our Boys*, 397-398.

by the time the fighting ended. "We stayed in sight of the battlefield all day," one of the Reserves noted in his diary on September 15, "and such a sight I never saw before, nor do I ever want to again. The dead lay in piles, so that they had to be carried to one side to make room for artillery to pass."[47]

Rodes reported heavy losses of 422 men: 61 killed, 157 wounded, and 204 captured, or more than one-third of his brigade. "We did not drive the enemy back or whip him," he candidly admitted, "but with 1,200 men we held his whole division at bay without assistance during four a half hours' steady fighting." Once more, the barb was sunk into the South Carolinians. Battle reports testify to the fight put up by the Palmetto soldiers. Of the 550 men Stevens guided into battle, 23 were killed, 142 were wounded, and 45 reported missing.[48]

In the battle's aftermath, many Confederates attempted to describe what, exactly, had transpired at Turner's Gap on the far Confederate left during the battle at South Mountain. Was Rodes defeated or did he gain a victory? "In view of the great force approaching to attack him, his fight seemed almost hopeless," Longstreet observed. "But he handled his troops with skill and delayed the enemy, with the little help that finally came, till night, breaking from time to time as he was forced nearer our center at the turnpike." That generally balanced view contrasted sharply with an account penned by Edward Porter Alexander, one of the Army of Northern Virginia's most capable gunners, who suggested that Rodes fought the enemy to a stalemate. As Alexander put it, "the action was kept up until darkness finally called its truce upon the field." Colonel Battle of the 3rd Alabama emphasized the desperate nature of the command: "Foot-sore and weary, almost hungry and almost naked, they had fought a great battle and added to their glory and their fame." D. H. Hill reported that Rodes' Brigade "immortalized itself," and during the postwar years paid tribute to its "heroic resistance." Hill concluded that it was "pitiable to see the gallant but hopeless struggle of those Alabamians against such mighty odds."[49]

---

47 Casualty figures have been culled from a survey of the regimental histories of the Reserves in Samuel P. Bates, *History of Pennsylvania Volunteers*, 2:698, 761; OR 1:186, 268; Sypher, *History of the Pennsylvania Reserve Corps*, 373; Carman, *The Maryland Campaign*, 447; "The Diary of a Pennsylvania Reserve," *National Tribune*, August 29, 1901.

48 OR 1:811, 941-942, 945, 946-947, 949, 1036; Carman, *The Maryland Campaign*, 160, 449, 451n14.

49 Longstreet, *From Manassas to Appomattox*, 224; Edward Porter Alexander, *Military Memoirs of a Confederate: A Critical Narrative*, ed. Gary W. Gallagher (1907; reprint, New York: Da Capo

Most recently, Rodes' first serious biographer concluded that "at South Mountain, Rodes rendered to the Confederacy an invaluable service, and certainly his most important of the war to date." Pushed off the crest during the engagement, the Alabamians held their ground until eleven that evening when Rodes ordered his command to proceed along the road to Sharpsburg and halt at Keedysville. "Oh that it had been daylight, that we might have pursued them at once!" lamented Sergeant Alonzo Hill of the 8th Pennsylvania Reserves.[50]

In the final analysis, widespread Rebel incredulity that the recently defeated blue-clad army could storm the steep sides of South Mountain and drive back veterans from Lee's invincible army—such as the disbelief expressed by Major Means of the 17th South Carolina to Captain Conner—necessitated an aggressive postwar revisionism. "They thought they could hold these passes against any force but they were considerably mistaken," observed John McQuaide, a veteran of Company C of the 8th Pennsylvania Reserves with no little pride. "I think they [the rebels] are full of Maryland now." Driving the Confederates off the mountain top was, as Colonel William Rogers of the 21st New York proclaimed, "one of the most brilliant little achievements of the war."[51]

Press, 1993), 231; OR, 1:1022; B&L, 2:574; Cullen Andrews Battle, "Boonsborough and Sharpsburg," in Beck, ed., Third Alabama!, 56.

50 Ibid; Hill, Our Boys, 398; Collins, Major General Robert E. Rodes, 162.

51 John McQuaide, letter to his brother, Thomas McQuaide, September 22, 1862, in Civil War Times Illustrated Collection, United States Army Military History Institute, Carlisle, Pennsylvania; William F. Rogers, as quoted in J. H. Mills, Chronicles of the Twenty-First Regiment, New York State Volunteers, 281.

"The success was complete"

Turner's Gap:
The Battle for the National Turnpike

"It is indeed true that we have beaten the enemy; these impetuous attacks
are only his last flurries; he is, though we do not know it, and
cannot discover it in the darkness, at his last gasp."

— *John Harrison Mills, 21st New York*[1]

W hen Nathan Evans sent his brigade of South Carolinians under
Colonel Peter Stevens to aid Robert Rodes' Alabamians, the
Palmetto soldiers expected to be reinforced on their right. There were only
three brigades from Major General David R. Jones' Division (Longstreet's
wing) available for the task. Two of these brigades—Brigadier General Thomas
Drayton's and Colonel George "Tige" Anderson's—had already been
forwarded to D. H. Hill, who had in turn thrust them south to plug embattled
Fox's Gap. The remaining brigade of Georgians under Brigadier General
Robert Toombs stood watch at Hagerstown, which General Lee prescribed as
James Longstreet's platform for invasion in Special Orders No. 191.

Longstreet stood atop Turner's Gap surveying the desperate situation.
While his trusted aide G. Moxley Sorrel later suggested that Longstreet's "quick
military instinct told him what was happening," the rebels' tenuous hold on
South Mountain was already readily apparent. "At first sight of the situation, as I
rode up the mountainside," recalled Longstreet, "it became evident that we

---

1 John Harrison Mills, *Chronicles of the Twenty-First Regiment, New York State Volunteers*, 284.

were not in time nor in sufficient force to secure our holding at Turner's Gap, and a note was sent to General Lee to prepare his mind for disappointment." At the same time, he summoned the three brigades of Jones' command to the mountain top "as rapidly as their exhausted condition would admit of."[2]

The brigades under James L. Kemper, Micah Jenkins, and George Pickett barely qualified as such, at least numerically speaking. Originally led by Longstreet on the Virginia peninsula and during the Second Manassas campaign, he divided his division and placed these three organizations under Kemper's command in a new, short-lived division. When the invasion of Maryland commenced, the bloodied brigades easily melted into Jones' Division. Only Kemper remained at the head of his brigade. Jenkins, wounded at Second Manassas, was replaced temporarily by Colonel Joseph Walker. Because he was still absent from a wound suffered at Gaines' Mill during the Seven Days' Battles, George Pickett's men were led by Brigadier General Richard B. Garnett. Kemper's and Garnett's commands combined numbered scarcely 850 men.[3]

Late on the afternoon of September 14, Kemper led his five Virginia regiments past the Mountain House and to the left on the road meandering just beyond Rodes' right flank. Captain George F. Norton commanded the 1st Virginia. The temporary head of the 7th Virginia was Major Arthur Herbert, and another major, Adam Clement, led the men of the 11th Virginia. Rounding out the brigade were Colonels Montgomery D. Corse and William R. Terry, who led the 17th Virginia and 24th Virginia regiments, respectively. Facing generally northeast, these regiments formed up across the Old Hagerstown Road "under very fierce shelling" from Captain George Durell's federal battery (Sturgis' division). Positioned deep in the lower valley, the guns enfiladed the

---

2 OR 1:839, 885-886, 1034-1035; Carman, *The Maryland Campaign*, 160; Longstreet, *From Manassas to Appomattox*, 227; G. Moxley Sorrel, *At the Right Hand of Longstreet: Recollections of a Confederate Staff Officer* (New York: Neal Publishing Company, 1905; reprint, Lincoln: University of Nebraska Press, 1999), 106. Considering Longstreet's earnest opposition to Lee's decision to divide the army to take Harpers Ferry, one wonders whether he felt a twinge of vindication or the pangs of deep frustration on the evening of September 14.

3 Harsh, *Sounding the Shallows*, 53-56; OR 1:804-805; Carman, *The Maryland Campaign*, 160-161. Unhappy with his performance in the Shenandoah Valley at First Kernstown, General Thomas Jackson placed Richard Garnett under arrest on April 1, 1862. Lee ordered Jackson to release the brigadier when the current campaign got underway. Garnett assumed command of his brigade on September 5, 1862, under Special Orders No. 188. OR 2:595. Unfortunately, available reports do not provide reliable estimates of Jenkins'/Walker's strength on September 14, 1862.

Virginians and wounded two of them. The 17th Virginia held Kemper's right flank. Extending the brigade to the left were, in order: the 11th, 1st, 7th, and 24th Virginia regiments. The latter three regiments rested in the woods left of the road, with the former regiments holding a position near the edge of a cornfield.[4]

Behind Kemper marched a frustrated Garnett, who also commanded five regiments of Virginians: Colonel Eppa Hunton's 8th, Major George C. Cabell's 18th, Colonel J. B. Strange's 19th, Captain William K. Wingfield's 28th, and Colonel William D. Stuart's 56th. When Garnett was ordered to move into position and support Kemper's right, all the aide could offer the brigadier was to "about-face . . . return the way I came until I reached a path, which I must take." When he asked for more information, the aide had none to give. The Virginian marched his men through the heavy terrain for some time before another courier found him with better instructions. By then, reported Garnett, "my men were almost exhausted. I consequently lost the services of a number of men by straggling." Garnett's paltry command of a few hundred men assumed an initial position facing generally south by southeast about 200 yards to the right of Kemper, with Hunton's regiment resting on the right flank and Stuart's 56th on the left. Between them (left to right) were the 28th, 19th, and 18th regiments. Because Garnett's men faced toward the Middletown Valley and the National road, his line was refused (angled) back from Kemper's right, meaning together they formed a broad V-shaped front with the tip facing the approaching enemy.[5]

Numerical strength was not the only factor working against these brigades on the late afternoon of September 14. A misinterpreted order had dispatched James Longstreet's already exhausted commands on an extended countermarch before they even reached the battlefield. "By the time we reached the top of the mountain at least half of the command has succumbed to the heat and wore fatigue of the long hasty march," Captain Henry T. Owen of the 18th Virginia recalled. According to Captain Owen, there were scarcely more than 400 men present for duty in Garnett's entire brigade. "Let it now be remembered that this army made fourteen miles to the immediate vicinity of the battleground in three and a half hours," maintained Private David Emmons Johnston of the 7th

---

4   *Ibid.*; OR 1:904-905.

5   *Ibid.*; see also Priest, *Before Antietam*, 254.

Virginia. That was very good time, insisted the private—even for a "Hamiltonian horse."[6]

The sight that greeted these arriving reinforcements did little to increase their enthusiasm. "Troops of the most demoralized stragglers are descending as we ascend, and long lines of wounded limping down the road," wrote the 1st Virginia's John Dooley. Hot, tired, hungry, and dusty by the time they reached their deployment line, when the initial artillery rounds from Durell's guns began finding their range, Dooley admitted experiencing real fear. "*I tell you*, I was frightened! These balls not content with making the ordinary scare, bounding over and above and around and among us, go crashing into the crags on our left, splintering into a thousand pieces large fragments of rock which wildly fly around our heads. . . . One shot went through a tree about three feet in diameter, splitting nothing but leaving a nice round smooth hole in the body."[7] Captain Owen of the 18th Virginia wrote about the same rain of iron. "A shell struck the fence . . . with a terrific explosion," he recalled, "splintering and throwing the pieces of broken fence nails high in air in every direction towards the rear."[8]

* * *

As the Virginians assumed their positions, John Hatch's federal division was in line and ready to knock them back up the slope. His four brigades shadowed the advance of the Pennsylvania Reserves that afternoon. One brigade, the Western regiments commanded by Brigadier General John Gibbon, had been detached from the balance of the division. The remaining trio—led by Colonel Walter Phelps Jr., Brigadier General Marsena Patrick, and Brigadier General Abner Doubleday—composed a fighting force of nearly 3,500 men. Phelps' six regiments included Lieutenant Colonel John McKie's 22nd New York, Captain John D. O'Brian's 24th New York, Colonel William

6   Henry T. Owen, "The Battle of South Mountain," handwritten manuscript, in Henry T. Owen Papers, Virginia Historical Society, Richmond, Virginia. Owen's estimate is consistent with Ezra Carman's figures. Carman, *The Maryland Campaign*, 160-161; OR 1:894; David Emmons Johnston, *The Story of a Confederate Boy* (Portland, Or.: Glass & Prudhomme Co., 1914), 139.

7   John Dooley, "South Mountain and Sharpsburg," in Joseph T. Durkin, S.J., ed., *John Dooley, Confederate Soldier: His War Journal* (Notre Dame: University of Notre Dame Press, 1963), 35-36.

8   Owen, "The Battle of South Mountain," Henry T. Owen Papers, Virginia Historical Society, Richmond, Virginia.

M. Searing's 30th New York, Major William H. De Bevoise's 84th New York (also known as the 14th New York State militia, raised from the borough of Brooklyn), and the 2nd United States Sharpshooters under Colonel Henry A. V. Post. Patrick's all-New York brigade included Colonel William F. Rogers' 21st, Colonel Henry C. Hoffman's 23rd, Colonel Newton B. Lord's 35th, and Lieutenant Colonel Theodore B. Gates' 20th State Militia. Finally, Doubleday rode at the head of the 7th Indiana, commanded by Major Ira G. Grover; the 76th New York under Colonel William Pratt Wainwright, the 95th New York under Major Edward Pye, and the 56th Pennsylvania under Lieutenant Colonel J. William Hoffman.[9]

Diverting to the right of the National Turnpike, Hatch encountered Joe Hooker at the Mount Tabor Church, where the I Corps leader presented him with the general order of battle. In essence, Hooker had divided the fight for Tuner's Gap into two main actions and a third latter smaller attack. The Frosttown Road partitioned the two larger assaults. George Meade's division of Pennsylvania Reserves would storm Robert Rodes' Alabama line north (or right) of the Frosttown Road, moving across the gorge and up to the heights of the northern crest. South (or left) of Meade's fight, in the space between the National Turnpike and the Frosttown Road, Hooker planned to engage Hatch's division (the brigades of Phelps, Patrick, and Doubleday) against what would be the inadequate defensive front comprised of the Virginians under Garnett and Kemper and, eventually, the South Carolinians under Joseph Walker. Finally, Hooker detached John Gibbon's brigade from Hatch's division. Once the primary strategic attacks were well underway—meaning Hooker's combined move against Rodes and the entire Confederate left, and Jesse Reno's IX Corps assault against the Confederate right at Fox's Gap—Gibbon's western regiments would demonstrate straight up the National Turnpike against Colonel Alfred Colquitt's Georgians.

With his orders in hand, Hatch directed his division, with Marsena Patrick's brigade in the lead, to move from column of divisions into line of battle. Hooker's schematic called for two regiments from Patrick's command to precede the advance of the main force in skirmish formation. He intended these regiments to not only ascertain the enemy's positions but potentially stymie any Confederate attempt to flank Jacob Cox's brigades left of the National Turnpike. Each of these advance units would be supported by one of Patrick's

Major General Joseph Hooker

Library of Congress

remaining regiments. In turn, at an interval of about 200 paces, these supporting regiments would be followed by Phelps' brigade, with Doubleday's men hurrying up the mountainside and following Phelps' command at an identical interval.[10]

Colonel Rogers' 21st New York was ordered forward to skirmish on the right. The men left behind the weight of their knapsacks as three companies from each flank went forward and deployed across the rocky slope. The remaining four companies followed, supporting from the center. As the men moved up the mountain, they encountered an elderly woman excited by the battle roaring on both flanks. She asked the skirmishers where they were heading.

"Don't you go there," she implored when one of Rogers' officers replied they were merely "going up the hill." Flailing her arms wildly in the air, she insisted, "There are hundreds of 'em up there," and then motioned the men to make for the rear. "Don't you go! Some of you will get hurt!" With rifled-muskets primed and ready for action, the Empire Staters continued up the mountainside, eager and anxious to confront and defeat "the hundreds" of Confederates near the summit. Like men always do to relieve combat stress, a

---

10 Mills, *Chronicles of the Twenty-first Regiment*, 279; Gates, *The Ulster Guard*, 295-296; OR 1:221, 241-242; Carman, *The Maryland Campaign*, 161; Marsena R. Patrick, diary entry, September 14, 1862, in David S. Sparks, ed., *Inside Lincoln's Army: The Diary of General Marsena Rudolph Patrick, Army of the Potomac* (New York: Thomas Yoseloff, 1964), 144-145.

few began cutting jokes. "Some of you will get hurt!" they mocked. "Some of you will get hurt!"[11]

The 20th New York State Militia supported the cloud of skirmishers on the right. Together, the regiments advanced, halting to re-form on the broken ground nearly every fifteen or twenty paces. Before too long they found the enemy posted behind a fence running north and south near the crest. "The enemy opened a brisk musketry fire as the Union lines approached the summit of the mountain," Lieutenant Colonel Theodore Gates wrote, "but most of their shot went over the heads of our men, doing execution only in the branches of the trees, among which they rattled like hail stones." Several Southern guns were ordered up from Lieutenant Colonel A. S. Cutts' Reserve Artillery and situated left of the National Turnpike. From this position they fired at the three lines with but little effect. "Owing to the little practice of the gunners and the sharp depression angle, the cannonade was as harmless as blank-cartridge salutes in honor of a militia general," D. H. Hill later explained. The enemy, lamented the general, "did not honor" these shells "by so much as a dodge."[12]

Even as these troops pressed within fifty paces of the fence line, the Confederate aim remained too high. The Southerners continued loading as fast as they could, "going through the motions" to overcome the nervous excitement of battle. Gates estimated at least eighty percent of their shots "flew harmlessly over the heads of the Federals. The trunks of the trees, among which they were standing, received a large proportion of the remaining 20 per cent." The lieutenant colonel speculated that this waste of ammunition was not the result of poorly drilled men, but the fact that they had never fired downhill during combat. "The fact is, that unless troops have been especially drilled in firing down the face of a mountain, they are sure to fire ninety per cent of their shots too high," explained Gates. "Indeed, this is the fault of the best drilled troops, as well as of tyros, on the most favorable ground—they fire too high."[13]

South of Colonel Rogers' jesting New York skirmishers, Colonel Lord's 35th New York marched on the left oblique, drifting away from the 23rd New York on its right as it approached the bed of the National Turnpike. In an effort

---

11 Mills, *Chronicles of the Twenty-first Regiment*, 280-281; Priest, *Before Antietam*, 251.

12 *Ibid.*; Gates, *The Ulster Guard*, 295-296; OR 1:221, 241-242, 1,020; Carman, *The Maryland Campaign*, 161; Marsena R. Patrick, diary entry, September 14, 1862, in Sparks, ed., *Inside Lincoln's Army*, 144-145; B&L 2:574.

13 Gates, *The Ulster Guard*, 297-298.

to close his front, Patrick ordered the 23rd New York to shift left to support Lord, while he sent the 80th New York edging rightward to support the 21st New York on the right side of his battle line. The result was a gaping hole in the center of his line. Patrick was losing control of his brigade at the worst possible time. When Phelps guided his brigade forward in accordance with the battle plan, he discovered the yawning space, halted his men, and dispatched one of his aides to find General Hatch. The division commander "immediately rode to the front" and issued orders to seal the dangerous gap. Phelps shoved his brigade forward into the breach, with two of Patrick's regiments on either side of his own men. With his front at least closed up once more, Hatch pushed his brigades forward as he rode through the lines cheering his soldiers.[14]

Hatch's federal line not only outnumbered the recently arrived Virginians, but overlapped them on both flanks by a wide margin. In addition, the Confederate V-shaped front meant that only a fraction of the defenders were in a position to deliver fire at the approaching Yankees. As the right side of Hatch's divisional line stepped within small arms range, a "fierce volley" was unleashed at the Virginians. "Rapid and continuous is the fusillade that follows," John Harrison Mills of the 21st New York wrote about the fire against Kemper's men. "The mountain top reeks with a sulphurous veil, out of which rises a horrid turmoil, and the echoes fly to hide in every nook and valley." Many of Kemper's Confederates were surprised by the sudden appearance of the federals. "On reaching the crest of the mountain we found ourselves face to face with the enemy and close up to them, and under fire before we were able to get into formation," Private David Johnston of the 17th Virginia recalled.[15]

The 18th Virginia on Garnett's side of the V-shaped front had only been crouched in position behind a rock ledge for about five minutes when a soldier spotted a federal soldier in Patrick's skirmish line. "Major Cabell," he said, "younder is a Yankee!"

Major George Cabell looked over the ridge and shouted, "Come in here and surrender you blue bellied rascal, or by guns I will have you shot!" Moments later, another Virginian warned, "There is two or three yankees down there

---

14 OR 1:220, 221-222, 231; Gates, *The Ulster Guard*, 296-297; William P. Maxson, *Camp Fires of the Twenty-third*, 98-99; Carman, *The Maryland Campaign*, 161; Martin Swarthout, diary entry, September 14, 1862, in Northwest Corner Civil War Roundtable Collection, United States Army Military History Institute, Carlisle, Pennsylvania.

15 David Emmons Johnston, *The Story of a Confederate Boy*, 140.

coming this way." Yet another private, this one curious as to why no one was shooting them down, yelled, "Who'll just look at em?"[16]

General Hatch rode along his front urging the men forward as the exchange of gunfire increased and he did his best to shout above the rattle of musketry. Within perhaps fifteen minutes, a bullet clipped the exposed general and forced him from the field. Command of his division devolved upon Abner Doubleday.[17]

As the 17th Virginia's Private Johnston later recalled, the fight rose to a desperate and even frenzied level. "A fire was soon opened upon the advancing enemy but they neither paused nor faltered and a fierce brief combat was held for the ridge," Owen recalled. General Phelps agreed, adding that "Although the enemy were strongly posted behind a fence . . . they could not withstand the terrific fire and steady veteran advance of my line." Parts of the Union line had moved to within about forty yards from the Virginians. James D. Forbes, an enlisted man who fought with Company B of the 22nd New York, part of Phelps' brigade, described the action as "sharp" and at times "hand to hand." As Forbes specifically recollected in a postwar piece for the *National Tribune*: "Well do I remember Lieutenant John J. Baker clinching a rebel soldier and pulling him through a rail fence. He sent him to the rear the most forlorn looking butternut I ever saw."[18]

While Phelps hammered the wide V-shaped front with most of his firepower ripping through Garnett's ranks, Patrick's regiments, still divided on either side of Phelps' brigade, had a bit farther to go before their full weight fell upon the defending Confederates. As the heavier federal battalions pressed forward, the Virginians began folding backward under the pressure. Darkness was falling over the field, and chaos—as it always does in combat—assumed a leading role. "There was great confusion, and the broken ranks were hard to rally and re-form," Captain Owen of the 18th Virginia admitted as twelve or fifteen men from different companies surrounded him. Major Cabell agreed, adding that the 18th Virginia "became a good deal scattered." Colonel Stuart's

---

16 Owen, "The Battle of South Mountain," Henry T. Owen Papers, Virginia Historical Society, Richmond, Virginia; OR 1:231; Mills, *Chronicles of the Twenty-First*, 282.

17 *OR* 1:220, 221-222, 232.

18 *Ibid.*, 231-232; Owen, "The Battle of South Mountain," Henry T. Owen Papers, Virginia Historical Society, Richmond, Virginia; James D. Forbes, "The 22nd New York," *National Tribune*, 24 September 1885.

56th Virginia had the unenviable task of fighting at the junction of the two brigades, and as the Yankees poured up the slope he realized his small regiment faced the very real possibility of being flanked, surrounded, and captured. Unable to identify the enemy because of the deepening gloom of dusk, Stuart wheeled back and attached his regiment to Kemper's right flank. In a stroke of amazing good fortune for the Confederates, Phelps—having suffered a loss which "at this point was much heavier than any other on the field"—halted his brigade to allow his men to catch their breath and reorganize. "This gave the Confederates time to rally and re-form in separate squads and detachments behind the rocks and fences and reopen a brisk fire," Captain Owen reported. Although "half of the brigade disappeared," many of the Virginians continued fighting as they fell back, hoping to hold back the enemy until reinforcements arrived. Once Phelps stopped shoving his men forward, wrote Private Johnston, "The firing [upon us] . . . ceased." The defenders soon learned the respite would not last long. "There was heard in our front the tramp of the enemy's feet," continued the private, "evidently preparing to renew the assault."[19]

During the brief lull in the center of Hatch's line, Phelps sought help from Doubleday's 1,000-man brigade (now under Colonel Wainwright of the 76th New York), to relieve his battered command. "Our Brigade cannot sustain itself much longer, as we are nearly out of ammunition!" one of Phelps' adjutants shouted to Wainwright. "For God's sake, to the front!"

Heeding the call, the colonel rushed to send the mixed brigade of Hoosiers, New Yorkers, and Pennsylvanians forward. "Steady, boys, steady!" he ordered over what one described as a "carnival of noise." Wainwright's 76th New York held the extreme left of the brigade, which coiled beyond Garnett's refused right. The balance of the line extended to the right by the 7th Indiana, 95th New York, and 56th Pennsylvania.[20]

---

19 Owen, "The Battle of South Mountain," Henry T. Owen Papers, Virginia Historical Society, Richmond, Virginia; Henry T. Owen, "Annals of the War—Chapters of Unwritten History: South Mountain," *Philadelphia Weekly Times*, July 31, 1880, quoted in Carman, *The Maryland Campaign*, 162; Maxson, *Campfires of the Twenty-Third*, 99; Carman, *The Maryland Campaign*, 162; OR 1:232, 899-900, 901-905; Johnston, *The Story of a Confederate Boy*, 140-141.

20 Abram P. Smith, *History of the Seventy-Sixth Regiment New York Volunteers* (Cortland: Truain, Smith, and Miles Printers, 1876), 152; George F. Noyes, *The Bivouac and the Battlefield* (New York: Harper and Brothers, 1863), 172-173; Priest, *Before Antietam*, 258; Carman, *The Maryland Campaign*, 162; OR 1:222, 232, 234-235, 238-240.

Within a short time, Abner Doubleday's men under Wainright gained the upper edge of the woods near the crest. They may have gone into combat more animated than usual. Earlier that day the soldiers enjoyed what one of them described as a "rare luxury"—a stop in a field of green turnips. "We halted, reformed the lines, fixed bayonets, and went forward again with a rush, cheering and yelling lustily . . . There was no need for the order to 'charge,'" Adjutant Edward Barnes of the 95th New York recalled. "The brigade, as if governed by one impulse, rushed impetuously forward and over the nearest fence, driving the enemy over the other and through a field of standing corn into the timber beyond and on either side." With a "deafening crash [the] sheets of flame" from the muskets of both Union and Confederate soldiers mingled as one.[21]

Color Sergeant Charles E. Stamp of Company A, 76th New York, carried the regimental colors into battle on this early evening. When the brigade received the orders to advance, Stamp rushed ahead of the regiment ignoring the bullets littering the air around him, leaped the stone wall outlining the crest, and planted his flagstaff firmly in the ground. With his hand clutching the colors, he urged his comrades forward. "There, come up to that!" he shouted with Garnett's embattled Virginians only yards away. Before the regiment could fall in line behind the stone wall, a bullet struck the young color sergeant through the head.

Stamp's conspicuous death sent a shiver of panic rippling through the men of 76th New York, some of whom broke for the rear. George Noyes, Doubleday's commissary sergeant, chased after several. "Why, boys, what are you running for?" he yelled after them. "We've beaten the enemy. Three cheers for victory!" Between the hearty cheers and the congratulations that "the baffled enemy has departed," intervals of "comparative calm" emerged. The onset of darkness only served to stir more confusion into the tumultuous situation. "An advance into the unknown localities in front would be [shear] madness," staffer Noyes observed. "The Seventy-sixth was probably never engaged in a more severe and deadly fight than at South Mountain," concluded Abram P. Smith, the regimental historian.[22]

---

21 *Ibid.*; Barnes, "The 95th New York at South Mountain," *National Tribune,* January 7, 1886; Longstreet, *From Manassas to Appomattox,* 223-224; Johnston, *The Story of a Confederate Boy,* 141.

22 Smith, *History of the Seventy-Sixth Regiment,* 153; Noyes, *The Bivouac and the Battlefield,* 173-174; Priest, *Before Antietam,* 259.

As Noyes yelled to the fleeing New Yorkers, everywhere else along the line the attack had been successful and ended almost as quickly as it had been inaugurated. Garnett's men had exhausted most of their cartridges and were streaming to the rear, and the 28th Virginia, having assumed the left flank of his brigade when Stuart slid over and joined Kemper's right, also fell back. William Henry Miller of the 56th Pennsylvania went into the fight on the right of Doubleday's brigade. "Of all the noise of musketry you ever heard," he wrote, "I think that was the worst. We were determined to drive them & drive them we did. They threw their arms & ran in all directions." In the ensuing chaos that followed, the 56th seized several prisoners.[23]

As it turned out, the celebration along this sector of the line proved premature. Despite their loose grip on the slope and thin defensive front, packs of Virginians somehow rallied once more, adamantly clinging to the rocky wooded hillside. The cloak of dusk worked to their advantage, masking their positions.[24] Riding along the federal division line on the far left, General Doubleday ordered the New Yorkers to cease firing and assume a recumbent position behind a fence, where the 76th New York remained until fragments of Garnett's command approached within fifteen paces. "The only thing to be done is to hold this fence at all hazards, lest the enemy, breaking through at this point, shall flank and put to rout the troops on both sides of us," wrote Noyes. "It remains for the staff to watch closely the line, cheer and encourage the men, look out for a moment of panic, and so keep all to their duty."[25]

Despite the overwhelming numbers aligned against them, the Virginians somehow organized the remnants of their scattered units, most of which were likely men from the 18th and 19th Virginia regiments, and advanced against Noyes and his comrades. During the lull, "Some two or three dozen stragglers fell into line very promptly but the majority were demoralized and acted very slowly, so that it became necessary to approach each separate individual soldier," recalled Captain Owen. Although some were placed back into line, one man refused to return to duty. "All sorts of appeals were made to him and he

---

23 William Henry Miller, letter to sister, September 1862, United States Army Military History Institute Collection, Carlisle, Pennsylvania; OR 1:904; Carman, *The Maryland Campaign*, 162.

24 *Ibid.*; Barnes, "The 95th New York at South Mountain," *National Tribune*, January 7, 1886; Longstreet, *From Manassas to Appomattox*, 223-224; Carman, *The Maryland Campaign*, 163.

25 OR 1:222, 901; Mills, *Chronicles of the Twenty-First Regiment*, 282-283; Noyes, *The Bivouac and the Battlefield*, 173-176; Smith, *History of the Seventy-Sixth Regiment*, 153.

replied that, 'There's no use talking about it for I don't care a cent. I am barefooted. I ain't had a mouthful to eat today. I have been a fighting and a charging, and a retreating ever since sunrise this morning and I believe I have fit over the best half of Maryland so I am done for today, unless the Yankees come right here I ain't going to fool with them any more tonight." Owen threatened to stab the man with his sword if he did not stand tall with his comrades. The unnamed soldier, however, turned his back to the captain and gave him permission to stick his sword through him. A frustrated and equally exhausted Owen ignored the man and moved on, leaving the confrontation behind him.

Just to Owen's left in the squad of men he reformed, someone yelled to the captain, "General Lee is up here and wants to see some of your officers." Owen called for Colonel Eppa Hunton of the 8th Virginia and, when he found him, repeated what the man told him. The two officers rode toward the rear and found the army commander astride his horse Traveller. "The first impulse I had was to take his horse by the bridle and lead him out of danger," Owen recalled. Before he could do so, Lee inquired as to the whereabouts of Joseph Walker and his brigade of South Carolinians. Lee had not been able to locate division commander David R. Jones.

Hunton replied, explaining to Lee that he did not know the location of either Walker or Jones.

"Then who commands these troops here?" asked Lee.

"This is Pickett's Brigade and commanded by General Garnett. The enemy are driving us back," Hunton answered. The news did not please the army leader, who knew exactly what was at stake in the fight for South Mountain.

"I will have reinforcement here in time to check them," he assured both officers. "Where is General Garnett? I want to send him a message to get these troops out of this place as quick as he can." Lee paused before turning once more to the colonel. "How many men have you here with you?" Hunton estimated his reformed squad at about forty men. Pausing once more, Lee turned to the rear and extended his finger. "Take all the men you have here and form a line back there in the road, facing toward the mountains," he said. "I have no troops out in that direction and I am afraid those rascally Yankees are going to try to flank us. If you hear any troops coming from that direction fire on them for you may know they belong to the enemy."[26]

---

26 Owen, "The Battle of South Mountain," Henry T. Owen Papers, Virginia Historical Society, Richmond, Virginia.

Before Hunton and Owen could reach their men, however, the squad of Confederates reopened the ball with the federals. A member of the 76th New York described it as "a well-directed and destructive fire" delivered from just fifteen paces. This "horrid game of death" continued as men from both sides, unable in most cases to pick out individuals, aimed their rounds at the orange musket flashes. "The flame from the respective muskets seemed to intermingle," Private Johnston observed, with the lines so close that both sides could clearly hear the shouts and screams of the other. Someone yelled, "There they are, men! Fire on them!" Lieutenant William Nathaniel Wood of Company A, 19th Virginia, heard someone give the command to "charge." Colonel John Bowie Strange of the 19th Virginia ordered his men to stand firm. As he did so, a musket ball struck him, and the officer buckled to the ground mortally wounded. "His voice was heard after he had received his wound, urging his men to stand firmly," Captain B. Brown of the 19th Virginia reported. General Garnett eulogized the fallen colonel in his report: "His tried valor on other fields, and heroic conduct in animating his men to advance upon the enemy with his latest breath, and after he had fallen mortally wounded, will secure imperishable honor for his name and memory." Command of the 19th Virginia was now in the hands of Captain John L. Cochran.[27]

The small but sharp attack ended the fighting here. Garnett's Brigade had been decimated, suffering losses of 196 men (35 killed, 142 wounded, and 19 captured or missing). "Again it seemed the noblest and best had fallen," lamented Lieutenant Wood. The casualty roster from Company B of the 19th Virginia included Sheppard brothers Mell and Dan. Enlisted man J. M. Brown, from that same regiment's Company F, lost his arm and became known to his comrades as "One Arm Brown." James Kemper's Brigade, which fought astride the Old Hagerstown Road and so did not suffer the full weight of the direct assault, suffered comparatively lighter losses. The victims of a raking, oblique fire, Kemper's Virginians lost 75 men: 11 killed, 57 wounded, and seven missing.[28]

27 Barnes, "The 95th New York at South Mountain," *National Tribune*, January 7, 1886; Johnston, *The Story of a Confederate Boy*, 140-141; OR 1:222, 895, 901; William Nathaniel Wood, *Reminiscences of Big I*, ed. Bell Irvin Wiley (Jackson, Tennessee: McCowat-Mercer Press, 1956), 35-36.

28 These figures have been culled from Ezra Carman's estimates of the losses at South Mountain, based largely on the official reports. See Carman, *The Maryland Campaign*, 449; see also OR 1:898, 901; Wood, *Reminiscences of Big I*, 35-36; Priest, *Before Antietam*, 260.

In accordance with Lee's instructions, Colonel Hunton and Captain Owen gathered up the survivors along their front headed for the rear. "Orders came to fall back to the road, and we did so in good order, waiting for the enemy to advance," the 19th Virginia's Lieutenant Wood wrote. "They did not, however, and after dark we moved down the western slope of the mountain and spent the remainder of the night."[29]

*   *   *

About 7:00 - 7:30 p.m., Micah Jenkins' small brigade of South Carolinians under Joseph Walker finally arrived at the front. The men had spent much of the day east of the Mountain House deployed in line of battle, shifting about per General Jones' orders to no effect whatsoever. Finally, with darkness descending and Garnett's command in shambles, Jones ordered Walker to move his men forward toward Garnett's right flank. Captain Owen heard the Palmetto soldiers moving about in the shadowy gloom as they deployed. "By Brigade Right Wheel!" Walker shouted. "Forward, Charge, bayonet!" The 1st, 5th, and 6th South Carolina regiments "advanced some 200 yards to the front behind a stone fence," reported Walker.

Federals also detected his arrival, the noise of which broke the relative silence that had blanketed this part of the battlefield. Wainwright believed the Confederates were attempting to turn his left flank, and ordered the 76th New York and the 7th Indiana to swing left to meet what one federal described as a "desperate effort." They made quick work of Walker's men. "[N]ot many cartridges were expended," Wainwright reported, but they sent the new arrivals tumbling back up the hill in a short defensive effort its colonel described as "brilliantly accomplished." Walker's report offered a more prosaic account when he claimed his men "engaged in a desultory fire with the enemy until dark, when the brigade was withdrawn to the [Mountain House]." Driven back or withdrawn meant little to the three dead and 29 wounded Palmetto soldiers left on the hillside. The 1st South Carolina suffered the heaviest losses, with one man killed and 15 wounded.[30]

---

29 Wood, *Reminiscences of Big I*, 35-36.

30 Owen, "The Battle of South Mountain," Henry T. Owen Papers, Virginia Historical Society, Richmond, Virginia; Ellison Capers, *South Carolina*, in *Confederate Military History* (Secaucus, New Jersey: Blue and Grey Press ed., 1993), 145-146; Carman, *The Maryland*

Other than a light skirmishing about to follow, Walker's rebuff marked the end of the fighting. Phelps' brigade, which fronted the center of the advance, reported 95 casualties, including 20 killed, 67 wounded, and eight men missing or captured. Patrick's brigade, divided on either side of Phelps' command, suffered fewer losses in its effort to close with the refused flanks of the Garnett-Kemper front, and reported only 23 casualties: three killed, 19 wounded, and one man missing. Doubleday (Wainwright) lost three killed and 52 wounded, and four missing or captured. One of those wounded was Colonel Wainwright, who relinquished command after being struck in the arm by a bullet.

Although Wainwright reported only light overall firing on his front, many other federals had only two or three rounds remaining in their cartridge boxes and recall the battle as a hard-fought affair. "Our loss in this stubborn contest for the possession of Turner's Gap, was . . . a large proportion, considering the number of men engaged and strength of our opponents, yet small when we remember the severity of the assailing fire, and the storm of bullets that swept our line," wrote John Harrison Mills of the 21st New York. Because of the rough terrain and growing darkness, Mills had no way of knowing just how few Confederates actually opposed he and his comrades that evening.[31]

Unlike the Confederates who had scrambled to collect any individuals willing and able to carry a musket and fight, the federals had brigades to spare. The fighting was winding down when four regiments of Colonel William A. Christian's brigade (the 26th and 94th New York, and 88th and 90th Pennsylvania), part of James Rickett's division, marched up by the left flank and engaged the few remaining enemy. "The firing was kept up until darkness put an end to the engagement," Colonel Peter Lyle reported. Christian's losses in this brief encounter were slight at two men killed and six wounded. The five regiments of Brigadier General George L. Hartsuff's brigade moved up on Christian's right and positioned itself on Doubleday's right flank, connecting his line with the left side of Meade's victorious Pennsylvania Reserves.[32]

"The victory is theirs," admitted John Dooley of the 1st Virginia, who used essentially the same reason to rationalize the defeat as that employed by Robert Rodes' Alabamians farther north. "Our men behave very well but we are too

---

Campaign, 163; OR 1:234-235, 237-239, 895-896, 902-903, 905-906; Mills, Chronicles of the Twenty-First Regiment, 284; Priest, Before Antietam, 260-263.

31 OR 1:184, 222, 237-238; Mills, Chronicles of the Twenty-First Regiment, 286.

32 Ibid., 1:185, 263, 264, 265; Carman, The Maryland Campaign, 163.

few and the blue coats are very many," Dooley added. The rebels were "too few in number" for many reasons, including the large numbers of demoralized stragglers Dooley himself reported on earlier. He went on to add: "Our regiment is sent to defend a position or line which a whole Brigade might be supposed able to protect. . . . There was not a fair fight here, and the bullets got so entirely *pranky, disorderly,* and *murderous* in their intent that although our brave fellows behave well and pay back with interest whatever favours were intended for them, still after about an hour and a half of retreating from position to position the Brigade gave it up as a hopeless business."[33]

As if in response to Dooley's account, Edward Barnes of the 95th New York, part of Doubleday's brigade, summarized the fight this way: "The advantage of position was originally with the Confederates, from whom it was wrested and held by the federals; although desperate efforts were made by the Confederates to regain it, it demonstrated that our army was not discouraged or demoralized. It further demonstrated, as was often shown during the war, that when good generalship was exercised, the soldiers gave it successful support."

When examining the advantages and disadvantages of the fight between the National Turnpike and the Frosttown Road, the physical condition and morale of the respective contenders must also be taken into consideration. As participants like Barnes, Captain Owen, William Henry Miller, and many others confirm, morale was in flux. The Virginians were hungry, demoralized, and exhausted, and many straggled out of the ranks in a scramble for the rear. Some who remained at or near the front simply refused to reform and fight. The federals, by way of contrast, were buoyed with an enthusiastic determination that animated their entire line. "There were no maneuvers on the Union side, and no surprises of the enemy," Theodore Gates summarized before concluding, "It was a victory won by square open fighting, where boldness, endurance and accuracy of fire won the day."[34]

*   *   *

While George Meade's Pennsylvania Reserves and John Hatch's three brigades advanced up the slope against Robert Rodes and Garnett-Kemper,

---

33 Dooley, "South Mountain and Sharpsburg," in Joseph T. Durkin, S.J., ed., 36-37.

34 Barnes, "The 95th New York at South Mountain," *National Tribune*, January 7, 1886; Gates, *The Ulster Guard*, 301.

respectively, John Gibbon's brigade of Westerners just a few hundred yards to the south engaged in the "third phase" of Joe Hooker's general orders for the storming of Turner's Gap. Donning the Regular Army's black dress hats in place of the standard-issue blue forage caps, the Western soldiers had fought together for the first time on August 28 at Gainesville (Brawner's Farm) in what was the opening encounter of the Battle of Second Bull Run. Gibbon's 1,300 men were divided into four regiments: Colonel Solomon Meredith's 19th Indiana, the 2nd Wisconsin under Colonel Lucius Fairchild, the 6th Wisconsin led by Lieutenant Colonel Edward S. Bragg, and the 7th Wisconsin under Captain John B. Callis. As events would quickly bear out, these were good marchers and hard fighters led by competent officers.[35]

Gibbon turned his command off the National Turnpike to the right with the rest of Hatch's division during the deployment phase that afternoon. When the brigade received its assignment from Hooker, Gibbon countermarched his regiments back to the federal road and advanced another one-half mile. He deployed his brigade on either side of the National Turnpike, with Captain John Callis' 7th Wisconsin on the right in line of battle and Colonel Solomon Meredith's 19th Indiana to the left. Gibbon directed the 6th Wisconsin to form in double column behind Callis' 7th, and he used the same formation with the 2nd Wisconsin, which fell in behind the Hoosiers. Lieutenant James Stewart's Battery B of the Fourth United States Artillery wheeled its guns into the middle of the road.[36]

Once they were in place it became a waiting game for Gibbon's men, who observed from afar the battle raging on their left at Fox's Gap and to their right under Hatch and Meade. "Two miles away on our right, long lines and heavy columns of dark blue infantry could be seen pressing up the green slopes of the mountain, their bayonets flashing like silver in the rays of the setting sun, and their banners waving in beautiful relief against the background of the green,"

---

35 On Gibbon's Brigade, see Alan D. Gaff, *Brave Men's Tears: The Iron Brigade at Brawner Farm* (Dayton, Ohio: Morningside Bookshop, Inc., 1988), Alan T. Nolan, *The Iron Brigade: A Military History* (Bloomington: Indiana University Press, 1994), and Nolan and Sharon Eggleston Vipond, eds., *Giants in Their Tall Black Hats: Essays on the Iron Brigade* (Bloomington: Indiana University Press, 1998). See also OR 1:170.

36 OR 1:247-248; Rufus R. Dawes, *Service with the Sixth Wisconsin Volunteers*, 80-81; Frank Haskell, letter, September 14, 1862, in Frank L. Byrne and Andrew T. Weaver, eds., *Haskell of Gettysburg: His Life and Civil War Papers* (Kent: Kent State University Press, 1989), 31-33; Carman, *The Maryland Campaign*, 163; Kent Gramm, "'They Must Be Made of Iron,'" in Noland and Vipond, eds., *Giants in Their Tall Black Hats*, 20.

recalled Major Rufus R. Dawes of the 6th Wisconsin. "For nearly an hour we laid upon the grassy knoll, passive spectators of the scene."[37]

Orders arrived about 5:00 p.m. With the simple command "Forward," Captain Wilson Colwell of the 2nd Wisconsin fanned out his Company B, from LaCrosse County, along with Company K of the 6th Wisconsin, from Juneau County, as skirmishers. "Nothing could be finer than the conduct of these two companies," boasted Dawes. The Badgers pushed up the side of the mountain and before long caught sight of enemy pickets from Colonel Alfred Colquitt's Brigade, which straddled the National Road waiting for the Western men. Large boulders afforded some shelter for the advancing troops from long-range Confederate fire. "Part of the men would fire and then rush forward while the others covered them and had at the rebels," Private James Patrick Sullivan of Company K recalled. The determined skirmishers fought for "every inch" of the ground. "The utmost enthusiasm prevailed and our fellows were as cool and collected as if at target practice," Sullivan continued. Indeed, on several occasions, as some of the men ducked behind the boulders, one man would select a target and then ask another to evaluate his shot. Dawes confirmed Sullivan's recollection, writing that "For half a mile of advance, our skirmishers played a deadly game of 'Bo-peep,' hiding behind logs, fences, rocks and bushes."[38]

In the middle of commanding this fine work, heavily bearded Captain Wilson Colwell was struck by a Georgia bullet. He lingered for an hour before dying. "His place can hardly be filled," lamented Colonel Lucius Fairchild of the 2nd Wisconsin. "He was a fine officer and beloved by the whole regiment."[39]

Stewart's two guns, meanwhile, continued rolling toward Colquitt's Georgians while the infantry advanced up the road under orders from a mounted General Gibbon, whose voice was "loud and clear as a bell and distinctly heard throughout the brigade." "Forward! Forward!" he yelled. The men needed little or no urging to maintain their steady advance. The brigade

---

37 Dawes, Service with the *Sixth Wisconsin Volunteers*, 80.

38 OR 1:249; James Patrick Sullivan, "A Private's Story of the Memorable Battle of South Mountain," in William J.K. Beaudot and Lance J. Herdegen, eds., *An Irishman in the Iron Brigade: The Civil War Memoirs of James P. Sullivan, Sergt., Company K, 6th Wisconsin Volunteers* (New York: Fordham University Press, 1993), 60; Byrne and Weaver, eds., *Haskell of Gettysburg*, 33; Dawes, *Service with the Sixth Wisconsin Volunteers*, 81.

39 OR 1:252-253; Dawes, *Service with the Sixth Wisconsin Volunteers*, 81; Gramm, "'They Must Be Made of Iron,'" in *Giants in Their Tall Black Hats*, 22.

was a "living machine"—an "impulsive force," remembered Dawes. "It was a most magnificent sight to see the boys of the Nineteenth going forward crowding the enemy, cheering all the time," Colonel Meredith reported.[40]

From their advanced height, Colquitt's 1,350 infantrymen observed their counterparts under the tall black hats ascending the National Turnpike. "I informed General Hill of the movement, and asked for supports," reported Colquitt. "Being pressed at other points, he had none to give me." Colquitt's five regiments would have to hold their position alone. North of the National Turnpike on Colquitt's left flank was Major Tully Graybill's 28th Georgia and on its right Colonel William P. Barclay's 23rd Georgia, with the 23rd's right flank resting on the edge of the road. Both regiments cut through a ravine in dense woods. The line continued on their right (south of the road) and on much higher wooded ground with two companies of Colonel L. B. Smith's 27th Georgia, Lieutenant Colonel J. M. Newton's 6th Georgia, the remaining companies of the 27th Georgia, and finally Colonel Birkett D. Fry's 13th Alabama on the far right. Fry had orders to stretch to his right to close the gap between Colquitt's right flank and Samuel Garland's left flank at Fox's Gap, but there were not enough men to seal the 400 yards. Four companies of infantry were concealed in the thick woods in front of the right side of the brigade under Capt. William Arnold of the 6th Georgia, and behind them were two companies of the 27th Georgia. Lane's artillery battery deployed beyond and behind Colquitt's right flank, unleashing shells and solid shot at Gibbon's approaching infantry. One of the federals on the receiving end observed, "his shot fly wild, making a good deal of hissing, but doing no harm."[41]

The intensity of Colquitt's fire slowly increased as the Westerners snaked their way up the tightening path and along both sides toward the summit. To cover the left flank of the advance, Colonel Meredith detached Captain William W. Dudley's Company B of the 19th Indiana on a skirmish line. When a sharp fire from a small cabin to the left of the road (concealed on the southwest and north by timber) harassed the Hoosiers, Stewart unlimbered his two guns and

---

40 Dawes, *Service with the Sixth Wisconsin Volunteers*, 81, 82-83; Nolan, *The Iron Brigade*, 124; *OR* 1:249-250.

41 *OR* 1:1052-1053; George D. Grattan, "The Battle of Boonsboro Gap or South Mountain," in *Southern Historical Society Papers*, 39 (Richmond: Southern Historical Association, 1914): 38; *B&L* 2:561-562; Carman, *The Maryland Campaign*, 163; Frank Haskell diary, September 14, 1862, as quoted in Frank Byrne, ed., *Haskell of Gettysburg: His Life and Civil War Papers* (Kent: Kent State University Press, 1989), 33.

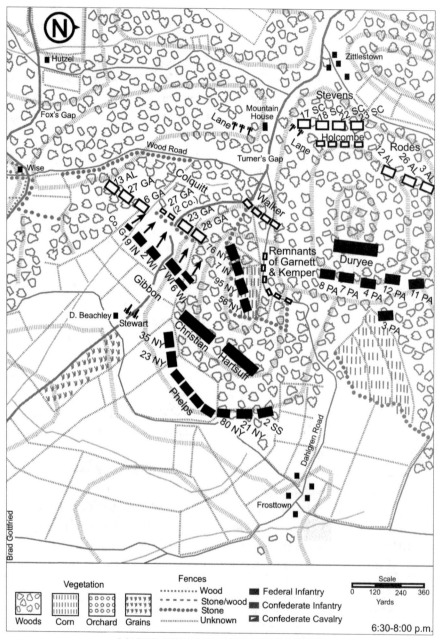

MAP 10. THE IRON BRIGADE'S FIGHT
FOR THE NATIONAL TURNPIKE

sent several shots into the cabin's roof. Smith's Georgians and Fry's Alabamians responded from the protection of the woods and within a short time the firing became general.[42]

Overseeing the fighting from a position north of the road, Colonel Colquitt wrote: "Confident in their superior numbers, the enemy's forces advanced to a short distance of our own lines, when, raising a shout, they came to a charge . . . they were met by a terrific musketry . . . this gave a sudden check to their advance. They rallied under cover of the uneven ground, and the fight opened in earnest. They made still another effort to advance, but were kept back by the steady fire of our men." Colquitt's regiments (including the two companies of the 27th Georgia) found good firing positions behind a low stone fence. Colonel Meredith, who admitted later that "At that point they were annoying us very much," ordered Captain John R. Clark of Company G to wheel his men to the left and pour an enfilading fire into the skirmishers (two companies of the 13th Alabama) in front of part of the line held by just two companies of the 27th Georgia. The Alabama troops fell back as did, apparently, the 27th Georgia companies, leaving a gap in the line between the right of the 23rd Georgia and the left of the 6th Georgia. As the Hoosiers were pressing forward, an opening developed on their right that Colonel Fairchild filled with his 2nd Wisconsin. Fairchild's men rested their right flank along the edge of the National Turnpike and began discharging ammunition as fast as they could stuff it down their barrels.[43]

At the same time on the opposite (north) side of the road, the 7th Wisconsin advanced through a cornfield for about one-half mile directly into the fire of the 23rd and 28th Georgia. "Suddenly the seventh Wisconsin halted and opened fire, and we could see a rapid spitting of musketry flashes from the woods above and in front of us," Dawes observed from the ranks of his 6th Wisconsin, which at this time was behind Captain Callis' men. The 7th kept advancing and firing until an enfilading fire opened with great intensity from behind a stone fence to the right front of the regiment, where "One color-bearer after another was shot down."[44]

---

42 OR 1:249-250; Carman, *The Maryland Campaign*, 163; Nolan, *The Iron Brigade*, 125.

43 *Ibid.*; OR 1:252-253.

44 *Ibid.*; Dawes, *Service with the Sixth Wisconsin Volunteers*, 81-82; Sullivan, "A Private's Story of the Memorable Battle of South Mountain," in William J.K. Beaudot and Lance J. Herdegen, eds., *An Irishman in the Iron Brigade*, 60-62; Nolan, *The Iron Brigade*, 125.

The steady enfilading musketry smothered Callis' Badgers and made it difficult to mount an effective response. Seeing that the right was in trouble and perhaps about to be turned, Gibbon directed an aide to order Lieutenant Colonel Bragg to deploy his 6th Wisconsin on the right of the threatened regiment. Captain Hollon Richardson raced to the rear to bring up Bragg's men. "Come forward, sixth!" his voice rang out in supplication. His shouts competed with those of Bragg. "Deploy column! By the right and left flanks, double quick, march!" the colonel commanded. Bragg's task to move quickly up the slope into the heavy small arms fire in an effort to stabilize the right and stop any flanking movement was a tall order. "The condition of the surface of the ground, and the steepness of the ascent up the mountain side, rendered this movement a difficult one," reported the colonel of the 6th Wisconsin. The tactical alignment at this time also complicated matters because the left companies of the 6th were hidden behind the rear ranks of the 7th Wisconsin, but the right companies were in the open and exposed to Georgia muskets at point-blank range. Colquitt's men had a good position, they knew it, and they were doing everything they could to throw back the attack.[45]

"Major!" Bragg shouted to Rufus Dawes. "Take command of the right wing and fire on the woods!"

Dawes, who would one day lead the regiment, called the right wing to attention, moved it forward at the right oblique, and ordered the men to load and fire at will.

These Badgers had just commenced doing so when Bragg barked out additional instructions for the major. "Have your men lie down on the ground, I am going over you!" he ordered.

The well-trained Westerners on the right went to ground as Bragg maneuvered the concealed companies on the left into the open firing range. The left companies fired a volley above their recumbent comrades into the tree- and rock-shrouded Georgians and advanced through their prone ranks. Amidst the heat of battle the companies repeated the process, with the left companies going to ground and the right companies standing, firing, and advancing. These alternating volleys continued as the regiments fitfully edged closer to the defiant Georgians.[46]

---

45 *Ibid.*; Carman, *The Maryland Campaign*, 164.

46 Dawes, *Service with the Sixth Wisconsin Volunteers*, 81-82; OR 1:247, 252-253, 257, 266.

Private Sullivan of the 6th Wisconsin's Company K had been suffering from the mumps for several days, so much so that his jaws had "reached a respectable rotundity." Before the fight, one of Sullivan's comrades provided him with a large silk handkerchief to tie about his face. As the firing into the Georgians grew more deadly, Sullivan—who was lying on the ground—decided to take off the scarf because it slipped over his eyes and obstructed his view. Sullivan reached up to untie the handkerchief when a bullet whizzed past his head and struck one of the boulders protruding from the mountainside. A fragment of the split lead round struck the enlisted man in his sore jaw, inciting "exquisite pain." Sullivan was considering whether to "run away or swear" when he felt "a stinging, burning sensation in my right foot followed by the most excruciating pain." The private sprang up and, using his rifled-musket as a crutch, limped his way down the steep slope in search of medical help. "In the darkness the sides of the mountain seemed in a blaze of flame, and the lines of the combatants did not appear more than three or four rods apart," Sullivan recalled. The mumps-suffering and now wounded Sullivan stole another glance at his besieged regiment. Although the pain in his foot and the persistence of the musketry—together with the enveloping darkness—prevented him from lengthy reflection, he looked long enough to see the men of the 6th once more "steadily advancing."[47]

"The fire became sharp," recalled Frank Haskell, one of Sullivan's comrades in the 6th Wisconsin, and cartridge boxes became lighter by the minute. "The whole brigade poured in a sharp and well directed fire upon the whole line of the enemy, and as darkness came on drove him to his last stand behind a stone wall near the summit of the mountain." Lyman Holford, another member of the 6th Wisconsin, echoed Haskell when he wrote, "We moved up and poured volley after volley into the enemy.... The balls flew thick and fast for nearly three hours."

By this time the opposing lines were so close and the combat so fierce that Alfred Colquitt estimated that the federals attacking him outnumbered his own troops by "at least five, perhaps ten" times. Fighting within shouting distance, one of Colquitt's embattled Georgians goaded, "Oh, you damned Yanks, we gave you hell again at Bull Run!" One of the Wisconsin boys heard the

---

47 James Patrick Sullivan, "A Private's Story of the Memorable Battle of South Mountain," in William J. K. Beaudot and Lance J. Herdegen, eds., *An Irishman in the Iron Brigade*, 61-62.

Southerner and snapped back, "Never mind, Johnny, it's no McDowell after you now. 'Little Mac' and 'Johnny Gibbon' are after you now!"[48]

While the 6th and 7th Wisconsin pressed hard against the Georgians on the right, the Hoosiers and Badgers of the 19th Indiana and 2nd Wisconsin—many of whom had already expended twenty rounds of ammunition or more—pressed against Colquitt's line in an effort to turn the right of the 23rd and 28th Georgia regiments north of the road. Protected by rock walls and trees, however, Colquitt's left regiments maintained their positions, at least for a time, despite the flanking position now held by the 2nd Wisconsin. The Confederate brigadier boasted in his report how well his men were performing. "Especial credit is due to Colonel Barclay, of the Twenty-third Georgia, and Major [Tully] Graybill, Twenty-eighth Georgia, who, with their regiments," declared Colquitt, "met and defeated the fiercest assaults of the enemy."[49]

It was now about 9:00 p.m., and the bulk of the firefight in the darkness played out near and beyond the north side of the National Turnpike. "Our cartridges were getting short and our guns were dirty with bad powder," Dawes of the 6th Wisconsin remembered. "Gradually by the direction of Colonel Bragg we ceased firing and lay still on the ground." The pop of musketry from the Georgians grew more sporadic, but still they held. One enlisted man in Company A of the 6th called out, "Captain Noyes, I am out of cartridges!" Likely overhearing this exclamation, the Georgians renewed a heavy fire for several minutes. When General Gibbon learned his men were out of ammunition, he ordered them to hold the mountain with their bayonets. Colquitt claims he did likewise. "The fight continued with fury until after dark. Not an inch of ground was yielded," reported the Georgia colonel. "The ammunition of many of the men was exhausted, but they stood with bayonets fixed." The fight for Turner's Gap was over.[50]

After dark, the Southern survivors made their way back farther uphill past the Mountain House and down the western slope on another exhausting journey that would eventually carry them to the undulating hills around

---

48 Frank Haskell, letter, September 14, 1862, in Byrne and Weaver, eds., *Haskell of Gettysburg*, 34; Lyman Holford, diary, pp. 113-114, in Lyman Holford Papers, Manuscript Division, Library of Congress, Washington, D.C.; OR 1:1053; Dawes, *Service with the Sixth Wisconsin Volunteers*, 82-83.

49 OR 1:252-253, 1,053; Carman, *The Maryland Campaign*, 164.

50 OR 1: 1,053; Dawes, *Service with the Sixth Wisconsin Volunteers*, 83.

Sharpsburg. Gibbon's soldiers, meanwhile, listened for the sounds of a withdrawing enemy amid the evening's fitful stillness. When he was sure Colquitt was falling back, Colonel Bragg sent volunteer skirmishers out to test his hypothesis. He was right: the skirmishers found no sign of the enemy's presence. Word of the enemy pullout eventually made its way back to the wounded Private Sullivan. "We heard that the brigade had covered itself with glory and had driven the enemy steadily to the top of the pass," he wrote proudly. Major Dawes' only regret was that darkness and a lack of ammunition rendered the pursuit of the fleeing Confederates impossible.

Confident the enemy had pulled out and that the day was theirs, Edward Bragg called for three cheers for the Badger state, which were delivered with enthusiasm. Gibbon's Westerners held their advanced position until relieved by Brigadier General Willis A. Gorman's brigade of Minnesota, Massachusetts, and New York troops from John Sedgwick's division of the Second Corps.[51]

"The loss of the brigade is again an evidence of its well-earned honors," Gibbon reported. All told, the brigade suffered 348 losses, with 68 killed, 275 wounded, and five reported missing or captured. Not surprisingly, Bragg's 6th Wisconsin suffered the heaviest losses with 11 killed and 79 wounded.[52]

The gruesome work of forcing Turner's Gap left an indelible impression on the men of Gibbon's brigade. In many ways the experience—ascending a steep wooded rocky slope, fighting hand-to-hand in places, using rotating fire, flanking a well-posted enemy, and then resting on arms on the ground they had won—were baptismal in nature. Momentum that afternoon had donned the Regular Army's black dress hat and ridden it to victory. The combat also forever named this band of Western comrades.

According to Jerome Watrous of the 6th Wisconsin, General George McClellan was within sight of the National Pike gorge that afternoon. "What

---

51 *Ibid.*, 83; Sullivan, "A Private's Story of the Memorable Battle of South Mountain," in William J. K. Beaudot and Lance J. Herdegen, eds., *An Irishman in the Iron Brigade*, 61-63; OR 1:247-250, 252, 254, 257, 1,052-1,053. It should be noted that the 6th Wisconsin held its hard-won position until 8:00 a.m. on September 15, when the 2nd New York from Gorman's brigade arrived to relieve it. Other regiments also gradually spilled onto the battlefield. Gorman claimed he could not send men into the woods at night, for all were cowards in the dark. "He forgot that the men whom he condemned to shivering and misery for the rest of the night had fought and won a bloody battle in the dark," Dawes caustically retorted. Lyman Holford of the 6th Wisconsin also commented on the necessity of holding the position the entire night. Lyman Holford, diary, pp. 113-114.

52 OR 1:249, 189; see also Carman, *The Maryland Campaign*, 447.

troops are those fighting on the Pike?" he allegedly asked Joe Hooker. When he learned their identity, the army commander concluded "they must be made of iron." "Why, General Hooker," McClellan proclaimed, "they fight equal to the best troops in the world." Together, these men had acquired a reputation as an "Iron Brigade," a moniker that would follow them as they advanced along the Hagerstown Turnpike three days later at Antietam, crossed the Rappahannock River with William Buell Franklin at Fredericksburg, and into the horrendous first day's fighting in Herbst's Woods on McPherson's Ridge just outside a town called Gettysburg.[53]

Despite the victory claimed by the Iron Brigade, Alfred Colquitt's Brigade fared significantly better. According to one careful analysis, the Alabamians and Georgians suffered just 18 men killed, 74 wounded, and 17 missing or captured. The advantage of fighting on higher ground from behind trees, rocks, and low stone walls is difficult to overstate. "When the advantages of the enemy's position are considered, and his preponderating numbers," boasted Joe Hooker, "the forcing of the passage of South Mountain will be classed among the most brilliant and satisfactory achievements of this army, and its principal glory will be awarded to the First Corps." Except for the relative strength of the combatants, Hooker had it about right.[54]

Although Colquitt later reported that "not an inch of ground was yielded" and that his men had "stood with bayonets fixed" throughout the evening, evidence suggests otherwise. Although the Confederates still held the National Road where it crested Turner's Gap at the Old Mountain House and wound down its back side, John Gibbon's attack forced Colquitt's regiments back from their original positions. Colonel Meredith was definitive on this point. His 19th Indiana moved forward with good effect after Fairchild's 2nd Wisconsin ran out of ammunition and fell back. "I then took forward my regiment and occupied the same position, and continued an enfilading fire upon the enemy," reported Meredith, "who soon fell back from their strong position, the Wisconsin and Indiana boys giving three hearty cheers as the fate of the day was thus decided. It was then after 9 o'clock in the night," continued Meredith, "and

---

53 OR 1:189; Nolan, *The Iron Brigade: A Military History*, 130. There are many stories about the naming of the Iron Brigade. For perhaps the best example, see Lance J. Herdegen, *The Men Stood Like Iron: How the Iron Brigade Won Its Name* (Bloomington: Indiana University Press, 1997), 143-153, 244n.

54 Carman, *The Maryland Campaign*, 449-450; OR 1:215.

pursuit being considered dangerous, we lay down on our arms, holding the battlefield."[55]

Even if we assume the "Iron Brigade" did not achieve an immediate decisive tactical victory on the tangled slopes of the mountain along the National Turnpike, Colquitt's distortion becomes irrelevant when the strategic view of what occurred on the rest of the loosely-knit Confederate lines is considered. The Confederate right suffered a decisive collapse at Fox's Gap under the weight of Jesse Reno's IX Corps. On the Confederate left, north of the National Turnpike at Turner's Gap, Hooker's I Corps gained the crests and enfiladed the opposing Rebel line, driving back brigades under Rodes, Garnett, Kemper, and eventually, Walker. Despite diligent and noteworthy defensive efforts in each of the battle's episodes, both ends of D. H. Hill's haphazard line of battle folded and broke. And in the center astride the National Turnpike, Colquitt's regiments—the thin and exposed hinge of the entire long Confederate line—was levered out of its original position and forced back "from their strong position" everywhere.

Assistant Adjutant General George D. Grattan, a member of Colquitt's staff, made several provocative postwar comments about battle. In the course of his writing, Grattan called the ascent of South Mountain by Gibbon's brigade "certainly brilliant," and in lock step with his commanding officer, repeated the claim that the Confederate regiments were not pushed "one foot from the ground they had held during the whole day." It is no surprise, then, that he labeled Hooker's report "shameful effrontery." But then Grattan tempered his claim by adding, "While we do not claim that this was a great victory, yet we can justly claim that this fight served the purpose of holding McClellan in check until Harpers Ferry was captured, and General Lee was enabled to bring his divided forces together for the great battle at Sharpsburg."[56] Grattan was, of course, silent on the effect of the battle on Confederate morale and the principle objective of Lee's invasion—a penetration into Pennsylvania.

Though bitter about having been left to fight such an important battle on his own under-strength hook, D. H. Hill's early description of the engagement portended his postwar revisionism. The battle, he wrote in his report, was "one

---

55 *OR* 1:249-250.

56 *Ibid.*, 1:1052-1053; George D. Grattan, "The Battle of Boonsboro Gap or South Mountain," in *Southern Historical Society Papers*, 39 (Richmond: Southern Historical Association, 1914), 43-44. Emphasis added by this author.

of the most remarkable and creditable of the war. The division had marched all the way from Richmond, and the straggling had been enormous in consequence of heavy marches, deficient commissariat, want of shoes, and inefficient officers . . . the division numbered less than 5,000 on the morning of September 14, and had five roads to guard, extending over a space of as many miles."

C hapter 9

"Knocking on the back door to Harpers Ferry"

The Fight for Crampton's Gap

It was a great sight to see, it made me feel sick to see so many dead
persons lying around over the ground and not buried.

— *Lewis Luckinbill, 96th Pennsylvania.*[1]

S ix miles south of Turner's Gap, the storm of battle broke out at another
South Mountain pass. Major General William Buel Franklin and his
federal VI Corps, consisting of 12,200 men in two divisions led by Major
Generals Henry W. Slocum and William Farrar Smith, squandered eleven
precious hours the previous evening. Following McClellan's declaration of
Franklin's independence—a vow of complete trust and confidence in his
protégé—the corps commander lingered until sunlight the next morning before
setting out to secure Crampton's Gap.

Securing this particular passage was absolutely vital because, along with the
narrower Brownsville Pass about one mile farther south, Crampton's Gap
offered ready access to Pleasant Valley which, in turn, opened the road to
Harpers Ferry. South Mountain bounded the rolling Maryland dale to the east,
while Elk Ridge extended in the mountain's shadow about two and a half miles
to the west. One arterial road extended along South Mountain, from its base at
Weverton, along the Potomac River, to Rohrersville. Two additional roads
traveled east to the west: one road crossed Israel's Creek and thrust over
Solomon's Gap, a depression through the middle of Elk Ridge, while the other

---

1 Lewis Luckinbill, diary entry, September 15, 1862, in Northwest Corner Civil War
Roundtable Collection, United States Army Military History Institute, Carlisle, Pennsylvania.

Major General William Buel Franklin. *Library of Congress*

road—a less traveled route in disrepair—connected Weverton and Sandy Hook on the eastern base of Elk Ridge.

The Potomac River was about 400 yards wide at this point as it snaked its way around the base of both ridges before converging with the Shenandoah River at the base of picturesque Elk Ridge. The lower town of Harpers Ferry—

the federal armory and arsenal held by nearly 12,000 Union infantry and cavalry under the hapless Colonel Dixon Stansburry Miles—was tightly ensconced in a natural basin at the confluence of the two rivers. Three eminences commanded the town: Loudoun Heights, south of the confluence; Bolivar Heights, situated to the west on the triangular landmass between the Potomac and the Shenandoah; and Maryland Heights, the highest of the three and the southern tip of Elk Ridge looming northeast of Harpers Ferry.

Lee's misplaced Special Orders No. 191 instructed Lafayette McLaws and Richard Heron Anderson to move their divisions (under McLaws) into Pleasant Valley and up to the high ground to wrest possession of Maryland Heights from any defenders. McLaws moved out on September 12, keenly aware of the importance of his assignment. "Harpers Ferry town being on the opposite side of the river but entirely commanded by Maryland Heights, from which a plunging fire, from musketry even, can be made into the place," McLaws reported. "So long as Maryland Heights was occupied by the enemy," he continued, "Harpers Ferry could never be occupied by us. If we gained possession of the heights, the town was no longer tenable to them."[2]

The South Carolinians of Brigadier General Joseph B. Kershaw's Brigade and the Mississippians of Brigadier General William Barksdale were assigned to carry Maryland Heights and removed any elements of the federal garrison posted there. Brigadier General Ambrose R. Wright's Brigade protected the river road stretching from Weverton, at the base of South Mountain, toward Sandy Hook and Harpers Ferry while Brigadier General Roger A. Pryor's Brigade took control of Weverton.

Brigadier General Paul J. Semmes' Brigade and William Mahone's Brigade under Colonel William A. Parham remained at Brownsville Pass. Both were under orders to protect Kershaw's rear from any enemy threat that might present itself from the direction of the South Mountain passes. Semmes dispatched Major Willis C. Holt's 10th Georgia to scout north along the Weverton-Rohrersville Road, while the 41st Virginia from Parham's command advanced to Solomon's Gap, where it would later be joined by the 61st Virginia. The piece to be placed was a brigade of Georgians and North Carolinians under Brigadier General Howell Cobb. Orders directed the brigadier, who had served nine years in the United States House of Representatives before becoming its Speaker, to cross Pleasant Valley and march along the eastern foot of Elk Ridge

---

2   OR 1:145-147, 852-854, 870.

in an effort to maintain contact with Kershaw. Should "any disaster render such necessary," McLaws wrote, Cobb's command would function as "a rallying force." Fortunately for the Confederates, no such disaster occurred. After what Kershaw described as a "very sharp and spirited engagement through the dense woods," his Palmetto command, with firm assistance from Barksdale's men, secured Maryland Heights by 4:30 p.m. on September 13. Because it was no longer necessary to maintain contact with Kershaw's troops, McLaws ordered Cobb to secure Sandy Hook.[3]

Throughout his deployment in Pleasant Valley, McLaws' focus was the ascent and capture of Maryland Heights and reduction of Harpers Ferry. He assumed no immediate enemy threat would interrupt his plans. Accordingly, he made arrangements to defend Kershaw's rear rather than to meet a potential federal advance across the mountain. According to campaign historian Ezra Carman, although McLaws did not "share in the belief" espoused by Lee, Jackson, and others that McClellan would offer no "serious trouble while in the execution of their plans," McLaws did assume any federal pursuit would be slow and deliberate. On September 13, for example, McLaws reported that he heard "heavy cannonading" to the east and northeast, and that various cavalry scouts "were constantly reporting the advance of the enemy from various directions." Instead of giving these statements credence, McLaws deemed their truth "questionable, as the lookouts from the mountains saw nothing to confirm them."[4]

There was some confusion within the Confederate ranks as to who was supposed to guard Crampton's Gap. General Semmes believed that if the federals moved against him it would be through Brownsville Pass, so he placed most of his brigade there. As the hours passed he grew more concerned and finally, on September 14, took matters into his own hands. "Having soon become more familiar with the roads and passes, on the morning of the 14th instant I ordered Colonel Parham, with his three remaining regiments and battery, to Crampton's Gap, for the purpose of guarding that pass," Semmes reported. He also told Parham that if he needed additional reinforcements to

---

3   *Ibid.*; *B&L* 2:601; Carman, *The Maryland Campaign*, 137; Reese, "Howell Cobb's Brigade at Crampton's Gap," *Blue & Gray* 15, no. 3 (February 1998): 13-15; Priest, *Before Antietam*, 273; see also William B. Henderson, *41st Virginia Infantry* (Lynchburg, Virginia: H.E. Howard, Inc., 1988), and Benjamin Trask, *16th Virginia Infantry* (Lynchburg, Virginia: H.E. Howard, Inc., 1988).

4   OR 1:854; Carman, *The Maryland Campaign*, 137.

defend the pass, he could recall the 10th Georgia from the Weverton-Rohrersville Road.[5]

Some of General Jeb Stuart's cavalry under Colonel Thomas T. Munford was operating near Crampton's Gap, which effectively left him in direct command of that sector. On September 12, Munford, with Lieutenant Colonel Richard H. Burk's 2nd Virginia Cavalry, Colonel Asher W. Harman's 12th Virginia Cavalry, and the three guns of Captain Roger P. Chew's Virginia Horse Artillery, occupied the tiny village of Jefferson. Captain Cary F. Grimes' Virginia Battery wheeled its naval howitzers behind Chew's guns. After "constant" skirmishing with the enemy's cavalry through the streets of Jefferson, Munford's troopers fell back to Burkittsville, at the base of Crampton's Gap.

After cavalry engagements near the Catoctin Creek and outside of Middletown, Stuart galloped a portion of his cavalry up South Mountain and, much to D. H. Hill's ire, left only Colonel Thomas Rosser's 5th Virginia Cavalry to defend Turner's Gap. Brigadier General Wade Hampton's cavalry brigade was sent south toward Burkittsville to aid Munford's thin regiments. Stuart, as Hill later grudgingly attested, repaired to Crampton's Gap on the morning of September 14, because he "had reason to believe [it] was as much threatened as any other." With Stonewall Jackson's men fast approaching Harpers Ferry, reasoned Stuart, and with McLaws' command occupying Maryland Heights, the trooper believed the enemy's main effort would be directed at the relief of the arsenal garrison—or, as he wrote, "against McLaws, probably by the route of Crampton's Gap."

Unfortunately, this sound reasoning did not translate into an adequate posting of troopers at the gap on the morning of September 14. Later that morning Stuart grew worried about an enemy movement along the banks of the Potomac River paralleling the bed of the Baltimore & Ohio Railroad—the most direct route to Harpers Ferry. "Next morning, upon my arrival, finding that the enemy had made no demonstration toward Crampton's Gap up to that time, and apprehending that he might move directly from Frederick to Harpers Ferry," Stuart reported, "I deemed it prudent to leave Munford to hold this point until he could be re-enforced with infantry, and moved Hampton nearer the Potomac." Before he galloped off, Stuart instructed Munford, now the

5   OR 1:872-873.

senior commander in the region of Crampton's Gap, to hold the pass "against the enemy at all hazards."

As discussed earlier, Jeb Stuart's move south deprived D. H. Hill's already isolated infantry division of both cavalry skirmishers and reconnaissance troops. In addition, Stuart's move down to the Potomac River to monitor and perhaps prevent an enemy thrust on the unkempt road along the river left his two cavalry regiments alone at Crampton's Gap. By the end of what would be a very long day, both Thomas Munford and William Parham would sympathize with D. H. Hill.[6]

*   *   *

The southern prong of the federal thrust that so concerned the Confederate commanders was part of the strategic movement General McClellan developed after procuring Special Orders No. 191. Drafted on September 13, this general strategy was designed to divide and defeat the Confederates in detail. Lee tied six infantry divisions to the Harpers Ferry operation, and McClellan aimed to relieve the besieged garrison by pressing Franklin's VI Corps through Crampton's Gap, South Mountain's "back door" to Harpers Ferry.

After Franklin passed through Crampton's Gap, his VI Corps would be in the perfect position to isolate and defeat McLaws' troops in Pleasant Valley. Once this was accomplished, Franklin would be able to march through the valley to relieve Harpers Ferry. This second step would effectively prevent Jackson from joining up with either D. H. Hill at Turner's Gap or Longstreet and Lee in Hagerstown, the staging ground for the continuation of the march north into Pennsylvania. Unable to maneuver, Jackson would have little choice but to beat a hasty retreat across the Potomac River into Virginia.

McClellan's plan for September 14 massed the right wing under Ambrose Burnside (Jesse Reno's IX Corps and Joe Hooker's I Corps) against Fox's and Turner's gaps. Leaving the tactical details in the hands of his commanders, Reno's and Hooker's men would drive through and defeat whatever Confederates were holding the passes (McClellan did not know with certainty whether the passes would be heavily defended when his men arrived, and by

---

6   OR 1:817-818, 825-826, 854, 872-873, 881-882; B&L 2:601-603; Priest, *Before Antietam*, 273.

whom). Once he seized one or both gaps and thrust beyond to the west side, the Army of Northern Virginia would be split in two.[7]

Setting out at dawn that Sabbath from the headquarters he had made in Buckeystown, General Franklin scribbled a quick note to his wife Anna. "We start out from here this morning for [Burkittsville] and will I think have a battle before the day is over," he predicted. Recalling the first fight at Bull Run in July 1861 and the more recent fight at Seven Pines the previous spring, Franklin added, "Is it not singular that everything seems to be done on a Sunday?" Not known as an aggressive marcher, Franklin continued temporizing that Sunday. At the hamlet of Jefferson, dirtied by the procession of cavalry that had passed through its streets the previous week, the general halted to wait for Darius Couch's division to arrive and unite with his VI Corps. Franklin waited for nearly an hour before learning Couch was still some distance to the rear. It was around ten that morning when the corps leader finally moved out of Jefferson and continued the advance without Couch.[8]

"The road from Burkittsville to Crampton's Pass lies through a beautiful rolling country," remembered Edward Burd Grubb from the 3rd New Jersey, "with the sweet pasture lands of Maryland lying on either side, thickly dotted with farm-houses. A short distance from Burkittsville the road rises to ascend the South Mountain, and passes over it, through a narrow gorge, walked on either side by very steep hills." A low stone wall outlined the densely wooded hills.[9]

---

7 See Timothy J. Reese, *High-Water Mark: The 1862 Maryland Campaign in Strategic Perspective* (Baltimore: Butternut and Blue, 2004), 26-33. Reese argues that Crampton's Gap looms much larger on the strategic horizons of the Maryland Campaign than the engagements for Turner's and Fox's gaps. Reese maintains this strategic significance is so large that it justifies an interpretive disconnection between the two northern gaps, which he labels "The Battle of South Mountain," and the Battle for Crampton's Gap. The reciprocal nature of McClellan's grand strategy, however, as outlined above, provides that the only distance between the "two" battles must be physical or geographic, and not strategic. See also Timothy J. Reese, *Sealed With Their Lives: The Battle for Crampton's Gap, Burkittsville, Maryland, September 14, 1862* (Baltimore: Butternut and Blue, 1998), and Timothy J. Reese, "Howell Cobb's Brigade at Crampton's Gap," *Blue & Gray* 15, no. 3 (February 1998): 6-21, 47-48, 50-56; *B&L* 2:592.

8 William Buel Franklin to Anna Franklin, September 14, 1862, as quoted in Mark A. Snell, *From First to Last: The Life of Major General. William Buel Franklin* (New York: Fordham University Press, 2002), 176; OR 1:374-375; Carman, *The Maryland Campaign*, 136; Priest, *Before Antietam*, 272.

9 Edward Burd Grubb, *An Account of the Battle of Crampton's Pass*, privately published pamphlet of an address given by Edward Grubb at the Reunion of Kearney's New Jersey Brigade at

Across this pastoral landscape, the men of the VI Corps advanced with Colonel Henry L. Cake's 96th Pennsylvania leading the column with the rest of Colonel Joseph Bartlett's brigade. Cake awoke that morning at 2:00 a.m. with orders directing him to march "at daylight" and "push on to Burkittsville." When his men reached Jefferson, Cake was informed, they would be augmented by three companies of Richard H. Rush's 6th Pennsylvania Cavalry that had been detailed as Franklin's headquarters escort. Armed with lances, Companies B, G, and I under Captain Henry P. Muirhead would be thrown out in front to scout and cover the advance of the infantry. An unidentified artillery piece (almost certainly one of Captain Emory Upton's guns) would support the movement.

Behind Cake's leading regiment tramped the other three units in Bartlett's brigade: Colonel Nathaniel J. Jackson's 5th Maine, and the 16th and 27th New York regiments under Lieutenant Colonels Joel J. Seaver and Alexander D. Adams, respectively. The remainder of Major General Slocum's division— New Yorkers and Pennsylvanians under John Newton and the New Jersey boys of the First Brigade commanded by Colonel Alfred T. A. Torbert—trailed behind.

"All morning we could see Reno and Burnside driving the Rebs along the top of South Mountain," recalled one enlisted man in Colonel Gustavus W. Town's 95th Pennsylvania, a regiment under Newton's command. Despite the distant sound of heavy combat, it was not yet apparent whether Franklin's troops were marching into similar danger. Colonel Cake was under orders to send back information "from time to time" as he closed on Crampton's Gap. "The enemy, however, did not want to be 'felt,'" explained Company A's Private Henry C. Boyer, "so we had force enough as it turned out, to do the work required of our hands."[10]

Boyer's assessment that the enemy did not want to be "felt" changed once the lead elements of Cake's 96th Pennsylvania marched around noon up the Burkittsville Road toward the village of Burkittsville at the foot of the gap.

Edgewater Park, September 20, 1888, pp. 2-3, Western Reserve Historical Society, Cleveland, Ohio..

10 Eric J. Wittenberg, *Rush's Lancers: The Sixth Pennsylvania Cavalry in the Civil War* (Yardley, Pennsylvania: Westholme Publishing, 2007), 59; Henry C. Boyer, "At Crampton's Pass," *The Shenandoah* (Pennsylvania) *Evening Herald*, August 31, 1886; Reese, Sealed With Their Lives, 290; OR 1:393, 176; *B&L* 592-593; Priest, *Before Antietam*, 272; J. Shaw, "Crampton's Gap," *National Tribune*, October 1, 1891.

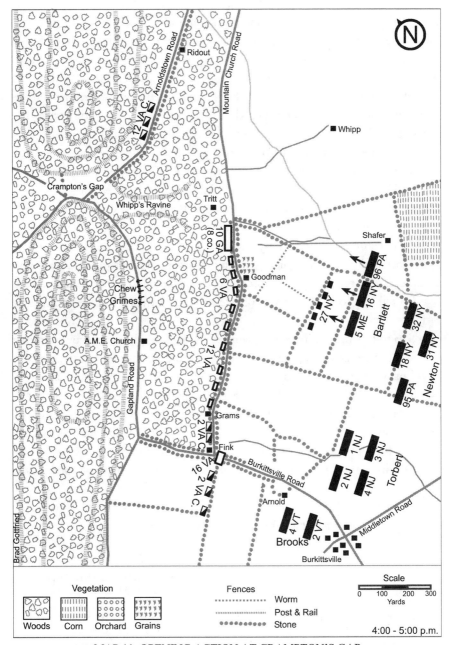

MAP 11. OPENING ACTION AT CRAMPTON'S GAP

Companies A and F fanned out in a skirmish line and began moving through the village, quickly dispersing a small contingent of Confederate cavalry. Major Lewis J. Martin, the regimental field officer in charge of the skirmishers, rode up to Company F's Lieutenant John Daugherty. Together, their "grave and important duty" was to develop the lines of the enemy and work through the town. As the skirmish line reached the western edge of Burkittsville, the remainder of the regiment moved into the village, stopping at the intersection of the Burkittsville and Middletown Roads. "A fine brick mansion" rose to the right in the "midst of a fresh, sweet-looking and well-kept lawn."[11]

Burkittsville was a predominately Union town founded in 1824 when Joshua Harley's Store was promoted to the status of "Post Office." That same year, a Pennsylvanian named Henry Burkitt arrived with the capital to develop the town Harley envisioned. By the autumn of 1862, Burkittsville's quaint streets boasted some fifty buildings, including a German Reformed Church and a Lutheran Church and 200 residents. Seven companies of skirmishers fanned out through the town at intervals of twenty feet, ready for trouble and further orders.[12]

"Up to this time neither man, woman or child had been seen by us in that village," Private Boyer recalled after the war. Hoping that one of the civilians could provide an adequate assessment of the enemy's strength and situation, Boyer received orders to collect all persons that he could to be interviewed. Major Martin had already galloped back from his observation of Dougherty's line to deliver the first report of the enemy's position. From his observatory post on the opposite side of Burkittsville, Martin had spied a Confederate skirmish line posted behind a strong stone wall he estimated to be about 1,000 yards distant.[13]

Boyer, meanwhile, rounded up a visibly shaken civilian named Otho Harley and dispatched him to Colonel Cake. "He began at once to beg that the battle

11 Boyer, "At Crampton's Pass," *Shenandoah Evening Herald*, August 31, 1886; Lewis Luckinbill, diary entry, September 15, 1862, in Northwest Corner Civil War Roundtable Collection, United States Army Military History Institute, Carlisle, Pennsylvania; Henry Keiser, diary entry, September 14, 1862, in Harrisburg Civil War Roundtable Collection, United States Army Military History Institute, Carlisle, Pennsylvania; Priest, *Before Antietam*, 275; Reese, *Sealed With Their Lives*, 54; John David Hoptak, *Our Boys Did Nobly: Schuylkill County, Pennsylvania Soldiers at the Battles of South Mountain and Antietam* (Self-Published, 2009), 101-102.

12 *Ibid.*; OR 1:393-395; Reese, *Sealed With Their Lives*, 61-63.

13 Boyer, "At Crampton's Pass," *Shenandoah Evening Herald*, August 31, 1886.

might not take place there," wrote Boyer. "He declared the town to be Union almost to a man—that all the Secessionists were off in the Southern army. He was assured that there would be no fight there—that if the enemy had men enough to make a stand it would be beyond the town, at the stone fence that appeared to run along just at the foot of the mountain." Cake asked Harley to be as specific as possible about the enemy's condition and strength. The old man told him "they intended to fight and did not dream of a defeat," and as to numbers, "They had 4,000 infantry, several hundred cavalry and two cannons."[14]

Not long after the meeting with Harley, a staff officer approached Cake with instructions to meet with Colonel Bartlett, General Slocum, and the staff officers of their division. These officers were weighing the various reports when a courier interrupted the planning conference with the written report of another army scout. According to this dispatch, the length of the enemy skirmish line indicated there were no more than 4,000 Confederate infantrymen, and only a single artillery piece had been spotted. The news excited usually unflappable Henry Slocum, who boasted that the enemy to their front consisted of "four cavalrymen, two guns and no infantry." The other officers agreed that the defenders were not present in large numbers. Orders rang out for the 96th Pennsylvania to advance through the town. "Attention! Steady now! Forward march!" Cake bellowed.[15]

"We was ordered to advance on them," Lewis Luckinbill recalled after the war, observing that "the firing was soon opened, they having artillery playing on us and we having none." The first indication that the reconnaissance was not as precise as indicated was when Captain Gary Grimes's Confederate battery, together with Lieutenant Colonel R. Preston Chew's horse artillery, opened a direct fire against the 96th Pennsylvania from Crampton's Gap, and Captain Basil Manly's North Carolina battery trained its guns on the approaching men from its position at Brownsville Gap. "At about ten o'clock we saw the first of the Yankee host, about three miles away, approaching our gap cautiously and slowly," recalled Private George Michael Neese, a gunner with Chew. The sight was both tremendous and terrifying. "They were so numerous that it looked as if they were creeping up out of the ground," he declared. "And what would or could our little force of some three or four hundred available men standing

14 *Ibid.*

15 *Ibid.*; Priest, *Before Antietam*, 276.

Colonel of the 27th New York, Joseph Bartlett. *Library of Congress*

halfway up a bushy, stony mountain side do with such a mighty host that was advancing on us with flying banners?"[16]

16 *B&L* 1:592-593; OR 1:393, 826-827; George M. Neese, *Three Years in the Confederate Horse Artillery* (New York: Neale Publishing Co., 1911), 119-121; Carman, *The Maryland Campaign*, 136; Lewis Luckinbill, diary entry, September 15, 1862, in Northwest Corner Civil War Roundtable Collection, United States Army Military History Institute, Carlisle, Pennsylvania.

About the only thing Neese and his Southern comrades could do at this point was unleash an impersonal rain of deadly solid shot, and that was something the artillerists could do very well. When the storm of iron shells arrived, recalled the 96th's Private Boyer, "The hint was taken. We were ordered to clamber back into the road; to lie down; after which we were not molested." According to Lewis Luckinbill of the same Pennsylvania regiment, he and his fellow soldiers remained recumbent for more than an hour. "An occasional shot was fired at our two mounted officers, who went back and forth on the road between the skirmish line and the regiment," Boyer continued, but for the greater part of their time on the ground, "there was no demonstration."[17]

While the 96th Pennsylvania acquired most of the long-range attention, Colonel Bartlett fanned his remaining regiments east of the scenic village. On the western side of the Middletown Road, his infantrymen were largely concealed from inquisitive Confederate eyes. "I was ordered by Major General Slocum to halt until he could mass his troops and arrange the plan of the assault," reported Bartlett, "as the appearance of the mountain pass convinced all that artillery was of no avail against it, and that nothing but a combined and vigorous charge of infantry would carry the mountain." For at least an hour, Bartlett's soldiers had little to do other than consume their rations and make anxious conversation while their commanders considered the best tactical plan for assaulting Crampton's Gap.[18]

After the war, Joe Barlett reflected on the sights of the pending conflict with the cadence and the rhythm of a poet:

> We could occasionally get a view of the troops in front of us—infantry, artillery, and cavalry—with the morning sun shining brightly upon their arms and accoutrements, winding down and stretching far out in the beautiful valley toward the Blue Ridge . . . Such scenes, which look tame upon canvas, are glorious to the young and enthusiastic soldier, who feels a thrill of pride as he looks upon the magnificent and real picture of war his comrades are presenting, and recalls to his mind the many battles they have already fought together, and is touched again with admiration and love for them as he

---

17 Lewis Luckinbill, diary entry, September 15, 1862; Boyer, "At Crampton's Pass," part two, *Shenandoah Evening Herald*, September 2, 1886.

18 OR 1:388; Carman, *The Maryland Campaign*, 136.

sees how willingly and eagerly they are marching to hurl themselves against their old enemy in one more struggle for victory before that glorious sun shall fall.[19]

*   *   *

It was about noon when Lafayette McLaws learned that the measured federal advance from Frederick that he had anticipated was not measured at all. Paul Semmes was so disturbed by the enemy advance that, after pushing Colonel Parham (Mahone's Brigade) out to Crampton's Gap, he galloped back up to Maryland Heights to inform McLaws of the imminent threat. The division commander ordered Brigadier General Howell Cobb's mixed brigade to countermarch from Sandy Hook to reunite with Semmes at Brownsville Pass. Once this was accomplished, Semmes could recall Parham and forward Cobb to the gap.

Even with Semmes at his side sounding the alarm, McLaws remained relatively untroubled by the situation. The explanation for his seeming nonchalance with respect to the potential disaster heading toward Pleasant Valley from South Mountain is revealed in his official report. "I was on Maryland Heights, directing and observing the fire of our guns, when I heard cannonading in the direction of Crampton's Gap," he wrote, "but I felt no particular concern about it, as there were three brigades of infantry in the vicinity," in addition to Tom Munford's cavalry. Further justifying his insouciance, McLaws reported that General Stuart, who was with him on Maryland Heights, told him that "he did not believe there was more than a brigade of the enemy" in opposition. "I, however, sent my adjutant-general to Cobb, as also Major Goggin, of my staff, with directions to hold the gap if he lost his last man in doing it, and shortly afterward went down the mountain and started toward the gap."[20]

*   *   *

19 Colonel Joseph J. Bartlett, "Crampton's Pass: The Start of the Great Maryland Campaign," *National Tribune*, December 19, 1889; see also Thomas T. Ellis, *Leaves from the Diary of an Army Surgeon, Or Incidents of Field, Camp, and Hospital Life* (New York: John Bradburn, 1863), 249.

20 OR 1:814-818; 853-854; Carman, *The Maryland Campaign*, 140. McLaws' report, of course, was written long after the event and with the benefit of hindsight. It is interesting to note that he left out any mention of Semmes' ride.

In time for the midday meal, General Franklin reached the front and established his headquarters at the Martin T. Shafer farm. As the corps leaders discovered, "The enemy was strongly posted on both sides of the road, which made a steep ascent through a narrow defile, wooded on both sides and offering great advantages of cover and position. Their advance was posted near the base of the mountain, in the rear of a stone wall, stretching to the right of the road at a point where the ascent was gradual, and for the most part over open fields." The general scrawled a note off to McClellan: "I think from appearances that we may have a heavy fight to get the pass." The position, Franklin resolved, "could only be carried" by an infantry attack.[21]

With difficult terrain possibly held by a strong veteran enemy, Franklin struggled to interpret McClellan's broad instructions. Was he to risk an advance at the cost of defeat, releasing the enemy instead of retaining them? Or did the directive that, upon reinforcement of his own troops, he was to follow "as rapidly as possible" authorize the delivery of a crushing blow? Colored by his interpretation of McClellan's role in Maryland—a reading which maintained that the army was to advance "slowly and cautiously"—Franklin delayed any attack.[22]

McClellan, meanwhile, wired back a murky response to Franklin's observations. "If you find the enemy in very great force at the pass let me know at once, and amuse them as best you can so as to retain them there," McClellan advised. Reiterating his general strategy of dividing and defeating the enemy in detail, he went on to make the strategic link between the fights for Fox's and Turner's gaps and the storming of Crampton's Gap. "In that event I probably will throw the mass of the Army on the pass in front of here. If I carry that it will clear the way for you, and you must then follow the enemy as rapidly as possible."[23]

While Franklin pondered his next move, General William "Baldy" Smith's division filtered in behind the VI Corps. Beginning about two that afternoon,

21 OR 1:374-375; William Buel Franklin to George B. McClellan, message, September 14, 1862, in Stephen W. Sears, ed., *McClellan Papers*, 460; *B&L* 1:592-593; on the establishment of Franklin's headquarters at the Shafer farm, see OR Atlas, Plate 27, Map 3, and Reese, *Sealed With Their Lives*, 58.

22 On Franklin's constructions of the Maryland Campaign, see his essay in *B&L* entitled "Notes on Crampton's Gap and Antietam," 2:591-597.

23 George B. McClellan to William Buel Franklin, message, September 14, 1862, in Stephen W. Sears, ed., *McClellan Papers*, 460; OR 1:380, 388-389.

the wing's commanding officers began to assemble in Martin Shafer's grove. Franklin pressed his subordinates with questions. "On which side of the Burkittsville Road would the main assault be launched? Who would initiate the attack?"

Without a moment's hesitation, General Slocum spat a terse single-word reply: "Bartlett."

When the war broke out, patriotic fervor swept the man commanding Slocum's Second Brigade away from his nascent law practice in Binghamton, New York, and into the ranks of the 27th New York. When the regiment's companies organized, Bartlett's comrades elected him their major. After Henry Slocum, the regiment's first colonel, was wounded at Manassas in July 1861, he personally assigned Bartlett to assume command of the regiment. On the Virginia peninsula the following spring, when Slocum was promoted to division command, Bartlett was offered Slocum's brigade and led it with skill. It was no surprise that, in the midst of the impending battle, Henry Slocum turned once again to young Joseph Bartlett.

"Then send for Bartlett and let him decide," replied Franklin.[24]

Colonel Bartlett had been resting his men for about an hour when Slocum's adjutant general Major Hiram C. Rodgers summoned him to join the conference. When Bartlett arrived, he found Franklin, Slocum, "Baldy" Smith, John Newton, and Brigadier General William T. H. Brooks (commander of the Vermont Brigade in Smith's division) lounging on the lawn at Franklin's headquarters. Bluish smoke from after-lunch cigars curled into the air. After some preliminary conversation not germane to the impending battle, Slocum turned to Bartlett and inquired which side of the road leading through the gap he would attack.

"On the right," Bartlett immediately replied.

"Well, gentlemen, that settles it," Franklin responded.

Unsure what his corps commander meant, Bartlett asked what, exactly, he had just resolved.

"The point of attack," replied Franklin.

The response infuriated the colonel. "I was naturally indignant that I should be called upon to give even an opinion upon such an important matter

24 Colonel Joseph J. Bartlett, "Crampton's Pass: The Start of the Great Maryland Campaign," *National Tribune*, December 19, 1889; see also Reese, *Sealed With Their Lives*, 66, and Charles B. Fairchild, *History of the 27th Regiment New York Volunteers* (Binghamton, New York: Carl & Matthews, Printers, 1888).

without previously hearing the views of such old and experienced officers upon such an important question," he recollected after the war.

Slocum, however, took some time to explain the situation. The road leading from Burkittsville through Crampton's Gap wound to the northwest up a considerable grade. Dense woods blanketed both sides of the road. Earlier in the day, General Brooks reconnoitered the ground to the left of the road and suggested that the assault pass over that ground. However, discussion between the high ranking commanders exposed a division of opinion. The narrow road at the crest and low stone walls afforded good cover to the enemy on both sides of the road. "Apart from this road, the side of the mountain is so steep and rocky that it is only with great difficulty one can climb it. The enemy had availed himself of every advantage of his position," federal surgeon Thomas T. Ellis noted.[25]

After discussing the strategic situation and the tactical lay of the terrain, Slocum turned to his most trusted brigade commander on the issue of where to go in. "As General Franklin has allowed you to decide the point of attack, on the ground that you were to lead it," he began, "it is no more than fair that I should leave to you the formation."

Bartlett suggested the formation of Slocum's three brigades—his own, Colonel Alfred Torbert's, and Brigadier General John Newton's—into a column of regiments deployed, two regiments front, with a 100-pace interval between the lines. The men, he continued, would be conducted to "a large field near the base of the mountain," where a ravine would screen the formations. This was the advantage of slating the main thrust on the right side of the road. From the ravine, the resulting six lines would be directed to strike northwest toward the crest. Bartlett's own brigade would lead the column, and Slocum's and Bartlett's former regiment, the 27th New York, would be deployed at the head as skirmishers. As Bartlett put it, the 27th New York would "skirmish into the teeth of their line of battle" and open the engagement. The colonel did not intend to halt the advance once he issued orders to move forward. Instead, the assault would proceed until the attackers reached the crest of the mountain on the Confederate left.

General Slocum issued his seal of approval and replicated Bartlett's sketch in his own written orders. Keeping in mind the suggestion of General Brooks,

---

25 *Ibid.*; OR 1:388-389; Carman, *The Maryland Campaign*, 137-139; Thomas Ellis, *Leaves from the Diary of an Army Surgeon, Or Incidents of Field, Camp, and Hospital Life*, 249.

though, Slocum also ordered "Baldy" Smith to throw Brook's Vermonters into the fight on the left. The main thrust would go in on the right while Brooks advanced on the left to create a diversion and, "if possible," turn the enemy's right flank.

Bartlett's formation assembled according to his instructions about 2:30 p.m. Lieutenant Colonel Seaver's 16th New York held the right of the first line, with Colonel Jackson and the 5th Maine extending the line to his left. Bartlett held his 121st New York under Colonel Richard Franchot in reserve to guard prisoners. His remaining regiment, Colonel Cake's 96th Pennsylvania, was still spread out in skirmish formation among the dwellings of Burkittsville, and received orders to follow up behind the advancing column.

Newton's command deployed in two lines behind Bartlett. Lieutenant Colonel George Myers, commanding the 18th New York, held the left of Newton's first line with the 32nd New York under Colonel Roderick Matheson on its right. In the second line, the men of the 31st New York and 95th Pennsylvania, led by Lieutenant Colonel Francis E. Pinto and Colonel Gustavus W. Town, respectively, stretched from left to right.

Colonel Torbert's New Jersey troops appeared next, likewise formed in two lines. Colonel Samuel L. Buck with the 2nd New Jersey held the left of the first line, while the 1st New Jersey filled in to the right. Colonel William B. Hatch's 4th New Jersey and Colonel Henry W. Brown's 3rd New Jersey maintained the second line, from left to right.[26]

*   *   *

While Bartlett and his fellow generals planned and deployed, meanwhile, the Confederates bolstered their lines along the Mountain Church Road running along the base of the mountain. As the ranking commander on scene, cavalryman Colonel Tom Munford grew increasingly unsettled by the strong federal presence gathering across his front. Only a scant force of infantry in the form of three under-strength Virginia regiments under Colonel William A.

---

26 Colonel Joseph J. Bartlett, "Crampton's Pass: The Start of the Great Maryland Campaign," *National Tribune*, December 19, 1889; OR 1:380, 401, 407-408; Grubb, *An Account of the Battle of Crampton's Pass*, privately published pamphlet of an address given by Edward Grubb at the Reunion of Kearney's New Jersey Brigade at Edgewater Park, September 20, 1888, pp. 2-3, Western Reserve Historical Society, Cleveland, Ohio; Boyer, "At Crampton's Pass," part two, *Shenandoah Evening Herald*, September 2, 1886.

Parham arrived that morning—the remnants of a brigade usually led by Brigadier General William Mahone, who had been wounded at Second Manassas. Earlier fighting on the Virginia peninsula and during the Seven Days' Battles, coupled with hard marching that produced an exodus of stragglers, further enervated the Virginia brigade. By the time they stood atop South Mountain, the effective strength of all three regiments combined was but 550 men.[27]

Tom Munford, however, had little choice but to arrange the regiments as best as possible on the terrain at hand and seek additional reinforcements. The first of Parham's regiments, the 16th Virginia, knelt behind a stone wall to form the right side of what would be a very thin line of infantry. The 12th Virginia filed into position on its left, north of the Burkittsville Road, trailed by the 6th Virginia, which deployed on the left of the 12th. "We were deployed eight feet apart, in order to extend our line as far as possible," Private Philip Brown from Company C of the 12th Virginia recalled. "We were behind a rail fence, with just enough distance from the road to lie down at full length, and rest our rifles on a low rail, where good aim could be taken." Munford also readied his two dismounted regiments of cavalry to bolster the weak flanks, situating the 2nd Virginia Cavalry on the right and the 12th Virginia Cavalry on the far left. Everyone had "strict orders" to hold their fire until the enemy was "within good rifle range."[28]

Although his skirmishers would end up playing more the role of spectators than actual participants in the ensuing combat, a thin picket line of 200 men from Colonel Edgar B. Montague's 32nd Virginia Infantry stationed themselves at the base of the mountain. General Semmes originally posted Montague about a mile to the south at Brownsville Pass, but on the morning of September 14, having become privy to Jeb Stuart's demand to defend Crampton's Gap "at all hazards," Semmes ordered Montague and his skirmishers to shift to the base of the mountain. There, they would be in a better

---

27 See OR 1:826-827, 843; Harsh, Sounding the Shallows, 71; Carman, *The Maryland Campaign*, 445; and Benjamin Trask, *16th Virginia Infantry*, passim. By the time Mahone's/Parham's Brigade reached Sharpsburg about sunrise on September 17, 1862, it had been whittled down to fewer than 100 effectives, and was consolidated into a single regiment and temporarily attached to Roger Pryor's Brigade.

28 OR 1:826-827; Carman, *The Maryland Campaign*, 138; Benjamin Trask, *16th Virginia Infantry*, passim; Philip F. Brown, *Reminiscences of the War of 1861-1865 by Philip F. Brown, Company C, 12th Virginia Infantry, Mahone's Brigade* (Roanoke, Virginia: Union Printing Co., 1912), 26.

position to ward off any enemy skirmishers who might advance directly through the village of Burkittsville.[29]

Finally, Semmes himself, as promised, forwarded Major Willis Holt's 10th Georgia from its position on the Weverton-Rohrersville Road. Holt had barely received Colonel Parham's instructions for deployment, however, before Semmes ordered the breathless regiment to countermarch back to its first position. Semmes was well acquainted with the local road network, and was simply unwilling to leave the arterial road through the Pleasant Valley unguarded.

With the enemy multitudes ready to storm his feeble line, Parham scoffed at what he believed was an unreasonable decision. "Seeing a large force of the enemy in line of battle approaching," Holt wrote, Parham gave the major preemptory orders to remain and to meet the emergency at hand. To help calm Semmes, however, Holt dispatched two companies of his 10th Georgia back to the Rohrersville Road. The companies that remained behind filed in on the left flank of Parham's line. Even with the addition of these Georgians and the Virginia cavalrymen, and taking into account the skirmishers of the 32nd Virginia, the Confederate defensive line boasted an effective strength of only some 1,200 men. It was this anemic front that was about to face the onslaught of an opponent roughly ten times its strength.[30]

*   *   *

"Almost as soon as the deployment was completed," Lieutenant Colonel Adams of the 27th New York reported, the enemy "briskly engaged" the federal skirmishers, who had fanned out into a broad arc to screen the advance. "I supposed we were in position nearly an hour before the enemy's advance column appeared in our front," Philip Brown recalled. The New Yorkers, dodging a hail of musketry fire and artillery from the heights above, halted behind a split rail fence 200 or 300 hundred yards away from the enemy.[31]

---

29 OR 1:817-818, 872-873, 876-877, 881-882; B&L 1:592-593; Reese, *Sealed With Their Lives*, 45, 47-51.

30 OR 1:872-873, 876-877; Priest, *Before Antietam*, 278, 280; Carman, *The Maryland Campaign*, 138.

31 OR 1:388-389, 392; Brown, *Reminiscences of the War of 1861-1865*, p. 26. Colonel Bartlett reported that the 27th New York halted about 300 yards in front of the enemy, but Private

The Confederate positions were now largely developed, and Slocum withdrew the skirmishers. Just as the other commanders had determined earlier that afternoon, Slocum expected an enemy infantry attack. "I had, therefore, left all the artillery of the division in [the] rear," he wrote, "but fearing that the stone wall behind which the enemy had taken cover would prove an insurmountable obstacle to the advance of my lines, I at once used every effort to bring forward a battery, with the view of driving the enemy from his position." Uncertain of the exact enemy strength, a closer inspection of the ground served to wither Slocum's morning bravado. This could be very serious work.

From the staging ravine to the rear of the advancing blue lines, a sergeant major from the 96th Pennsylvania observed the commotion to the front and joked, "General Slocum's four cavalrymen and two guns before us," a reference to Slocum's earlier scoff at the thin enemy awaiting them.

"Yes, we are going to have a fight," Private Boyer agreed.[32]

The combat began in earnest when Slocum advanced Bartlett's first line— the 5th Maine and 16th New York—to the front. For ten or fifteen minutes, however, the pair of regiments hesitated in making the charge. "Finally, a great cheering, as if greeting some welcome reinforcements, swelled along the line," recalled Private Brown of the 12th Virginia, "and over the fence they clambered, and started for us at double quick time." Bartlett's regiments advanced about fifty yards. "Here we opened on them, and continued a brisk fire for nearly three quarters of an hour," the 16th New York's Lieutenant Colonel Seaver reported. According to Colonel Jackson from the 5th Maine, the assault was made "under a severe and galling fire." The deadly exchange of fire left a line of killed and wounded bluecoats and rebuffed, if temporarily, the survivors several yards.[33]

Many men in the embattled regiments looked to the rear for reinforcements and were surprised by what they saw—or didn't see. "By some unexplained and unaccountable mistake, more than 1,000 yards intervened between the head of

Brown, with a more commanding view of the battlefield, estimated the distance at only 200 yards. See also, Reese, *Sealed with Their Lives*, passim.

32 *OR* 1:380; Boyer, "At Crampton's Pass," part two, *Shenandoah Evening Herald*, September 2, 1886.

33 *Ibid.*; *OR* 1:389, 389-390; Brown, *Reminiscences of the War of 1861-1865*, p. 26; see also Newton Martin Curtis, *From Bull Run to Chancellorsville* (New York: G.P. Putnam's Sons, 1906), 170.

the column of General Newton's brigade and my own line," the frustrated Colonel Bartlett later reported. Without support, the men from New York and Maine maintained the battle, added Bartlett, with "nothing but the most undaunted courage and steadiness," nearly exhausting their ammunition.[34]

The 32nd New York and 18th New York finally moved up by the right flank to relieve Bartlett's embattled line which, once relieved moved twenty paces to the rear to catch its breath and reorganize before renewing the assault. Newton's second line, consisting of the 31st New York and 95th Pennsylvania, tracked behind this relief. They swept through the gap and assumed a position to the left of their comrades before the whole line was ordered to resume the advance. Cheers went up once more as the federals rushed forward and scaled the split rail fence. "I was in the act of firing my rifle when the cheering commenced," Confederate Private Brown of the 12th Virginia remembered, "and, seeing an officer with his hat lifted on the point of his sword, as he mounted the fence I took deliberate aim, but the smoke of my rifle prevented my seeing what effect it had." While leading the charge at the head of the 18th New York, a rebel ball (likely fired from someone in the 6th Virginia) claimed the life of Captain William Horsfall, whose subordinates Lieutenants Daniel Daley and William Ellis also fell seriously wounded. Southern artillery continued exploding above the federal lines, wrote Private Brown, and "though we popped our rifles as rapidly as possible, it seemed evident that we would soon be overwhelmed."[35]

Newton's regiments only moved forward a short distance before falling back to the relative safety offered by the captured rail fence. From behind the heavy wooden rails the federal soldiers awaited the arrival of their own artillery, which was still some distance to the rear. Alfred Torbert's New Jersey brigade, meanwhile, arrived in supporting distance after a confounded advance through a large field of ripe September corn. "The Jerseymen did not take rows fairly and much confusion resulted in their march through the obstruction," recalled Private Boyer, who shadowed Torbert's advance with men of the 96th Pennsylvania.[36]

34 OR 1:389, 390, 391, 392.

35 *Ibid*; OR 1:398, 398-399; Brown, *Reminiscences of the War of 1861-1865*, p. 26.

36 *Ibid*; Carman, *The Maryland Campaign*, 139; Grubb, *An Account of the Battle of Crampton's Pass*, pp. 3-4, Western Reserve Historical Society, Cleveland, Ohio; Boyer, "At Crampton's Pass," *Shenandoah Evening Herald*, part two, September 2, 1886.

The attack's fits and starts agitated Slocum. It was now after 4:00 p.m., and his troops had been up and moving since two that morning. "We have no artillery and I have sent in vain to have a battery brought forward," he explained to Colonel Cake when he saw the 96th Pennsylvania snaking up behind the New Jersey men. "We can do nothing without it. If you will take the 96th into that field to the right and charge the wall it would be glorious work," Slocum insisted.[37]

Orders went out and the 96th Pennsylvania prepared to move behind the front into the plowed field on the extreme right of the federal line to storm the Confederate left held by the 10th Georgia. "Brisk musketry firing was in progress on our left, but the good cover in possession of the enemy and the distance at which we stood rendered it quite certain that we could gain nothing at a stand-off fight . . . it was evident that nothing but a rush forward would win," explained Colonel Cake. "We was ordered to advance on them and the firing was soon opened they having artillery playing on us and we having none," Lewis Luckinbill wrote in his diary. "We advanced under the fire in double quick until we got within musket range they being behind stone fences as usual and we in the clear." According to Henry Keiser from the 96th's Company G, a "deadly volley" opened as they rushed forward at the double quick. "Bursting shell now hailed around us," Boyer wrote. "They had our range nicely and the 'piff' of lead told a near approach to danger."[38]

Fence rails and scattered piles of rubbish made it difficult for Cake to keep his lines formed. Some of the boys looked to their left down the federal lines to guide their speed and movement. Torbert's men, who formed on the opposite flank, had not advanced a step. "To encourage the Jerseymen on our left we fired another volley on gaining the last sheltering fence row," Boyer wrote. "The Jerseymen were evidently thinking it over, and we were alone to the right and front, in point-blank range," he emphasized. After a brief respite at this last fence line, the men fixed bayonets. "We got orders to charge," Luckinbill wrote.

37 Boyer, "At Crampton's Pass," part two, *Shenandoah Evening Herald*, September 2, 1886; *OR* 1:389, 393-394.

38 *Ibid.*; Boyer, "At Crampton's Pass," part three, *Shenandoah Evening Herald*, September 3, 1886; Lewis Luckinbill, diary entry, September 15, 1862, in Northwest Corner Civil War Roundtable Collection, United States Army Military History Institute, Carlisle, Pennsylvania; Henry Keiser, diary entry, September 14, 1862, in Harrisburg Civil War Roundtable Collection, United States Army Military History Institute, Carlisle, Pennsylvania.

"Forward into the road and give them the bayonet—it is death for all to hesitate now!" Cake screamed.[39]

The Georgians of the 10th regiment hunkered down behind their stone wall along Mountain Church Road, together with Howell Cobb's 24th Georgia stationed higher up on the side of the mountain, and opened a steady fire against the approaching Pennsylvanians. The five guns deployed at Brownsville Pass kept up their firing as well. Confederate troops supporting these guns enjoyed a panoramic view of the field and attacking enemy lines. "It was a grand sight," admitted one Southerner. "I will never forget it." Cake recalled that his men were "shocked" by the solid firing ripping through the ranks, "but not repulsed [and] the men bounded forward, determined to end it with the bayonet." "We followed them up sharp, driving them as we went," Lieutenant John K. Fernsler from the 96th Pennsylvania's Company H explained to his diary. Some of the Georgians took up a position in and around the stone Tritt house and opened fire against the right side of the 96th Pennsylvania. Cake moved some of his men in that direction, swept away the defenders, and continued on. With the front pressing heavily against the main Georgia line and the right side of the 96th overlapping the luckless Georgians, the men from the Deep South had little choice but to fall back from the protection of the wall and into the road, and then up the side of the mountain toward Whipp's Ravine. Luckinbill remembered having "routed them out from behind stone fences and ran them clear off the mountain going up." Brief hand-to-hand combat broke out along the line but the attackers had every advantage by this point. "We thought we had bayoneted a hundred and fifty in that road, but when we returned to bury them we found but twelve," Boyer recalled, demonstrating how the frenzy of close-quarter fighting doesn't always produce the most accurate of recollections.[40]

If any of Cake's men took the opportunity to glance left, they might have seen the impressive sight of most of the long federal line of battle assaulting the heavily outnumbered defenders. The cold steel of their bayonets glimmered in the twilight amidst the incessant roar of screaming men and artillery and small arms fire. Newton's brigade (95th Pennsylvania, and 31st, 18th, and 32nd New

---

39 *Ibid.*

40 *Ibid.*; John K. Fernsler, diary entry, September 14, 1862, in James F. Haas Collection of the Harrisburg Civil War Roundtable, United States Army Military History Institute, Carlisle, Pennsylvania; Carman, *The Maryland Campaign*, 139. The arrival of Howell Cobb's troops is treated later in this chapter.

York, from left to right) advanced to the fight on Colonel Cake's immediate left. Exhausted though they were, Bartlett's 5th Maine and 16th New York were also driving forward and may have merged into Newton's line, with Newton's 31st New York and the 95th Pennsylvania pressed between Bartlett and Torbert's New Jersey troops farther left. When the order to commence firing rang out, Torbert still had his brigade in column of regiments. Brooks' Vermont troops were just getting their diversion underway on the far left of the entire line, opposed by the dismounted troopers of the 2nd Virginia Cavalry and a small portion of the 16th Virginia infantry. [41]

After five minutes of volleying, Torbert ordered his front line to scale the fence behind which it had engaged the rebels and head for the "shingly sides of the hill," where the enemy stood blazing away in their direction. His rear regiments received orders to rush over the fence that had sheltered the front line. The men of the 3rd and 4th New Jersey sprang up with a cheer and enthusiastically joined the front line. "This charge is described by every one who saw it, as one of the most magnificent, best sustained, and most gallant charges that was ever seen," Edward Grubb of the 3rd New Jersey reflected. A member of the 16th Virginia on the receiving end of this attack agreed: "They came over the field grandly, the officers all in place and cheering."[42]

"When they were about twenty yards distant, I was shot in the arm, about three inches below the elbow" explained Philip Brown of the 12th Virginia, "the bullet passing between the two bones, then through the elbow joint, and lodged in the muscle of the arm. I do not know whether it was the excitement, or what, but I felt no more pain at the time, than if a brush had hit me, but the blood trickling to my finger tips, and the utter uselessness of, or inability to move the arm, made me realize that it was broken," he continued.[43]

"The enemy fell back before our men could reach the wall," recalled Grubb of the 3rd New Jersey, fighting on Torbert's right front. These heavily outnumbered defenders extending the line beyond the right of the embattled 10th Georgia had been fighting for some time and were exhausted and even

41 OR 1:384-386, 389-394, 396-401; Carman, *The Maryland Campaign*, 139-140.

42 Grubb, "An Account of the Battle of Crampton's Pass," 4, Western Reserve Historical Society, Cleveland, Ohio; James Toomer, as quoted in Reese, *Sealed With Their Lives*, 130; see also Curtis, *From Bull Run to Chancellorsville*, 170, and Ellis, Leaves, 250.

43 OR 1:384-386, 389-394, 396-401; Grubb, *An Account of the Battle of Crampton's Pass*, 4, Western Reserve Historical Society, Cleveland, Ohio; Brown, *Reminiscences of the War of 1861-1865*, p. 27.

more spread out than before. Their muskets continued to fire, "but nothing could withstand the onset of our men," the 3rd New Jersey's Colonel Henry Brown. As Torbert later put it, "The enemy, although holding a very strong position, and having the advantage of artillery, could not stand these charges, so broke and fled up the mountain side in great disorder, closely pursued by our men, who drove them through the pass, and some distance in the valley on the other side."[44]

On Torbert's left, Newton's and Bartlett's men rushed across the ground in grand style. According to Brigadier General Winfield Scott Hancock, observing from his position in reserve, the advance was "the perfect poetry of war." The Union men pressed "naturally forward," scaling the stone wall and shaking the enemy. "At our approach the rebels retreated from the breastworks up the steep mountain side," wrote one private from Bartlett's 16th New York. The federals called out for them to surrender, and many prisoners were bagged up and down the line. The 32nd New York alone captured 130 men, and the 16th Virginia admitted to having surrendered at least 74 prisoners. Reporting from the Union right flank, Private Boyer expressed no grief for "horribly killing or wounding all we could of those who resisted or would not stop."[45]

"The men fought nobly and pressed on up the steep ascent under a perfect shower of bullets, and their example encouraged others," wrote Lieutenant Colonel Seaver of the 16th New York, Bartlett's brigade. "'Down went the men at my order, and *down* came a volley from a full regiment or more, and we returned the fire. We had them started, and—they could not help it—*they ran*."[46]

When the 95th Pennsylvania reached the crest, a group of enemy soldiers endeavored to make a final stand, opening a volley into the oncoming federals and wounding several. The Pennsylvanians returned the fire and the rebels broke and ran, many smashing their guns on the rocks. Farther down the line, the men of the 18th New York had run out of ammunition. "Colonel, my men are out of cartridges," their major coolly called out to Bartlett. "Never mind, Major, push on, we have got 'em on the run!" bellowed the aggressive brigade

---

44 *OR* 1: 382-388, 396-397, 881-882.

45 James Allen, as quoted in W. F. Beyer and O. F. Kendel, eds., *Deeds of Valor: How America's Civil War Heroes Won the Congressional Medal of Honor* (Detroit: Perrien-Keydel Co., 1903), 73; *OR* 1:399; Benjamin Trask, *16th Virginia Infantry*, passim; Boyer, "At Crampton's Pass," part three, *Shenandoah Evening Herald*, September 3, 1886.

46 Joel Seaver, as quoted in Newton Martin Curtis, *From Bull Run to Chancellorsville*, 170.

leader. "The regiments each side of you have got ammunition, and are using it."[47]

James Allen, an Irish-born private from Company F of the 16th New York followed a band of retreating rebels clawing their way up a steep slope. "By this time they had reached a road running up the mountain which was skirted on our side by another wall," he wrote. "The only thing for me to do was to climb also." The rebels stopped several times to fire at Allen, and one of the balls slightly wounded him. In an attempt to deceive the Southerners, Allen waved his arms and ordered an imaginary company to push on from behind him. "Up, men, up!" he cried. "The rebels, thinking that they were cornered, stacked their arms in response to my order to surrender," boasted the resourceful Irishman. "I made haste to get between them and the guns, and found that I had fourteen prisoners and a flag taken from the color-guard." Spying the commotion, Colonel Seaver came up, removed his glasses, and proudly inspected Allen's party before riding back for guards to receive the prisoners, all the while knowing that the regiment had secured the crest. A proud Seaver called for three hearty cheers. This bold episode earned Private Allen the Congressional Medal of Honor.[48]

* * *

While the three federal brigades were making their successful main attack on the right side of the Burkittsville Road, Brooks' Vermont Brigade was slowly unfolding its "diversion" designed to assist their comrades on the right. The Vermont men had snaked through Burkittsville under a galling artillery fire from Brownsville Gap before halting at the edge of town. "We found the enemy in position behind a stone wall at right angles with the road," Brooks reported. Lieutenant Abel K. Parsons from Company A of the Fourth Vermont turned to General Brooks with a most evident observation—Confederate infantry fire filled the woods before them. "I don't think there are quite so many as all that," Brooks determined. As soon as the enemy line was developed, he dispatched Lieutenant Colonel Charles B. Stoughton's 4th regiment as

---

47 Bartlett, "Crampton's Pass," *National Tribune*, 19 December 1889; J. Shaw, "Crampton's Gap," *National Tribune*, 1 October 1891.

48 W.F. Beyer and O.F. Kendel, eds., *Deeds of Valor: How America's Civil War Heroes Won the Congressional Medal of Honor*, 73-74.

The David Arnold barn screened the advance of the Vermont Brigade.

Henry F. Ballone

skirmishers into the fields on the left of the road. Major James H. Walbridge's 2nd Vermont trailed close behind in support. Colonel Breed N. Hyde's 3rd Vermont, Colonel Lewis A. Grant's 5th Vermont, and Major Oscar L. Tuttle's 6th Vermont remained at the edge of Burkittsville awaiting orders. Col. William Irwin brought up his brigade behind Brooks' men.[49]

When his skirmishers had little effect, Brooks prepared the rest of the brigade to advance. "The instant the line was ready, we charged, with bayonets fixed, at double quick, across the open level field to the stone wall where the enemy was posted. Before we got to the wall, the rebels began to run singly, then in little squads of three or four, and finally, as we were about to reach the wall, they all broke pell mell up the slightly inclined open plain, from the wall to the foot of the mountain," recalled Private John Conline of the 1st Vermont. The Confederates, wrote the 2nd Vermont's Edson Emery, were driven away and up the hill "in fine style."

According to "Baldy" Smith, the Vermont Brigade "added materially to the day's result by carrying out General Franklin's idea of threatening the enemy's right flank." Indeed, the entire Confederate line at Crampton's Gap had been rolled up the slopes of the mountain.[50]

*   *   *

49 OR 1:407-408; Carman, *The Maryland Campaign*, 140; John Conline, "Recollections of the Battle of Antietam and the Maryland Campaign," paper read January 7, 1897, in *War Papers, Being Papers Read Before the Commandery of the State of Michigan, Military Order of the Loyal Legion of the United States*, vol. 2 (reprint, Wilmington, North Carolina: Broadfoot Publishing Company, 1993), 114-115; Priest, *Before Antietam*, 287.

50 *Ibid*; Edson Emery, diary entry, September 14, 1862, in Civil War Miscellaneous Collection, United States Army Military History Institute, Carlisle, Pennsylvania.

Although they started fitfully, the federal attacks were short in duration and decisively delivered once they got underway. "All orders were carried out in detail. No more and no less was done than to execute the plan during the fiercely contested assault which was so clearly expressed in the bivouac," was Bartlett's matter-of-fact explanation. "The line of musketry smoke was evidently advancing up the ascent, and that indicated a victory there," one federal soldier recalled. Tucked away on the other side of Burkittsville, General William Franklin watched the unfolding battle with at least some level of surprise at its success. "The men swept forward with a cheer, over the stone-wall, dislodging the enemy, and pursuing him up the mountain-side to the crest of the hill and down the opposite slope," reported the VI Corps leader. "This single charge, sustained as it was over a great distance, and on a rough ascent of unusual steepness, was decisive." Franklin was not the only astonished observer. "It is hardly possible to conceive how this position could have been carried; but it was, with little delay and loss by our men," reminisced federal surgeon Ellis. "Our boys struggled up, with courage, while the foe above poured down upon them a perfect storm of balls, and drove him from the very summit of the hill, flying down the further side in one wild and confused mass." New Jersey's Lieutenant Colonel Seaver reflected that "the line of our advance was marked by a train of cold and lifeless rebellious mortality, from the base to the summit of the mountain."[51]

*   *   *

The federal victory, however, was not yet complete. Hours earlier that day, about noon, Lafayette McLaws had ordered the 1,341 men of Howell Cobb's Confederate brigade to countermarch from Sandy Hook to Brownsville Pass. There, Cobb could reunite with brigade commander Paul Semmes, whose worries about Crampton's Gap had all but consumed him. At the same time McLaws issued this order, he attempted to allay Semmes' fears by instructing him to direct Cobb's command to seal the problematic gap.[52]

Cobb received the orders from McLaws about one hour later and began a languid countermarch that did not reach Brownsville—a mere five miles

---

51 OR 1:375, 389; *Harpers New Monthly Magazine*, 36 (February 1868): 278; Ellis, *Leaves*, 250; Seaver as quoted in Curtis, *From Bull Run to Chancellorsville*, 170-171.

52 OR 1:852-854, 861, 870-873.

Brigadier General Howell Cobb. *Library of Congress*

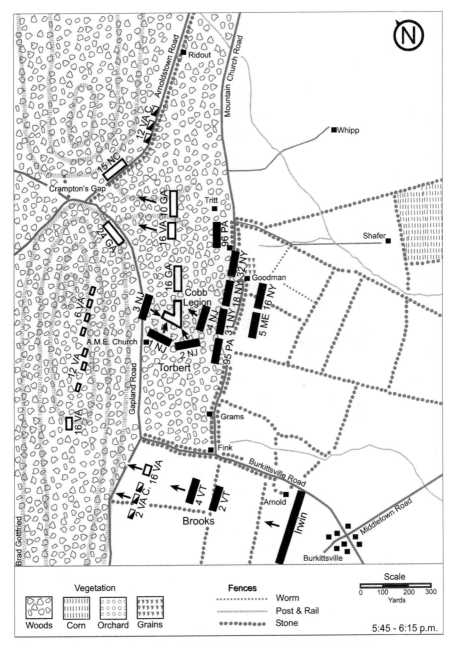

MAP 12. CONFEDERATE ROUT AT CRAMPTON'S GAP

away—until three hours later. Because he had no further instructions from McLaws, Cobb went into camp, wasting an hour of precious time. "General Cobb was inexperienced enough not to realize that as ranking officer he was responsible for everything that might happen in the rear, where his inferiors in rank were stationed, unless they were under the immediate orders of others superior to himself," McLaws wrote in 1888. "If he had had more experience as to the responsibility which rank confers he would not have waited an hour in camp upon contingencies, but would have gone in person in advance to inform himself as to the best way to provide against misfortune."[53]

When a frustrated Thomas Munford ordered Cobb to come up at once to Crampton's Gap, a sense of urgency finally gripped Howell Cobb. "I immediately ordered my two strongest regiments (24th Georgia and 15th North Carolina) to march to their support," he reported. "Before, however, the head of the column had filed into the road I received a message from Colonel Parham, who was in command of Mahone's brigade at the gap, to the effect that the enemy was pressing him hard with overwhelming numbers, and appealing for all the support I could bring to him." Cobb formed up his remaining two regiments, the 16th Georgia and the Georgia (Cobb) Legion, and accompanied them in person. This time Cobb marched his men as quickly as possible, their commander "impressed with the importance of the position."[54]

By the time Cobb reached the battlefront, however, Crampton's Gap was already as good as lost. The entire line was under fire and the pressure was growing heavier by the second. Virginians and Georgians were already streaming up the wooded slope in retreat. "When the general himself came up, I explained the position of the troops, and of course turned over to him the command," Munford wrote. Despite his seniority, Cobb wanted no such responsibility. At his request, Munford personally positioned the 24th Georgia and 15th North Carolina, deploying them on the left. The Georgians of the 24th

---

53 *Ibid.*; OR 1:826; Lafayette McLaws, "The Capture of Harpers Ferry," *Philadelphia Weekly Press*, 12 September 1888. If McLaws was looking to distance himself from the disaster at Crampton's Gap, he only further demonstrated his own complicity in the state of affairs. In the initial Confederate deployment in Pleasant Valley, McLaws designated Cobb's Brigade as the "wild card," the "rallying force." If the division commander was aware of the brigadier's inexperience (which as division commander he most certainly was), then his selection of Cobb for this critical role underscores the extent to which McLaws underestimated the threat of the federal advance and the strategic importance of the valley.

54 OR 1:870; Reese, "Howell Cobb's Brigade at Crampton's Gap," *Blue & Gray* 15, no. 3 (February 1998): 14.

assumed the relative shelter of Whipp's Ravine, supporting the embattled 10th Georgia, while the Tarheels aligned themselves higher up the slope along a low stone wall paralleling the Arnoldstown Road.

Munford directed Cobb to guide his remaining smaller regiments down the Gapland Road to support the embattled right. These units—the Cobb Legion under Lieutenant Colonel Jefferson Lamar and the 16th Georgia under Lieutenant Colonel Philip Thomas—moved off the Gapland Road onto the wooded slope above the Mountain Church Road, with Thomas' regiment on the left and Lamar's on the right. Munford was attempting to bring them into line, but "they behaved badly and did not get into position before the wildest confusion commenced." Wounded men making for the rear passed through their makeshift line, enlarging the chaos and reinforcing the permeating sense of hopelessness. "General Cobb attempted to rally the men," Munford added, "but without the least effect, and it would have been as useless to attempt to rally a flock of frightened sheep."[55]

In all fairness to Cobb, he and his men reached the battlefield with just enough time to get into a position no troops could have held, ensnared by the pincers of Bartlett, Torbert, Newton, and Brooks in one of the most terrifying situations any of them would experience during the war.

By now, the 96th Pennsylvania and New Yorkers from the 32nd and 18th regiments had pushed some distance up Whipp's Ravine on the far right of the Union line. With the 10th Georgia in full rout, Cobb's 24th Georgia and soon thereafter his 15th North Carolina likewise turned and fled. While the Pennsylvanians and New Yorkers collapsed the Confederate left, Torbert's New Jersey troops on the other end of the line, buoyed by their victory against the Virginians, spotted enemy troops ahead and to their right. The federals swung around and headed directly for what would prove to be Cobb's Legion. The slope-climbing New Jerseyans numbered perhaps 1,200 men, and so outnumbered the 250-man Legion by nearly five to one. Whether Lieutenant Colonel Jefferson Lamar realized how heavily he was outnumbered is open to question, but he and his men stayed put and opened fire on the approaching enemy. In an attempt to repel the oncoming federals, some of Lamar's men "madly leaped the [stone] wall" in front of them—the last remaining barrier that offered any sort of protection from enemy fire—and "rushed the [federal] advance column." As Federal surgeon Thomas Ellis concluded, "it was a

---

55 *Ibid.*; OR 1:826-827.

madness that led them to death." Lamar's command was pinned down under heavy pressure when federals were discovered threatening his right flank. Lamar refused his right in an effort to prevent his line from being flanked, and was now fighting the enemy on two sides. The 3rd New Jersey worked its way behind the Legion as men from the 1st, 2nd, and 4th New Jersey regiments slammed into the balance of the thinning line. Georgians fell thick and fast on a slope so steep that it was just as hard to defend the ground as it was to attack up it. As far as Lieutenant Wiley C. Howard of Cobb's Legion was concerned, "It seemed McClellan's whole army was coming up the road."

Captain Gib J. Wright from Company D of Cobb's Legion was struck in the foot. "Wright will long be remembered as he lay holding up his bleeding foot and cried to us as we passed, 'give 'em hell, boys, they've got me down!'" one of his comrades noted. "By jaunties, give 'em hell anyhow." Many from the Legion broke and scrambled uphill as Lamar pleaded with them to stop and fight. Lamar finally ordered a retreat by the left flank, but was mortally wounded before he could make his own exit.[56]

"[We] rushed with exultant yells" upon Cobb's Legion," recalled Edward Grubb of the 3rd New Jersey. "Well did the brigade avenge them that day, and well did they avenge themselves, for three hundred prisoners, three stands of colors, over seven hundred stands of arms of the most approved pattern, one piece of artillery and a large number of haversacks and blankets were the spoils of the top of the hill at Crampton's Pass." Lamar's small command lost nearly 80% of its men on the Maryland mountainside. The small 16th Georgia, aligned on the Legion's left, was also struck hard in the attack and melted away soon after Cobb's Legion broke apart and fled uphill.[57]

"When I reached the gap I found both Colonel Munford and Colonel Parham active and energetic in the discharge of their duty," reported General Cobb, "which continued to the end of the fight. At the road intersection atop South Mountain, Cobb and other commanders did their best to rally the beaten commands, grouping together bits and pieces from the Legion, and the 10th,

56 Reese, "Howell Cobb's Brigade at Crampton's Gap," 18; Ellis, *Leaves*, 252; Bartlett, "Crampton's Pass," December 19, 1889; Joseph T. Derry, A. M., *Georgia*, in *Confederate Military History* (reprint, Secaucus, New Jersey: The Blue & Grey Press, 1993), 186; *Southern Historical Society Papers*, vol. 12, (Richmond, Virginia), 522-523; Wiley C. Howard, *Sketch of Cobb Legion Cavalry and Some Incidents and Scenes Remembered* (Atlanta: n.p., 1901), 3.

57 Grubb, *An Account of the Battle of Crampton's Pass*, 4-5, Western Reserve Historical Society, Cleveland, Ohio.

16th, and 24th Georgia regiments. "Shortly after the lines were broken," reported Cobb, "I was endeavoring to rally the troops, General Semmes appeared on the field, and, at great exposure and with great coolness and courage, gave me his cordial aid and co-operation. All of the members of my staff were on the field, and did all that could be done under the circumstances," he continued. "One of them, Colonel John B. Lamar, of Georgia, volunteer aide, whilst near my side, earnestly rallying the men, received a mortal wound, of which he died the next day. No nobler nor braver man has fallen in this war." Those soldiers who heeded the pleas took up positions behind low stone walls lining a clearing called Padgett's Field.

The only support arrived in the form of Lieutenant Henry Jennings' 2-gun section of Captain H. H. Carlton's Troup Light Artillery, which Cobb ordered unlimbered at the intersection of the Arnoldstown and Gapland roads. The brigadier pointed a 12-pounder brass howitzer dubbed "Jennie" down the Arnoldstown Road toward the federal right and aimed the remaining gun, a 6-pounder howitzer affectionately named "Sallie Craig," down the Gapland Road toward Burkittsville and the federal left. This placed the guns well in advance of their paltry infantry support, and with limited fields of fire amidst nearly pitch blackness.[58]

Edgar Richardson, a member of the gun crew working "Sallie Craig," remembered coming up with the artillery at the double quick. As they approached the front they met some of Cobb's men already running for their lives. "General Cobb was doing his best to rally his men, but he could not stop them," Richardson recalled. "When we passed him he hollored here is the Troup Artillery men, rally to it, but there was but one man that would come back." By this time the federals were less than 100 yards away, the "Sallie Craig" lobbed five rounds in an effort to stop them. "General Cobb hollowed and told me to look at the Yankees coming up the road close at us," Richardson recollected. The federals streaming toward the summit from several directions had little if any regimental organization, thrusting up from Whipp's Ravine, through the trees, over the rocks, and up the Gapland Road. "I fired into the head of the column," continued Richardson. "I cut their colors down and I think I must have killed several of them." Richardson's comrades manning

58 *Ibid.*; Reese, *Sealed With Their Lives*, 118-119, 161; Reese, "Howell Cobb's Brigade at Crampton's Gap," 18. While the origin of the name "Jennie" is unknown, the "Sallie Craig" honored a 16-year-old girl of the same name from Bethlehem, Pennsylvania, who sewed a Confederate banner and became the South's version of Barbara Freitchie.

"Jennie" were not as successful. That gun, he recalled, only managed to get off three rounds before thick musketry fire tore apart her axle and rendered further service useless. Fearing the loss of the guns, the artillerists limbered and fled, leaving Jennie behind. The few remaining Confederate infantry did likewise, effectively ending the Battle for Crampton's Gap.[59]

"As long as [we] could pursue [we] did pursue, but human breath and human legs cannot go very far over a mountain-top," explained the 3rd New Jersey's Edward Grubb. One of his federal comrades, a soldier from Company K of the 2nd New Jersey, agreed: "We pursued them until we were so fatigued we could go no further, and achieved a complete victory. Our loss was comparatively small, but that of the rebels was very severe, as the appearance of the field after the action bore evidence . . . the ground in every direction being strewn with their dead and wounded."[60]

As the Georgians dissolved into the darkness, crumbling down the far side of the mountain in abject retreat, Generals McLaws and Stuart approached the pass from their perch atop Maryland Heights. "Hearing of the attack at Crampton's Gap, I rode at full speed to reach that point," Stuart explained. As they drew near the pass, McLaws asked Stuart for his advice. The cavalryman suggested an attempt be made to reclaim Crampton's Gap, but McLaws would hear nothing of it. His focus remained on Maryland Heights and the reduction of Harpers Ferry. Now, however, he had to draw up a plan to resist the untimely federal thrust through Crampton's Gap into Pleasant Valley.[61]

When Cobb arrived, he told Stuart and McLaws that the enemy was but two hundred yards behind him. Major Heros von Borcke, one of Stuart's staff officers, recalled the chaotic scene. "The poor General was in a state of the saddest excitement and disgust at the conduct of his men," began Major von Borke. "As soon as he recognized us in the dusk of the evening, he cried out in heartbroken accents of alarm and despair, 'Dismount, gentlemen, dismount, if your lives are dear to you!'" When the dour Georgia politician recognized the

---

59 *Ibid.*; OR 1:400; Reese, *Sealed With Their Lives*, 162-166; Edgar Richardson, letter to his mother and sister, dated September 25, 1862, as reproduced in Timothy J. Reese, *Letters from the Battlefield: Crampton's Gap, September 14, 1862* (Burkittsville, Maryland: South Mountain Heritage Society, 1994), no pagination.

60 *Newark* (Ohio) *Daily Advertiser*, September 20, 1862; see also OR 1:382-388, 396-397, 881-882.

61 *Ibid.*, 1:819, 854-855; *Carman, The Maryland Campaign*, 142.

cavalry chieftain he cried out, "Oh! My dear Stuart, that I should live to experience such a disaster!"[62]

Stuart tried to comfort Cobb and threw out several parties of pickets to reconnoiter the enemy front. Darkness (and in some cases an exhaustion of ammunition) prevented the federals from pursuing. About 9:00 p.m., the federals bivouacked for the night where they had stopped their advance. "We came down to the road in the Pass, and halted for the night," Henry Keiser noted in his diary.[63]

The sharp victory cost the federals 533 casualties. Official returns reported 113 killed, 418 wounded, and just two missing or captured. While regiments like the 6th Vermont and 31st New York suffered relatively light losses, with just three and four wounded, respectively, Colonel Cake's 96th Pennsylvania suffered far heavier losses with 20 killed and 71 wounded, including Lieutenant Dougherty and Major Martin among the dead. Burial crews sent the bodies home to be interred in Pottsville, whose residents shrouded the town in fresh mourning crepe. "Our work was fortuitous, but none of our officers and men ever thought they had done more than their simple duty," reflected Private Boyer.[64]

*   *   *

"I guess you have heard before now of the sad fate of Cobb's Legion," member Samuel A. Burney wrote home to his wife ten days later. "They were cut to pieces on Sunday the 14th." Burney told her of the rough, rocky mountain side and estimated fairly closely the odds against the Confederates at ten to one. "The Yankees flanked our men on right & left. It is believed that many of the missing are unhurt & prisoners. The seven companies of infantry now number 138 men," Burney continued. "It is sad to see our Legion so badly

62 *Ibid.*; Heros von Borcke, *Memoirs of the Confederate War for Independence* (Philadelphia: Lippincott, 1867), 150.

63 OR 1:383, 386; Henry Keiser, diary entry, September 14, 1862, in Harrisburg Civil War Roundtable Collection, United States Army Military History Institute, Carlisle, Pennsylvania; Lewis Luckinbill, diary entry, September 15, 1862, in Northwest Corner Civil War Roundtable Collection, United States Army Military History Institute, Carlisle, Pennsylvania; Grubb, *An Account of the Battle of Crampton's Pass*, p. 5, Western Reserve Historical Society, Cleveland, Ohio.

64 OR 1:183; Boyer, "At Crampton's Pass," part three, *Shenandoah Evening Herald*, September 3, 1886.

cut up. They would not have suffered so badly if they had not stood their ground so well. They say that no men ever fought with more superior gallantry than the Georgia legion."[65]

Howell Cobb agreed that his troops performed well on September 14. "There were many [acts] of personal courage which circumstances prevent me from mentioning at present," he observed. Losses were another matter. "It is impossible for me to report the casualties, as the fate of only a few of the large number missing is certainly known," he reported mournfully. "Of the number who went into the battle there are now missing and unaccounted for over 800." When the official accounting was complete, the returns depicted a grisly toll: 59 killed, 189 wounded, and 442 men missing or captured, or more than one-half of Cobb's command. Like division leader McLaws, Thomas Munford had no doubt about who was to blame for the fiasco that was Crampton's Gap. "Had General Cobb's brigade given the support to the first troops engaged which they deserved, the gap would have been held," Munford reported, before writing the even more damning: "Had General Cobb come up in time, the result might have been otherwise. There were two stone walls at the base of the mountain parallel to each other, and one commanding the other, which could have been held against great odds had the troops been in position.[66]

Losses in other Southern commands were also noteworthy. William Mahone's Brigade under Parham counted 203 casualties: five killed, 74 wounded, and 124 men missing or captured. In Paul Semmes' Brigade, the 10th Georgia suffered three killed, 21 wounded, and 37 missing. Munford's two cavalry regiments contributed eight additional casualties. All told, Franklin's VI Corps attack against the back door to Harpers Ferry left stripped away nearly 900 Confederates from Lee's already depleted Army of Northern Virginia.[67]

In retrospect, the outcome of the battle for Crampton's Gap was no surprise given Franklin's heavy numerical advantage. Like their comrades defending the two gaps farther north, the rebels at Crampton's used the steep, wooded, and rocky slope and stone walls to slow down the enemy advance for an entire afternoon. Despite his uncertain grasp of McClellan's general strategy,

---

65 Samuel A. Burney to his wife, letter, September 24, 1862, in Nat S. Turner, III, ed., *A Southern Soldier's Letters Home: The Civil War Letters of Samuel A. Burney, Cobb's Georgia Legion, Army of Northern Virginia* (Macon, Georgia: Mercer University Press, 2002), 211-213.

66 OR 1:827, 861, 870-871; Carman, *The Maryland Campaign*, 445.

67 *Ibid.*

Franklin scored an important triumph at Crampton's Gap. "The victory was complete," he reported frankly. To his wife Anna, Franklin wrote that the struggle on South Mountain was "one of the prettiest fights of the war," before erroneously adding, "I arranged the details of it myself."[68]

Edward Grubb echoed his corps commander when he proclaimed, "This was a clear and undisputed victory, one of the few fights in the whole war, so far as I know, that the enemy made no claim to having won." Colonel Bartlett, who would soon christen his horse "Crampton" in celebration of the victory, wrote, "Congratulations were generously and feelingly exchanged all around and renewed confidence expressed in our brave fellows, who never had failed us when given a fair chance."[69]

Private Boyer of the 96th Pennsylvania reflected on the battle long after the war in a series of informative essays published in the Shenandoah, Pennsylvania *Evening Herald.* In an effort to acknowledge and defend the critical role his regiment played, he lamented that the battle "was overshadowed by the grander affairs [Antietam] that followed." The conversation about the significance of the engagement, however, was not initiated in the newspapers or other publications after the war. It began instead that evening on the battlefield, where the federal troops experienced, for the first time, the exhilaration of holding a piece of ground wrested from the enemy. The Union men on Fox's and Turner's gaps farther north experienced the same unique opportunity.[70]

When he finally rose from his restive slumber on the field the next morning, the 16th New York's Lieutenant William H. Walling penned a brief note to his sister. "Another eventful day has passed," he began. "Yesterday we went to meeting—not that peaceful, quiet kind that you probably participated in, but that kind in which graves are peopled." Indeed, for all involved it had been a most unholy Sabbath.[71]

68 OR 1:375; William Buel Franklin to Anna Franklin, September 15, 1862, as quoted in Mark A. Snell, *From First to Last: The Life of Major General William B. Franklin,* 184.

69 Grubb, *An Account of the Battle of Crampton's Pass,* p. 5, Western Reserve Historical Society, Cleveland, Ohio; Bartlett, "Crampton's Pass," *National Tribune,* December 19, 1889.

70 Boyer, "At Crampton's Pass," part three, *Shenandoah Evening Herald,* September 3, 1886.

71 William H. Walling to his sister, letter, September 15, 1862, in Curtis, *From Bull Run to Chancellorsville,* 171.

C hapter 10

"The day has gone against us"

Losing South Mountain

D arkness blanketed South Mountain on September 14 while the sounds of murderous battle fitfully gave way to the horror and suffering left in its wake. The great irony of war is that in all of the inhumanity of battle, the combat itself often brings out humane and holy purposes. Often the first examples emanate from the field hospitals, where civilians and soldiers alike face the enormous challenges of aiding the wounded and consoling the dying.

"They kept up a mournful noise all night," Lieutenant Colonel Adoniram Judson Warner recalled. "Some of them [died] in great agony." The night air was cold and brisk, and men wounded or not shivered in various stages of misery. Some of the federals allowed the wounded rebels to use their blankets while others attempted to comfort their erstwhile enemies as best they could. "We also found a number of wounded & we gave them water & Covered them with thear Blankets," wrote the 48th Pennsylvania's Captain James Wren. "Our wounded were scattered over a great distance up and down the mountain, and were suffering untold agonies," Rufus Dawes of the 6th Wisconsin remembered. "Owing to the difficulties of the ground and the night, no stretcher bearers had come upon the field. Several dying men were pleading piteously for water, of which there was not a drop. . . . The dread reality of war was before us in this frightful death, upon the cold, hard stones."[1]

---

1 Lieutenant Colonel Adoniram Judson Warner in James B. Casey, ed., "The Ordeal of Adoniram Judson Warner: His Minutes of South Mountain and Antietam," in *Civil War History: A Journal of the Middle Period* 28, no. 3 (September 1982), 213-236; James Wren, diary entry, September 15, 1862, in John Michael Priest, ed., *From New Bern to Fredericksburg* (Shippensburg, PA: White Mane Publishing Co., Inc., 1990), 68; Rufus R. Dawes, *Service with the Sixth Wisconsin Volunteers*, 84.

"The road was completely blocked up with army wagons and ambulances," Connecticut veteran B. F. Blakeslee recalled. "The road was narrow over the mountain, and terribly dusty. The ambulances were filled with the wounded, and rebel prisoners under guard were trying to go to the rear. Infantry, baggage wagons, provision and ammunition trains, were eagerly pushing to the front. The result was a stand-still for over an hour. On both sides of the road, shot and shell had pierced the trees and houses. The fences were riddled with bullets, telegraph poles were down, and the earth was ploughed by solid shot. The dead lay by the road-side, and the ambulances were scouring the mountainsides with men detailed to pick up the wounded."[2]

Bodies littered the battlefield. "They were lying about the yard in such numbers that it was with difficulty we rode through without treading on them," recalled one federal veteran of the fighting. "The battle-field gives evidence of the desperate fighting of yesterday," observed Theodore Reichardt, who passed through the battlefield with Battery A of the First Rhode Island Light Artillery on September 15. "All about us lay the dead and dying," William Richard Todd of the 79th New York remembered. "Oh my God my dear wife I am sick at heart from the sights I have seen. The town is filled with dead and dying, and I am told hundreds of poor wounded still lay on the field dying by inches," James Brisbin wrote home.[3]

Union Major George Hildt described one part of the field where "17 of their dead were lying[,] touching each other." Sergeant George Magusta Englis of the 89th New York made a similar observation. "I counted over 20 dead Rebbles in front of our lines," he penned his family days later. "I measured the ground and in 40 feet square I counted 16 of the enemy lying dead on it," James Wren wrote. Surgeon Thomas Ellis offered the most graphic description of the grisly field: "On the battle-field, bodies of the dead lay about in every direction, and in every imaginable position. Here fell an officer, sword in hand, urging on his men; one was drinking from his canteen as the fatal bullet pierced his brain; another, in the act of discharging his piece; and others, while loading their

2 B. F. Blakeslee, *History of the 16th Connecticut Volunteers* (Hartford: Case, Lockwood & Brainard Company, 1875), 9-11.

3 *Harper's New Monthly Magazine*, 36 (February 1868), 278; Theodore Reichardt, *Diary of Battery A, First Rhode Island Light Artillery* (Providence: N.B. Williams, 1865), 153; William Richard Todd, *The Seventy-ninth Highlanders, New York Volunteers* (Albany, 1886), 235-236. James Brisbin, letter to his wife, September 16, 1862, in Civil War Times Illustrated Collection, United States Army Military History Institute, Carlisle, Pennsylvania.

The dead litter the Fox's Gap battlefield. *Battles & Leaders of the Civil War*

muskets. Most of the killed were shot in the head, which is owing to the elevated position on which the enemy was posted," he wrote. "I have seen all of war I ever wish to," one New Hampshire boy lamented. "The thing is indescribable. Oh, horrors!"[4]

On Monday, September 15, squads of men fanned out to bury the dead. "Near the summit we saw several burial-parties digging trenches for our own dead, which had been gathered up and lay in ranks, their faces decently covered with hats or blankets," wrote an observer. "I counted one hundred and twenty bodies thus laid out."[5] Martin Deady of the 23rd Ohio's Company A, one of those detailed to a burial squad of seventy-five men, described his experience by simply writing, "Buried 200 Rebes they lay pretty thick." Deady did not complete his horrendous task until Thursday the 18th. "Same old work . . . awful smell to work by." His experiences atop the mountain haunted him for the rest of his life. "After the battle of South Mountain . . . in our work of laying away our comrades we came across a young Confederate officer on whose coat was pinned a slip giving the name Capt. H. C. Hyers, Mad River Lodge, North Carolina," Deady advertised in *Confederate Veteran* magazine six decades later in

4   Hildt, letter, September 22, 1862, in Hildt Papers, Ohio Historical Society, Columbus, Ohio; George Magusta Englis, letter, September 20, 1862, in Eileen Mae Knapp Patch, ed., *This From George* (Binghamton, New York: Broome County Historical Society, 2001), 39; James Wren, diary entry, September 15, 1862, in Priest, ed., *From New Bern to Fredericksburg*, 68; Thomas T. Ellis, diary, September 1862, in *Leaves from the Diary of an Army Surgeon: or, Incidents of Field, Camp, and Hospital Life*, 312; Edward O. Lord, ed., *History of the Ninth Regiment New Hampshire Volunteers in the War of the Rebellion* (Concord: Republican Press Association, 1895), 90.

5   *Harper's New Monthly Magazine*, 36 (February 1868), 279.

an effort to locate a member of the captain's family. "We buried him, and I cut the name on a piece of board at the head of his grave."[6]

Locals, hardened veterans, and others who for any variety of reasons had not been present during the vicious fighting flocked in droves to the new battlefield to witness firsthand the wake of the widespread combat. "Some of the country people living thereabout, who had been scared away by the firing, ventured back, making big eyes at all they saw, and asking more ridiculous questions," one federal enlisted man recalled.[7] For these veterans, discussions with locals on a field victorious were simply unprecedented. "Burnside permitted the troops to view the Battlefield they fought on yesterday, being the first time, he said . . . this being a victory . . . he would grant them the privilege," explained James Wren.[8]

"This was my first experience in gathering the wounded from a battlefield after it was won," admitted Wilson Hopkins of the 16th New York, who was in command of the ambulance corps for Henry Slocum's division. "Many have visited such places and reported the sickening sights, but I cannot describe their ghastly realities. Later I became more familiar with such scenes, yet I can never forget that dreadful night; its horrors overshadow all spectacles I witnessed on other battlefields, and the memory of what I there saw will remain with me to the end."[9]

Benjamin Hirst, a member of Company D of the 14th Connecticut, wrote candidly about his encampment on the "Blood Stained Fields" of South Mountain—his first encounter with the macabre and terrifying aftermath of a major battle.[10] Dr. James Oliver, who was busy amputating arms and legs, likewise discussed the impact these sights and sounds had on him. "I never saw in my three years of service, so many dead bodies as lay on a few acres of ground

6   Martin Deady, diary entry, September 16 and 18, 1862, in *Diary of Michael Deady, Co. H, 23rd Regiment O.V.I.*, Rutherford B. Hayes Presidential Center; Deady, advertisement, *Confederate Veteran*, 31 (1923), 282.

7   Kathleen A. Ernst, *Too Afraid to Cry: Maryland Civilians in the Antietam Campaign* (Mechanicsburg: Stackpole Books, 1999), 104.

8   *Confederate Veteran*, 31 (1923), 282.

9   Hopkins, as quoted in Schildt, *Roads to Antietam*, 107.

10 Benjamin Hirst, as quoted in *The Boys from Rockville: Civil War Narratives of Sgt. Benjamin Hirst, Company D, 14th Connecticut Volunteers*, ed. Robert L. Bee (Knoxville: University of Tennessee Press, 1998).

on top of South Mountain," wrote Dr. Oliver. "That hideous night, I shall always remember."[11]

The whirlwind of death and destruction had taken its greatest toll around the Daniel Wise farm at Fox's Gap, where both Generals Jesse Reno and Samuel Garland met with their demise. One Confederate, picked off by a federal musket as he was in the act of climbing one of the fences, remained entwined between the rails. A Pennsylvanian recalled that the rebel casualties lay "actually two and three deep. . . . In a log house near by, [a dead soldier] sat with his eye to a chink between the logs with a bullet through his head."[12] "I saw a number of dead bodies, and among them several still living, but too far gone to bear moving. One sat up, his head supported by a musket thrust bayonet-end into the ground. . . . Amidst all this agony, blood, and distortion, I remarked one dead face, white as wax, and wearing a sweet, placid smile, as if life had passed in a pleasant dream. The expression of that face was startling and unspeakably touching. I have never seen any thing like it, before or since, on the field of battle," shuddered another veteran.[13] In addition to the dead and wounded, the Wise cabin had been looted and the farmer's daughter, Cecilia, returned to find a dead man sprawled across her mattress.[14]

The macabre display of groaning wounded and stiffening bodies marked the farm as the site of South Mountain's fiercest combat. Brigadier General Willcox described the scene as "such a picture of the killed and wounded as . . . was rarely seen during the war." Willcox recalled one particularly moving incident: "Sitting on the stone fence [was] the body of a little boy in gray, a musician, perfectly dead and rigid, his arm extended and finger pointing towards our lines."[15]

Wise's farm became infamous for more than its gruesome litter and frequent mentions in diary entries. Someone dumped dozens of Confederate

11 James Oliver, as quoted in John W. Schildt, *Roads to Antietam* (Shippensburg, PA: Burd Street Press, 1997), 98-99.

12 *Ibid.*

13 *Harper's New Monthly Magazine*, 36 (February 1868): 279.

14 Ernst, *Too Afraid To Cry*, 102-103.

15 Orlando Willcox is quoted in Ernst, *To Afraid to Cry*, 102, and in Steven R. Stotelmyer, "The Truth About Wise's Well: Setting the Record Straight on South Mountain," *Blue and Gray* (October 1990). The "little incident" is recounted by Willcox in the chapter of his memoirs entitled "South Mountain and Antietam," in Scott, ed., *Forgotten Valor*, 357.

corpses into a well adjacent to the Wise property. Although local lore implicated farmer Wise himself, the culprits turned out to be Ohio soldiers. On September 16, "Some Ohio troops had been detailed to bury [the dead], but not relishing the task, and finding the ground hard to dig, soon removed the covering of a deep well connected with Wise's house on the summit, and lightened their toil by throwing a few bodies into the well," recorded Massachusetts veteran Charles Wolcott. The bodies remained in the well until 1874, when they were removed and re-interred in the Washington Confederate Cemetery in Hagerstown.[16]

Hoping to escape its macabre history, the Wise family sold the property four years later. Still, the myriad experiences encountered on those mountainous acres would never abandon the elder farmer or his family members. Indeed, before the war's end, the self-described "old pedlar" took up his pen to write poetry. In one sentimental piece he dedicated to the "Young People of the United States," Wise made clear his utter disdain for the Southern rebellion:

> Now I old and bald,
> And always true enough my country to uphold;
> Our government always has been good enough for me
> And why should it not for others be?
> This is to let my young Union friends know
> That they should never join a rebel foe,
> For it is a dirty show,
> Put together your thought, and study
> How General Washington fought for this country,
> To set it free and give us liberty;

Wise went out of his way to note the rebels' "great mistakes" and to overtly instruct the "ladies too" of their implicit patriotic duty to "stick up for the red, white and blue," for "this will give the soldiers courage too." Ending with yet another supplication to the young to "fight on, fight on" and to "never give up on such a glorious land," Wise confirmed his ardent devotion to his country and

---

16 Walcott's regimental history is quoted in Stotelmyer, "The Truth About Wise's Well," 28. For more information, generally, on death, burial, retrieval, and the Civil War, see Drew Gilpin Faust, *This Republic of Suffering: Death and the American Civil War* (New York: Alfred A Knoft, 2008).

cause—a devotion bolstered by the maelstrom of war that had engulfed his property and, in some respects, consumed his reputation.[17]

*   *   *

Driven by their curiosity, some of the locals walked around the battlefield to catch a glimpse of the carnage firsthand. Frank P. Firey and his father found the body of the 3rd South Carolina Infantry Battalion's Lieutenant Colonel George Strother James, who had been killed in action late in the day while fighting as part of Thomas Drayton's Brigade. After cutting off the dead officer's uniform buttons as mementos, the Fireys gave Colonel James a proper burial. The two put the incident behind them until the following summer, when Confederate troops tramped across South Mountain on their way to Gettysburg and the elder Firey and his son offered water to some of the thirsty Southern infantry. When they discovered they were South Carolinians, they recounted the story of having buried a colonel after the South Mountain fight of September 14. One of the Palmetto soldiers exclaimed, "Colonel James! My God! He was the colonel of our regiment, and his brother is the captain of our company." A few of the South Carolinians "immediately ran for the ranks and in a few minutes returned with their captain," Benjamin S. James. The elder Firey presented the buttons to the young officer, who folded the small treasures into his handkerchief with a promise to return that summer to exhume his brother's remains for a proper burial in South Carolina.[18]

17 Daniel Wise, "To The Young People of the United States." An original copy of this poem was found in the Rutherford B. Hayes Papers, Hayes Presidential Center, Fremont, Ohio. In the left margin, Hayes noted in his own hand, "Written by an old man living on South Mountain about the time of the battle 1862 - H."

18 Frank P. Firey, "On the Battlefield of South Mountain," *Confederate Veteran*, 23 (February 1915): 71-72. The 3rd South Carolina Volunteer Infantry Battalion (also known as the James Battalion or the Laurens Battalion) lost 132 men from all causes out of only about 250 men engaged at Fox's Gap on September 14, 1862. Despite his promise, Captain Benjamin James never returned that summer to claim his brother's remains. Landowner Frank Firey moved west after the war and became the postmaster and eventually mayor of Pomona, California. Frank P. Firey, *City of Pomona in the Making* (Pomona: Pomona Valley Historical Society, 1935). In a February 1915 article published in *Confederate Veteran* magazine, Firey wrote that he assumed Captain James did not return in 1863 because he had been killed at Gettysburg during Pickett's Charge. Why the captain did not return to locate his brother's corpse is open to speculation, but he survived the war to become a doctor and died in Clayton, South Carolina, on August 19, 1895. *Clayton* [South Carolina] *Courier*, as noted on http://genforum. genealogy. com/james/messages/32773.html.

Although civilian compassion was nearly ubiquitous, so too was confusion in the makeshift hospitals. Burkittsville, Middletown, and Frederick, along with many other small communities and local churches opened their doors to the deluge of patients spewed from South Mountain. The Mountain House, of late the headquarters for D. H. Hill, became a refuge for both bleeding bodies and weary warriors. "You can have no idea of a hospital soon after a battle," admonished James Denton to his mother. "The wounded lay on the ground till the afternoon the day after the Battle, when they was removed to Burkittsville, about a mile from the Battlefield. There they were laid on straw on the floor, most of them without blankets."[19] The inhabitants of Burkittsville, explained a grateful surgeon Thomas Ellis, "opened their houses with alacrity for the reception of the wounded, and offered the kindest attentions to the sufferers."[20]

Daniel M. Holt, the surgeon of the 121st New York, was also posted near Burkittsville. Even though a man of medicine, he was not prepared for the aftermath of combat. "I have never seen what I never once expected I should see—a battlefield—a field of blood and carnage," he candidly admitted to his wife Louisa. "Oh! The terrible sight which met our eyes on the morning after that short and terrible conflict as we marched up those rugged steeps!" Holt's diary also recorded a variety of gruesome sights: A dead horse; a rebel with his brains blown out and stiffened arms permanently extended; Union men mortally wounded and gasping for air. "I cannot describe, neither can I [have you] realize what we have passed through," Dr. Holt continued. "[W]e are in the thickest of the fray." Holt, a caring and passionate man, worried because he grew entirely numb by exposure to so much death and destruction. "I pass over the putrifying bodies of the dead and feel as little unconcerned as though they were two hundred pigs. Their protruding bowels, glassy eyes, open mouths, ejecting blood and gases . . . affect me not." Holt's personal views about slavery, however, infused his duty with a certain vengeful sentiment. "They have with open eyes entered into a conspiracy to break up and destroy our free institutions and entail slavery dark and eternal upon us. As a free, an enlightened and a Christian people, we are bound to subdue this rebellion. . . . This is perhaps

---

19 James Denton to Mrs. Gordon Phillips, letter, November 19, 1862, from Pension File of Sgt. George A. Phillips, Co. B., 32nd New York Infantry, as quoted in Timothy J. Reese, ed., *Letters from the Battlefield* (Burkittsville: South Mountain Heritage Society, 1994), n.p.

20 Ellis, diary, September 1862, 312.

wrong, but I cannot help having all the bitterness of my heart stirred up against them."[21]

"It is hard to see the Wounded in the Hospitals, to see what they have to suffer," explained one wounded Maine soldier to his mother from Burkittsville. "Thankfully," he added too optimistically, "I don't think it will last much longer."[22] Another Union soldier described a hospital atop Fox's Gap as "an awful sight, being a little house, by itself, & in the yard thear [sic] was 3 or 4 Large [operation] tables in it . . . you Could see many legs Laying in the yard with the shoes & stockings still on—not taken off when amputated . . . in a field to the Left of this house was a long line of dead Soldiers Laying side by side with a Little inscription on thear [sic] breasts, giving thear [sic] Names & thear [sic] Compny & Regt & the state they ware from . . . the pioneer or ambulance Corps [was] engaged [in] digging a long trench, 7 feet wide to bury them in. . . ."[23] Another witness wrote home that "The doctors attend to the amputations first, and if a wounded man has not got a friend with him, he suffers severely."[24]

A few years after the war, a federal veteran described another hospital located in one of the many brick houses lining the main thoroughfare through Middletown. "The surgeons occupied one of the rooms amputating and dressing the wounds, and the patients were then lain in the yard, bedded on wisps of straw, pillowed on knapsacks, and covered with blankets or over-coats. There they seemed to lie comfortably enough, some nibbling crackers; others, assisted by a comrade, taking a little drink."[25] Most of the patients were sent to the campaign's medical center at Frederick. "The old general hospital [in Frederick], which had contained six hundred beds, was so crowded with patients that one thousand were of necessity placed in the wards, and one thousand eight hundred men were fed at its tables and slept somewhere," Acting Assistant Surgeon W. W. Keen reported. The tight quarters and lack of

---

21 Daniel M. Holt to Louisa Holt, letter, September 16, 1862, in James M. Greiner, Janet L. Coryell, and James R. Smither, eds., *A Surgeon's Civil War: The Letters and Diary of Daniel M. Holt, M.D.* (Kent, Ohio: Kent State University Press), 18-19.

22 Abraham Chase to his mother, letter, November 11, 1862, in Timothy J. Reese, ed., *Letters from the Battlefield.*

23 James Wren, diary entry, September 15, 1862, in Priest, ed., *From New Bern to Fredericksburg,* 69.

24 Denton to Phillips, letter, November 19, 1862, in Reese, ed., *Letters from the Battlefield.*

25 *Harper's New Monthly Magazine,* 36 (February 1868), 278.

proper ventilation contributed to a serious outbreak of gangrene the following month, forcing dozens of patients to spend weeks marinating in a vile mixture of blood and pus. Surprisingly, only two of the cases proved fatal.[26]

The especially forbidding wounds also troubled the overtaxed surgeons. A minie ball entered the left side of the face of Sergeant Augustus Reinwald of the 42nd Pennsylvania and emerged from behind his right ear. Pale, weak, emaciated, and insensible, the unfortunate Reinwald was unable to swallow or open his mouth and bled from the mouth, ear, and eye. With some of his nerves paralyzed, he lost vision in his right eye and all sensation on his right side before receiving a medical discharge from the army. Private Charles Mullen of the 69th Pennsylvania offered another grisly example of what can befall unlucky men on a field of combat. Mullen fell to the ground unconscious after a saber cut sliced off the left side of his scalp. His months-long ordeal carried him through numerous hospitals, with the flap created by the gruesome wound exposing a portion of his blackened dead skull bone. Forceps finally removed the flap and allowed his scalp to heal, but he was left with a permanent mental disability.[27]

And yet the suffering was only beginning for thousands of families and new widows and orphans back home. "It becomes my painful duty to inform you that your Brother, Lieut. Louis Wright, was killed in action at this place while gallantly leading his Company in a charge upon the enemy," the quartermaster of the 32nd New York wrote to the sister of a comrade. "He left your address with me for the reason that you would break the sad news to his Mother more gently than a letter direct would." W. H. Aubery, the steward of Hospital D in Burkittsville, penned a similar letter to an anxious father waiting back home in New Jersey. "I take pen in hand to inform you of the Death of your dear Son. It is sad for you to hear this news. . . . He had me to promise him to write to you and I told him I would." Likewise, the horrors lingered for the mountaintop civilians who tilled up human remains for years to come. "Today is Ascension Day," John Koogle wrote on May 14, 1863. "Henry and I were over the South Mountain battlefield, some citizens were burying bones."[28]

---

26 *Medical and Surgical History of the War of the Rebellion*, 12: 826. Hereafter cited as *MSHWR*.

27 *MSHWR*, 7:165.

28 W. H. Forbes to Mrs. Jacob Reitler, letter, n.d.; W. H. Aubery to Mr. B. Exner, letter, October 22, 1862, as quoted in Reese, ed., *Letters from the Battlefield*; John Koogle, diary entry, as quoted by Steven R. Stotelmyer, *The Bivouacs of the Dead: The Story of Those Who Died at Antietam and South Mountain* (Baltimore: Toomey Press, 1992), 16.

*   *   *

The cheerless circumstances on the battlefield and in the field hospitals mirrored the dismal mood permeating D. H. Hill's headquarters at the old Mountain House. After an entire day of reverses, the rebel leaders were, as Ezra Carman described them, "an anxious and disheartened group." The victorious federals held ground so near the headquarters that the Confederate leaders' voices were, by necessity, reduced to whispers. "As I approached, I inquired, in an ordinary tone of voice, as to the condition of affairs on our left," John Bell Hood wrote, "and to my surprise was met with a mysterious 'Pshe—Pshe'—; a voice added in an audible whisper, 'The enemy is just there in the corn field; he has forced us back.'"[29] Hood suggested that the cadre abandon the mountain. The grim situation was inscribed on Robert E. Lee's face. "General Lee inquired of the prospects for continuing the fight," Longstreet recalled in his memoir. Hill, who had defended the passes through the day, was more suited to deliver the report. "He explained that the enemy was in great force with commanding positions on both flanks, which would give a cross-fire for his batteries, in good range on our front, making the cramped position of the Confederates at the Mountain House untenable," Longstreet summarized. "His explanation was too forcible to admit of further deliberation."[30]

A Union prisoner provided information that the II and XII corps were marching up the National Pike for Bolivar. "It became manifest that our forces were not sufficient to resist the renewed attacks of the entire army of McClellan," Longstreet reported. "He would require but little time to turn either flank, and our command must then be at his mercy." After nightfall, when Lee realized the day had gone against him, "[he] took immediate measures to reunite with McLaws and recross the Potomac in Virginia."[31]

Lee's dispatch to address the dire situation—the first order of retreat he issued as a field commander—went to McLaws at 8:00 p.m. "The day has gone against us," he wrote, "and this army will go by Sharpsburg and cross the river." Lee continued:

29 Carman, *The Maryland Campaign*, 165; Hood, *Advance and Retreat*, 41.

30 *Ibid.*; Longstreet, *From Manassas to Appomattox*, 227.

31 *Ibid.*; OR 1:840; Carman, *The Maryland Campaign*, 169.

It is necessary for you to abandon your position tonight. Send your trains not required on the road to cross the river. Your troops you must have well in hand to unite with this command, which will retire by Sharpsburg. Send forward officers to explore the way, ascertain the best crossing of the Potomac, and if you can find any between you and Shepherdstown leave Shepherdstown Ford for this command. Send an officer to report to me on the Sharpsburg road, where you are and what crossing you will take. You will of course bring Anderson's division with you.[32]

About ten that evening, the supply trains wheeled out and the infantry and artillery followed through the night. At Sharpsburg, as he wrote, he could easily reunite his forces and prepare to cross the Potomac. "The effort to force the passage of the mountains had failed," he reported. "Under these circumstances, it was determined to retire to Sharpsburg, where we would be upon the flank and rear of the enemy should he move against McLaws, and where we could more readily unite with the rest of the army."[33]

Gone was the ebullience, the pomp, the pageantry, the proclamations, and the poised confidence of Lee and the Army of Northern Virginia. With a single Sabbath battle, the "most propitious time" for the rebel army to invade above the Potomac River and "throw off the oppression" metamorphosed into a period of desperation and defeatism that threatened the abandonment of the entire campaign. South Mountain opened a season of opportunity for McClellan's army. The rebel ebb had begun. While those with Lee suggested that he exhibited no sign of disappointment or depression, it requires no imaginative leap to conclude, as Ezra Carman did, that "it was with a swelling heart" that Lee delivered the order for retreat.[34] Even some of the most unapologetic rebel veterans reached the same conclusion. "General Lee was evidently much depressed,"[35] one survivor of his army, R. K. Charles, concluded in *Confederate Veteran*.

Once the fighting died away, explained William W. Sherwood, "We had to fall back. As I fell back being barefooted I cut my foot and I came out of the fight about dark the fight ceased and about ten o'clock the army commenced to fall back. We marched all night. We had to leave some of our wounded at

32 *WPREL*, 307-308.

33 OR 1:147; Carman, *The Maryland Campaign*, 166.

34 *Ibid.*; Carman, *The Maryland Campaign*, 169-170.

35 R. K. Charles, "Events in the Battle of Fredericksburg," *Confederate Veteran*, 14:65.

Boonsborough."[36] "The victory is theirs," asserted a Virginian from James Kemper's Brigade. "In fact, long before we arrived, the most important points had been carried, and all that remained was to check this tide of triumphant blue coats and secure a safe retreat. . . . The remnant of our little army began its retreat in silence, so silently that according to their own account the enemy knew nothing of it until the next morning when even our rear guard was out of danger."[37]

Events continued to move apace. In response to events and conditions on the ground, Lee's precise strategy of withdrawal from Maryland shifted several times during the evening of September 14 and into the early morning hours of September 15. News that the federals had forced Crampton's Gap and that General McLaws was in danger of being trapped in Pleasant Valley exacerbated the Army of Northern Virginia's perilous situation. General Lee had to reunite his army at any cost, and quickly. About fifteen minutes past eleven that evening, Lee issued an often overlooked dispatch to McLaws informing him that Generals Longstreet and D. H. Hill would assume a blocking position some two and one-half miles west of Boonsboro on the road leading to Sharpsburg. "This portion of the army will take position at . . . Keedysville . . . with a view of preventing the enemy that may enter the gap at Boonsborough turnpike from cutting you off, and enabling you to make a junction with it," Lee instructed McLaws. "If you can pass tonight on the river road, by Harper's Ferry, or cross the mountain below Crampton's Gap toward Sharpsburg, let me know."[38]

Lee, Longstreet's men, and D. H. Hill's battered division, which had been the first to slip down the mountain, arrived in Keedysville about 5:00 a.m. They remained there no more than one hour. Still unsure of the fate of Harpers Ferry, ignorant of McClellan's plans for pursuit, and realizing that the ground around Keedysville offered few tactical advantages, Lee determined to continue three miles west to Sharpsburg. The high ground there offered the Army of Northern Virginia a strong defensive position from which to ward off any potential Union attack that might threaten a reunification with McLaws. This position also put Antietam Creek, meandering roughly parallel to the Potomac River,

---

36 William W. Sherwood, diary entry, September 14, 1862, in Sherwood Papers, Virginia Historical Society, Richmond, Virginia.

37 John Dooley, *John Dooley Confederate Soldier: His War Journal*, 36-38.

38 Harsh, *Sounding the Shallows*, 181-182; OR 2:608.

between the Confederates and their pursuers. As a result, Lee's move to Sharpsburg early on the morning of September 15 was intended to coalesce the fragments of his army for a safe and orderly withdrawal below the Potomac River.[39]

Did Lee believe his daring campaign might still be salvaged with a victory somewhere between South Mountain and Harpers Ferry? Considering the frenetic pace and reactive character of his decision-making in the immediate aftermath of the defeat at South Mountain, it is doubtful Lee was thinking along these lines on the night of September 14. He was entirely unaware that earlier that evening (8:15 p.m.) Jackson had dispatched a courier to him with the following message: "Through God's blessing, Harpers Ferry and its garrison are to be surrendered. I write at this time in order that you may be apprised of the condition of things."[40] This welcome and important news, however, did not reach the army commander until at least 8:00 a.m. the following morning on September 15—long after Lee had already decided to reunite his army at Sharpsburg. The situation facing the Confederate army, however, was still perilous. If McClellan struck before Lee could reunite his troops, the outnumbered and exhausted Army of Northern Virginia faced potential destruction on Northern soil. Lee hurried Jackson's men to Sharpsburg to reinforce his position there, though he still intended to execute a safe withdrawal below the Potomac. Once Jackson arrived, however, Lee felt better about his situation and decided to keep his options open in Maryland for at least one more day, though he made no definitive plans to bring on a major battle along Antietam Creek and almost certainly did not want one.[41]

Many historians, excising the tortuous and apprehensive hours following the Confederate defeat at South Mountain from their narratives, seize upon the surrender of Harpers Ferry as the decisive turning point of the campaign. With the news of Jackson's victory, they argue, Lee regained his momentum and made a bold strike to salvage the campaign with "a stand in these hills [at

39 Benjamin Frankling Cooling, *Counter-Thrust: From the Peninsula to the Antietam* (Lincoln: University of Nebraska Press, 2007), 222-223; Harsh, *Sounding the Shallows*, 182; Carman, *The Maryland Campaign*, 169-170, 186-187.

40 *OR* 1:951.

41 Harsh, *Sounding the Shallows*, 182. The uncharacteristically defensive nature of the battle Lee waged at Sharpsburg on September 17, 1862, which has garnered criticism from even Lee's most impassioned defenders, lends support to this conclusion.

Sharpsburg]." "General Lee decided not to risk another battle north of the Potomac," writes Stephen Sears, but, upon hearing word of Harpers Ferry's surrender, "the pendulum swung back. . . . Robert E. Lee was now thinking aggressively again." This analysis underestimates the deleterious effect South Mountain had on Lee and his strategic plans. "The moral effect of our movement into Maryland has been lost by our discomfiture at South Mountain, and it was then evident that we could not hope to concentrate in time to do more than make a respectable retreat," Longstreet explained after the war.

Any Confederate dream of ending the war in Maryland with a single grand battle was now gone forever.[42]

* * *

As might be expected after forcing the mountain gaps, the strategic view of the unfolding Maryland campaign looked quite different from federal eyes. General McClellan, having achieved his most complete battlefield victory of the war, wired General Halleck: "After a very severe engagement the Corps of Hooker and Reno have carried the heights commanding the Hagerstown road. The troops behaved magnificently." His telegraph continued with palpable evidence of ebullience:

> They never fought better. Franklin has been hotly engaged on the extreme left. . . . It has been a glorious victory; I cannot yet tell whether the enemy will retreat during the night or appear in increased force in the morning. I am hurrying up everything from the rear to be prepared for any eventuality . . .

Most importantly, the magnificently behaved troops were in high spirits. "The morale of our men is now restored!" confirmed McClellan, whose own confidence grew with each report he wired.[43] "We attacked a large force of the enemy yesterday . . . our troops, old and new regiments, behaved most valiantly and gained a signal victory. The rebels routed, and retreating in disorder this morning," he informed Lieutenant General Winfield Scott at West Point on September 15. "I do not consider that any danger to Washington is now to be

---

42 Harsh, *Taken at the Flood*, 305; Stephen W. Sears, *Landscape Turned Red: The Battle of Antietam* (Boston and New York: Houghton Mifflin Company, 1983), 150-151. *B&L* 2:666-667.

43 McClellan to Halleck, September 14, 1862, in *McClellan Papers*.

feared from the north side of the river," McClellan wired Major General Nathaniel Banks.[44]

McClellan's most important communiqués went to the commander-in-chief. "Gen Lee last night stated publicly that he must admit they had been shockingly whipped," he wrote President Lincoln, to which Lincoln responded, "God bless you, and all with you. Destroy the rebel army, if possible."[45] The president's optimism remained evident in a dispatch to Illinois politician Jesse K. Dubois a few hours later. "I now consider it safe to say that General McClellan has gained a great victory over the great rebel army in Maryland, between Frederick and Hagerstown. He is now pursuing a flying foe."[46] McClellan's dispatches deeply moved Lincoln, but Navy Secretary Gideon Welles remained justifiably skeptical. "A tale like this from Pope would have been classed as one of his lies," he confessed to his diary. "I am afraid it is not as decisive as it should be. . . . I shall rejoice if McClellan has actually overtaken the Rebels which is not altogether clear."[47]

McClellan's initial reports of the battle exaggerated the Confederate death toll at South Mountain, but he did not overestimate how the army viewed the engagement. Other commanders reached similar conclusions about the meaning of the battle and its impact on the ranks. "Moving all together, [the federals] drove the enemy from behind the stone fences in the Gap with great slaughter," James Harrison Wilson recalled. "The victory was a signal and encouraging one. It was here that I first saw infantry attacking after nightfall. The flash of the rebel rifles lit the mountain side like fireflies," and Union guns responded "like continuous streaks of lightning and kept steadily on without wavering or faltering till it had crowned the ridge, we knew the victory was surely ours."[48] In a letter to his wife Marie dated September 15, Orlando B. Willcox explained, "We have had a glorious victory . . . God be praised for his mercy." Likewise, in his official report Joseph Hooker noted, "When the advantages of the enemy's position are considered, and his preponderating

44 OR 2:294-5.

45 *Ibid.*; *CWAL*, 5:426.

46 OR 2:295.

47 Welles, diary entry, 1:30.

48 James Harrison Wilson, *Under the Old Flag: Recollections of Military Operations in the War for the Union, The Spanish War, The Boxer Rebellion, Etc.*, 2 vols. (New York: D. Appleton and Company, 1912), 1:105-106.

numbers, the forcing of the passage of South Mountain will be classed among the most brilliant and satisfactory achievements of this army. "[49]

McClellan's decided victory wrested the strategic initiative from Lee and denied him the opportunity to continue north. Compelled to abandon his visions of rebel tents along the Susquehanna River, Lee now sought to reunite his fractured army for an orderly withdrawal across the Potomac, risking in the process a bloody showdown with McClellan's forces at Sharpsburg he certainly was not hoping to fight. "Until the passes of the South Mountain were forced, General Lee does not appear to have seriously contemplated a battle; in which, from the scattered condition of his command, he had nothing to gain and everything to lose," federal veteran George B. Davis wrote after the war.[50]

*　　*　　*

Just three days after South Mountain, the respective armies, hardened and worn by long marches and the September 14 combat, faced off in the fields and farm lanes of Sharpsburg. It was a battle Lee never intended to fight, though he was apparently content with the powerful nature of the rolling terrain. "Lee's position west of Antietam Creek was more suited to lateral defensive maneuver than to the tactical defensive," explained historian Brian Holden Reid. "Close study of the ground reveals that it is not as strong as it appears. That Lee might have thought in terms of bluffing McClellan behind these rolling crests rather than in fighting him there is confirmed by Lee's decision not to order the digging of entrenchments, which was unusual for him."[51]

Cornered, under strength, and denied the clear vistas required to make good command decisions, Lee's beleaguered army withstood waves of federal assaults from dawn until nearly sunset. Heavy fighting swept across D. R. Miller's thirty acres—forever after known simply as "The Cornfield"—around the Dunker Church and West Woods, along a sunken farm road known to

---

49 O. B. Willcox to M.F. Willcox, September 15, 1862, in Scott, ed., *Forgotten Valor: The Memoirs, Journals, and Civil War Letters of Orlando B. Willcox*, 365-366; OR op. cit.

50 George B. Davis, "The Antietam Campaign," in *Papers of the Military Historical Society of Massachusetts*, 3:53.

51 Reid, *America's Civil War: The Operational Battlefield*, 190. Reid was not using "entrenchments" to mean circa 1864 Petersburg-style breastworks, but rather operation breastworks, which included throwing up dirt, stacking fence rails to improve a position, and so forth.

history as the Bloody Lane and, finally, along the banks of shallow Antietam Creek and beyond. Only dusk and timely Southern reinforcements in the form of A. P. Hill's "Light" Division, which arrived after a grueling march from Harpers Ferry, put an end to the bloodiest day in American history. Miscommunication, uncoordinated attacks, and a failure of leadership plagued McClellan's army throughout the day. Because the fighting had trickled into dusk, and with only one ford behind him on the Potomac, it was impossible for Lee to have evacuated his infantry, artillery, and associated wagons before daylight. He had no choice but to shorten his lines, send his wagons and other material over the river, and prepare to fight again the next day. Neither army was eager to renew the bloodshed on September 18, and except for sporadic skirmishing, the federal attack Lee and his lieutenants feared never materialized. The Army of Northern Virginia withdrew during the night, leaving in its wake 1,550 killed, 7,750 wounded, and more than 1,000 missing and/or captured. Federal losses were heavier at 2,100 killed, 9,550 wounded, and 750 missing and or captured. On September 19, McClellan reported to Halleck that Maryland was "entirely freed from the presence of the enemy," and that "no fears need now be entertained for the safety of Pennsylvania."[52]

Tactically speaking the September 17 battle was a bloody draw, but the strategic ramifications of the Confederate withdrawal below the Potomac offered President Lincoln the opportunity to change the entire face of the American Civil War. The beleaguered president's long-awaited moment to strike at the institution of slavery had arrived. "I think the time has come now," the president averred. In stark contrast to the optimism he had displayed upon receiving McClellan's dispatch from South Mountain, in the wake of the seemingly meaningless slaughter along the Antietam, Lincoln grew more ambivalent. "I wish it was a better time," he implored, explaining that "the action of the army against the rebels had not been quite what I should have best liked. But they have been driven out of Maryland." As the president told Republican Congressman George Boutwell of Massachusetts, "When Lee came over the river, I made a resolve that when McClellan drove him back—and I expected he would do it sometime or other—I would send the Proclamation after him." Secretary of the Treasury Salmon Chase agreed with Lincoln: the Union army had thwarted Confederate designs for Maryland and Pennsylvania, and the season for emancipation had arrived. "The Rebels are driven out of

52 McClellan to Halleck, September 19, 1862, in McClellan Papers, 470.

Maryland: but they have taken out with them all their artillery, trains, & spoils. Still it is much that their audacious designs on Maryland, Pennsylvania, and Washington are defeated," Chase told Robert Dale Owen. The thread that unraveled the Confederate canvas was pulled in the gaps of South Mountain. On September 22, Lincoln issued the preliminary Emancipation Proclamation, instructing the rebellious regions that unless they returned their loyalties to the Union by January 1, 1863, the slaves held there would be "then, thenceforward, and forever free."[53]

Lincoln's simple gesture revolutionized the Union war effort. After making it clear that the proclamation was a military act, enforceable by federal bayonets, Lincoln reminded "all officers or persons in the military or naval service of the United States" that they were prohibited from returning any of the fugitives who made their way to Union lines. Indeed, recognizing, as did Joseph Medill, that "the slaves must not only be emancipated, but armed and set in battle on the side of the Union," Lincoln provided for the enlistment of free blacks and former slaves in the Union armies and navies.[54] Two days after announcing the preliminary proclamation, the president issued his second suspension of the writ of *habeas corpus.* "It is the beginning of the end of the rebellion; the beginning of the new life of the nation," insisted the *New York Tribune.*[55]

England and France, meanwhile, held their collective breath awaiting the outcome of Lee's thrust into Maryland. In a September 24 memorandum to Gladstone, Lord Palmerston wrote, "A great Battle appeared by the last accounts to be coming on [and] if McClellan is badly defeated the Federal Cause will be manifestly hopeless." However, Palmerston continued, "a few days will bring us important accounts."[56] When those "accounts" arrived, and the British read of the "glorious victory" at South Mountain, of the bloody stalemate at Antietam Creek, and of Lee's decision to cross the Potomac back into Virginia, the Prime Minister hesitated on the important question of intervention, observing that "the results accomplished" on the battlefield rendered "the

---

53 WAL, 5:434; George Boutwell, as quoted in Guelzo, *Lincoln's Emancipation Proclamation,* The End of Slavery in America (New York: Simon & Schuster, 2004), 169; Salmon Chase to Robert Dale Owen, letter, September 20, 1862, in Niven, ed., *The Papers of Salmon Chase,* 3:276-277.

54 Joseph Medill to Salmon Chase, in Niven, ed., *The Papers of Salmon Chase,* 3:265.

55 *New York Tribune,* September 23, 1862. Guelzo's *Lincoln's Emancipation Proclamation* remains the best treatment of the Emancipation Proclamation.

56 Palmerston to Gladstone, September 24, 1862, in Palmerston Papers.

whole matter full of difficulty." The dilemma, he determined, could "only be cleared up by some more decided events between the contending armies."[57]

Whether McClellan recognized this as well is open to some debate. His opportunity to pursue and to destroy Lee's weakened army slipped away as late summer faded into late October. Throughout, Lincoln urged McClellan to slip below the Potomac and move against Lee. "I have read your dispatch about sore-tongued and fatigued horses," Lincoln wrote in reply to one of McClellan's reasons for not advancing against Lee. "Will you pardon me for asking what the horses of your army have done since the battle of Antietam that fatigues anything?"[58]

By the time McClellan began moving into northern Virginia it was too late. Lincoln removed him from command on November 5 and replaced him with Major General Ambrose E. Burnside. McClellan immediately registered his objections. "They [the administration] have made a great mistake—alas for my poor country—I know in my innermost heart she never had a truer servant," he wrote his wife Mary Ellen. "I have done the best I could for my country . . . to the last I have done my duty as I understand it."[59] His farewell words waxed sarcastic: "I cannot omit this expression of my thanks to the President for the constant evidence given me of his sincere and personal regard, and his desire to sustain the military plans which my judgment led me to urge for adoption and execution." Nonetheless, McClellan was confident that the Maryland Campaign would one day emerge as his crowning achievement. "I am devoutly grateful to God that my last campaign with this brave army was crowned with a victory which saved the nation from the greatest peril it had then undergone."[60]

"McClellan is gone," Major George H. Hildt of the 30th Ohio wrote to his father back home in Canal Dover, Ohio. Unlike many comrades who were moved by McClellan's emotional farewell, Hildt was less sentimental and more practical in his assessment of McClellan's demise. "I am satisfied," he

---

57 Palmerston to Russell, October 2, 1862, in Palmerston Papers; see also James McPherson, "The Saratoga That Wasn't: The Impact of Antietam Abroad," in *This Mighty Scourge: Perspectives on the Civil War* (New York: Oxford University Press, 2007), 65-76.

58 *CWAL*, 5: 474.

59 Sears, ed., *McClellan Papers*, 519-520.

60 Isaac W. Heysinger, "The Maryland Campaign of 1862, from September 7th to November 16th," paper read May 10, 1905, in *Military Essays and Recollections of the Pennsylvania Commandery, Military Order of the Loyal Legion of the United States*, vol. 2, comp. Michael A. Cavanaugh (reprint, Wilmington, North Carolina: Broadfoot Publishing Company, 1995), 80-81.

continued. "Burnside is the better man by great odds. I was much pleased with him at South Mountain and Antietam, and think him to be the right man in the right place," Hildt concluded before describing the Rhode Islander's customary checkered shirt and pleasant countenance.[61]

For Major Hildt, flushed with the memory of storming South Mountain and the victory that followed, Burnside embodied the newfound resolve of the federal army. This firmness of purpose held that the blue coats could once and for all whip the rebels and, at long last, end this ungodly war.

---

61 Maj. George H. Hildt to John Hildt, Jr., letter, November 22, 1862, in Hildt Papers, Ohio Historical Society, Columbus, Ohio.

C hapter 11

"One of the great critical points in the history of the war."

South Mountain in History and Memory

The battle of South Mountain, Sept. 14, 1862, would have been
recorded in the annals of our nation as a great battle, had it not been
followed . . . by the more fatal and important contest at Antietam," Russell
Conwell observed in the 1876 presidential campaign biography he authored for
Rutherford B. Hayes.[1]

Union veterans routinely agreed upon both the strategic significance and
immediate consequences of the South Mountain fight, and went to great
lengths to fiercely defend the battle's place among the significant combats of
the Civil War. By the turn of the century, however, the Battle of South
Mountain had faded into distant memory, a minor footnote in the romanticized
Civil War narrative devoured by late nineteenth-century Americans. Faced with
the inexorable passing away of its staunchest advocates, South Mountain
gradually but surely slipped into historical oblivion. Unwilling to acknowledge
the unexpected defeat atop the wooded rocky slopes that had sabotaged the
Army of Northern Virginia's plan for sustained operations north of the
Potomac River, architects of the Lost Cause helped shepherd the Maryland
mountain combat off the main stage. The September 14 engagement suffered at

---

1 Russell Conwell, *The Life and Public Services of Governor Rutherford B. Hayes* (Boston: B. B.
Russell, 1876), 81. Conwell mistakenly assigns the battle of Antietam to September 15 rather
than September 17, but the premise of his argument remains valid.

the hands of later historians who, captivated by the staggering casualty rolls and the first images of battlefield dead, were eager to explain Antietam's horrific carnage. This concluding chapter considers the demise of the battle's reputation over time.

'That We Would Finally Win'

On July 3, 1862, federal enlisted man John Beatty asked, "Shall we hail the Fourth as the birthday of a great nation, or weep over it as the beginning of a political enterprise that resulted in dissolution, anarchy, and ruin?"[2] Indeed, as historian Michael C. C. Adams demonstrated, the gloom of the fighting on the Virginia peninsula, followed by the horrendous defeats that were the Seven Days' Battles and Second Manassas, coupled with racial and political divides on the home front, disillusioned federal soldiers on the eve of the Maryland Campaign. For the doubt-ridden men of the Union army, emasculated by these defeats, the victory at South Mountain loomed larger than life. "After the depressing scenes, weary marches, and fierce battles of August, the veterans were inspired with new life by the attractions on every side as we forced our way towards the enemy holding the passes of the South Mountain range," Rutherford Hayes explained to a regimental historian, encouraging him to underscore the significance of the fight for Fox's Gap in his narrative.[3] "You may not remember, but after the defeats which were inflicted upon McClellan by Lee, in the Seven Days campaign and at Bull Run, everywhere throughout the country, the confederates were victorious and were in the highest spirits," echoed William Brearly of the 17th Michigan Volunteers. "With the full belief that they would be successful, and that there was no army that could seriously obstruct their way, [the rebels] entered upon their first Maryland campaign. Unexpectedly to Lee, he was thrown upon the defensive, and the results you know as well as I do."[4]

---

2   Beatty, as quoted in Michael C. C. Adams, *Our Masters the Rebels: A Speculation on Union Military Failure in the East, 1861-1865* (Cambridge: Harvard University Press, 1978), 105.

3   Hayes, undated letter fragment [remainder missing], in Charles Richard Williams, ed., *Diary and Letters of Rutherford Birchard Hayes*, 5:154-155.

4   William Brearly to Century Magazine, letter, July 29, 1886, in Century Collection, Civil War Correspondence, Box 117, Rare Book and Manuscripts Division, New York Public Library, New York, New York.

Adoniram Judson Warner of the 10th Pennsylvania Reserves likewise articulated the psychic importance of the South Mountain victory for the discouraged ranks of federal enlisted men that critical September of 1862. According to Warner, when he threw his Pennsylvanians into the engagement north of the National Pike, they hesitated. "This was the effect of the defeat at Bull Run," Warner reasonably concluded. "I did all in my power to push them rapidly forward and soon nearly all were in the ravine and beyond it and the rebels were running . . . I never felt before as then. The skies never seemed so near or so clear." Because the Army of the Potomac had "been baffled on the Peninsula [and] had been beaten and discomfited at Bull Run," Warner argued, the result of South Mountain was particularly affecting for its blue-coated participants. "The consciousness that we had by sheer hard fighting, beaten the enemy and driven him from his strong positions filled me to overflowing," he admitted, and "gave me confidence that we would finally win and the country be safe." Andrew Fitch of the 79th New York concurred with Warner's assessment, adding in a letter to his father, "We have been a little more successful than in Virginia."[5]

"Through mismanagement, or through whatever cause to which it may be attributed," a military historian wrote in 1867, "the Army of Northern Virginia had driven the Army of the Potomac, or, at all events, had fought sufficiently well to find itself, back beyond the point from which it had started, upward of a year previous; and now to see that same Union army, so maltreated, so mishandled, so misjudged, climbing those rugged heights and advancing to the attack as calmly as if they had never met with a check or experienced a disaster, was something perfectly sublime. If no further than this," he concluded, "South Mountain was decisive in first showing to their countrymen and to the world of what glorious stuff the rank and file of the 'Army of the Potomac' was composed."[6]

In the leaves of their diaries and in their letters home, Union soldiers recorded their newfound confidence. For many, the victory was a peculiar new

5   Adoniram Judson Warner, as quoted in James B. Casey, ed., "The Ordeal of Adoniram Judson Warner: His Minutes of South Mountain and Antietam," *Civil War History* 28, no. 3 (September 1982); Andrew Fitch, letter to his father, September 25, 1862, in Leigh Collection, Book 5, United States Army Military History Institute, Carlisle, Pennsylvania.

6   John Watts de Peyster, "The Maryland Battles of September, 1862," in *The Decisive Conflict of the Late Civil War, or Slaveholder's Rebellion*, no. 1 (New York: MacDonald & Co., Printers, 1867), 39-40.

experience that began with resting under arms on a battlefield won from the enemy. "At sundown we held the Pass, and last night, for the first time, we slept on the field of battle," Joel Seaver explained in a letter home.[7] "We laid on our arms in line of battle on the place where we fought all night," Lyman Holford recorded.[8] Echoing this commentary, and that of James Wren and so many of those who had slept upon their arms, cared for the wounded, and buried the dead, William Richard Todd of the 79th New York marveled at the phenomenon. "The weather was cold and as we stood in line shivering and wishing for morning, we conversed in low tones with each other, congratulating ourselves on this our first victory in the new campaign," recorded Todd. "Would the enemy now retrace his steps into Virginia? We hoped not, but that he would remain north of the Potomac long enough for us to annihilate him, horse, foot and artillery!"[9]

One correspondent for the *New York Times* seems to have understood the influence that wresting the physical battlefield away from the enemy had on veterans. His visit to Turner's Gap revealed "a carnage of which I had previously no conception." Recalling the battle as "one of the most memorable battles which has occurred during the war," he, too, noted that the rebels fled "precipitately, leaving the road strewn with dead whom they never stopped to bury." The reporter interviewed General Ambrose Burnside, "who spent the night in the field, with his staff. . . . As [Burnside] passed over the hill the troops greeted him with prolonged and earnest cheers. The General and the whole army regard the battle and its results as one of the greatest victories of the war."[10]

Observing so many dead Confederates on the field aided the federals in sizing up the exact dimensions of their hard-fought victory. "The dead rebels are lying around us thick as gooseberries. We are on the site of the recent battle in which General McClellan routed them right and left slaughtering thousands," exaggerated James Jenkins Gillette in a letter to his mother. In the same missive,

---

7   Joel Seaver to Howland, letter, September 15, 1862, in Curtis, *From Bull Run to Chancellorsville*, 171.

8   Lyman Holford, diary entry, pp. 113-114, in Lyman Holford Papers, Manuscript Division, Library of Congress.

9   William Richard Todd, as quoted in Schildt, *Roads to Antietam*, 94-95.

10   *New York Times*, September 14-18, 1862, as quoted in Paul and Rita Gordon, *Never the Like Again: Frederick County, Maryland* (Frederick: The Heritage Partnership, 1995), 176-177.

he described the opposing army as "despicable."[11] For one of the first times in the war, Gillette was able to make the connection between battlefield news and battlefield slaughter. "A lot of gray clothes, old knapsacks, and equipments thrown own by the road showed us how precipitate had been the retreat of the rebels, which made us feel all the better," Thomas Leonard Livermore observed.[12]

These sights were so important that participation in the battle was not even requisite to enjoy the fruits of the victory. David Rice of the 108th New York neither fought in the battle nor bivouacked on the battlefield, but he did pass through it with a comrade on September 15. "Heard all the news about the battle the day before," he wrote. "Hank and I left . . . and set on afoot about 4 miles to the Battlefield on top of a high mountain where we beheld the greatest sight we ever saw—the rebels had run and left their men scattered over the ground just as they were shot down. Some places there was fifteen or twenty in a file some with eight or ten bullet holes in them . . . the rebels had to skedaddle this time."[13]

For J. D. Brougher of the 130th Pennsylvania, South Mountain was "where the enemy had made a stand, where we fought and they were compelled to retreat off the field leaving their dead and wounded on the field."[14] Such debris rendered the rebel defeat indisputable. "Passed over the battle ground of the previous evening," commented Indiana cavalryman Samuel J. B. V. Gilpin, whose regiment had not been engaged during the battle. "The principal feature of the morning was the dead, dying, wounded, prisoners, stragglers, skirmishers, abandoned artillery, dust and excitement." In his diary the day before, Gilpin confirmed the victory on South Mountain by noting, "the enemy retired having their dead and wounded on the field."[15] The detritus littering the battlefield on that Sabbath animated the blue-coated soldiers simply because it

11 James Jenkins Gillette to his mother, letter, September 16, 1862, in Gillette Papers, Manuscript Division, Library of Congress.

12 Thomas Leonard Livermore, *Days and Events, 1860-1866*, 121.

13 David Rice, diary entry, 15 September 1862, in *Diary of David Rice*, Manuscript Division, Library of Congress.

14 J. D. Brougher to William Orland Bourne, letter, November 23, 1867, in William Orland Bourne Papers, Manuscript Division, Library of Congress.

15 Samuel J. B. V. Gilpin, 1st Indiana Cavalry, diary entries, September 14 and 15, 1862, in E. N. Gilpin Papers, Manuscript Division, Library of Congress.

was evidence of a successful combat—a visible validation of their hard-fought victory.

The South Mountain battlefield continued to inspire federal troops long after the fighting on its slopes ceased. The following summer, as the blue columns again moved northward to confront an invading Army of Northern Virginia, the federals negotiated the passes of South Mountain once more. "We had a glimpse of the South Mountain battlefield, where McClellan and his troops had, the year before, won victory for our flag, the spot where the gallant Major General Reno fell being pointed out to us," a captain of the 61st Ohio recalled. "The inspiration of this historic battlefield is to me one of the precious memories of this eventful march from Stafford Heights to Gettysburg."[16] Having been humiliated on the open plains before Marye's Heights at Fredericksburg in December, mired in the mud under Burnside in January, and debased by Joe Hooker at Chancellorsville in May, South Mountain was an unwonted victory.

*   *   *

When explaining why the battle of South Mountain was significant for federal troops, Brigadier General Regis de Trobriand emphasized not the gruesome evidence of victory littering the captured battlefield, but the honor of having defended Northern soil from being defiled by invasion. "The morale of our troops was marvelously raised since they had return to the loyal states. On Maryland soil they were at home; they were now fighting for their firesides, to save the threatened capital and with it perhaps the Republic," de Trobriand explained. "An enthusiasm of valor animated them. This was shown by the vigor with which the enemy had just been attacked and driven from position after position in the passes of South Mountain. This first victory was of good augury. It had increased the confidence both of officers and men."[17]

16 Leonidas M. Jewett, "From Stafford Heights to Gettysburg in 1863," in *Sketches of War History 1861-1865: Papers Prepared for the Commandery of the State of Ohio, Military Order of the Loyal Legion of the United States, 1896-1903*, ed. W.H. Chamberlin, A. M. Van Dyke, and George A. Thayer (1903; reprint, Wilmington, North Carolina: Broadfoot Publishing Company, 1992), 215-216.

17 Regis de Trobriand, *Four Years with the Potomac Army* (Ticknor and Company, 1888), 320-321.

The confidence and enthusiasm were contagious. Louis Richards from Company G of the 2nd Pennsylvania Emergency Militia of 1862 described the scene in camp after the much-awaited news of South Mountain arrived. "The anxiety increased to hear something from the army," he recalled. "Reports circulated, which were afterwards verified, that fighting had commenced between the corps of Generals Hooker and Reno and the rebels, and that General Reno had been killed. When the campfires were lighted, after nightfall, the woods resounded with martial music, song, and cheers, and the scene was a highly animating and inspiring one. Such sights are seldom witnessed, and are not to be soon forgotten."[18] The battle of the 14th, Gilbert Frederick of the 57th New York Volunteers proclaimed, "was a victory for our forces. The success of Franklin on the left endangered Lee's communications, thwarted his purpose to push into Pennsylvania, and compelled him to give battle near the Potomac. It also gave the Union Army that esprit de corps which victory always brings."[19] Corporal Frederick Pettit of the 100th Pennsylvania acknowledged the adrenaline rush of victory, but gave in to the physical needs of his body when he admitted, "Notwithstanding the excitement of the day I slept soundly."[20]

When the men reviewed the extreme topographical challenges the gaps presented to them, jubilance in the federal ranks swelled to even greater heights and appeared all the more warranted. "The rebels had all the advantage of ground but they still lost the most men," marveled Edward Schweitzer of the 30th Ohio.[21] Alfred Lewis Castleman of the 5th Wisconsin illustrated the impact that storming the mountain had on federal morale. "Hurrah again!" he exclaimed when learning of the victory at Crampton's Gap:

> This is a terrible pass, and it seems wonderful that any army could force it against an opposing foe. It is in the shape of a triangle, the base being at the top of the mountain,

18 Louis Richards, diary for September 1862, in *Eleven Days in the Militia During the War of the Rebellion: Being a Journal of the Emergency Campaign of 1862* (Philadelphia: Collins Printer, 1883), 28.

19 Gilbert Frederick, *The Story of a Regiment*, 85-86.

20 Frederick Pettit to "parents, brothers, and sisters," letter, September 23, 1862, in *Infantryman Pettit: The Civil War Letters of Corporal Frederick Pettit*, ed. William Gilfillan Gavin (New York: Avon Books, 1990), 15-16.

21 Edward Schweitzer, diary entry, September 14, 1862, in Civil War Times Illustrated Collection, United States Army Military History Institute, Carlisle, Pennsylvania.

the apex at the bottom. Into this narrow point our army had to crowd its way, up a mountain almost perpendicular, whilst musketry and artillery enfiladed our advancing lines at every point. Yet our men, with the cool determination of veterans, forced their way steadily through the Gap, up the precipitous sides of the mountain, and drove the enemy from his stronghold.[22]

In an ode to the "Bloody Seventeenth," Gabriel Campbell reminded that neither "rebel steel, nor walls of stone" could check the "loyal flood" of Michiganders over the mountain top. "Our victory shouts sent to the sky/Proclaim the Battle won."[23] According to Ozro N. Hubbard, the Confederates "did not give us battle until we came to South Mountain. They could not have selected a more fitting place for a battle as nature had done more than enough to have made it almost impregnable for men to ascend without additional obstacles in the form of armed men. We dashed at charged bayonets among the foe. They could not withstand such furious onset and they fled up and over the mountain having their dead and wounded in our lines," he concluded.[24] "If there was ever a victory gained, in any way, in any campaign, the Battle of South Mountain resulted in a most decided and complete Union victory," Alonzo Hill determined.[25] "The victory of South Mountain was one of the most brilliant achievements of the Federals during the war," Theodore Gates echoed.[26] "The enemy has been badly beaten . . . you have reason to be proud of your son," James Wyatt, the chaplain of the 79th New York, wrote to the mother of a comrade.[27]

Calvin S. Locke, a Unitarian minister from West Dedham, Massachusetts, assured the grieving family that mortally wounded George F. Whiting, a

22 Alfred Castleman, diary entry, September 14, 1862, in *The Army of the Potomac, Behind the Scenes: a Diary of Unwritten History: from the Organization of the Army . . . to the Close of the Campaign in Virginia, About the First Day of January, 1863.* (Milwaukee, WI: Strickland & Co., 1863), 223-224.

23 Gabriel Campbell, "The Charge at South Mountain by the Stonewall Regiment: A Poem By the Captain of a Company of Students, Seventeenth Michigan Infantry," imprint from *Dartmouth Magazine*, 1903, Western Reserve Historical Society, Cleveland, Ohio.

24 Ozro N. Hubbard to William Orland Bourne, letter, July 6, 1867, in Bourne Papers, Manuscript Division, Library of Congress.

25 Alonzo F. Hill, *Our Boys*, 398.

26 Gates, *The Ulster Guard*, 301.

27 Chaplain James C. Wyatt to Elizabeth Freeman Lusk, letter, September 15, 1862, in *War Letters of William Thompson Lusk* (New York: W. C. Lusk, 1911), 197.

member of the 35th Massachusetts, was a "patriotic volunteer" who did not die in vain. "He was not taken from the world simply by sickness, which is the divinely appointed method of our departure," Locke began, "but he fell, wounded by the enemy of his country, in the severe struggle by which their efforts at invasion were rendered futile."[28]

*   *   *

Northern newspapers also celebrated the notion that the long-luckless Army of the Potomac "would finally win." Yearning for a federal military success in the Eastern Theater, newspapers seized quickly and easily upon the victory at South Mountain, determining that the tide had indeed turned. John Forney, the owner of the *Philadelphia Press*, was so impressed by the success of the mountain combat that, following the "victory," he sent a telegram to one of his correspondents, hopeful that the rebellion would be crushed before winter. The *Capital City Fact*, from Columbus, Ohio, reported a "great and decisive defeat of the Rebels near Middletown, Md. The victory is complete, the rebels are routed and disorganized and fleeing . . . for this great achievement, besides obtaining an ascendancy over the enemy, we have further cause for thankfulness . . . if our successes continue, of which we have no reason for doubt, from the present efficient state of our army . . . we may look forward with faith."[29]

On September 15, the *Boston Evening Transcript*, in its most bold and confident typeface, noted by telegraph that South Mountain, or the "Capture of Hagerstown Heights," was a "glorious federal victory" following "terrible fighting." Reports continued about a "badly cut up" enemy, and the rebel retreat out of Maryland was fully described. This was "important news," announced the paper, for the "defeat of the rebels" meant an enemy "army in a panic." A day later, glowing reports saturated the pages of the *Transcript*. Editors "confirmed" the "glorious victory" in the headlines with a reprint of McClellan's message to Halleck, followed by a careful review of the

28 Calvin S. Locke, *The Patriotic Volunteer, A Sermon, Delivered October 19, 1862 at the Funeral of George F. Whiting* (Boston: Press of John Wilson and Son, 1862), in the collection of the Western Reserve Historical Society, Cleveland, Ohio.

29 On Forney, see J. Cutler Andrews, *The North Reports the Civil War* (Pittsburgh: University of Pittsburgh Press, 1955), 274; *Capital City Fact*, September 17, 1862.

"particulars" of the engagement.[30] The excitement in the pages was unmistakable. The gallant charges of the 12th and 23rd Ohio, as well as the heroic stand of the 17th Michigan, were some of the first images of the Maryland Campaign savored by readers. The editors, relying chiefly on McClellan's reports, delivered to the citizenry the news of a decisive victory; similar to South Mountain's effect on participants, the battle helped instill hope on the home front that the rebel ebb tide had indeed begun. As the *Capital City Fact* noted, "The news from the Seat of War in Maryland still continues to redound to the credit of the brave men now engaged in deadly strife with the enemies of our country. . . . The long and dark days spent a week ago in suspense as to the final result of the struggle for the maintenance of our Government are passed, and giving place to cheerful hours in which congratulations are exchanged, that the good time long expected has come at last, and that Right and Justice at length triumphs over our foes. Jeff Davis had better postpone his day of thanksgiving. . . . The days of the rebel government are numbered, and the end is at hand."[31]

Not surprisingly, Southerners dismissed the enthusiastic response of the Northern press to the battle. "South Mountain was heralded abroad by our antagonists as a great victory," Daniel Harvey Hill noted. "Favors of that sort have been few and far between, and this seemed to call for special gratulation and congratulation."[32] Confederate soldier J. C. Ives told his mother that his comrades had "read with great amusement the accounts from Maryland" circulating in Yankee newspapers.[33] "If we have been thus badly beaten, why is no use made of the victory? Why has McClellan not crossed the river and destroyed the army of General Lee?" the *Richmond Dispatch* queried. "The truth is this: The victory, though not so decisive as that of Manassas, was certainly a Confederate victory."[34]

Most Southern newspapers simply avoided addressing South Mountain in their accounts of the invasion, brushing aside the obvious defeat as an

---

30 *Boston Evening Transcript*, September 15, 1862.

31 *Capital City Fact*, September 18, 1862.

32 D. H. Hill, "Reunion of Virginia Division, A.N.V. Association," in *Southern Historical Society Papers*, 13:271.

33 J. C. Ives to his mother, letter, September 23, 1862, in J. C. Ives Papers, Manuscript Division, Library of Congress, Washington, DC.

34 *Richmond Dispatch*, September 30, 1862.

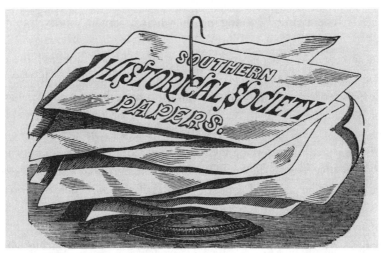

The masthead of the *Southern Historical Society Papers*, one of the most influential organs of the Lost Cause. *Southern Historical Society Papers*

inconsequential obstacle on the road to Sharpsburg. In retrospect, these careful and deliberate omissions mirrored General Lee's disappointment in ceding the campaign's initiative to McClellan and the Army of the Potomac.[35]

These immediate post-battle accounts were but the first drafts of what would be more than a generation of unapologetic Confederate revisionism. In the pages of veterans' periodicals, magazines, newspapers, and other outlets of the Lost Cause, ex-Confederates spilled ink in their efforts to diminish the strategic significance of the sharp defeat that was South Mountain. "The battle of South Mountain was one of extraordinary illusions and delusions," began the principle Confederate account of the battle in *Century* magazine's enormously popular *Battles & Leaders of the Civil War* series. "The Federals were under the self-imposed illusion that there was a very large force opposed to them, whereas there was only one weak division until late in the afternoon. They might have brushed it aside almost without halting, but for this illusion. It was a battle of delusions, also," continued the writer, "for, by moving about from point to point and meeting the foe wherever he presented himself, the Confederates

---

35 Gary W. Gallagher, "The Net Result of the Campaign was in Our Favor: Confederate Reaction to the Maryland Campaign," in Gallagher, ed. *The Antietam Campaign* (Kent: Kent State University Press, 1999), 32.

deluded the federals into believing that the whole mountain was swarming with rebels."[36]

Because the Confederate forces were so heavily outnumbered, the battle became a ready-made target for exponents of Confederate mythology, who were always ready to point out the numerical superiority of the federal armies and navies during the Civil War. Moreover, the prominent battlefield role played by D. H. Hill—who, as editor of *The Land We Love*, a popular postwar magazine devoted to preserving the memory of Confederate soldiers, was one of the ablest advocates of the Lost Cause—gave many unreconstructed rebels a motive for wielding pens in defense of their version of the events of September 14, 1862. Hill, for example, described the Confederate defenses on South Mountain as "a thin curtain of men extending for miles along the crests of the mountains on that bright Sabbath day in September," while facing what he described as "a vast, perfectly organized and magnificently equipped [federal] army. . . . Lee's army was never so small." One of Hill's admirers echoed these sentiments in a piece published in the *Southern Historical Society Papers*: "At South Mountain, by an obstinate rear-guard fight against enormous odds, he had secured and protected the concentration of General Lee's army on the field of Sharpsburg."[37] These assessments conveniently overlooked the rebels' superior defensive perch atop South Mountain, as well as the rugged heights the federals were forced to scale to achieve their victory.

Perhaps the most substantial revision made by Confederate apologists concerned the objective of Lee's operations north of the Potomac River. Insisting that the reduction of Harpers Ferry was always a principal goal of the invasion, some ex-Confederates refused to concede that Lee had surrendered any initiative on the bloodied mountain passes. In this revised narrative, the rebel stand at South Mountain became at worst a trifling skirmish, and at best the boldly calculated holding action that had sealed the fate of Harpers Ferry. "If the battle of South Mountain was fought to prevent the advance of McClellan, it was a failure on the part of the Confederates," Hill conceded. But, he continued, "if it was fought to save Lee's trains and artillery, and to reunite his scattered forces, it was a Confederate success." In the future, concluded Hill, the battle of South Mountain would be of interest to the military reader, as

---

36 *B&L* 2:559-560.

37 *Southern Historical Society Papers*, 13:268; 9:390.

it showed "the effect of a hallucination in enabling 9,000 men to hold 30,000 at bay for so many hours . . . robbing victory of its fruits."[38]

Richmond Examiner editor Edward A. Pollard's treatment of the battle in his *Southern History of the War*—the inaugural salvo of the Lost Cause—stressed Lee's perfect prescience in posting rebels on the mountain top for the purpose of defending Harpers Ferry until its reduction, noting that "it was certainly not part of the original plan to fight a pitched battle here, except to secure this one desirable result."[39] In 1890, Jefferson Davis's apologetic history of the Confederacy echoed Pollard's sentiments when the former Confederate president claimed the stand on South Mountain "gave Jackson time to complete the reduction of Harpers Ferry."[40]

Sentiments such as these raised a storm of indignation among hardened Union veterans of the battle. South Mountain, veteran Eliakim Scammon later expounded, was something he and his comrades could "never forget."[41] Caught between their horrific knowledge of the war and an emerging culture of sectional reconciliation, these men already felt marginalized, and believed they had a moral obligation to ensure that the historical record stood corrected. "This we did consider a grand affair, and rightly too, as our Six Regiments whipped Longstreet's thirty thousand men," John Hughes wrote to the famous Union nurse Mary Ball Bickerdyke after the war.[42] "Lee had only gained a short interval of freedom of movement to end at Antietam," Gilbert Thompson maintained. "Lee's Maryland Campaign was a failure, he came near losing his army."[43] In 1885, William H. Brearly, a veteran of the 17th Michigan, complained that *Century* magazine had unjustly overlooked the South Mountain

38 *B&L* 2:580.

39 Edward A. Pollard, *Southern History of the War: The Second Year of the War* (New York: Charles B. Richardson, 1864), 125-127. See also, Dennis E. Frye, "Drama between the Rivers: Harper's Ferry in the 1862 Maryland Campaign," in Gallagher, ed., *Antietam: Essays on the 1862 Maryland Campaign* (Kent: Kent State University Press, 1989), 14-34, and John W. Daniel, "Unveiling of Valentine's Recumbent Figure of Lee," in *Southern Historical Society Papers*, 11:351.

40 Jefferson Davis, *A Short History of the Confederate States of America* (New York: Belford Company Publishers, 1890), 286.

41 Eliakim Scammon to James M. Comly, letter, May 5, 1864, in James M. Comly Papers, microfilm reel 1, Rutherford B. Hayes President Center, Fremont, Ohio.

42 John Hughes to Mary Bickerdyke, February 3, 1899, Bickerdyke Papers, Box 3, General Correspondence, Manuscript Division, Library of Congress, Washington, DC.

43 Gilbert Thompson Papers, Manuscript Division, Library of Congress.

fight, which he deemed "one of the great critical points in the history of the war." "I think you have done the Union side of this matter an injustice, by allowing this to be all passed over in absolute silence," he fumed. "Considering all of the circumstances," he continued, "I consider South Mt. as a crisis to the Confederates, and indeed to us, no small importance, and one deserving of more mention, than the casual and obscure admission of a defeated General, that one of his brigades 'broke.'" Recounting how the Michiganders "utterly routed" the rebels at Fox's Gap, Brearly insisted the rebel forces "'broke' because they had good reason."[44]

Although the battle had many Union defenders, none was more vocal than Rutherford B. Hayes, who never failed to reflect upon what he called "South Mountain Day." "Sunday a year ago was the fourteenth," he penned in his diary in 1863. "South Mountain and its losses and glories. How the sadness for the former fades and the satisfaction with the latter grows!" In 1881 Hayes, as president of the United States, remembered "the anniversary of South Mountain" by removing "the old coat which I wore when wounded" from its "anti-moth box." Three years later, September 14 was again the Sabbath. "Our little squad remembered to talk over the battle at South Mountain, fought on such a day as this twenty-two years ago today." His tribute was even more effusive the following year. "The battle of South Mountain was fought twenty-three years ago today! I think of it with great satisfaction. The wound and Lucy's search after her husband! What a flood of recollections comes to me!" The battle had left an indelible impression on his mind. "This is South Mountain Day," he recorded in his diary in 1891, two years before his death. "Twenty-nine years ago this morning we marched up the old National Road . . . We had gained the victory!"[45]

Perhaps most tellingly, however, whenever federal veterans listed the important engagements in which they had participated, they consistently placed

44 William Brearly to Century Magazine, letter, July 29, 1886, in Century Collection, Civil War Letters, Box 117, Rate Books and Manuscripts Division, New York Public Library, New York, New York.

45 Rutherford B. Hayes, diary entries, September 13, 1863; September 14, 1881; September 14, 1884; September 14, 1885; September 14, 1891, in Charles Richard Williams, ed., *Diary and Letters of Rutherford Birchard Hayes* (Columbus: Ohio State Archeological and Historical Society, 1922). On Hayes' personal memory of the Civil War, see Brooks D. Simpson, "The Good Colonel: Rutherford B. Hayes Remembers the Civil War," 14th Hayes Lecture on the Presidency, February 16, 2003, Rutherford B. Hayes Presidential Center, Fremont, Ohio.

South Mountain among the ranks of the war's most storied and recognized battles, including Bull Run, Antietam, and Gettysburg.[46] Federal memoirs of the Maryland Campaign and regimental histories routinely considered, as did Russell Hastings of the 23rd Ohio Volunteers, the "two great and glorious battles" fought to repel Lee's invasion.[47] Likewise, when novelist and poet John W. Trowbridge made his celebrated journey to the seminal sites of the late rebellion, he inspected Cemetery Hill at Gettysburg; walked amongst the ruins of Chambersburg, torched by a Confederate raid in 1864; and, in his first stop below the Mason-Dixon, hired a local guide named Lewy Smith to take him across the South Mountain battleground. "The Mountain rose before us, leopard-colored, spotted with sun and cloud," announced Trowbridge.[48]

In an attempt to grapple with the searing experiences of their youth, many Union veterans followed in Trowbridge's footsteps, driven to return to the former fields of battle. They, too, flocked to the sites that they deemed most significant and most haunting. Bates Alexander, a veteran of the 7th Pennsylvania Reserves, was one of those veterans. Accompanied by his daughter, he traversed the fields of South Mountain, Antietam, and Gettysburg in 1889. "I readily found where our regiment fought, in front of the famous Cornfield near the Hagerstown Pike. But at South Mountain I was less fortunate, mainly for want of time, though as I expect to 'move on the Mountain in force' next Summer, I shall find the place on top of the mountain where our regiment stood when firing ceased on Sunday evening, Sept. 14,

---

46 This widespread but overlooked phenomenon is encountered in various veterans' writings, regimental histories, and Grand Army of the Republic record books. For only a few examples, see Private W. Treadwell, notation in *Memorials of Hours Among the Brave, Central Park Hospital*, vol. 3, in William Orland Bourne Papers, Manuscript Division, Library of Congress; "Monthly Record of Events," *Harper's New Monthly Magazine*, 25 (November 1862), 837; Israel N. Stiles, "On to Richmond in 1862," paper read March 10, 1887, in *Military Essays and Recollections: Papers Read Before the Commandery of the State of Illinois, Military Order of the Loyal Legion of the United States*, vol. 3 (1899; reprint, Wilmington, North Carolina: Broadfoot Publishing, 1992), 53; Douglas A. Brown, "The Commemoration of The Lincoln Centenary by the Ohio Commandery of the Military Order of the Loyal Legion of the United States at their Headquarters, February 12, 1909," in *Sketches of War History 1861-1865: A Compilation of Miscellaneous Papers Compiled for the Ohio Commandery of the Loyal Legion, February 1885 - February 1909* (reprint, Wilmington, North Carolina: Broadfoot Publishing, 1993), 293.

47 Russell Hastings' Civil War memoirs are found with the Rutherford B. Hayes Papers, "R. B. Hayes and the 23rd O.V.I. Folder 1," Rutherford B. Hayes Presidential Center, Fremont, Ohio.

48 John T. Trowbridge, *The South: A Tour of Its Battlefields and Ruined Cities* (1866; reprint, New York: Arno Press, 1969), 49.

1862. . . . It would afford one some satisfaction to stand at that point next Summer and notice how far our column was away."[49]

A few years later, another of the so-called 'boys in blue,' "having a few days of vacation to spare," determined to "take a trip to South Mountain and Antietam . . . thinking perhaps some of the boys of the old Ninth Corps, and especially those of my own dear regiment, the 45th Pa., would like to hear how those battlefields look after the lapse of nearly 30 years." Leaving Philadelphia on August 19, he traveled to Frederick, where he found an old friend named Gaver and took the stagecoach to Middletown. "I assure you I appreciated the drive much better than I did our march over the same road," joked the aging veteran. Arriving at Middletown, "a town of one street, all down hill one way and up hill the other," he boarded at the City Hotel, where he found "plenty to eat and a good bed."

Early the next day, the comrades "started for old South Mountain." Disparate recollections soon swelled into an almost overwhelming flood of memories:

> Do you remember at the edge of the town the little creek which we forded dry-shod, the rebs having burned the bridge on the right of the road? On the left was the still-smoking ruins of a barn and a smith shop. How after marching a short distance out the National Pike the rebs got the range on us and commenced shelling us? We then fled off to our left, under the brow of the hills, their shells then flying high over our heads. Soon after we climbed the mountain road. Well do I remember that Sunday morning.

The veterans found the old stone wall at Fox's Gap unchanged. Nearby, two houses that witnessed the battle remained, as did the trees under which the regiment once sought refuge. "When I stood on top of it, and looked down the road over which we had marched, I can assure you I did some thinking." The men proceeded to amble through the woods "where so many of our boys lay down their lives." Soon, the pair encountered the newly erected Reno monument. "I think it is about time that we were erecting a stone to mark the ground over which we fought," he determined. The Pennsylvania veteran was loath to leave the field. "After taking a view of the surrounding country—for it is grand beyond description—and once again going over our battle-ground and saying farewell to old South Mountain, I think for the last time, feeling more

---

than sad for the many dear boys who fell, we started for the old Stone Bridge [at Antietam]." He and his comrade remained in Sharpsburg only a brief time, offering reverence at the National Cemetery and ambling across the Burnside Bridge. But even while touring the Antietam field the veteran remained fixed on the mountain. "To my right I can see old South Mountain looming up again. There is a sort of fascination about it for me, and I sit and gaze at it as long as it is in sight."[50]

Although they were overwhelmed by the commercial success and romantic appeal of the Lost Cause, the insistent voices of these Union veterans were not lost entirely. The earliest Antietam guidebooks made interpretive links between South Mountain and Sharpsburg. The very first guide to the Antietam National Cemetery, printed in 1869, noted that "the Cemetery itself is located on a gentle rise, from whence a survey of almost the entire battlefield may be enjoyed, while within the scope of the eye's range lies an unobstructed tract of country, miles in extent, taking in the distant South Mountain, memorable as the spot where Lee received his first check during the invasion of Maryland, and which caused him gradually to fall back with his army until it rested on the waters of the Antietam and made a final stand only to be again defeated."[51] George Hess, the Superintendent of the Antietam National Cemetery and a veteran of Company I, 28th Pennsylvania, published the earliest of these tourist guidebooks in 1890. His booklet, "Battle-Field Guide of the Battles of South Mountain and Antietam," argued for the significance of both engagements. An 1898 guidebook, in addition to documenting the battles of South Mountain and Antietam, considered Harpers Ferry as well. [52]

Early defenders of both George McClellan and James Longstreet, two leaders who emerged from the war with sullied reputations, naturally underscored South Mountain's strategic consequences. Paul Frothingham held

---

50 "Battlefields Revisited," *National Tribune*, October 13, 1892.

51 *History of Antietam National Cemetery* (Baltimore: John Woods, 1869), 19-20.

52 George Hess, *Battle-Field Guide of the Battles of South Mountain and Antietam* (Hagerstown: Globe Job Rooms Prints, 1890); *Souvenir and Guide Book of Harper's Ferry, Antietam, and South Mountain Battlefields* (n.p.: Edward Grave, 1898). Compare these early interpretive tools with the National Park Service's map and guide printed in 2006. In the latter, the actions on South Mountain are rendered utterly insignificant in a single sentence. A map outlining a driving tour of Maryland Campaign points of interest conveniently leads visitors to Ferry Hill and Shepherdstown (the site of Lee's Headquarters during the Battle of Antietam), and the Pry House Field Hospital—but does not offer directions to the South Mountain passes.

that the Young Napoleon firmly grasped that the sole objective of the Army of the Potomac was forcing Lee's army into a battle that could halt his invasion. "This result was accomplished by the very fact of McClellan's bringing the Union army into position across Lee's path," he wrote. McClellan, in his estimation, had "created a military situation which, in itself, nipped in the bud the most dangerous campaign of the Confederacy."[53] Similarly, Longstreet biographers H. J. Eckenrode and Bryan Conrad concluded, "the battle of South Mountain was important, in as much as it marked the ruin of Lee's Maryland Campaign.... If he had been dreaming of the Susquehanna ... that dream now came to an end."[54] Even one ex-rebel endorsed the federal veterans' efforts to deem the battle significant, calling it the "slight error that decided the first campaign into Maryland and sent our troops back across the Potomac discomfited."[55] But all this was too little too late. By the turn of the century, the rebels had won the interpretive war and the Lost Cause's triumph became the nation's history. As its participants and defenders faded away with the heavy hand of time, South Mountain settled into the shadows as little more than an appendix to Antietam.

In the last decades of the twentieth century, housing developments snaked their way up the slopes of the mountain in the footsteps of the federal armies. Few granite monuments dot the hills and valleys where men laid down their lives on an unassuming September Sabbath. In recent years, however, laudable efforts to preserve the battlefield generated a wider awareness and appreciation of the battle "before Antietam." On September 13, 1986, the state of Michigan erected an historical tablet at Fox's Gap commemorating the charge of the Wolverine regiment. Only a few years later, a small stone was unveiled nearby to mark the location of Confedeate Brigadier General Samuel Garland's mortal wounding. In 1989, a group of local citizen-activists led by George Brigham formed the non-profit Central Maryland Heritage League. Their mission was to preserve ten critical acres on the Fox's Gap battlefield from impending development. Since then, the League has worked with living history

---

53 Paul Frothingham, as quoted in William Myers, *General George Brinton McClellan: A Study in Personality* (New York: D. Appleton-Century Company, 1934), 359.

54 H. J. Eckenrode and Bryan Conrad, *James Longstreet: Lee's War Horse* (1936; reprint, Chapel Hill: University of North Carolina Press, 1986, with a Foreword by Gary W. Gallagher), 122-123.

55 R. K. Charles, "Events in Battle of Fredericksburg," *Confederate Veteran*, 14, 65.

organizations and the Civil War Trust to secure additional battlefield tracts. At present, the organization, which owns two historic structures and twenty-two acres of battleground, has blossomed into a civic charity concerned with educating Marylanders about their rich cultural heritage. Finally, in October 2003, the Living History Association of Mecklenburg County, North Carolina, dedicated a sculpture, completed by artist Gary Casteel, to honor all of the Tarheels who fought on South Mountain. The monument depicts a color-bearer from North Carolina endeavoring to keep his colors hoisted into the air. The original stone wall that shielded Garland's Brigade stands but a few feet away as a most haunting and silent witness.

*   *   *

In 1867, John Watts de Peyster, a veteran of the Regular Army in both the Mexican War and the late rebellion, and one of the nation's first military scientists, contributed a selection on Antietam to a series of essays collectively titled "Decisive Battles of the War." In his essay "The Maryland Battles in September 1862," de Peyster began by arguing that "it was impossible to treat of Antietam without devoting a large space to South Mountain or Boonsboro," for "whatever was won in the cornfields and woods of Antietam was decidedly initiated in the gaps of the South Mountain." When one considered the performance of the Union troops in the "bloody gorges of the Blue Ridge," he argued, it was rather effortless to conclude that the battle of South Mountain was "a very remarkable event, and a decisive demonstration of the enormous capabilities and striking characteristics of our Northern people."[56]

By wresting the initiative from Lee at South Mountain, the men of the Army of the Potomac had done more than achieve a simple tactical victory. Now, Horace Greeley later reflected, "our soldiers, flushed with unwonted victory, and dull in the faith that they had just wrested two strong mountain-passes from the entire rebel army, were ready for any effort, any peril."[57]

---

56 de Peyster, "The Maryland Battles in September, 1862," 38-39.

57 Horace Greeley, "The American Conflict: Lee's Invasion," *National Tribune*, September 15, 1898.

A ppendix 1[1]

Union Order of Battle and Losses

ARMY OF THE POTOMAC
Major General George B. McClellan

Burnside's Wing
Major General Ambrose Everett Burnside

I Corps
Major General Joseph Hooker

First Division
Brigadier General Rufus King
Brigadier General John Hatch
Brigadier General Abner Doubleday

First Brigade
Colonel Walter Phelps Jr.
22nd New York: Lieutenant Colonel John McKie Jr.
10 (k), 20 (w)
24th New York: Captain John D. O'Brian
1 (k), 25 (w)
30th New York: Colonel William M. Searing
4 (k), 5 (w)
84th New York: Major William H. de Bevoise

1   OR 1, 183-187.

5 (k), 15 (w), 8 (m)
2nd U.S. Sharpshooters: Colonel Henry A. V. Post
2 (w)

Total Casualties 1st Brigade: 20 (k), 67 (w), 8 (m)
First Brigade Aggregate Losses: 95

Second Brigade
Brigadier General Abner Doubleday
Colonel William Wainwright (w)
Lieutenant Colonel J. William Hofmann
7th Indiana: Major Ira G. Grover
12 (w)
76th New York: Colonel William P. Wainwright, Captain John W. Young
2 (k), 18 (w)
95th New York: Major Edward Pye
11 (w), 1 (m)
56th Pennsylvania: Lieutenant Colonel J. William Hofmann, Captain
Frederick Williams
1 (k), 11 (w), 3 (m)

Total Casualties Second Brigade: 3 (k), 52 (w), 4 (m)
2nd Brigade Aggregate Losses: 59

Third Brigade
Brigadier General Marsena R. Patrick
21st New York: Colonel William F. Rogers
1 (k), 3 (w)
23rd New York: Colonel Henry C. Hoffmann
6 (w)
35th New York: Colonel Newton B. Lord
2 (k), 10 (w), 1 (m)
80th New York: Lieutenant Colonel Theodore B. Gates

Total Casualties 3rd Brigade: 3 (k), 19 (w), 1 (m)
3rd Brigade Aggregate Losses: 23

Fourth Brigade (Iron Brigade)
Brigadier General John Gibbon
19th Indiana: Colonel Solomon Meredith
9 (k), 37 (w), 7 (m)
2nd Wisconsin: Colonel Lucius Fairchild
6 (k), 19 (w), 1 (m)
6th Wisconsin: Lieutenant Colonel Edward S. Bragg
11 (k), 79 (w), 2 (m)
7th Wisconsin: Captain John B. Callis
11 (k), 116 (w), 20 (m)

Total Casualties 4th Brigade: 37 (k), 251 (w), 30 (m)
4th Brigade Aggregate Losses: 318

First Division Artillery
Captain J. Albert Monroe

New Hampshire Light, 1st Battery, Lieutenant Frederick Edgell
1st Rhode Island Light, Battery D, Captain J. Albert Monroe
1st New York Light, Battery L, Captain John A. Reynolds
4th U.S., Battery B, Captain Joseph Campbell

Second Division
Brigadier General James Ricketts

First Brigade
Brigadier General Abram Duryee
97th New York: Major Charles Northrup
2 (k), 3 (w)
104th New York: Major Lewis C. Skinner
1 (w)
105th New York: Colonel Howard Carroll
1 (k), 2 (w)
107th Pennsylvania: Captain James MacThomason
2 (k), 10 (w)

Total Casualties First Brigade: 5 (k), 16 (w)
First Brigade Aggregate Losses: 21

Second Brigade
Colonel William Christian
26th New York: Lieutenant Colonel Richard H. Richardson
2 (w)
94th New York: Lieutenant Colonel Calvin Littlefield
2 (k), 2 (w)
88th Pennsylvania: Lieutenant Colonel George W. Gile
90th Pennsylvania: Colonel Peter Lyle
2 (w)

Total Casualties Second Brigade: 2 (k), 6 (w)
Second Brigade Aggregate Losses: 8

Third Brigade
Brigadier General George L. Hartsuff
12th Massachusetts: Major Elisha Burbank: Captain Benjamin F. Cook
1 (k), 1 (w)
13th Massachusetts: Major J. Parker Gould
83rd New York: Lieutenant Colonel William Atterbury
1 (k), 1 (w)
11th Pennsylvania: Colonel Richard Coulter
2 (w)

Total Casualties Third Brigade: 2 (k), 4 (w)
3rd Brigade Aggregate Losses: 6

Second Division Artillery
1st Pennsylvania Light, Battery F, Captain Ezra W. Matthews
1st Pennsylvania Light, Battery C, Captain James Thompson

Third Division (Pennsylvania Reserves)
Brigadier General George G. Meade

First Brigade
Brigadier General Truman Seymour
1st Pennsylvania Reserves: Colonel R. Biddle Roberts
10 (k), 30 (w)

2nd Pennsylvania Reserves: Captain James N. Byrnes
5 (k), 12 (w)
5th Pennsylvania Reserves: Colonel Joseph W. Fisher
1 (k), 9 (w)
6th Pennsylvania Reserves: Colonel William Sinclair
11 (k), 43 (w)
13th Pennsylvania Reserves: Colonel Hugh W. McNeil
11 (k), 39 (w)

Total Casualties First Brigade: 38 (k), 133 (w)
First Brigade Aggregate Losses: 171

Second Brigade
Colonel Albert Magilton
3rd Pennsylvania Reserves: Lieutenant Colonel John Clark
4th Pennsylvania Reserves: Major John Nyee
5 (k), 22 (w)
7th Pennsylvania Reserves: Colonel Henry C. Bollinger
5 (k), 7 (w)
8th Pennsylvania Reserves: Major Silas M. Baily
15 (k), 34 (w), 1 (m)

Total Casualties Second Brigade: 25 (k), 63 (w), 1 (m)
Second Brigade Aggregate Losses: 89

Third Brigade
Colonel Thomas Gallagher (w)
Lieutenant Colonel Robert Anderson
9th Pennsylvania Reserves: Lieutenant Colonel Robert Anderson,
Captain Samuel B. Dick
10 (k), 33 (w)
10th Pennsylvania Reserves: Lieutenant Colonel Adoniram Judson Warner
4 (k), 18 (w)
11th Pennsylvania Reserves: Lieutenant Colonel Samuel M. Jackson
12 (k), 30 (w)
12th Pennsylvania Reserves: Captain Richard Gustin
6 (k), 19 (w)

Total Casualties Third Brigade: 32 (k), 100 (w)
Third Brigade Aggregate Losses: 132

Third Division Artillery
1st Pennsylvania Light, Battery A, Lieutenant John G. Simpson
1st Pennsylvania Light, Battery B, Captain James H. Cooper
5th U.S. Battery C, Captain Dunbar R. Ransom

IX CORPS
Major General Jesse Lee Reno (k)
Brigadier General Jacob Dolson Cox

First Division
Brigadier General Orlando Bolivar Willcox

First Brigade
Colonel Benjamin C. Christ
28th Massachusetts: Captain Andrew P. Caraher
7 (w)
8th Michigan: Lieutenant Colonel Frank Graves
8 (w)
17th Michigan: Colonel William H. Withington
26 (k), 106 (w)
79th New York: Lieutenant Colonel David Morrison
12 (w)
50th Pennsylvania: Major Edward Overton
3 (w)

Total Casualties First Brigade: 26 (k), 136 (w)
First Brigade Aggregate Losses: 162

Second Brigade
Colonel Thomas Welsh
46th New York: Lieutenant Colonel Joseph Gerhardt
2 (k), 7 (w)
45th Pennsylvania: Lieutenant Colonel John I. Curtin
27 (k), 107 (w)

100th Pennsylvania: Lieutenant Colonel David A. Leckey
8 (k), 37 (w)

Total Casualties Second Brigade: 37 (k), 151 (w)
Second Brigade Aggregate Losses: 188

Artillery
Massachusetts Light, Eighth Battery, Captain Asa M. Cook
1 (k), 4 (w)
2nd U.S., Battery E, Lieutenant Samuel N. Benjamin

Second Division
Brigadier General Samuel D. Sturgis

First Brigade
Brigadier General James Nagle
2nd Maryland: Lieutenant Colonel J. Eugene Duryea
6th New Hampshire: Colonel Simon G. Griffin
9th New Hampshire: Colonel Enoch Q. Fellows
23 (w), 6 (m)
48th Pennsylvania: Lieutenant Colonel Joshua K. Sigfried
11 (w), 1 (m)

Total Casualties First Brigade: 34 (w), 7 (m)
First Brigade Aggregate Losses: 41

Second Brigade
Brigadier General Edward Ferrero
21st Massachusetts: Colonel William S. Clark
7 (w)
35th Massachusetts: Colonel Edward A. Wild
3 (k), 37 (w), 23 (m)
51st New York: Colonel Robert B. Potter
4 (k), 12 (w)
51st Pennsylvania: Colonel John F. Hartranft
3 (k), 27 (w)

Total Casualties Second Brigade: 10 (k), 83 (w), 23 (m)
Second Brigade Aggregate Losses: 116

Artillery
Pennsylvania Light, Battery D, Captain Geore W. Durell
4th United States, Battery E, Captain Joseph C. Clark, Jr.

Third Division
Brigadier General Isaac P. Rodman

First Brigade
Colonel Harrison Fairchild
9th New York: Lieutenant Colonel Edgar A. Kimball
89th New York: Major Edward Jardine
2 (k), 18 (w)
103rd New York: Major Benjamin Ringold

Total Casualties First Brigade: 2 (k), 18 (w)
First Brigade Aggregate Losses: 20

Second Brigade [not engaged]
Colonel Edward Harland
8th Connecticut: Lieutenant Colonel Hiram Appleman
11th Connecticut: Colonel Henry W. Kingsbury
16th Connecticut: Colonel Francis Beach
4th Rhode Island: Colonel William P. Steere

Third Division Artillery
5th U.S., Battery A, Lieutenant Charles P. Muhlenberg

Kanawha Division
Brigadier General Jacob Dolson Cox

First Brigade
Colonel Eliakim P. Scammon
12th Ohio: Colonel Carr B. White
13 (k), 47 (w), 5 (m)

23rd Ohio: Lieutenant Colonel Rutherford B. Hayes (w),
Major James M. Comly
32 (k), 95 (w), 3 (m)
30th Ohio: Colonel Hugh Ewing
17 (k), 53 (w)

Total Casualties First Brigade: 62 (k), 195 (w), 8 (m)
First Brigade Aggregate Losses: 265

Second Brigade
Colonel George Crook
Lieutenant Colonel Melvin Clark
11th Ohio: Lieutenant Colonel Augustus Coleman
7 (k), 34 (w), 3 (m)
28th Ohio: Lieutenant Colonel Gottfried Becker
3 (k), 12 (w)
36th Ohio: Lieutenant Colonel Melvin Clark
7 (k), 18 (w)

Total Casualties Second Brigade: 17 (k), 64 (w), 3 (m)
Second Brigade Aggregate Losses: 84

Artillery
Ohio Light Artillery, First Battery, Schambeck's Company, Chicago,
Captain James McMullin Dragoons
1(k), 6 (w)
Gilmore's Company, West Virginia Cavalry, Kentucky Light Artillery,
Lieutenant James Abraham
Simmond's Battery, Harrison's Company, West Virginia Cavalry, Lieutenant
Dennis Delaney

Franklin's Wing
Major General William B. Franklin

VI Corps
Major General William B. Franklin

First Division

Major General Henry W. Slocum

First Brigade (New Jersey Brigade)
Colonel Alfred T. A. Torbert
1st New Jersey: Lieutenant Colonel Mark W. Collet
7 (k), 34 (w)
2nd New Jersey: Colonel Samuel L. Buck
10 (k), 45 (w)
3rd New Jersey: Colonel Henry W. Brown
11 (k), 29 (w)
4th New Jersey: Colonel William B. Hatch
10 (k), 26 (w)

Total Casualties First Brigade: 38 (k), 134 (w)
First Brigade Aggregate Losses: 172

Second Brigade
Colonel Joseph J. Bartlett
5th Maine: Colonel Nathaniel J. Jackson
4 (k), 28 (w)
16th New York: Lieutenant Colonel Joel J. Seaver
20 (k), 41 (w)
27th New York: Lieutenant Colonel Alexander D. Adams
6 (k), 27 (w)
96th Pennsylvania: Colonel Henry L. Cake
20 (k), 71 (w)

Total Casualties Second Brigade: 50 (k), 167 (w)
Second Brigade Aggregate Losses: 217

Third Brigade
Brigadier General John Newton
18th New York: Lieutenant Colonel George R. Myers
11 (k), 41 (w), 2 (m)
31st New York: Lieutenant Colonel Francis E. Pinto
1 (k), 3 (w)

32nd New York: Colonel Roderick Matheson

11 (k), 40 (w)
95th Pennsylvania: Colonel Gustavus W. Town
1 (k), 14 (w)

Total Casualties Third Brigade: 24 (k), 98 (w), 2 (m)
Third Brigade Aggregate Losses: 124

First Division Artillery
Captain Emory Upton
Maryland Light Battery, Battery A, Captain John Wolcott
Massachusetts Light, Battery A, Captain Josiah Porter
New Jersey Light, Battery A, Captain William Hexamer
2nd U.S., Battery D, Lieutenant Edward Williston

Second Division
Major General William Farrar Smith

First Brigade [no casualties]
Brigadier General Winfield Scott Hancock
6th Maine: Colonel Hiram Burnham
43rd New York: Major John Wilson
49th Pennsylvania: Lieutenant Colonel William Brisbane
137th Pennsylvania: Colonel Henry M. Bossert
5th Wisconsin: Colonel Amasa Cobb

Second Brigade (Vermont Brigade)
Brigadier General W. T. H. Brooks
2nd Vermont: Major James H. Walbridge
5 (w)
3rd Vermont: Colonel Breed N. Hyde
4th Vermont: Lieutenant Colonel Charles B. Stoughton
1 (k), 10 (w)
5th Vermont: Colonel Lewis A. Grant
6th Vermont: Major Oscar L. Tuttle
3 (w)

Total Casualties Second Brigade: 1 (k), 18 (w)
Second Brigade Aggregate Losses: 19

Third Brigade [not engaged]
Colonel William H. Irwin
7th Maine: Major Thomas W. Hyde
20th New York: Colonel Ernes von Vegesack
33rd New York: Lieutenant Colonel Joseph W. Corning
49th New York: Lieutenant Colonel William C. Alberger
77th New York: Captain Nathan S. Babcock

Second Division Artillery
Captain Romeyn B. Ayres
Maryland Light, Battery B, Lieutenant Theodore J. Vanneman
New York Light, 1st Battery, Captain Andrew Cowan
5th U.S., Battery F, Lieutenant Leonard Martin

Cavalry Division
Brigadier General Alfred Pleasonton

First Brigade
Major Charles Whiting
5th U.S. Cavalry: Captain Joseph McArthur
6th U.S. Cavalry: Captain William P. Sanders

Second Brigade
Colonel John Farnsworth
8th Illinois Cavalry: Major William Medill
3rd Indiana Cavalry: Major George Chapman
1st Massachusetts Cavalry: Captain Casper Crowninshield
8th Pennsylvania Cavalry: Captain Peter Keenan

Third Brigade
Colonel Richard H. Rush
4th Pennsylvania Cavalry: Colonel James Childs
6th Pennsylvania Cavalry: Lieutenant Colonel C. Ross Smith

Fourth Brigade
Colonel Andrew T. McReynolds
1st New York Cavalry: Major Alonzo Adams
12th Pennsylvania Cavalry: Major James Congdon

Fifth Brigade
Colonel Benjamin F. Davis
8th New York Cavalry: Colonel Benjamin F. Davis
3rd Pennsylvania Cavalry: Lieutenant Colonel Samuel Owen

Artillery
2nd U.S., Battery A, Captain John Tidball
2nd U.S., Batteries B and L, Captain James M. Robertson
2nd U.S., Battery M, Lieutenant Peter Hains
3rd U.S., Batteries C and G, Captain Horatio G. Gibson

Unattached
15th Pennsylvania Cavalry: Colonel William Palmer

A ppendix 2[1]

Confederate Order of Battle and Losses

ARMY OF NORTHERN VIRGINIA
General Robert E. Lee

MCLAWS' DIVISION
Major General Lafayette McLaws

Cobb's Brigade
Brigadier General Howell Cobb
16th Georgia
24th Georgia: Lieutenant Colonel C. C. Sanders
Cobb's (Georgia) Legion
15th North Carolina: Lieutenant Colonel William MacRae

Total Casualties Cobb's Brigade: 58 (k), 186 (w), 442 (m)
Cobb's Brigade Aggregate Losses: 686

Semmes's Brigade
Brigadier General Paul J. Semmes
10th Georgia: Major Willis Holt
3 (k), 21, (w), 37 (m)
53rd Georgia: Lieutenant Colonel Thomas Sloan
15th Virginia: Captain E. M. Morrison
32nd Virginia: Colonel E. B. Montague

1   Carman, *The Maryland Campaign*, 445; 449.

Total Casualties Semmes's Brigade: 3 (k), 21 (w), 37 (m)
Semmes's Brigade Aggregate Losses: 61

Artillery
Troup Light Artillery
1 (k), 3 (w)
1st North Carolina Artillery
Richmond Fayette Artillery
Magruder Light Artillery

R. H. Anderson's Division

Mahone's Brigade
Colonel William A. Parham
6th Virginia
12th Virginia
16th Virginia
41st Virginia

Total Casualties Mahone's Brigade: 5 (k), 74 (w), 124 (m)
Mahone's Brigade Aggregate Losses: 203

Artillery
Portsmouth Light Artillery

David Rumph Jones' Division
Brigadier General David Rumph Jones

Toombs' Brigade
Brigadier General Robert Toombs
2nd Georgia: Lieutenant Colonel William Holmes
15th Georgia: Colonel William Millican
17th Georgia: Captain J.A. McGregor
20th Georgia: Colonel John Cumming

Drayton's Brigade
Brigadier General Thomas F. Drayton
50th Georgia: Lieutenant Colonel F. Kearse

51st Georgia
3rd South Carolina Battalion
15th South Carolina: Colonel W. D. DeSaussure
Phillips (Georgia) Legion

Total Casualties Drayton's Brigade: 49 (k), 164 (w), 176 (m)
Drayton's Brigade Aggregate Losses: 389

Pickett's Brigade
Brigadier General Richard B. Garnett
8th Virginia: Colonel Eppa Hunton
18th Virginia: Major George Cabell
19th Virginia: Colonel J. B. Strange (mw), Captain John L. Cochran
28th Virginia: Captain W. L. Wingfield
56th Virginia: Colonel William Stuart

Total Casualties Pickett's Brigade: 35 (k), 142 (w), 19 (m)
Pickett's Brigade Aggregate Losses: 196

Kemper's Brigade
Brigadier General James L. Kemper
1st Virginia
7th Virginia
11th Virginia: Major Adam Clement
17th Virginia: Colonel Montgomery Corse
24th Virginia

Total Casualties Kemper's Brigade: 11 (k), 57 (w), 7 (m)
Kemper's Brigade Aggregate Losses: 75

Jenkin's Brigade
Colonel Joseph Walker
1st South Carolina (Volunteers): Lieutenant Colonel D. Livingston
2nd South Carolina
5th South Carolina: Captain T. C. Beckham
6th South Carolina: Lieutenant J. M. Steedman
4th South Carolina Battalion
Palmetto (South Carolina) Sharpshooters

Total Casualties Jenkin's Brigade: 3 (k), 29 (w)
Jenkin's Brigade Aggregate Losses: 32

G. T. Anderson's Brigade
Colonel George T. Anderson
1st Georgia (Regulars): Colonel William Magill
7th Georgia
8th Georgia
9th Georgia
11th Georgia: Major F. H. Little

Total Casualties G. T. Anderson's Brigade: 3 (w), 4 (m)
G.T. Anderson's Brigade Aggregate Losses: 7

Hood's Division
Brigadier General John B. Hood

Wofford's Brigade
Colonel William T. Wofford
18th Georgia: Lieutenant Colonel S. Z. Ruff
Hampton (South Carolina) Legion
1st Texas: Lieutenant Colonel P. A. Work
4th Texas: Lieutenant Colonel B. F. Carter
5th Texas: Captain I. N. M. Turner

Total Casualties Wofford's Brigade: 3 (w), 2 (m)
Wofford's Brigade Aggregate Losses: 5

Law's Brigade
Colonel Evander M. Law
4th Alabama: Lieutenant Colonel O. K. McLemore
2nd Mississippi: Colonel J. M. Stone
11th Mississippi: Colonel P. F. Liddell
6th North Carolina: Major Robert Webb

Total Casualties Law's Brigade: 3 (k): 11 (w), 5 (m)
Law's Brigade Aggregate Losses: 19

Evans' Brigade
Colonel Peter F. Stevens
17th South Carolina: Colonel F. W. McMaster
18th South Carolina: Colonel W. H. Wallace
22nd South Carolina: Lieutenant Colonel Thomas Watkins
23rd South Carolina: Captain S. A. Durham
Holcombe (South Carolina) Legion
Macbeth (South Carolina) Artillery

Total Casualties Evans's Brigade: 23 (k), 142 (w), 45 (m)
Evans's Brigade Aggregate Losses: 210

D. H. Hill's Division
Major General Daniel Harvey Hill

Ripley's Brigade [no casualties]
Brigadier General Roswell Ripley
1st North Carolina: Colonel Hamilton Brown
3rd North Carolina: Colonel William L. DeRosset
4th Georgia: Colonel George Pierce Doles
44th Georgia: Captain John Key

Garland's Brigade
Brigadier General Samuel Garland, Jr. (k)
Colonel Duncan K. McRae
5th North Carolina: Colonel Duncan K. McRae, Captain Thomas Garrett
12th North Carolina: Captain S. Snow
13th North Carolina: Lieutenant Colonel Thomas Ruffin, Jr.
20th North Carolina: Colonel Alfred Iverson
23rd North Carolina: Colonel Daniel Christie

Total Casualties Garland's Brigade: 37 (k), 168 (w), 154 (m)
Garland's Brigade Aggregate Losses: 359

G. B. Anderson's Brigade
Brigadier General George Burgwyn Anderson
2nd North Carolina: Colonel C. C. Tew
4th North Carolina: Colonel Bryan Grimes

14th North Carolina: Colonel R. T. Bennett
30th North Carolina: Colonel F. M. Parker

Total Casualties G.B. Anderson's Brigade: 7 (k), 54 (w), 29 (m)
G. B. Anderson's Brigade Aggregate Losses: 90

Colquitt's Brigade
Colonel Alfred Colquitt
13th Alabama: Colonel B. D. Fry
6th Georgia: Lieutenant Colonel J. M. Newton
23rd Georgia: Colonel W. P. Barclay
27th Georgia: Colonel Levi B. Smith
28th Georgia: Major Tully Graybill

Total Casualties Colquitt's Brigade: 18 (k), 74 (w), 17 (m)
Colquitt's Brigade Aggregate Losses: 109

Artillery
Major S. F. Pierson
Alabama Battery, Captain R.A. Hardaway
Jefferson Davis Artillery, Captain J.W. Bondurant
Virginia Battery, Captain William B. Jones
King William Artillery, Captain Thomas Carter

Cavalry
Major General James Ewell Brown Stuart

Munford's Brigade
Colonel Thomas T. Munford
2nd Virginia Cavalry
6th Virginia Cavalry
7th Virginia Cavalry
12th Virginia Cavalry
17th Virginia Cavalry

Total Casualties Munford's Brigade: 3 (k), 5 (w)
Munford's Brigade Aggregate Losses: 8

Hampton's Brigade
Brigadier General Wade Hampton
1st North Carolina Cavalry
2nd South Carolina Cavalry
10th Virginia Cavalry
Cobb's (Georgia) Legion
Jeff Davis Legion

Lee's Brigade
Brigadier General Fitzhugh Lee
1st Virginia Cavalry
3rd Virginia Cavalry
4th Virginia Cavalry
5th Virginia Cavalry
9th Virginia Cavalry

Horse Artillery
Captain John Pelham
Chew's Battery
Hart's Battery
Pelham's Battery

A ppendix 3

An Interview with
Author Brian Matthew Jordan

Author Brian Jordan recently discussed his new book, the research and writing process, and the importance of South Mountain with Lindy Gervin of Savas Beatie.

LG: What inspired you to write a book about South Mountain, Brian?

BMJ: I have always been interested in the Maryland Campaign of 1862. I found it perplexing, however, that Antietam—traditionally described as a tactical stalemate—somehow provided President Lincoln the necessary courage to issue the preliminary Emancipation Proclamation on September 22, 1862.

LG: So a major turning point of the war . . .

BMJ: Yes. I set out to determine why and whether Civil War-era Americans viewed the Maryland Campaign as a turning point, and in the process I discovered South Mountain. Little had been written about that September 14th fight, and most historians deemed it a trifling skirmish—nothing more than an insignificant clash three days prior to Antietam.

LG: And you found something different?

BMJ: I did. In veterans' accounts, regimental histories, diaries, letters, as well as regimental standards heralding the great battles of the war, South Mountain consistently earned a prominent place. Many of the men who fought there considered the battle to be the decisive turning point of the Maryland

Campaign. That really surprised me. When I first visited Antietam National Battlefield, I expected the story of South Mountain would be prominently told. I asked for directions to the mountaintop and its passes, only to discover that much of the land had been developed. There was hardly any available interpretation of the battle. It was treated as unimportant and trivial. So I decided to research it, and eventually, write something about it.

LG: How did you conduct your research?

BMJ: I used diaries, letters, and manuscript collections from the rich holdings of all the usual suspects, including the Library of Congress, National Archives, the U.S. Army Military History Institute, the Rutherford B. Hayes Presidential Center, Ohio Historical Society, Western Reserve Historical Society, Virginia Historical Society, and New York Public Library, among others. I also surveyed a wide array of regimental histories, published letters and diaries, newspapers and magazines, and the official reports of commanders. Future students of the battle will have an easier time of it with the publication of Ezra Carman's seminal manuscript on the Antietam campaign—*The Maryland Campaign of September 1862*, edited and annotated by Tom Clemens.

LG: I think we published that! (Laughter)

BMJ: Yes, and it is a tremendous resource.

LG: Why has the Battle of South Mountain received so little attention from historians?

BMJ: First and foremost, Antietam (or Sharpsburg as the fighting was called in the South) completely overshadowed South Mountain. The staggering losses alone shoved the September 14th fight for the mountain passes off the main stage completely. A dozen hours of combat one unassuming September day added some 23,000 men to the Civil War's grisly register of men killed, wounded, missing, or captured, rendering Antietam the single bloodiest day in American history.

LG: And of course, the photographs of the dead. . . .

BMJ: Alexander Gardner's display, "The Dead of Antietam," depicts individuals, and in some cases, entire rows, of stiff bullet-riddled bodies strewn along the Hagerstown Turnpike and in the Sunken Road. Those are some of the most vivid images of the entire Civil War, and certainly of the Maryland Campaign. I think there is a tendency among Civil War chroniclers to consign great significance to great slaughter. In an attempt to rationalize such catastrophic losses, modern historians have "explained away" the staggering death toll by informing readers that the end of slavery and the future of freedom demanded such unprecedented sacrifices. I think the tragedy of Antietam is minimized by the notion that it prompted the issuance of the preliminary Emancipation Proclamation—a reassuring explanation of what Antietam's harvest of death accomplished. We remain uncomfortable and are reluctant to acknowledge that sometime small, random, unplanned events force large ripples into the stream of history.

LG: The Confederates remembered the battle differently, didn't they?

BMJ: Yes they did. The real meaning and import of the fighting suffered from the active postwar revisionism of its Rebel participants. Confederates had little desire to remember a battle in which the Federals wrestled away the higher, better ground from an army that had never been driven from the field, and in doing so, score an unprecedented victory that changed the course of the entire campaign by disrupting General Lee's plans completely. There was much more romance in the story of an exhausted, barefoot army boldly striking north across the Potomac River, fighting it out against a larger and better equipped Army of the Potomac at Sharpsburg, standing on the field all the following day, and then making an organized (but not demoralized) retreat back to Virginia. South Mountain was a problem for the Confederates to overcome historically speaking, but the remedy was ready-made in the Lost Cause mythology, which I explain in the last chapter of *Unholy Sabbath*.

LG: Why should we remember the Battle of South Mountain?

BMJ: Many reasons. South Mountain served as one of the war's earliest high-profile examples of hand-to-hand combat in the Civil War. The fight involved two future presidents, including one, Rutherford B. Hayes, who was seriously wounded. It was while fighting for one of the passes that a brigade of Midwestern men earned its now immortal moniker "Iron Brigade." But more importantly, Union veterans remembered South Mountain as a decisive turning point in the Maryland Campaign—the critical moment that transferred the momentum of the campaign from the Army of Northern Virginia to the Army of the Potomac.

LG: So are you arguing that it was a decisive battle?

BMJ: Absolutely. It is completely uncertain what Lee's smaller army would have been able to accomplish if Special Orders 191 had not been lost, or if McClellan had moved slower, or if the South Mountain passes had held. But the September 14th battle dashed forever General Lee's hopes for a smooth campaign north of the Potomac waged on his initiative and timetable. South Mountain was the first decisive Federal victory in the Eastern Theater—but how many people really realize that? Lee's plans were foiled, his initiative halted. He found himself in the unprecedented position of having to issue orders for a complete and hasty retreat—the clearest admission we have that he deemed the battle significant enough to unravel his dreams of tenting on the Susquehanna River.

LG: Any other reasons?

BMJ: Yes. South Mountain is a cautionary tale for students of the Civil War. What we in the 21st century deem "significant" often has little or no correlation to what the men themselves felt and experienced at the time.

LG: How does Unholy Sabbath *differ from other works about the Battle of South Mountain?*

BMJ: Because of the confusing nature of the various fights, historians seeking to understand the battle have narrowly focused on tactics, neglecting South Mountain's larger strategic significance within the campaign . . .

LG: And by focusing on the tactics, the story gets lost in the weeds.

BMJ: It does. *Unholy Sabbath* considers the three mountain gaps (Fox's, Turner's, and Crampton's) as a part of a strategic whole, and situates the campaign not only within the context of Lee's invasion of Maryland, but also within the larger political, social, and military history of the Civil War. My hope is that readers come away with a stronger sense of South Mountain's overall significance. My book is also the only existing study of the battle that considers its aftermath—the experience of tenting on a battleground wrestled from the enemy, the task of burying the dead, and the contested process veterans faced when remembering (or, conversely, forgetting) the past. Finally, the book contains a unique chapter on South Mountain in historical memory.

LG: I was glad to see all the maps in the book.

BMJ: Me too (laughter). The narrative is supplemented with a dozen state-of-the-art maps by skilled Civil War cartographer and historian Bradley M. Gottfried. Every previous work on South Mountain have relied on rather incomprehensible and often hand-drawn maps, most of which are presented completely out of context. I think the maps alone are worth the price of the book! The narrative is also enhanced by some great battlefield photography by Henry F. Ballone. I am thankful to both men for helping me with this project.

LG: What was your approach to research and writing Unholy Sabbath?

BMJ: I attempted to write a book that seamlessly blended academic history and military history in a way that would appeal to both general readers and students of the war. To their peril, I think many historians within the academy are reluctant to embrace military history, just as military historians too often dismiss the work of academics. This book isn't just another account of rectangles and arrows moving across the battlefield. I really tried to avoid that (although a big portion of the book naturally deals with micro-tactics). I hope *Unholy Sabbath* is an example of the type of work that can be realized when academic history and military history merge with one another.

LG: Anything else you would like to share with readers?

BMJ: My sincere hope is that *Unholy Sabbath* fosters a greater public appreciation for the events of September 14, 1862. This is especially important when you consider that the South Mountain battlefield routinely makes the Civil War Trust's list of the top ten most endangered battlefields in the nation. To be sure, the battlefield still retains some hidden gems: large portions of all three gaps are meticulously preserved, the original stone wall held by the North Carolinians at Fox's Gap still stands, and the Old Mountain House (now the Old South Mountain Inn) remains perched atop Turner's Gap. Maryland's Gathland State Park operates a small visitor contact station which recently launched an in-depth walking tour of the Crampton's Gap battlefield. But my ultimate dream is that we will one day have the South Mountain Unit of Antietam National Battlefield, and that the interpretive experiences for visitors will continue to expand in the coming years.

LG: What are you working on now?

BMJ: I am writing a cultural history of Union veterans tentatively titled, *When Billy Came Marching Home*. Recently, my interest has shifted to the postwar years and the veteran experience. I suppose you can already see that interest in the pages of *Unholy Sabbath*. My next book will offer, I hope, the most detailed exploration that we have to date of the experience of coming home from the Civil War, the challenges of being a veteran, and the complicated tensions between veterans who could never forget, and civilians who refused to remember.

LG: Thank you for your time, Brian, we appreciate it.

BMJ: You're welcome.

Bibliography

Manuscripts

Manuscript Division, Library of Congress, Washington, DC
Mary Ball Bickerdyke Papers
William Oland Bourne Papers
Ezra Ayers Carman Papers
James Jenkins Gillette Papers
E.N. Gilpin Papers
George Washington Hall Diary
Lyman Holford Papers
J.C. Ives Papers
David Rice Diary
Michael Shuler Diary
Gilbert Thompson Papers
Dennis Tuttle Papers

Ohio Historical Society, Columbus, Ohio
George H. Hildt Papers

Rare Book and Manuscript Division, New York Public Library, New York City
Century Collection

Rutherford B. Hayes Presidential Center, Fremont, Ohio
Martin Deady Diary
John McNulty Clugston Diary
James M. Comly Papers
Rutherford B. Hayes Papers
Daniel Wise Poem

United States Army Military History Institute, Carlisle, Pennsylvania
  Civil War Miscellaneous Collection
  Edson Emery Diary
  John Morton Letter
Civil War Times Illustrated Collection
  James Brisbin Letter
  John McQuaide Letter
  Frederick Petitt Letter
  Edward Schweitzer Diary
  Martin Sheets Diary
Harrisburg Civil War Round Table Collection
  James F. Haas Collection [John K. Fernsler Diary]
  Robert B. Cornwall Letter
  Henry Keiser Diary
William Marvel Collection
Northwest Corner Civil War Roundtable Collection
  Lewis Luckinbill Diary
  Martin Swathout Diary
James and Charlotte Pratt Collection
United States Army Military History Institute Collection
  James H. McIlwain Letter
  William Henry Miller Letter

Virginia Historical Society, Richmond, Virginia
  Osmun Latrobe Papers
  Henry T. Owen Papers
  William W. Sherwood Papers

Western Reserve Historical Society, Cleveland, Ohio
  Gabriel Campbell Poem
  Edward Burd Grubb Pamphlet

Newspapers & Periodicals

Baltimore Sun
Boston Evening Transcript
Canton [Ohio] *Repository*
Capital City Fact [Columbus, Ohio]

Century Magazine
Confederate Veteran
Dayton [Ohio] *Daily Journal*
Harper's New Monthly Magazine
National Tribune
New York Tribune
New York Times
Newark [Ohio] *Daily Advertiser*
Norwalk [Ohio] *Weekly Register*
Philadelphia Inquirer
Philadelphia Weekly Press
Richmond Examiner
Shenandoah [Pennsylvania] *Evening Herald*
Southern Historical Society Papers
Summit County [Ohio] *Beacon*
Wellsboro [Pennsylvania] *Agitator*

Government Documents

U.S. War Department. *The War of the Rebellion: The Official Records of the Union and Confederate Armies.* 128 vols. Washington: Government Printing Office, 1880-1901.

Barnes, Joseph K., Ed., *The Medical and Surgical History of the War of the Rebellion, 1861-1865.* 6 vols. Washington, D. C.: Government Printing Office, 1870-1888.

Primary Sources

Abraham, James. *With the Army of West Virginia, 1861-1864.* Lancaster, Pennsylvania: Evelyn A. Benson, 1974.

Alexander, E. Porter. *Military Memoirs of a Confederate: A Critical Narrative,* ed. T. Harry Williams. Bloomington: Indiana University Press, 1962.

Allan, William. "The Strategy of the Campaign of Sharpsburg or Antietam, September 1862." *Papers of the Military Historical Society of Massachusetts* 3 (1888): 73-103.

Allen, Albert D. ed., *History of the Forty-Fifth Regiment Pennsylvania Veteran Volunteer Infantry.* Williamsport, Pennsylvania: Grit Publishing, Co. 1912.

Barney, C.H. ed. *The Reno Memorial, South Mountain, Maryland, Unveiled September 14, 1889: Its Inception, Erection, and Dedication.* Portland, Maine: Society of the Burnside Expedition and the Ninth Army Corps, 1891.

Basler, Roy P., ed. *The Collected Works of Abraham Lincoln.* New Brunswick, New Jersey: Rutgers University Press, 1953.

Bates, Samuel P. *History of the Pennsylvania Volunteers*. Harrisburg: B. Singerly, State Printer, 1869.

Battle, Cullen Andrews. *Third Alabama! The Civil War Memoir of Brigadier General Cullen Andrews Battle, CSA*, ed. Brandon H. Beck. Tuscaloosa: The University of Alabama Press, 2000.

Battles and Leaders of the Civil War, ed. Robert Underwood Johnson and Clarence Buel. New York and London: Thomas Yoseloff, 1956.

Beale, Howard K., ed. *The Diary of Gideon Welles*. New York: W.W. Norton & Co., 1960.

Beaudot, William J.K. and Lance J. Herdegen, eds. *An Irishman in the Iron Brigade: The Civil War Memoirs of James P. Sullivan, Sergt. Company K, 6th Wisconsin Volunteers*. New York: Fordham University Press, 1993.

Blakeslee, B.F. *History of the 16th Connecticut Volunteers*. Hartford: Case, Lockwood & Brainard Company, 1875.

Bosbyshell, Oliver C. *The 48th in the War*. Philadelphia: Anvil Printing Co., 1895.

Brinkerhoff, Henry R. *Thirtieth Regiment Ohio Volunteer Infantry*. Columbus, Ohio: James W. Osgood, Printer, 1863.

Brown, Philip F. *Reminiscences of the War of 1861-1865 by Philip F. Brown, Company C, 12th Virginia Infantry, Mahone's Brigade*. Roanoke, Virginia: Union Printing Co. 1912.

Buck, Samuel D. *With the Old Confeds, Actual Experiences of a Captain in the Line*. Baltimore: H.E. Houck and Co., 1925.

Burlingame, Michael, ed. *Lincoln's Journalist: John Hay's Anonymous Writings for the Press, 1860–1864*. Carbondale: Southern Illinois University Press, 1998.

Carman, Ezra. *The Maryland Campaign of September 1862*, ed. Joseph Pierro. New York: Routledge Press, 2008.

Castleman, Alfred Lewis. *The Army of the Potomac, Behind the Scenes: A Diary of Unwritten History from the Organization of the Army to the Close of the Campaign in Virginia, About the First Day of January, 1863*. Milwaukee, Wisconsin: Strickland & Co., 1863.

Cavanaugh, Michael A., comp. *Military Essays and Recollections of the Pennsylvania Commandery, Military Order of the Loyal Legion of the United States*. Wilmington, North Carolina: Broadfoot Publishing Company, 1995.

Coles, R.T. *From Huntsville to Appomattox*, ed. Jeffrey D. Stocker. Knoxville: The University of Tennessee Press, 1996.

Committee of the Regimental Association. *A History of the Thirty-Fifth Regiment, Massachusetts Volunteers*. Boston: Mills, Knight, & Co., 1884.

Conwell, Russell. *Life and Public Services of Governor Rutherford B. Hayes*. Boston: B.B. Russell, 1876.

Cox, Jacob Dolson. *Military Reminiscences of the Civil War*. New York: Charles Scribner's, 1900.

Crater, Louis. *History of the Fiftieth Regiment Pennsylvania Veteran Volunteer Infantry*. Reading, Pennsylvania: Coleman Printing House, 1884.

Crist, Lynda Lasswell and Mary Seaton Dix, eds. *The Papers of Jefferson Davis*. Baton Rouge: Louisiana State University Press, 1971-1995.

Crownshield, Benjamin W. *A History of the First Regiment of Massachusetts Cavalry Volunteers.* Boston: Houghton, Mifflin, and Co., 1891.

Curtis, Newton Martin. *From Bull Run to Chancellorsville.* New York: G.P. Putnam's Sons, 1906.

Cussel, Charles A. *Durell's Battery in the Civil War.* Philadelphia: Craig, Finley, & Co., 1900.

Dawes, Rufus R. *Service with the Sixth Wisconsin Volunteers.* Marietta, Ohio: E.R. Alderman & Sons, 1890.

de Peyster, John Watts. "The Maryland Battles in September 1862," in *The Decisive Conflict of the Late Civil War, or Slaveholder's Rebellion.* New York: MacDonald & Printers, 1867.

Dickert, Augustus. *History of Kershaw's Brigade.* Dayton, Ohio: Morningside Bookshop, 1976.

Dowdey, Clifford, and Louis H. Manarin, eds. *The Wartime Papers of R.E. Lee.* New York: Bramhall House Publishers, 1961.

Durkin, Joseph T., ed. *John Dooley, Confederate Soldier: His War Journal.* South Bend, Indiana: University of Notre Dame Press, 1963.

Ellis, Thomas T. *Leaves From the Diary of an Army Surgeon: or, Incidents of the Field, Camp, and Hospital Life.* New York: John Bradburn, 1863.

Fairchild, Charles B. *History of the 27th Regiment New York Volunteers.* Binghamton, New York: Carl & Matthews, Printers, 1888.

Ferguson, Garland S. "Twenty-Fifth Infantry," in Walter Clark, ed. *Histories of the Several Regiments and Battalions from North Carolina in the Great War 1861-'65.* Goldsboro, North Carolina: Nash Brothers, 1901.

Firey, Frank P. *City of Pomona in the Making.* Pomona: Pomona Valley Historical Society, 1935.

Foner, Phillip S, ed. "The President and His Speeches," in *The Life and Writings of Frederick Douglass.* New York: International Publishers, 1975.

Ford, Worthington Chauncey, ed. *A Cycle of Adams Letters.* Boston: Houghton, Mifflin, and Co., 1920.

Frederick, Gilbert. *The Story of a Regiment.* Chicago: C.H. Morgan Co., 1895.

Gates, Theodore B. *The Ulster Guard.* New York: Benjamin H. Tyrrel, 1879.

Gavin, William Gilfillan, ed. *Infantryman Pettit: The Civil War Letters of Corporal Frederick Pettit.* New York: Avon Books, 1990.

Gibbon, John. *Personal Recollections of the Civil War.* New York: G.P. Putnam's Sons, 1928.

Gibbs, Joseph. *Three Years in the 'Bloody Eleventh': The Campaigns of a Pennsylvania Reserves Regiment.* University Park: Pennsylvania State University Press, 2002.

Gould, Joseph. *The Story of the Forty-Eighth.* Mt. Carmel, Pennsylvania: The 48th Pennsylvania Regimental Association, 1908.

Graham, Matthew J. *History of the Ninth New York Volunteers (Hawkins' Zouaves): Being a History of the Regiment and Veteran Association from 1860 to 1900.* New York: E.P. Coby & Co., 1900.

Grattan, George D. "The Battle of Boonsboro Gap or South Mountain." *Southern Historical Society Papers* 29 (1914): 31-44.

Greiner, James M., Janet L. Coryell, and James R. Smither, eds. *A Surgeon's Civil War: The Letters and Diary of Daniel M. Holt, M.D.* Kent, Ohio: Kent State University Press, 1994.

Guedalla, Philip, ed. *Gladstone and Palmerston: Being the Correspondence of Lord Palmerston with Mr. Gladstone, 1851-1865.* London and Southampton: The Camelot Press Ltd., 1928.

Hall, Isaac. *History of the Ninety-Seventh Regiment, New York Volunteers.* Utica: L.C. Childs & Son, 1870.

Hess, George. *Battle-Field Guide of the Battles of South Mountain and Antietam.* Hagerstown: Globe Job Room Prints, 1890.

Heysinger, Isaac. "Introductory—Inaccuracy of All the Current Histories," in *Antietam and the Maryland and Virginia Campaigns of 1862,* 1912.

Hill, Alonzo F. *Our Boys.* Philadelphia: John E. Potter, 1864.

Hirst, Benjamin. *The Boys From Rockville: Civil War Narrative of Sgt. Benjamin Hirst, Company D, 14th Connecticut Volunteers,* ed. Robert L. Bee. Knoxville: University of Tennessee Press, 1998.

History of Antietam National Cemetery. Baltimore: John Woods, 1869.

Hood, John Bell. *Advance and Retreat: Personal Experiences in the United States and Confederate States Armies.* New Orleans: For the Hood Orphan Memorial Fund by P.G.T. Beauregard, 1880.

Horton, J.H. and Solomon Treverbaugh. *A History of the Eleventh Regiment, Ohio Volunteer Infantry.* Dayton, Ohio: W.J. Shuey, 1866.

Hough, Franklin B. *History of Duryee's Brigade.* Albany, New York: J. Munsell, 1864.

Hubbs, G. Ward, ed., *Voices From Company D: Diaries by the Greensboro Guards, Fifth Alabama Infantry Regiment, Army of Northern Virginia.* Athens: University of Georgia Press, 2003.

Huebner, Richard Alden, ed. *Meserve Civil War Record.* Oak Park, Michigan, 1987.

Jewett, Leonidas M. "From Stafford Heights to Gettysburg in 1863." *Sketches of War History 1861-1865: Papers Prepared for the Commandery of the State of Ohio Military Order of the Loyal Legion of the United States,* ed. W.H. Chamerlain et al. Reprinted edition. Wilmington, North Carolina: Broadfoot Publishing Company, 1992.

Johnson, Bradley Tyler. "Address on the First Maryland Campaign." *Southern Historical Society Papers* 12 (1882): 503-504.

Johnson, Charles F. *The Long Roll.* East Aurora, New York: The Roycrofters, 1911.

Johnston, David Emmons. *The Story of a Confederate Boy.* Portland, Oregon: Glass & Prudhomme Co., 1914.

Jones, J.B. *A Rebel War Clerk's Diary,* ed. Howard Swiggett. New York: Old Hickory Bookshop, 1935.

Keeler, Roger S. *Crossroads of War: Washington County, Maryland in the Civil War.* Shippensburg, Pennsylvania: Burd Street Press, 1997.

Lane, David. *A Soldier's Diary: The Story of a Volunteer, 1862-1865.* n.p. 1905.

Livermore, Thomas Leonard. *Days and Events, 1860-1866.* Boston: Houghton, Mifflin, & Co., 1920.

Locke, Calvin S. *The Patriotic Volunteer.* Boston: Press of John Wilson and Son, 1862.

Long, A.L. *Memoirs of Robert E. Lee, His Military and Personal History.* Philadelphia: J.M. Stoddart & Co., 1886.

Longstreet, James. *From Manassas to Appomattox: Memoirs of the Civil War in America.* Bloomington: Indiana University Press, 1960.

Lord, Edward O., ed. *History of the Ninth Regiment New Hampshire Volunteers.* Concord: Republican Press Association, 1895.

Loving, Jerome M. ed. *Civil War Letters of George Washington Whitman.* Durham, North Carolina: Duke University Press, 1975.

Lusk, William Thompson. *War Letters of William Thompson Lusk.* New York: W.C. Lusk, 1911.

Lyle, William. *Lights and Shadows of Army Life.* Cincinnati: R.W. Carroll and Co., 1865.

Marshall, Charles, *An Aide-de-Camp of Lee, Being the Papers of Colonel Charles Marshall, Sometimes Aide-de-Camp, Military Secretary, and Assistant Adjutant General on the Staff of Robert E. Lee, 1862-1865*, ed. Sr. Frederick Maurice. Boston: Little, Brown & Co., 1927.

Massachusetts Soldiers, Sailors, and Marines in the Civil War. 6 vols. Norwood, Massachusetts: Norwood Press, 1933.

Maxson, William P. *Camp Fires of the Twenty-Third.* New York: Davies & Kent, 1863.

Mills, John Harrison. *Chronicles of the Twenty-First Regiment, New York State Volunteers.* Buffalo: 21st Regiment Veteran Association, 1887.

Mitchell, Charles W., ed. *Maryland Voices of the Civil War.* Baltimore: Johns Hopkins University Press, 2007.

Neese, George. *Three Years in the Confederate Horse Artillery.* New York: Neale Publishing Company, 1911.

Nevins, Allan and Milton Halsey Thomas, eds., *The Diary of George Templeton Strong.* New York: The Macmillan Company, 1952.

Niven, John, ed., *The Papers of Salmon P. Chase.* Kent, Ohio: Kent State University Press, 1996.

Noyes, George Freeman. *The Bivouac and the Battlefield: Or, Campaign Sketches in Virginia and Maryland.* New York: Harper & Brothers, Publishers, 1863.

Palfrey, Francis Winthrop. *The Antietam and Fredericksburg.* New York: Charles Scribner's, 1882.

Parker, Thomas H. *History of the 51st Regiment of Pennsylvania Volunteers and Veteran Volunteers.* Philadelphia: King and Baird Printers, 1869.

Patch, Eileen Mae Knapp, ed., *This From George: The Civil War Letters of Sergeant George Magusta English, Company K, 89th New York Regiment of Volunteer Infantry.* Binghamton, New York: Broome County Historical Society, 2001.

Pollard, Edward A. *Southern History of the War: The Second Year of the War*. New York: Charles B. Richardson, 1864.

Pratt, Fletcher, ed. *My Diary North and South*. New York, 1954.

Priest, John Michael, ed. *Captain James Wren's Diary: From New Bern to Fredericksburg*. Shippensburg, Pennsylvania: White Mane Publishing Co., Inc., 1990.

Prime, William C., ed. *McClellan's Own Story: The War For the Union, The Soldiers Who Fought It, The Civilians Who Directed It, and His Relations to It and Them*. New York: Charles L. Webster, 1887.

Reichardt, Theodore. *Diary of Battery A, First Rhode Island Light Artillery*. Providence: N.B. Williams, 1865.

Reno, Conrad. "General Jesse Lee Reno at Frederick: Barbara Fritchie and Her Flag," in *Civil War Papers Read Before the Commandery of the State of Massachusetts Military Order of the Loyal Legion of the United States*. Boston, 1900.

Report of the Antietam Battlefield Memorial Commission of Pennsylvania and Ceremonies at the Dedication of the Monuments Erected by the Commonwealth of Pennsylvania. Harrisburg: State Printer, 1906.

Richards, Louis. *Eleven Days in the Militia During the War of the Rebellion: Being a Journal of the Emergency Campaign of 1862*. Philadelphia: Collins Printer, 1883.

Richardson, James D., comp. *Messages and Papers of the Presidents*. New York: Bureau of National Literature, 1887.

Richardson, James D., comp. and ed. *Messages and Papers of Jefferson Davis and the Confederacy, Including Diplomatic Correspondence 1861-1865*. New York: Chelsea House-Robert Hector Publishers, 1966.

Ropes, John Codman. *The Army Under Pope*. Boston: Charles Scribner's, 1881.

Russell, William Howard. *My Diary North and South*, ed. Fletcher Pratt. New York: Harper Brothers, 1954.

Scott, Robert Garth, ed. *Forgotten Valor: The Memoirs, Journals, and Letters of Orlando B. Wilcox*. Kent, Ohio: Kent State University Press, 1999.

Sears, Stephen W., ed. *For Country, Cause, and Leader: The Civil War Journal of Charles B. Hayden*. New York: Ticknor & Fields, 1993.

Sears, Stephen W., ed. *The Civil War Papers of George B. McClellan: Selected Correspondence, 1860–1865*. New York: Ticknor & Fields, 1989.

Smith, Abraham P. *History of the Seventy-Sixth Regiment in New York Volunteers*. Cortland, New York: Truain, Smith, and Miles Printers, 1876.

Sorrell, Moxley G., *At the Right Hand of Longstreet: Recollections of a Confederate Staff Officer*. New York: Neal Publishing Company, 1905.

Souvenir Guide and Guide Book of Harper's Ferry, Antietam, and South Mountain Battlefields. n.p.: Edward Grave, 1898.

Sparks, David S., ed. *Inside Lincoln's Army: The Diary of General Marsena Rudolph Patrick, Army of the Potomac*. New York: Thomas Yoseloff, 1964.

Stone, James Madison. *Personal Recollections of the Civil War*. Boston: By the Author, 1918.

Sypher, Josiah. *History of the Pennsylvania Reserve Corps*. Lancaster, Pennsylvania: Elias Barr & Co., 1865.

Taylor, Walter H. *Four Years With General Lee*, ed. James I. Robertson, Jr. Bloomington: Indiana University Press, 1962.

Todd, William. *The Seventy-Ninth Highlanders, New York Volunteers in the War of the Rebellion, 1861-1865*. Albany: Barton & Co., 1886.

Tower, Lockwood R., ed. *Lee's Adjutant: The Wartime Letters of Colonel Walter Herron Taylor, 1862-1865*. Columbia: University of South Carolina Press, 1995.

Turner III, Nat S. *A Southern Soldier's Letters Home: The Civil War Letters of Samuel A. Burney, Cobb's Georgia Legion, Army of Northern Virginia*. Macon, Georgia: Mercer University Press, 2002.

Urban, John W. *My Experiences Mid Shot and Shell and in Rebel Den*. Lancaster, Pennsylvania: n.p. 1882.

Von Borcke, Heros. *Memoirs of the Confederate War for Independence*. New York: Peter Smith, 1938.

Walcott, Charles F. *History of the 21st Massachusetts Volunteers in the War for the Preservation of the Union*. Boston: Houghton Mifflin, 1882.

Wall, Henry Clay. *Historical Sketch of the Pee Dee Guards, Co. D, 23rd North Carolina*. Raleigh: Edewards, Broughton, & Co., 1876.

War Papers, Being Papers Read Before the Commandery of the State of Michigan, Military Order of the Loyal Legion of the United States. Wilmington, North Carolina: Broadfoot Publishing Company, 1993.

Ward, J.E.D. *Twelfth Ohio Volunteer Infantry*. Ripley, Ohio: J.E.D. Ward, 1864.

Wiggins, Sarah Woolfolk, ed. *The Journals of Josiah Gorgas, 1857-1878*. Tuscaloosa: University of Alabama Press, 1995.

Williams, Charles Richard, ed. *The Diary and Letters of Rutherford Birchard Hayes: Nineteenth President of the United States*, 5 vols. Columbus: Ohio Archaeological and Historical Society, 1922-1926.

Wilson, James Harrison. *Under the Old Flag: Recollections of Military Operations in the War for the Union, The Spanish War, The Boxer Rebellion, Etc*. New York: D. Appleton and Company, 1912.

Wood, William Nathaniel. *Reminiscnes of Big I*, ed. Bell Irvin Wiley. Jackson, Tennessee: McCowat-Mercer Press, 1956.

Woodward, E. Morrison. *Our Campaigns: The Second Regiment Pennsylvania Reserve Volunteers, 1861-1864*. Philadelphia: J.E. Porter, 1865.

Secondary Sources

Adams, Michael C.C. *Our Masters the Rebels*. Cambridge: Harvard University Press, 1978.

Andrews, J. Cutler. *The North Reports the Civil War*. Pittsburgh: University of Pittsburgh Press, 1955.

Ayers, Edward L. "Worrying About the Civil War," in *What Caused the Civil War? Reflections on the South and Southern History*. New York, W. W. Norton, 2005.

Beyer, W.F. and O.F. Keydel, eds., *Deeds of Valor: How America's Civil War Heroes Won the Congressional Medal of Honor*. Detroit: Perrin-Keydel Co., 1907.

Bigelow, John Jr. *The Campaigns of Chancellorsville*. New Haven: Yale University Press, 1910.

Blight, David W. *Frederick Douglass' Civil War: Keeping Faith in Jubilee*. Baton Rouge: The Louisiana State University Press, 1989.

Boritt, Gabor S. *Lincoln and the Economics of the American Dream*. Memphis: Memphis State University Press, 1978.

Bridges, Hal. *Lee's Maverick General: Daniel Harvey Hill*. New York: McGraw Hill, 1961.

Burton, Brian K. *Extraordinary Circumstances: The Seven Days Battles*. Bloomington and Indianapolis: Indiana University Press, 2001.

Byrne, Frank L. and Andrew T. Weaver, eds. *Haskell of Gettysburg: His Life and Civil War Papers*. Kent, Ohio: Kent State University Press, 1989.

Cannan, John. *The Antietam Campaign: July–November, 1862*. New York: Wieser & Wieser, Inc. 1990.

Capers, Ellison. *South Carolina in Confederate Military History*. Secaucus, New Jersey: Blue and Grey Press ed., 1993.

Case, Lynn M. and Warren F. Spencer. *The United States and France: Civil War Diplomacy*. Philadelphia: University of Pennsylvania Press, 1970.

Casey, James B. "The Ordeal of Adoniram Judson Warner: His Minutes of South Mountain and Antietam." *Civil War History* 28, no. 3 (September 1982), 217.

Clinton, Catherine and Nina Silber, eds. *Divided Houses: Gender and the Civil War*. New York and Oxford: Oxford University Press, 1992.

Collins, Darrell, L. *Major General Robert E. Rodes of the Army of Northern Virginia: A Biography*. New York and California: Savas Beatie, 2008.

Connelly, Thomas Lawrence and Archer Jones. *The Politics of Command, Factions, and Ideas in Confederate Strategy*. Baton Rouge: Louisiana State University Press, 1973.

Cooling, Benjamin, *Counter-Thrust: From the Peninsula to the Antietam*. Lincoln: University of Nebraska Press, 2007.

Cox, LaWanda F. *Lincoln and Black Freedom: A Study in Presidential Leadership*. Columbia: University of South Carolina Press, 1981.

Cozzens, Peter. *Shenandoah 1862*. Chapel Hill: University of North Carolina Press, 2008.

Davis, Burke. *J.E.B. Stuart: The Last Cavalier*. New York: Rinehart, 1957.

Dean, Jr., Eric T. "'We Live Under a Government of Men and Morning Newspapers': Image, Expectation, and the Peninsula Campaign of 1862." *The Virginia Magazine of History and Biography* 103, no. 1 (January 1995): 5-28.

Dew, Charles B. "How Samuel E. Pittman Validated Lee's 'Lost Orders' Prior to Antietam: A Historical Note." *Journal of Southern History* 70, no. 4 (November 2004): 865-870.

Duncan, Richard R. "Marylanders and the Invasion of 1862." *Civil War History: A Journal of the Middle Period* 11, no. 4 (December 1965): 370-383.

Eicher, David J. and John H. Eicher. *Civil War High Commands.* Stanford: Stanford University Press, 2001.

Ernst, Kathleen A. *Too Afraid To Cry: Maryland Civilians in the Antietam Campaign.* Mechanicsburg: Stackpole Books, 1999.

Escott, Paul D. *After Secession.* Baton Rouge: Louisiana State University Press, 1992.

Everett, Donald E., ed. *Chaplain Davis and Hoods Texas Brigade.* San Antonio: Principia Press of Trinity University, 1962.

Faust, Drew Gilpin. *Mothers of Invention: Women of the Slaveholding South in the American Civil War.* Chapel Hill: The University of North Carolina Press, 1996.

——. *The Creation of Confederate Nationalism: Ideology and Identity in the Civil War South.* Baton Rouge: Louisiana State University Press, 1988.

——. "We should Grow to Fond of It: Why we Love the Civil War." *Civil War History,* 50, no. 4 (December 2004), 368-383.

Faust, Patricia L., ed. *Historical Times Illustrated Encyclopedia of the Civil War.* New York: Harper & Row, 1986.

Flaherty, Darwin L. "The Naming of Reno, Nevada: A Century Old Mystery." *Nevada Historical Society Quarterly* 27, no. 3 (1984): 154-181.

Foner, Eric. *Free Soil, Free Labor, Free Men.* New York: Oxford University Press, 1970.

Frassanito, William A. *Antietam: The Photographic Legacy of America's Bloodiest Day.* New York: Scribner's, 1978.

Freeman, Douglas Southall. *R. E. Lee. A Biography.* 4 vols. New York: Scribners, 1934-1935.

Frye, Dennis E. *Antietam Revealed.* Collingswood, New Jersey: C.W. Historicals, 2004.

Gaff, Alan D. *Brave Men's Tears: The Iron Brigade at Brawner Farm.* Dayton, Ohio: Morningside Bookshop, Inc. 1988.

Gallagher, Gary W. ed. *Antietam: Essays on the 1862 Maryland Campaign.* Kent, Ohio: Kent State University Press, 1989.

Gallagher, Gary W., ed. *Lee: The Soldier.* Lincoln: University of Nebraska Press, 1996.

Geary, James W. and John T. Hubbell, eds. *Biographical Dictionary of the Union: Northern Leaders of the Civil War.* Westport, Connecticut: Greenwood Press, 1995.

Goodwin, Doris Kearns. *Team of Rivals: The Political Genius of Abraham Lincoln.* New York: Simon & Schuster, 2005.

Gordon, Paul and Rita Gordon. *Never the Like Again: Frederick County, Maryland.* Frederick: n.p., 1995.

Grimsley, Mark. *The Hard Hand of War: Union Military Policy Toward Southern Civilians, 1861–1865.* New York: Cambridge University Press, 1995.

Guelzo, Allen C. *Lincoln's Emancipation Proclamation: The End of Slavery in America.* New York: Simon & Schuster, 2004.

Guelzo, Allen C. *The Crisis of the American Republic.* New York: St. Martins, 1995.

Hagerman, Edward. *The American Civil War and the Origins of Modern Warfare: Ideas, Organization, and Field Command.* Bloomington and Indianapolis: Indiana University Press, 1988.

Harsh, Joseph L. "On the McClellan-Go-Round." *Civil War History: A Journal of the Middle Period* 19, no. 2 (1973): 117.

Harsh, Joseph L. *Sounding the Shallows: A Confederate Companion for the Maryland Campaign of 1862.* Kent, Ohio: Kent State University Press, 2000.

Hartwig, D. Scott. "'It Looked Like a Task to Storm': The Pennsylvania Reserves Assault South Mountain." *North and South* 5, no. 7 (October 2002): 36-49.

Hartwig, D. Scott. "'My God! Be Careful!' Morning Battle at Fox's Gap, September 14, 1862." *Civil War Regiments: A Journal of the American Civil War* 5, no. 3 (1996).

Hassler, Jr., Warren W. "The Battle of South Mountain." *Maryland Historical Magazine* 52 (March 1957): 53.

Hassler, William Woods. *Colonel John Pelham: Lee's Boy General.* Richmond: Garrett and Massie, Inc., 1960.

Hattaway, Herman and Richard E. Beringer. *Jefferson Davis, Confederate President.* Lawrence: The University Press of Kansas, 2002.

Heidler, David S. and Jeanne T. Heidler, eds. *Encyclopedia of the American Civil War: A Political, Social, and Military History.* New York: W.W. Norton & Company, 2000.

Henderson, William B. *41st Virginia Infantry.* Lynchburg: Virginia: H.E. Howard, Inc. 1988.

Herdegen, Lance J. *The Men Stood Like Iron: How the Iron Brigade Won Its Name.* Bloomington: Indiana University Press, 1997.

Hess, Earl J. *The Union Soldier in Battle: Enduring the Ordeal of Combat.* Lawrence: University Press of Kansas, 1997.

Hesseltine, William B. *Lincoln and the War Governors.* New York: Alfred A. Knopf, 1948.

Hoptak, John. *Our Boys Did Nobly: Schuylkill County, Pennsylvania, Soldiers at the Battles of South Mountain and Antietam.* Self-published, 2009.

Howard, Wiley C. *Sketch of Cobb Legion Cavalry and Some Incidents and Scenes Remembered.* Atlanta: n.p. 1901.

Howe, Daniel Walker. *What Hath God Wrought: The Transformation of America, 1815–1848.* New York: Oxford University Press, 2008.

Jermann, Donald R. *Antietam: The Lost Order.* Gretna, Louisiana: Pelican Publishing Company, 2006.

Jones, Howard. *Abraham Lincoln and a New Birth of Freedom: The Union and Slavery in the Diplomacy of the Civil War.* Lincoln: University of Nebraska Press, 1999.

——. *Blue and Gray Diplomacy: A History of Union and Confederate Foreign Relations.* Chapel Hill: University of North Carolina Press, 2010.

Jones, Wilbur. *Giants in the Cornfield: The 27th Indiana Infantry.* Shippensburg, Pennsylvania: White Mane Publishing, Inc., 1997.

Kempfer, Lester L. *The Salem Light Guard: Company G, 36th Regiment Ohio Volunteer Infantry.* Chicago: Adams Press, 1973.

Klement, Frank L. *The Limits of Dissent: Clement L. Vallandingham and the Civil War.* Lexington: The University Press of Kentucky, 1970.

Krick, Robert E.L., *Staff Officers in Gray: A Biographical Register of the Staff Officers in the Army of Northern Virginia.* Chapel Hill: University of North Carolina Press, 2003.

Krick, Robert K. *Stonewall Jackson at Cedar Mountain.* Chapel Hill: The University of North Carolina Press, 1990.

Manarin, Louis H. "A Proclamation: 'To the People of _____'." *North Carolina Historical Review 41*, no. 2 (April 1964): 246-251.

Marvel, William. *Race of the Soil: The Ninth New Hampshire Regiment in the Civil War.* Wilmington, North Carolina: Broadfoot Publishing, 1988.

McClure, Alexander Kelly. *Abraham Lincoln and Men of War-Time.* Philadelphia: Times Publishing Company, 1892.

McConnell, William F. *Remember Reno: A Biography of Major General Jesse Lee Reno.* Shippensburg, Pennsylvania: White Mane Publishing Co., Inc., 1996.

McMurry, Richard M. *John Bell Hood and the War for Southern Independence.* Lincoln: University of Nebraska Press, 1992.

McPherson, James M. *Crossroads of Freedom: Antietam.* Oxford and New York: Oxford University Press, 2002.

McPherson, James M. *This Mighty Scourge: Perspectives on the Civil War.* New York: Oxford University Press, 2007.

McWhiney, Grady. "'Who Whipped Whom?' Confederate Defeat Reexamined." *Civil War History: A Journal of the Middle Period* 11, no. 1 (March 1965): 17-18.

Mingus, Sr., Scott L. *Human Interest Stories from Antietam.* Ortanna, Pennsylvania: Colecraft Industries, 2007.

Monaghan, Jay. *Diplomat in Carpet Slippers: Abraham Lincoln Deals with Foreign Affairs.* Indianapolis and New York: Bobbs Merrill, 1945.

Murfin, James V. *The Gleam of Bayonets: The Battle of Antietam and Robert E. Lee's Maryland Campaign September 1862.* Baton Rouge: Louisiana State University Press, 1965.

Neely, Mark E. *The Union Divided: Party Conflict in the Civil War North.* Cambridge London: Harvard University Press, 2002.

Older, Curtis L. *The Land Tracts of the Battlefield of South Mountain.* Westminster, Maryland: Willow Bend Books, 1999.

Owsley, Frank L., ed. *King Cotton Diplomacy: Foreign Relations of the Confederate States of America.* Chicago: University of Chicago Press, 1959.

Pinsker, Matthew. *Lincoln's Sanctuary: Abraham Lincoln and the Soldiers' Home.* New York: Oxford University Press, 2003.

Priest, John Michael. *Before Antietam: The Battle for South Mountain.* Shippensburg, Pennsylvania: White Mane Publishing Co., Inc., 1992.

Reese, Timothy J. *High Water Mark: The 1862 Maryland Campaign in Strategic Perspective.* Baltimore: Butternut and Blue, 2004.

———. *Letters from the Battlefield: Crampton's Gap, September 14, 1862.* Burkittsville, Maryland: South Mountain Heritage Society, 1994.

——. *Sealed With Their Lives: The Battle for Crampton's Gap, September 14, 1862.* Baltimore: Butternut and Blue, 1998.

——. "The Cavalry Clash at Quebec Schoolhouse." *Blue and Gray Magazine* (February 1993): 24-30.

Reid, Brian Holden. *America's Civil War: The Operational Battlefield, 1861–1863.* Amherst, New York: Prometheus Books, 2008.

Reid, Robert L. "William E. Gladstone's 'Insincere Neutraility' During the Civil War." *Civil War History: A Journal of the Middle Period* 15, no. 4 (December 1969): 293-307.

Rocha, Guy. "Wanted: The Real Reno." *Sierra Sage* (September 2007): 23.

Rotundo, E. Anthony. *American Manhood.* New York: Basic Books, 1993.

Rowland, Thomas J. *George B. McClellan and Civil War History: In the Shadow of Grant and Sherman.* Kent, Ohio: Kent State University Press, 1998.

Rubin, Anne Sarah. *A Shattered Nation.* Chapel Hill: The University of North Carolina Press, 2005.

Schildt, John W. *Roads to Antietam.* Hagerston, Maryland: Antietam Publications, 1985.

Silber, Nina. *The Romance of Reunion: Northerners and the South, 1865-1900.* Chapel Hill: University of North Carolina Press, 1993.

Simpson, Brooks D. "The Good Colonel: Rutherford B. Hayes Remembers the Civil War" Fourteenth Annual Hayes Lecture on the Presidency, 16 February 2003.

Snell, Mark A. *From First to Last: The Life of Major General William Buel Franklin.* New York: Fordham University Press, 2002.

Stotelmyer, Steven R. *The Bivouacs of the Dead: The Story of Those Who Died at Antietam and South Mountain.* Baltimore: Toomey Press, 1992.

Stotelmyer, Steven R. "The Truth About Wise's Well: Setting the Record Straight on South Mountain." *Blue and Gray* (October 1990), 28-35.

Taylor, Paul. *He Hath Loosened the Fateful Lightning: The Battle of Ox Hill (Chantilly) September 1, 1862.* Shippensburg, Pennsylvania: White Mane, 2003.

Trask, Benjamin. *16th Virginia Infantry.* Lynchburg, Virginia: H.E. Howard, Inc., 1988.

Vinond, Nolan and Sharon Vinond, eds. *Giants in the Their Tall Black Hats: Essays on the Iron Brigade.* Bloomington: Indiana University Press, 1998.

Wakelyn, Jon, ed. *Biographical Dictionary of the Confederacy.* Westport, Connecticut: Greenwood Press, 1977.

Warner, Ezra J. *Generals in Blue: Lives of the Union Commanders.* Baton Rouge: Louisiana State University Press, 1964.

Warner, Ezra J. *Generals in Gray: Lives of the Confederate Commanders.* Baton Rouge: Louisiana State University Press, 1959.

Welker, David A. *Tempest at Ox Hill: The Battle of Chantilly.* Cambridge: Da Capo Press, 2002.

Wheeler, Richard. *Lee's Terrible Swift Sword.* New York: Harper Collins, 1992.

Wiley, Bell Irvin. *The Life of Billy Yank.* Indianapolis: Bobbs Merrill, 1952.

Williams, Byron L. *The Old South Mountain Inn.* Shippensburg, Pennsylvania: Beidel Printing House, 1990.

Williams, Harry T. *Hayes of the Twenty-Third: The Civil War Volunteer Officer.* New York: Alfred A. Knopf, 1965.

Wittenberg, Eric J. *Rush's Lancers: The Sixth Pennsylvania Cavalry in the Civil War.* Yardley, Pennsylvania: Westholme Publishing, 2007.

Index

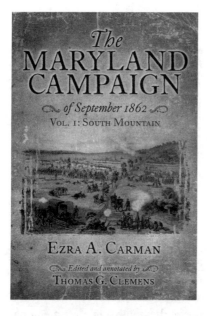

South Mountain (Fox's Gap)
September 14, 1862

PARTIAL EXCERPT: *The Maryland Campaign of 1862, Vol. 1: South Mountain*, by Ezra A. Carman (edited and annotated by Thomas G. Clemens), Savas Beatie LLC, 2010.

W hile Franklin, with the Sixth Corps, was forcing Crampton's Gap, Burnside, at the head of the First and Ninth Corps, was severely engaged at Turner's Gap, six miles northeast of Crampton's. The engagement was most severe at and south of Fox's Gap, a mile and more south of Turner's, and there was a sharp and fierce contest north, but as both these were for the possession of the main road, which ran through Turner's Gap, this place has given the Union name to the battle. The Confederates call it the battle of Boonsboro.

At this point the South Mountain runs, in a general direction northeast and southwest, and its crests are about 1300 feet above sea-level and 1000 feet above the general level of the Catoctin or Middletown Valley. The National road or turnpike between Frederick and Hagerstown crosses the mountain at Turner's Gap, a depression some 300 feet below the crests on either side.

The mountain on the north side of the turnpike is divided into two crests or ridges, by a narrow valley, which, though deep at the gap, becomes a slight depression about a mile to the north. There are country roads, both to the right of the Gap and to the left, which give access to the crests overlooking the National road. The principal one on the left, or south, called the Old Sharpsburg road, is nearly parallel to, and about three-fourths of a mile distant from the road through the Gap, until it reaches the crest of the mountain at Fox's Gap, where it bends to the left and, leaving Boonsboro far to the right, goes to Sharpsburg. A road on the right, known as the Old Hagerstown Road, passes up a ravine in the mountain about a mile from the National road and, bending to the left over and along the first crest, enters the National road just east of the Mountain House. By the National road the summit of the Gap is reached by easy grades. On the east side of the mountain, on either side of the road, almost to the very summit, the land was cleared and under cultivation. At the summit, on the south side of the road, is the Mountain House or old Inn, a famous hostelry of the olden days, when stage-coach and wagon formed the chief means of communication between Baltimore and Wheeling.

Some years after the war Mrs. Dahlgren, widow of Adm. John A. Dahlgren, purchased the Mountain House and much of the surrounding field and forest. The house was renovated, the field and forest improved, and a charming summer home established. North of the road and nearly opposite the house a modest memorial chapel was erected, in which were placed the remains of Adm. Dahlgren and Col. Ulric Dahlgren. In May 1898, the remains of Mrs. Dahlgren were laid to rest by the side of those of her husband and son.[1]

From the opposition displayed by the Confederates to his advance from Frederick, on the 13th, Pleasonton was convinced that they would make a determined stand at Turner's Gap, with an accession of force, and called upon Burnside for infantry support; awaiting its arrival he utilized the declining hours of the day (the 13th), by sending some dismounted cavalry up the mountain, on the right of the National road, to examine the position. This brought on some skirmish and caused the Confederates to concentrate on that flank. Pleasonton learned of the two roads, one on the right, another to the left of the Gap, both entering the National road beyond it, and favoring the movement of turning both flanks of the Confederate position. As the infantry support requested of Burnside did not come up on the 13th, Pleasonton made no effort to force the Gap and bivouacked in the valley, near its foot.[2]

---

1   Carman's description of the terrain follows the pattern established earlier in the manuscript. The "Mountain House" as Carman called it, is today a restaurant and the postwar chapel is restored. Carman is mistaken, however: Ulric was never buried there. For more information, see generally, Eric J. Wittenberg, *Like a Meteor Blazing Brightly: The Short but Controversial Life of Colonel Ulric Dahlgren* (Roseville MN: Edinborough Press, 2009).

2   See Pleasonton's report, *OR* 19, pt. 1, pp. 209-10.

Early on the morning of the 14th Pleasonton renewed his reconnaissance of the Gap and soon ascertained that the Confederates were in some force, upon which he awaited the arrival of infantry. Meanwhile Benjamin's and Gibson's batteries had come up to within a short distance of Bolivar and took position to the left of the National road, on a high knoll, about a half mile beyond the forks of the Old Sharpsburg road with the turnpike, commanding a portion of the Gap, and began an engagement with the Confederate artillery well up in the Gap.[3] Later in the day McMullin's Ohio battery came up and engaged the Confederates, about a mile distant.

General J. D. Cox, commanding the Kanawha Division, of the Ninth Corps, bivouacked on the night of the 13th, a little west of Middletown. He did not receive an order from Burnside to support Pleasonton on the evening of the 13th, as Pleasonton was led to believe, but was ordered that evening to support him with a brigade next morning. Cox detailed the brigade, commanded by Colonel E. P. Scammon, to report to Pleasonton and, at 6 a. m., Sunday, September 14th, it left camp and marched out on the National road. The brigade consisted of the 12th, 23d and 30th Ohio regiments and numbered nearly 1500 men. Cox was on the road when Scammon marched out and, impelled by a laudable curiosity, to know how Pleasonton intended to use the brigade, rode forward with Scammon, when, just after crossing Catoctin Creek, he was greatly surprised to see, standing at the road is Colonel Moor, who, two days before, had been taken prisoner in the streets of Frederick. Cox asked for an explanation and Moor replied that he had been paroled and was on the way back to the Union camps. Upon learning that the object of Scammon's movement was a reconnaissance into the Gap, Moor made an involuntary start and uttered an unintended note of warning, then, remembering that he was under parole, checked himself and turned away.[4]

The incident was not lost on Cox, who now realized that there was more serious work to be done by his brigade than merely supporting a cavalry reconnaissance. He says:

> I galloped to Scammon and told him that I should follow him in close support with Crook's Brigade, and as I went back along the column I spoke to each regimental commander, warning them to be prepared for anything, big or little,—it might be a skirmish, it might be a battle. Hurrying back to the camp, I ordered Crook to turn out his brigade prepared to march at once. I then wrote a dispatch to General Reno, saying

---

3   Cox, *B&L*, p. 585, and Burnside's report, *ibid.*, p. 417.

4   Cox, *ibid.*, pp. 585-6, and Cox, Reminiscences, p. 280.

I suspected we should find the enemy in force on the mountain-top, and should go forward with both brigades instead of sending one. Starting a courier with this, I rode forward to find Pleasonton, who was about a mile in front of my camp, where the old Sharpsburg road leaves the turnpike. I found that he was convinced that the enemy's position in the gap was too strong to be carried by a direct attack, and that he had determined to let his horsemen demonstrate on the main road, supporting the batteries (Benjamin's and Gibson's) while Scammon should march by the Sharpsburg road and try to reach the flank of the force on the summit. Telling him of my suspicion as to the enemy, I also informed him that I had determined to support Scammon with Crook, and if it became necessary to fight with the whole division I should do so, in which case I should assume the responsibility myself as his superior officer. To this he cordially assented.

One of my batteries (Simmonds') contained a section of 20-pounder Parrotts, and as these were too heavy to take up the rough mountain road, I ordered them to go into action beside Benjamin's battery, near the turnpike, and to remain with it till further orders. Our artillery at this time was occupying a knoll about a half mile in front of the forks of the road, and was exchanging shots with a battery of the enemy well up toward the gap. It was about half past 7 o'clock when Crook's column filed off on the old Sharpsburg road, Scammon's having perhaps half an hour's start. We had fully two miles to go before we should reach the place where our attack was made and, as it was a pretty steep road, the men marched slowly with frequent rests. On our way up we were overtaken by my courier who had returned from Reno with approval of my action, and the assurance that the rest of the Ninth Corps would come forward to my support."[5]

The engagement about to be opened by Cox was confined entirely to the south of the National road. It began early in the day and continued until after dark and shall be first considered.

When General Cox left the column, to order out Crook's Brigade, Scammon continued the march and reported to Pleasonton, on the National road, about a mile beyond the Catoctin. By this time Pleasonton had come to the conclusion to send him to the left, by the old Sharpsburg road, to feel the enemy and ascertain whether they held the crest of South Mountain, on that side, in any considerable force. About 7 a. m. Scammon turned off the National road at Ripp's and taking a cross road, passing a school house, entered the old Sharpsburg road, which was followed a quarter of a mile beyond Mentzer's Mill, when an artillery shot from the summit of the mountain, revealed the presence of an enemy and compelled more caution in movement. A detachment of the 30th Ohio continued the direct

5   *Ibid.*, p. 586.

movement up the mountain by the main road, and the main column turned off, at what is now the Reno school house, into a country road, leading still farther to the left and running nearly parallel to the crest of the mountain. It had the advantage of cover of the forest. When the head of the column reached the extreme southern limit of the open fields south of the gap on the east slope of the mountain, the 23d Ohio, Lieutenant-Colonel Rutherford B. Hayes, was deployed to the left to move through the woods on the left of the road and up to the crest of the mountain, gaining, if possible, the enemy's right to attack and turn it. The remainder of the brigade advanced on Hayes' right and rear, the 12th Ohio, Colonel C. B. White, in the center, and the 30th Ohio, Colonel Hugh Ewing, on the right. The entire line soon became engaged with an enemy, whose preparation we now note.[6]

We have seen that General D. H. Hill, with five brigades, was halted near Boonsboro, on the night of the 10th, to guard the wagon trains and park of artillery of the Confederate army and to watch all the roads leading from Harper's Ferry up Pleasant Valley. This required a considerable separation of his command on the various roads; his headquarters were about the center of his five brigades, and not less than three miles from Turner's Gap. As Stuart, with his cavalry, had been charged with the duty of observing the movements and checking the advance of the Union army, Hill did not consider it necessary to leave any infantry to defend the Gap but, when, on the forenoon of the 13th, he received a message from Stuart that he was being pushed back by two brigades of Union infantry, and requesting that a brigade of infantry be sent back to check the Union pursuit at Turner's Gap, Hill sent him the two brigades of Garland and Colquitt and the batteries of Bondurant and Lane, of four guns each, and it was the presence of this force that caused Pleasonton to pause in his advance on the evening of that day and call upon Burnside for a brigade of infantry.[7]

---

6 Carman did not state how he knew the details of Scammon's route, but he was a friend of Rutherford B. Hayes and visited him many times. Hayes was there, so he may have told Carman the details. The places mentioned are in the OR *Atlas*, Plate XXVII, 3, which shows the battle of South Mountain and the roads near it. The troops and movements are found in Scammon's report, OR 19, pt. 1, pp. 461-2, and the cannon shot alerting the Union soldiers is found in a letter from R. B. Wilson, 12th Ohio Infantry, Library of Congress, Manuscript Division, Ezra Carman Papers. The 23rd Ohio leading the column is also confirmed in a letter to Carman from President Rutherford B. Hayes, on Executive Mansion stationery, NYPL, Box 10, Folder 23.

7 D. H. Hill, *B&L*, p. 560. Hill's OR report is vague, but other sources show the second brigade, Garland's, was not sent until later in the evening and did not arrive at the Mountain House until the morning of the 14th. Garland did, however, go up to the Mountain House and spoke with D. H. Hill that night. See McRae's report, *ibid.*, 19, pt. 1, p. 1,039; and George Grattan, "Battle of Boonsboro Gap or South Mountain," *SHSP*, 39 (April 1914), pp. 37-8. Although not printed until after Carman was dead, it is obvious that Carman knew of Grattan's

At the same time Hill ordered the three other brigades to be drawn in nearer to Boonsboro and directed Ripley to send, at daybreak next morning, a regiment to hold the Hamburg Pass road, between two and three miles north of Turner's Gap. About midnight Hill received a note from General Lee saying that he was not satisfied with the condition of things on the National road and directing him to go in person to Turner's Gap, next morning, and assist Stuart in its defense. Hill made an early start and, upon reaching the Mountain House, at the summit of the Gap, between daylight and sunrise of the 14th, received a message from Stuart that he had gone to Crampton's Gap. The cavalry pickets had all been withdrawn and, as far as Hill then knew, Stuart had taken all his command with him. Garland's Brigade was found at the Mountain House and Colquitt's at the foot of the mountain, on the east side, without cavalry videttes in front, and with no information of the Union forces but under the impression that they had retired, when, in fact, says Hill: "General Cox's Federal division was at that very time marching up the old Sharpsburg or Braddock road, a mile to the south, seizing the heights on our right and establishing those heavy batteries which afterwards commanded the pike and all the approaches to it."[8]

Nor did Hill know of or suspect this movement and he was ignorant of the topography of the country. He has been criticized as being slow to learn the character of his surroundings and for not accompanying his two brigades to the mountain on the afternoon of the 13th, and examining the ground upon which, it was probable, he would be called upon to fight. He had, however, depended entirely upon Stuart to defend his rear, and Stuart parries criticism by reporting that the Gap was no place for cavalry operations; that he had put Hill's two brigades in position, directed Rosser with a detachment of cavalry and the Stuart Horse Artillery, to occupy Braddock's Gap and then started to join the main position of his command at Crampton's Gap. He says:

---

account. Grattan also mentioned in the article that he corresponding with Carman. Although those letters have not yet been found in the various repositories, Carman's use of Grattan's account is unmistakable. E. M. Dugand, 5th North Carolina Infantry, to John A. Gould, April 1892, "We arrived at the gap at sunrise. . ." NYPL Carman Papers, Box 9, Folder 2.

8   Ripley sent the 4th Georgia Infantry to guard what he called "Hamburg Pass." This slight gap in South Mountain is shown on local maps as Orr's Gap, after a nearby property owner. Apparently Ripley confused this gap with a gap ten miles to the east in Catoctin Mountain, where a village named Hamburg was located. See Ripley's report, OR 19, pt. 1, p. 1,031, Dennis Griffith map of Maryland 1794, and Varle Map 1808 (Washington County Free Library). Historians seem to have perpetuated this mistake. In addition to the direct quote, much of this paragraph comes from Hill, *B&L*, pp. 560-1.

I had not, up to this time, seen General D. H. Hill, but about midnight he sent General Ripley to me to get information concerning roads and gaps in the locality where General Hill had been lying for two days with his command. All the information I had was cheerfully given, and the situation of the gaps explained by maps. I confidently hoped by this time to have received the information which was expected from Brig. Gen. Fitz Lee. All the information I possessed, or had the means of possessing, had been laid before General D. H. Hill and the commanding general. His troops were duly notified of the advance of the enemy, and I saw them in line of battle awaiting his approach, and, myself, gave some general directions concerning the location of his lines during the afternoon, in his absence."[9]

Once on the ground, it took Hill but a hasty examination to decide that the Gap could only be held by a force larger than he had at his disposal and was wholly indefensible by a small one. General Lee was so informed and Hill ordered up General George B. Anderson's Brigade back near the summit and ordered it in line of battle, on either side of the National Road, three regiments on the right and two on the left.[10] Having posted Colquitt across the road, he then rode to the right, on a ridge road, to reconnoiter and, much to his surprise, found Colonel Thomas L. Rosser with the 5th Virginia Cavalry and two guns of Pelham's Battery, guarding Fox's Gap on the old Sharpsburg or Braddock road. Rosser had been ordered to that point by Stuart, who had not informed Hill of the fact, nor had Rosser been told that he would have infantry support. While here Hill became convinced that there were movements of troops on the mountain side below, screened from view by the forest, and, at the foot of the mountain, Cox's men could be seen advancing.

This was a menacing condition of affairs and Hill took measures to meet it. He rode back to the Mountain House and found Garland prepared for action. That gallant and enterprising officer had heard the report of a gun on the right front and the hurtling of a shell, and put his brigade under arms. Hill explained the situation to him and ordered him to sweep through the woods, on the right, to the old Sharpsburg road and hold it all hazards, as the safety of Lee's large trains depended upon its retention. He had already ordered up George B. Anderson to assist Colquitt and Garland, but was reluctant to order up Ripley and Rodes from the

---

9   Stuart's report, *OR* 19, pt. 1, p. 817. Carman made no comment, but it appears that Hill and Stuart were not acting in complete concert on the night of September 13. Hill's tone in his *B&L* account, pp. 560-1, is mildly critical.

10   Carman confused George B. Anderson's Brigade, perhaps with Garland's Brigade. Anderson only had four regiments, and he could not have posted five regiments as Carman described. See Chapter Eleven, which contains the Order of Battle for the two armies.

important points held by them near Boonsboro, until something definite was known of the strength and designs of the Union advance.[11]

From the National road or turnpike, at the Mountain House, where Garland was drawn up, a rough road runs southerly, first on the east slope and then along the crest of the mountain, nearly a mile, where it is intersected, at right angles, by a road diverging from the National road, about a mile west of Middletown. This road was followed by General Braddock in his march on Fort Duquesne, in 1755, and for many years was known as the Braddock road, later it became known as the old Sharpsburg road. The point where this road intersects the road on the crest of the mountain is generally known as Fox's Gap—sometimes as Braddock's Gap.[12]

About three-quarters of a mile beyond Fox's Gap, another road reaches the mountain top and connects with the crest road. This road branches from the old Sharpsburg road at the foot of the mountain, runs southerly some distance along its base and reaches the crest by a northwest course. It was by this road that Scammon marched. From Fox's Gap the crest road runs southerly a half mile, then follows the terrain of the mountain westerly, a quarter of a mile, and intersects the road reaching the crest by the northwest course, and at the point of this intersection on the crest, several wagon roads and trails lead down the west side of the mountain, into the valley south of Boonsboro. West of the crest road there is a slight depression beyond which are spurs and ridges covered by a dense forest. In front of Fox's Gap, and between it and the roads farther south, is a plateau of open ground; at the time some was wheat stubble, some in corn and some in grass. The ground sloping eastward from this plateau was open and under cultivation and heavy stone fences separated many of the fields.[13]

Garland's orders were to move quickly to the right and defend Fox's Gap and the road south of it, where it crossed the mountain. He was immediately in motion and, passing through the first belt of woods, south of the National road, found Rosser and, after a short conference with him, formed line. He had five regiments of North Carolina infantry, aggregating about 1000 men, and Bondurant's Alabama battery of four guns. The 5th North Carolina was placed on the left [right], north of

---

11 Hill, *B&L*, pp. 561-2. Hill's postwar memoirs make it clear that Hill did not know Rosser was at Fox's Gap. Hill's report, *OR* 19, pt. 1, p. 1,020, states that "Rosser, who had reported to me," is ambiguous. Likely, only later in the day did Hill learn of Rosser's presence there.

12 This description is from Jacob Cox, *Military Reminiscences of the Civil War* (New York: Charles Scribner & Sons, 1900), pp. 281-2.

13 This byroad, viable in its day for horses and artillery, was noted by Cox in his book, *ibid.*, p. 282 and in his *B&L* article, p. 587. The rest of the description is similar to Col. Duncan McRae's in *OR* 19, pt. 1, pp. 1,039-40. Part of the crest road is now the path of the Appalacian Trail.

the farther road and quite near it. The 12th and 23d North Carolina were on the left of the 5th on the mountain or crest road, the 12th on the open ground, the 23d behind a low stone wall. These three regiments filled the line between the two roads crossing the mountain south of Turner's Gap. Then came the 20th and 13th North Carolina on the left, north of Fox's Gap. From the nature of the ground and the duty to be performed by an inadequate force, the regiments were not in contact with each other, the 13th being 250 yards to the left of the 20th. There were intervals between the regiments south of Fox's Gap also, but this part of the line was strengthened by Bondurant's Alabama battery of four guns, which took position near the right, in a small clearing with a stone fence on either flank. Later, as we shall see, the 20th and 13th North Carolina were moved to the right, south of the Gap, but the interval between them was not closed.[14]

Garland and Colonel D. K. McRae, commanding 5th North Carolina, went forward to reconnoiter. McRae reports:

> Immediately in front of the ridge road were stubble fields and cornfields, and, for about forty paces to the front, a plateau, which suddenly broke on the left into a succession of ravines, and, farther beyond and in front a ravine, of greater length and depth, extended from the road which ran along the base of the mountain far out into the fields, and, connected with the ravine on our left, formed natural parallel approaches to our position. Between and beyond these ravines to our right was a dense growth of small forest trees and mountain laurel, through which the intersecting road ran for some distance, and on the mountain side to the top this growth was continued. General Garland and I had been but a few moments in the field when our attention was directed to persons moving at some distance on this road, and, apprehending that the enemy might be preparing to make a lodgment upon the mountain side, he ordered me to advance a body of fifty skirmishers into the woods to our right oblique front to go as far as possible to explore. This was done, and they had not passed fifty steps . . . when they encountered the enemy's skirmishers and the fight commenced."[15]

The skirmishers then encountered were those of the 23d Ohio and the time was 9 a. m. Hayes was moving through the woods on the left of the road, by the

---

14 The placement of the 5th North Carolina is an error by Carman, who obviously meant the "right." Hill, *B&L*, p. 563. See also McRae, *OR* 19, pt. 1, p. 1,040. Bondurant's position description is from a letter by John Purifoy dated July 15, 1899, LOC, Carman Papers.

15 McRae's report, *OR* 19, pt. 1, p. 1,040.

right flank, one company deployed in front as skirmishers, one on the right and another on the left as flankers.[16]

As soon as the skirmish lines became engaged Garland ordered McRae to support those of the 5th North Carolina and McRae led his entire regiment forward. The forest growth of small trees was so dense that it was almost impossible to advance in line of battle, and, as he cleared some of it, coming into partly open ground and approaching the near edge of another woods, he was met by the advance of the 23d Ohio. Hayes had seen McRae coming down hill on his right, and, while yet in the woods, faced his regiment by the rear rank and pushed through the thicket and over the rocky, broken ground to meet the advancing 5th North Carolina. The skirmishing at close quarters was very severe, many falling on both sides. As the skirmishing soon involved his whole regiment, Hayes ordered an advance, which was quickly responded to, and some conscripts on the right of the 5th North Carolina, never before under fire, fled from the field, upon which McRae fell back a short distance. Hayes halted, reformed line, and the engagement was soon resumed and became so hot that he ordered a charge, which was made in gallant style, driving the Confederates clear out of the woods, the 5th North Carolina falling back to its original position. While this was transpiring, the 12th North Carolina, numbering about 70 men, came to the support of the 5th North Carolina, gave one wild volley and retreated in disorder. About half the regiment halted on the line of the 13th North Carolina and continued with it the remainder of the day. The 23d North Carolina now advanced from the crest road about 40 yards into the field in front of the 23d Ohio, and, under cover of a hedge row and an old stone fence, partly fallen down, opened with some effect upon it and upon the 12th Ohio on the right of the 23d. This advance of the 23d North Carolina was followed by Garland's order to the 20th and 13th North Carolina to move from the left to the right to support the 5th North Carolina.[17]

The 23d Ohio halted at a stone fence, just out of the woods, and kept up a brisk fire upon the 23d North Carolina behind the old stone fence, on an opposite hill, not more than 100 yards distant. Its loss was heavy, among the wounded was its gallant commander. Soon after giving the command to charge, and when but a few

16 The information about skirmisher and flank companies is inferred in R. B. Wilson's letters and maps, July 11 and 22, 1899, NA-AS, but not directly stated. It is confirmed by Hayes's memoirs of South Mountain sent to Carman. See Hayes, undated letter, NYPL Collection, Box 10, Folder 23.

17 The description of the fighting comes from the reports of Scammon's brigade, OR 19, pt. 1, pp. 461-2; Hugh Ewing, *ibid.*, p. 469; James M. Comley, *ibid.*, pp. 466-7; Carr White, *ibid.*, pp. 464-5; and McRae, *ibid.*, p. 1,040.

yards out of the woods, Hayes was severely wounded, a musket ball shattering the bone of his left arm, above the elbow, but he remained in command. Weak from loss of blood, he was compelled to lie down. Fearing an attack on the left he ordered his regiment to leave the stone fence and fall back to the edge of the woods. In falling back he was left in the field; requesting to be carried back a few men stepped out of the woods for that purpose, but drew upon themselves such a heavy fire from the 23d North Carolina that Hayes ordered them back. A few moments later Lieutenant Benjamin W. Jackson ran forward, brought his wounded commander back into the woods and laid him down behind a log. Here he relinquished the command to Major J. M. Comly; had his wound dressed and walked to the Widow Coogle house, near a mile distant, and taken to Middletown.[18]

On the right of the 23d, and in the center of the brigade line, was the 12th Ohio, which, after moving nearly a fourth of a mile through a pine wood, was obliged to advance over open pasture ground, under a most galling fire from the 23d North Carolina. It was halted and ordered to lie down for shelter and await the coming up of the 30th Ohio on its right, when a general advance of the entire brigade was to be made.

The movement convinced McRae that a strong Union force had been massed in the woods, with the intention to turn his right, and he suggested that the woods be shelled, but there were no guns available, as Bondurant's Battery had been so heavily pressed by the Ohio skirmishers, who advanced to the stone fence on its right and opened fire on its flank, that Garland ordered it away. Garland now rode to the left to bring up the 20th and 13th North Carolina, that he had ordered to the support of the 5th. He met these two regiments after they had crossed the Sharpsburg road, when, perceiving that some of the skirmishers of the 30th Ohio were apparently endeavoring to turn the left of his line, he halted the 13th North Carolina at the Wise house, and the 20th North Carolina 250 yards farther to the right. The 13th was in an open field, upon the brow of a hill and, immediately in front of it, in a dense wood, were the Ohio skirmishers, some of whom, farther to the left, were threatening the flank of the 13th. . . . **END OF EXCERPT** . . .

---

18 Carman may have been deceived here by "old soldier's stories." It is unlikely from reading the reports mentioned in the previous footnote that the like-numbered regiments ever directly opposed one another. Carman described Rutherford B. Hayes's wounding in words strikingly similar to his diary, which was not published until 1922, but was taken from Hayes's undated memoir. See NYPL Carman Papers, Box 10, Folder 23. The "Widow Koolge house"(Carman's spelling is incorrect, but is more correct than Hayes's diary, which has "Kugler"), where Hayes was taken, is shown on OR Atlas Plate XXVII-3. See Charles R. Williams, ed., *Diary and Letters of Rutherford B. Hayes, Nineteenth President of the United States* (Columbus: Ohio State Archeological & Historical Society, 1922), vol. 2, p. 357.

About the Author

Author

Brian Matthew Jordan graduated in 2009 with a Bachelor of Arts in History and Civil War Era Studies from Gettysburg College. The native of northeastern Ohio discovered a passion for history at an early age. He is a frequent speaker at Civil War Round Tables nationwide, delivers popular tours for Gettysburg College's Civil War Institute and the Gilder Lehrman Institute of American History, and conducts seminars for various Teaching American History grant recipients. His published work has appeared in multiple journals including *Civil War History*. Jordan is currently working on a Ph.D. in History at Yale University.